WITHDRAWN

The Album

The Album

A Guide to Pop Music's Most Provocative, Influential, and Important Creations

Adding Punk Attitude to the Mix, 1974–1988

3

James E. Perone, Editor

James E. Perone, Series Editor

PRAEGER

AN IMPRINT OF ABC-CLIO, LLC
Santa Barbara, California • Denver, Colorado • Oxford, England

Library of Congress Cataloging-in-Publication Data

The album : a guide to pop music's most provocative, influential, and important creations / James E. Perone, editor.
    v. cm. — (The Praeger singer-songwriter collection)
    Includes bibliographical references and index.
    Contents: Vol. 1. Country, rock, soul, pop, and blues : the 1960s —Vol. 2. The golden age of the singer-songwriter : 1970–1973 — Vol. 3. Adding punk attitude to the mix : 1974–1988 — Vol. 4. An explosion of diversity : 1989–Present.
    ISBN 978-0-313-37906-2 (hardcover : alk. paper) — ISBN 978-0-313-37907-9 (ebook)
1. Popular music—History and criticism.   I. Perone, James E.
    ML3470.A24 2012
    781.6409—dc23   2012026593

ISBN: 978-0-313-37906-2
EISBN: 978-0-313-37907-9

16 15 14 13 12   1 2 3 4 5

This book is also available on the World Wide Web as an eBook.
Visit www.abc-clio.com for details.

Praeger
An Imprint of ABC-CLIO, LLC

ABC-CLIO, LLC
130 Cremona Drive, P.O. Box 1911
Santa Barbara, California 93116–1911

This book is printed on acid-free paper ∞
Manufactured in the United States of America

Some content appearing in these volumes was originally published in the following titles:

Kirkpatrick, Rob, *The Words and Music of Bruce Springsteen* (Santa Barbara, CA: Praeger, 2006); Bennighof, James, *The Words and Music of Paul Simon* (Santa Barbara, CA: Praeger, 2007); Bielen, Ken, and Ben Urish, *The Words and Music of John Lennon* (Santa Barbara, CA: Praeger, 2007); Moskowitz, David, *The Words and Music of Bob Marley* (Santa Barbara, CA: Praeger, 2007); Bielen, Ken, *The Words and Music of Neil Young* (Santa Barbara, CA: Praeger, 2008); Gable, Christopher, *The Words and Music of Sting* (Santa Barbara, CA: Praeger, 2008); Kessel, Corinne, *The Words and Music of Tom Waits* (Santa Barbara, CA: Praeger, 2008); Tarr, Joe, *The Words and Music of Patti Smith* (Santa Barbara, CA: Praeger, 2008); Woldu, Gail Hilson, *The Words and Music of Ice Cube* (Santa Barbara, CA: Praeger, 2008); Hage, Erik, *The Words and Music of Van Morrison* (Santa Barbara, CA: Praeger, 2009); Benitez, Vincent P., *The Words and Music of Paul McCartney: The Solo Years* (Santa Barbara, CA: Praeger, 2010); Bennighof, James, *The Words and Music of Joni Mitchell* (Santa Barbara, CA: Praeger, 2010); Inglis, Ian, *The Words and Music of George Harrison* (Santa Barbara, CA: Praeger, 2010); Moskowitz, David, *The Words and Music of Jimi Hendrix* (Santa Barbara, CA: Praeger, 2010); Bielen, Ken, *The Words and Music of Billy Joel* (Santa Barbara, CA: Praeger, 2011).

Contents

Introduction

In large part because volume 3 of *The Album* covers a relatively long time span (1974–1988), the albums that are analyzed in this volume exhibit an especially wide range of diversity. The early 1970s' singer-songwriter movement broadened out in style such that some performers turned inward to an even greater extent than their predecessors, while others attempted to maintain a level of introspection that would reach the widest possible audience. The integration of country and rock continued to move forward, but this was also a time period in which some massive changes were afoot. For one thing, disco music—love it or hate it—entered the public consciousness and seemed for a time to be all over the radio and television. Partially in reaction to the popularity and the slickness of disco, though, punk rock entered the scene, first with American performers such as the Patti Smith Group, Television, and the Ramones and then with a host of British bands such as the Sex Pistols, the Clash, the Jam, the Damned, and numerous others. A number of singer-songwriters maintained a punk-like edginess to their lyrics but were much wider ranging in their musical influences, including such artists as Warren Zevon and Elvis Costello. Also in the mid-1970s, one of the most consistently influential American artists of the rock era, Bruce Springsteen, came to prominence, as did the Top 40 pop favorite Billy Joel. As the 1970s gave way to the 1980s, Michael Jackson, Madonna, and Prince burst on the scene, with music that seemed to be particularly well tailored to the age of the music video. Curiously, though, by the end of the time period covered in this volume, a new cadre of singer-songwriters, mostly women, renewed the focus on individual, personal human emotions of the early 1970s' singer-songwriter movement but with an edgier outlook on life.

At the start of the 1974–1988 period, the singer-songwriter movement continued to diversify. Joni Mitchell, who was a mainstay of the style from the start, continued to experiment with musical forms and also continued to integrate jazz, folk, and rock unlike that of any other recording artist. Jackson Browne made his first commercial inroads and gave the listening public an even more introspective, starkly personal view of the artist's emotional life than any of his predecessors. In fact, because Browne wrote and recorded so many songs about the life of the artist/touring musician, his music tended to sound more immediately autobiographical than the work of others in the singer-songwriter movement.

Autobiography also was found in the work of Emmylou Harris in her 1975 album *Pieces of the Sky*, in which her own writing and in well-chosen covers she comments on the life of her recently deceased friend and mentor, Gram Parsons. Joan Baez returned to prominence with her 1975 album *Diamonds & Rust*. This album was even more directly autobiographical than Harris's, especially because of the way in which Baez fans heard references to the relationship between Baez and Bob Dylan in Baez's writing and in her selection of repertoire. Janis Ian, too, probed her own life and extended her experiences to those of other young women in the songs of her 1975 album *Between the Lines*.

Singer-songwriters such as Ian and Browne brought out quite a bit of personal angst in their lyrics, and the others mentioned above certainly did not gloss over the pain and hurt they had experienced in life. Some singer-songwriters, though, referenced their emotions and experience but maintained a different balance between raw expression and popular appeal. John Denver, for example, wrote much of his own material on *Back Home Again*, but melancholy is tempered by exuberance, and sadness is tempered by fondness. Denver, too, was a rare musician who generally performed in a country style but whose primary appeal was to listeners who did not necessarily consider themselves to be fans of country music.

Among the singer-songwriters, Harry Chapin held a curious position. Chapin enjoyed some commercial success with several singles (e.g., "Taxi," "Cats in the Cradle," and "WOLD") but was not particularly well thought of by pop music critics. He was also a performer whose live appearances tended to make his studio recordings seem somewhat thin and cold. An essay on Chapin's *Greatest Stories Live* double album is included in this volume because it documents Chapin at his best and shows the near-cultlike following that he enjoyed among his audience.

It is difficult to say if the Eagles represented the culmination of Gram Parsons's ideal of fully merging country and rock into an American popular roots music that would break down genre boundaries, but the group was among the most successful acts of the 1970s, and their album *Hotel California* was one of the best of the entire decade. And if the Eagles did not represent the culmination of the integration of the disparate styles, then they were the leaders until the 1990s, when Garth Brooks may have taken one step beyond their work at integrating the styles.

A perfectionist in the studio who could work on an album for months and months, Stevie Wonder topped even his successful earlier effort such as *Innervisions* and *Talking Book* with his 1976 double album (plus a bonus extended-play disc) *Songs in the Key of Life*. On possibly his greatest achievement as an artist, Wonder mixed seriousness, levity, introspection, social commentary, simple person-to-person emotions, and danceability like no other musician of the day, and *Songs in the Key of Life* remains one of the greatest and most-beloved albums by any artist ever.

This volume of *The Album* does not include any detailed analyses of disco albums; however, disco was an extremely popular and important genre in the 1970s and into the 1980s. Kool and the Gang, the Bee Gees, K. C. and the Sunshine Band, Gloria Gaynor, Donna Summer, Barry White and the Love Unlimited Orchestra, and a host of other performers took to the radio airwaves and the sound systems of discotheques with their solid, four-beats-to-the-bar, usually heavily orchestrated, slick, fashion-conscious recordings. One of the most popular movies of the 1970s, *Saturday Night Fever*, chronicled the disco subculture and generated a highly successful soundtrack album and numerous hit singles. As one considers the album as an entity, it is worth noting that disco tended to be more about individual songs than albums. In fact, a fair number of disco records were issued as 45-rpm 12-inch vinyl extended-play singles (as opposed to 45-rpm 7-inch plastic records). The extended mixes kept dancers on the floor longer, and the format allowed for easier segues from song to song by disc jockeys in dance clubs.

As I noted in *Music of the Counterculture Era*,[1] perhaps in the overall scheme of things, though, the sociological aspects of disco were more important than the music itself. Robert McRuer, in his article "Gay Gatherings," emphasizes the importance of disco music and the entire disco scene in the emergence of an openly gay subculture. According to McRuer, the popularity among male homosexuals of black female singers such as Grace Jones, Donna Summer, and Gloria Gaynor reflected a transference of "black" as a minority status to "gay" as a minority status.[2] Braunstein puts it another way, writing that "For the first half of the 1970s, disco was an extended conversation between black musicians and gay dancers."[3] To put it in even more general terms, the disco scene helped to break down the barriers of sexual orientation and race.

Disco also played an important role in the development of rap and hip-hop. New York City–area disc jockeys, particularly immigrants from Jamaica, were known to rap during the transitions between the records they spun in dance clubs. While rap became better known and developed further as it became a competitive street poetry, it owes the 1970s' disco scene at least partial credit for its existence as a musically based entertainment form. By the late 1970s, block parties in some New York neighborhoods included competitive rapping. The hip-hop genre really began with the Sugarhill Gang's single "Rapper's Delight," a piece that includes the kind of competitive street rapping that developed out of the earlier work of Jamaican disco DJs. The first song to include rap that made it to the top of the pop charts was, ironically, the all-white group Blondie's 1981 single "Rapture."

Partially in reaction to the slickness of disco music, the fact that discotheques relied on a recorded product (and therefore negated the importance of live musicians), and the glamour of the disco scene, punk rock developed in the New York City area around the middle of the 1970s. The New York club CBGB was the center of activity for artists such as the Patti Smith Group, the Ramones, Tom Verlaine and Television, Blondie, and others. Within the diversity that was punk rock, there were some common elements, such as lyrics about disenfranchisement, angst, and alienation, as well as music that featured harmonic and melodic minimalism, distorted electric guitars, and sometimes screamed vocals. The genre also was associated with its own fashion, which included torn and tattered jeans, torn T-shirts, and piercings. Patti Smith's *Horses* and *Easter* and the Ramones' *Rocket to Russia*, all of which are analyzed in this volume, represent American punk rock of the time. In these three albums, however, the listener will find much diversity.

Mid-1970s' youths in the United Kingdom perhaps had more reason to be attracted to punk rock than did American youths, in part because of worse economic conditions and also because of questions that arose over the validity of the monarchy. The first British punk rock band, the Sex Pistols, was largely the construction of impresario Malcolm McLaren, who was inspired by a stay in New York City, where he became associated with the glam/punk band the New York Dolls. In 1976 and 1977, the Sex Pistols performed and recorded songs that were meant to take back music from the arena rock bands that dominated British music and that expressed anger with British government policies and the monarchy. With members with stage names such as Sid Vicious and Johnny Rotten, there is no doubt that the band was meant to incite controversy. The Sex Pistols released one album, *Never Mind the Bollocks Here's the Sex Pistols*, that has become one of the most iconic rock albums of all time.

While the Sex Pistols had a short life as a functioning band and offered very little recorded output, some British punk bands continued to evolve the style into the 1980s. The Clash, along with their 1979 album *London Calling*, were more finely focused on the politics of Britain and the rest of the world and were instrumental in introducing touches of Jamaican reggae into the punk style. The Police, which started off life as a punk rock band, reflects the emergence of new wave rock out of punk in the late 1970s and into the 1980s. The band's 1980 album *Zenyatta Mondatta* includes numerous references to Jamaican reggae and ska and includes lyrics that are reflective on world politics as well as on personal intrigues of a more local nature.

As punk gave way to new wave rock in the United States, American bands seemed to focus less on politics, when compared with their British counterparts. In fact, some focused on escapism and fun, presumably as a reaction against the seriousness of the world situation. Hailing from Athens, Georgia, the B-52's (later spelled by the band without the apostrophe) became arguably

America's party band of the early 1980s. Their self-titled debut album includes ample humor and a stark minimalistic musical return to the simplicity of the prepsychedelic 1960s. Other American and British new wave bands that are not represented in the major essays in this volume turned increasingly to synthesizers in the early 1980s, and some bridged the gap between punk and disco, which ironically turned new wave into a sort of punk-disco hybrid.

The early 1980s witnessed the real birth of the video age in music. Back in the 1960s, some acts produced promotional films for their latest singles. These ranged from mimed performances of the music to the innovative psychedelic films that were produced in support of the Beatles' double A-side single "Penny Lane" and "Strawberry Fields Forever." With the advent of MTV and other music video networks on cable television in the early 1980s, though, the video age really began. Early in the video age, there were relatively few music videos available; therefore, one might see a video by an experimental composer such as Philip Glass or Laurie Anderson included in the rotation with well-known pop culture icons such as Michael Jackson. So, although an album such as Laurie Anderson's *Big Science* might seem to be off the radar of the early 1980s' pop music world, this work—which actually does reflect the New York City loft scene of the day—gained considerable exposure because of the video for the song "O Superman." Several artists, though, were naturals for the new medium, including Michael Jackson, Madonna, and Prince. Jackson's 1982 album *Thriller* was accompanied by elaborate videos that interpreted the stories of the songs and included production on such a grand scale that they set the standard for all music videos that followed. The videos of the songs from Madonna's 1984 album *Like a Virgin* perhaps were better known than the unadorned audio-only versions. It might be argued that the music video decreased listener creativity in interpreting the words and music because they offered a single interpretation. It might also be argued that some artists might have been more focused on the spectacle of their videos than on the music itself, to the music's detriment. However, the best combinations of musicians, producers, video writers, and video directors created miniature films that remained vivid and relevant long after they were viewed for the first or second time.

Prince's feature-length film *Purple Rain* combined the music video, live performance, and film drama in a way that might not have been conceivable before the advent of the music video. The *Purple Rain* album contains some of Prince's greatest music of the mid-1980s and also generated controversy (as some of his work has done throughout his lengthy and prolific career). Most notably, after witnessing her daughter listening to the song "Darling Nikki," which includes references to kinky sex and masturbation, Tipper Gore, along with other wives of Washington, D.C., politicians, founded the Parents Music Resource Center (PMRC). The national PTA and the PMRC lobbied the music industry to place warning labels on recordings that included lyrical references to sex, drugs, and violence, a practice that is still in place today.

Another 1984 album, Bruce Springsteen's *Born in the U.S.A.*, became the center of a different sort of controversy. Some Washington politicians heard the refrain of the album's title track as an expression of patriotic pride rather than as the sarcastic statement that it really is, that is, in the context of the pointed adversity that Springsteen's Vietnam veteran character describes in the verses. Some considered using "Born in the U.S.A." as a campaign song but generally were dissuaded from doing so. This album resonated with the underemployed, disenfranchised, and the working class but was especially important at adding fuel to the discussion over veterans' rights and benefits.

The early 1980s were also notable for the introduction of the compact disc (CD). Earlier innovations in the physical medium used for the album (e.g., the introduction of audio cassettes and eight-track tapes in the 1960s) largely resulted in changes in the ways and locations in which consumers listened to music. For example, the two competing tape media could be used in automobiles and watercraft and, with the later portable cassette machines, while out for a walk or a jog. The CD, however, produced greater impact on how albums were made. Perhaps most importantly, the CD offered record companies the opportunity to release an hour's worth of high audio fidelity music on a single disc. Anecdotally, from having lived through that time, I think it is probably safe to say that consumers came to expect more product than the 40–50 minutes of music contained on the pre–CD-age albums.[4] Some artists included more songs on their albums, some artists built songs with longer rhythmic groove sections, and some artists incorporated longer introductions and longer fade-outs. The CD made an impact on classical music and jazz, too. For example, repertoire that could not be issued on one vinyl disc or that had to be split in nonoptimal ways on classical albums could now be sequenced as it would be in a concert hall, without having to turn over the record. In the mid-1980s, the development of CD players and multidisc changers for automobiles and the popularity of Sony Corporation's Discman portable CD player both combined to diminish the importance of the audio cassette, which itself had earlier supplanted the eight-track.

The second half of the 1980s was a time period in which pop music fans became more exposed to and more enamored with the influence of world music. Although American and British rock musicians had incorporated aspects of Jamaican, Indian, Arabian, Peruvian, and some African music into their recordings as early as the 1960s, Paul Simon's 1986 album *Graceland* fully integrated South African township music and musicians almost entirely throughout. The album also exhibited the influence of Cajun and zydeco music. It might not be remembered today that when *Graceland* was released, it was highly controversial in large part because Simon's work with South African musicians in their homeland violated a widespread embargo of the country because of its system of apartheid. As I wrote in *Paul Simon: A Bio-Bibliography*, Simon "justified his work by saying that he was (1) paying the black musicians significantly above union scale; (2) giving the South Africans full credit on the album (including songwriting credit and the attendant royalties, and (3) giving this beautiful musical style a chance to be heard and appreciated by the entire world."[5] Despite the controversy, including protests against Simon and *Graceland* at Howard University, once the system of apartheid broke down, black South African leader Nelson Mandela supported Simon's work, and some former critics altered their stances and agreed that *Graceland*, in its own way, probably helped in the move toward a more just political system in South Africa.

The late 1980s were also the time of the emergence of the Irish rock band U2 as international superstars. Although the group had been around since the punk rock scene of the late 1970s and although U2 had been moderately successful as a recording band and successful as a touring act, the 1987 album *The Joshua Tree* established them as the best-known, most important, and among the most popular rock bands of the era. U2's continuing work as recording artists and as a major concert draw, as well as Bono's outspoken political activism, have kept U2 in the musical and news spotlight into the second decade of the 21st century.

The late 1980s also brought the dawning of a new vibrant singer-songwriter movement. Unlike the singer-songwriter genre of the age of Carole King, James Taylor, Joni Mitchell, and Jackson Browne, the focus was now fully on women. Suzanne Vega (*Solitude Standing*), Enya (*Watermark*), Melissa Etheridge (*Melissa Etheridge*), and Tracy Chapman (*Tracy Chapman*) all have their work included in this volume; however, the analyses in volume 4 of *The Album* continue this edition of the singer-songwriter movement well into the 1990s. The female singer-songwriter movement included more stylistic diversity and seemed in some respects to be less market driven; therefore, it is easy to hear the work of the women listed above and their 1990s' colleagues as some of the most personally expressive work of any edition of the singer-songwriter movement.

Notes

1. James E. Perone, *Music of the Counterculture Era* (Westport, CT: Greenwood, 2004), 89–90.
2. Robert McRuer, "Gay Gatherings: Reimagining the Counterculture," in *Imagine Nation: The American Counterculture of the 1960s and '70s*, edited by Peter Braunstein and Michael William Doyle, 215–240 (New York: Routledge, 2001).
3. Peter Braunstein, "Disco," *American Heritage* 50(7) (November 1999): 55.
4. Some albums of the 1960s that I have in my collection contain even less than 40 minutes of music.
5. James E. Perone, *Paul Simon: A Bio-Bibliography* (Westport, CT: Greenwood, 2000), 8–9.

Jackson Browne

Late for the Sky (1974)

James E. Perone

Jackson Browne enjoyed a tremendous run of popularity in the mid-1970s. The Browne style combined an easygoing voice, instantly recognizable electric slide guitar, touches of country rock, and lyrics that often were more deeply personal, introspective, and confessional than those of other members of the singer-songwriter cadre. Several of Jackson Browne's albums exhibit his approach to the singer-songwriter style well; however, perhaps none is better or more personal sounding than *Late for the Sky*.

Even back in the predigital days of vinyl albums, most pop albums contained more than the eight songs of *Late for the Sky*. This is not, however, a thin collection of Jackson Browne's music: the shortest song is just over three minutes long, and five of the songs exceed five minutes in duration. The album opens with its title track, a moderately slow anthem-like song. In this piece, Browne explores the feeling of being alone after a relationship has ended, the mystery of why two people fall in love with each other, and the process of coming to grips with all of the questions that surround the end of a relationship. As he often does, Browne uses somewhat obscure, metaphorical language as he contemplates subjects about which there are more questions than firm answers. In particular, his use of certain verbs (e.g., "dreaming," "drifting," "sleeping," and "running") is interesting. The first three concern nebulous states of awareness and thus suggest the unexplainable nature of love. Browne's use of the word "running" is also telling of his character's emotional state and suggests the eternal quest. This is borne out in numerous Jackson Browne songs throughout the 1970s: his characters may run toward a goal or an understanding, but seldom does Browne tell the listener that they arrive.

Browne's music for "Late for the Sky" and other songs on this album is not as compact and to-the-point as most Top 40 pop of the era, and this is not necessarily a bad thing. The fact that verse, chorus, and middle eight sections are not as clearly defined as in conventional pop music, the fact that Browne tends to emphasize more minor harmonies in major-key pieces than some songwriters, the fact that the sections tend to be longer and more complex in structure than those in conventional pop music, and the fact that Browne's melodic contours meander somewhat all contribute to the overall effect and support the questioning, searching nature of his lyrics. The introspective nature of Browne's lyrics is also supported by the instrumental arrangement, which on "Late for the Sky" incorporates acoustic guitar, slide electric guitar, organ, bass, and drums—an uncomplicated band-oriented texture that stood apart from the bigger productions that marked the mid-1970s.

Although Browne's work in the 1970s tends to be grouped with the singer-songwriter style of artists such as Joni Mitchell and James Taylor, it also was tied to the California country rock style of groups such as Poco and the Eagles. The song "Fountain of Sorrow" is a particularly good example of the country rock side of Browne's style. In fact, the vocal harmony arrangement sounds a bit like a combination of the work of the Eagles and Crosby, Stills, Nash and Young. Compared with some of the work of some of Browne's contemporaries, however, "Fountain of Sorrow" is more expansive. Not only is the song nearly seven minutes in length, but the chorus section is longer and more complex than was typical of the era. The performance, too, feels more expansive because of the sudden thinning of the texture approximately five minutes into the song. After a brief, quiet piano interlude, Browne enters singing one final statement of the chorus, this time without the assistance of the backing singers. The dramatic textural thinning can be heard in other Jackson Browne recordings of the period and tends to focus the listener's attention back onto the personal nature of Browne's lyrics.

The title, "Fountain of Sorrow," might leave the listener with the preconceived notion that Browne focuses on sadness. In reality, although there is a bittersweet quality to the text, the focus is on overcoming sadness. Although Browne is somewhat vague as to the exact nature of the relationship of his character and the character to whom he sings, it appears most likely that the two were former lovers. Apparently his former partner ran "off in search of a perfect stranger"; however, the two now seem to be on good terms. The lyrics are formed around the premise that Browne's character found some old photographs of the other person and was struck by the bittersweet look in (presumably) her eyes. Then as Browne encounters her years later and sees that now she appears completely happy, it pleases him that she has come to grips with all of the pain of the past.

In the next track, "Farther On," Browne turns inward, or at least he sings from the perspective of an inward-looking character. He sings of having hidden his feelings and emotions earlier in life and having sought solace in a fantasy world of books and movies. He intimates to the audience that he still is a romantic, for he still looks "for the beauty in songs." His character's dreams of the past largely have been unrealized, and this has tested his faith and resolve. Still, he continues to move "farther on" down the metaphorical road of life. The searching, the yearning, and the restlessness of Browne's character in this song resonated with the youths of the day. *Late for the Sky* was released just at the tail end of the Vietnam War, a time that also saw the continuing unfolding of the Watergate Scandal and its aftermath. This was a time in which the United States and its population were in need of healing. For youths, the peace, love, and understanding of the hippie era was giving way to the glitz, glamour, and superficiality of disco and early stirrings of the violent discontent of punk. In short, this was a time period of uncertainty, and Browne's characters in "Farther On" and in his other work captured the yearning for healing and closure that defined the mid-1970s.

> ## SIBLING POP
>
> The first half of the 1970s saw the emergence of heavy metal and the introspective singer-songwriter style, gender-defying glam rock, swamp rock, R&B and soul styles that increasingly focused on political and social commentary, and many other genres and subgenres. Today it seems far too easy to forget that the U.S. pop charts of that same time period were dominated by recordings of Karen and Richard Carpenter, known professionally as the Carpenters. On some of the duo's hits, Richard Carpenter shared writing credits with Richard Bettis, while other Carpenters hits came from the pens of Paul Williams as well as Burt Bacharach and Hal David, and still others were covers of older pop material. The most successful singles by the duo included "(They Long to Be) Close to You," "We've Only Just Begun," "Rainy Days and Mondays," "Goodbye to Love," "Top of the World," and "Superstar." The duo's 1970 album *Close to You* remains a favorite, but their work largely was defined by singles that featured Richard Carpenter's full, lush arrangements and production, multitracked backing vocals, and Karen Carpenter's often-haunting alto voice.

There is no doubt that Browne could write punchy to-the-point music with a strong commercial hook and strong Top 40 appeal. For example, "Take It Easy," which he cowrote with Glenn Frey, was a significant hit for Frey's group, the Eagles, and Browne's musically upbeat songs "Doctor My Eyes" and "Running on Empty" were significant hits for their writer. All three of these songs have engaging, instantly recognizable melodies and musically are to the point, in contrast to most of the songs on *Late for the Sky*, which include melodies that tend to meander somewhat and have more complex formal structures. "Farther On" is a particularly strong example of how Browne linked meandering words and music to an extent on *Late for the Sky* that far exceeded his earlier (e.g., "Doctor My Eyes") and later (e.g., "Running on Empty") more commercial work.

The next song, "The Late Show," is another slow, introspective ballad. This time, though, Browne's melancholy is heightened even more. The key word that he uses in this piece is "emptiness." His character contemplates well-wishers and is torn between hearing their encouragement as genuine and hearing their encouragement as their inability to express their true feelings. As if sensing that the musical and lyrical move toward the profoundly melancholy requires some emotional relief for the listener, Browne turns to straight-ahead rock and roll for "The Road and the Sky." His lyrical message, however, is remarkably consistent with the general tenor of the album's other tracks. Once again, Browne's character has more questions than answers about life. Instead of focusing on a feeling of melancholia, though, this character has become reckless (e.g., driving in "a stolen Chevrolet") and uses the excitement that he receives from risk-taking as the "high" that takes his mind off of his troubles and persistent angst. This combination of upbeat, rollicking rock and roll and lyrics about grappling with the meaning of life and how to come to grips with life's disappointments and difficulties is the hallmark of Browne's most commercially successful work. In fact, "The Road and the Sky" is not all that far removed thematically or musically from songs such as "Doctor My Eyes" and "Running on Empty."

For the most part, coproducers Browne and Al Schmitt achieved a consistent band-oriented sound on *Late for the Sky*. With the exception of elaborate multipart backing vocals, most of the arrangements sound as though they could be reproduced live. The treatment of Browne's voice also for the most part is consistent, with little artificial reverberation. This gives his voice an immediate natural-sounding quality that meshes with the introspective, personal nature of the lyrics. It may seem curious, then, that on "For a Dancer" there is an uncharacteristic spaciousness that surrounds Browne's lead vocals. There are some other notable sonic differences that make this song stand out from its predecessors, most importantly David Lindley's contribution on a featured fiddle/violin obbligato that runs through much of the piece. That the piece stands out and that it steers the closest of any on the album to American roots music are both important features, because this is also perhaps the most universal and most mature song on *Late for the Sky*. In "For a Dancer," Browne uses the metaphor of the dance as he ponders the ultimate meaning of life in the face of certain mortality. Although it is not the last track on the album, "For a Dancer" tends to bring closure to the questions and the angst of the preceding songs. Browne concludes that ultimately one cannot know the answers to the questions of life, to the question of what happens when one dies, or how one's life will be judged. In the face of what could sound like hopelessness, Browne offers encouragement to the dancer to continue with life's dance until that final "dance you'll do alone."

The subject of death also plays a role in "Walking Slow." Over an upbeat musical setting, Browne sings about walking through his old neighborhood and expresses the belief that if he were to die on his walk, life would go on. In a sense, then, and despite the fact that "For a Dancer" seems to bring closure to the album's first five songs, "Walking Slow" is a natural follow-up— Browne has shifted the focus from each individual's shared mortality to the bigger picture of life in general continuing. However, the mood of the music is not entirely happy. Browne walks the line between happy and melancholic by making extensive use of the submediant (vi) chord, ending some phrases that sound as though they should end on the major tonic (I) chord deceptively on the minor quality submediant.

Late for the Sky began with an anthem-like musical and lyrical statement, and its finale, "Before the Deluge," forms a similarly grand closing bookend. As he views the apocalypse, an apocalypse caused by the destruction of the environment, he observes the surprise of those who had fought against environmental degradation. Not only are the lyrics a call to rescue the global environment from the abyss, but they also sum up the feelings of members of Browne's generation who, in 1974, must have had serious questions about hope for the future. Although Browne does not speak anywhere on *Late for the Sky* about the specific events of the five years that led up to the time of the album, the destruction of the environment in "Before the Deluge" can be heard as a metaphor for the fragile state of the collective psyche of members of Browne's generation in the wake of the Vietnam War, the Manson murders, the Kent State University shootings, the Watergate Scandal, and so on. Interestingly, the phrase structure of music and lyrics calls to mind Bob Dylan's song "Chimes of Freedom." In fact, the numerous suspended fourth chords of "Before the Deluge" also call to mind the Byrds' recording of the Dylan song on their 1965 album, *Mr. Tambourine Man*.

Members of Jackson Browne's generation were in their mid-20s at the time of the release of *Late for the Sky*. The songs can be heard as deeply personal statements from the soul of Browne and from the souls of his characters; however, they can also be heard as symptomatic of the search for meaning of a generation. The war in Vietnam was all but lost, so questions abounded about the sacrifice of the killed and those who had returned physically and psychologically broken as well as those who had sought refuge in Canada to avoid the military draft. The communal peace, love, and understanding of the 1960s was giving way to the so-called Me Decade, so questions arose about the idealism and dreams of the 1960s: Would the dreams of Jackson Browne's generation ever be realized? It is also possible to hear the album as a collection of anthems for male emotional liberation—the ability to reflect inwardly and express one's emotions, even if it meant crying. Still, it is important to keep in mind that despite the fact that it is possible to interpret *Late for the Sky* on a deeper generational level or as a symbol of increasing male expression of emotion, the album is not just a metaphor for the angst of its time; it remains a vibrant collection of songs in which Jackson Browne portrays and observes characters who are universally human enough that they still resonate more than 35 years later.

2

Gram Parsons

Grievous Angel (1974)

James E. Perone

When one discusses the development of country rock in the late 1960s, the names Michael Nesmith, Rick Nelson, Gram Parsons, and Bob Dylan frequently come up. Nelson had been a star in popular music and on television from the 1950s, Dylan has been one of the most iconic of all figures in American vernacular music since the dawn of the 1960s, and Nesmith was well known in the mid-1960s as a member of the Monkees as well as one of the stars of the television series of the same name. Members of the general public are much less likely to be familiar with Parsons by name. Gram Parsons—through his groundbreaking 1967–1968 work with the short-lived International Submarine Band; his work with the Byrds on the 1968 *Sweetheart of the Rodeo* album and tour; his association with Keith Richards and Mick Jagger when the Rolling Stones made forays into merging country, blues, and rock in the late 1960s; his subsequent work with the Flying Burrito Brothers; his duets with Emmylou Harris; and his solo work into 1973—turned out to be one of the most influential artists in the merger of rock and country as well as a major influence on the development of the later alternative country (alt-country) genre. The album *Grievous Angel* was recorded in 1973 and issued in 1974 after Parsons's death from a drug overdose. It was not a great commercial success, but it remains one of Parsons's most highly acclaimed recordings.

One of the first things that the listener might notice when hearing *Grievous Angel*—or Parsons's first solo album or the 1960s work of Dylan, Nesmith, and Nelson, for that matter—is that Parsons did not so much create the hybrid of country, folk, and rock that became most popular through the 1970s' recordings by the Eagles and Poco. Most of the material and the arrangements on

Grievous Angel are closer to traditional country than the more popular country rock hybrids of the 1970s. What Parsons did with the Byrds, in his association with the Rolling Stones, and in his other work was to show that young people, hippies even, could be one with country music. As such, he is as much an antecedent of the Eagles and Poco as he is of the outlaw country that emerged later in the 1970s, not to mention the forays into country that artists such as Elvis Costello would make within a few years of Parsons's death.

Grievous Angel contains a mixture of fairly recent country songs by a variety of writers, new songs written or cowritten by Parsons, one of Parsons' songs from the 1960s, and two long-standing country standards that go back more than a decade. The album begins with the Parsons composition "Return of the Grievous Angel." Here, as on most of the tracks on *Grievous Angel*, Parsons is joined by instrumentalists from Elvis Presley's backing band (including lead guitarist James Burton), Bernie Leadon (at the time the lead guitarist of the Eagles), and, perhaps most importantly, vocalist Emmylou Harris. This song of wandering, homesickness, and various experiences on the road is typical of the works that Parsons wrote on the album: the text is lengthy, and the music and lyrics meander somewhat, suggesting the influence of folk revival and old traditional country music (as opposed to commercial Nashville country) on Parsons's writing style. In particular, the song contains extended musical sections that seem to be coming to a harmonic and melodic cadence, only to continue for another four-measure phrase. In the case of "Return of the Grievous Angel," this somewhat conversational approach to songwriting fits well with the wanderings about which Parsons (lead) and Harris (harmony) sing. Among the more interesting images that Parsons presents are that of "the King" who wore "on his head, an amphetamine crown" and the "twenty thousand roads I went down . . . and they all led me straight back home to you." The first of these refers to Elvis Presley, widely known as the King of Rock and Roll, who would increasingly from this time until his death in 1977 become known for his widely fluctuating weight and drug addictions. The second of these lyrical images lent itself to the title of David Meyer's 2007 biography of Parsons, *Twenty Thousand Roads: The Ballad of Gram Parsons and His Cosmic American Music*.[1]

While Parsons adopts a somewhat conversational approach to musical phrase structure and rhyme scheme in "Return of the Grievous Angel" and in other songs he wrote, he was not alone: other relatively young songwriters who were blurring the lines of country, rock, and pop were experimenting in the same way. For example, one need only listen to the opening verse of Michael Nesmith's song "Don't Wait for Me" (a May 1968 recording[2] released on the 1969 Monkees album *Instant Replay*) to hear how a rhythmic change on a soft rhyme (a quick "comin'" and a drawn-out "something") can allow a writer to turn what might be anticipated to be a conventional 8-measure phrase into a 10-measure vocal phrase, followed by a 2-measure instrumental interlude.

And although the general phrase structure is considerably more conventional, Jimmy Webb's "Galveston," which was a 1969 country and pop hit for Glen Campbell, contains a phrase extension on the line "on the beach where we used to run" that lends a conversational realism to the song. Gram Parsons, on songs such as "Return of the Grievous Angel" and "$1000 Wedding" in particular, went a bit further than his contemporaries and predecessors in moving from predictable pop song structure in the direction of a freer-flowing narrative.

The next track, the country ballad "Hearts on Fire," was written by Tom Guidera and Walter Egan. It is more conventional in structure, which only serves to highlight the conversational aspects of Parsons's writing style. It is a song about a yearlong love that has flamed out, only to cause sleepless nights. The gist of the text is that the more intense a relationship is, the more intense the feeling of loss and blame when it ends. Significantly, the album's seventh track, Boudleaux Bryant's "Love Hurts," a slow country ballad best known before *Grievous Angel* through early 1960s' recordings by the Everly Brothers and Roy Orbison, presents similar ideas about lost love. The duet work of Parsons and Emmylou Harris on "Love Hurts" is one of the highlights of the album.

Back in the mid-1960s, Tom T. Hall might have been best known as the author of several songs that supported U.S. efforts in Vietnam; however, Hall's 1970 composition "I Can't Dance" is about as far from politics as it could be. The song is a humorous high-energy roadhouse dance number. While it serves to lighten the album's focus on songs of heartache, longing, homesickness, and brokenness, it does tend to stand out just because it is so different in general mood than the rest of the songs.

In 2000, Sundazed Music released *Another Side of This Life*, a CD collection of previously unissued 1965–1966 demo recordings of Gram Parsons. The song "Brass Buttons" is included among these home recordings, making it the oldest Parsons composition on *Grievous Angel*. In keeping with the folk revival style of the mid-1960s, the song can be understood on several levels. Some Parsons fans interpret the song as a reference to the singer-songwriter's alcoholic mother. Certainly Parsons's reference to "bottle of blues" and his remembrance of "everything she said" could be understood that way. However, even the "bottle of blues" image—the one that comes closest to a direct acknowledgment of alcohol abuse—can be understood in other ways. For example, perhaps "bottle of blues" is just a color image that goes along with the "green silks and silver shoes" found earlier in the lyrics. In any case, in folksinger-songwriter style, Parsons makes the text vague enough that the song can be read as a recollection of a deceased mother, a lost lover, or even a lost child. Dating as it does from Parsons's early days as a writer, the phrase structure is much more conventional than that of his more narrative-form works of the 1970s. In its form and arrangement, "Brass Buttons" is perhaps the closest song on *Grievous Angel* to the prevailing Eagles/Poco-style folk–country rock hybrid that was enjoying considerable commercial success at the time. The arrangement and Parsons's understated singing style help to create a mood of bittersweet nostalgia and a twinge of melancholy that matches that of the text.

Parsons uses his impressionistic imagery to tell the story of a bride who presumably dies shortly before her wedding in "$1000 Wedding." He also keeps the narrative conversational by means of extended phrase structure. Despite the fact that it is a strophic song, it gives the listener the impression that it is at least in part through-composed, mostly because the stanzas are so long.

Ira and Charlie Louvin's "Cash on the Barrelhead" lightens the mood considerably. Despite the fact that Parsons portrays a character who clearly is down on his luck, with "no money down, no credit plan," this up-tempo country rock adaptation of 1950s' bluegrass is a rollicking roadhouse dance piece. This feel is confirmed by the presence of friends and associates of Parsons who turn the recording studio into what sounds like a live concert atmosphere. In fact, Parsons, as the record's producer, labels the Louvin Brothers' "Cash on the Barrelhead" and his own "Hickory Wind" as "Medley Live from Northern Quebec." The studio trickery that makes the two tracks sound like a live concert recording is a bit too much on the obvious side. It tends to do more of a disservice, however, to "Hickory Wind" than it does to the rocking Louvin Brothers song.

"Hickory Wind," credited to Parsons and Bob Buchanan,[3] dates from Parsons's days as a folksinger-songwriter, although the song did appear on the Byrds' *Sweetheart of the Rodeo*. One of the great tragedies of the Byrds album is that although it was later acknowledged as one of the most important attempts to reconcile rock and country, in part through Parsons's contributions, Parsons's vocals were erased from the finished mix of the album because of contractual difficulties. While a "Hickory Wind" absent the fake audience sounds of the "Medley Live from Northern Quebec" tracks on *Grievous Angel* would have been preferable, at least this album presents the song as interpreted by Parsons. Despite the fact that the authorship of the song is in dispute and that Parsons had been associated with it for perhaps six years before the recording of *Grievous Angel*, "Hickory Wind," with its recollections of growing up in an easier time in South Carolina, fits in with the album's other songs of longing for the innocence and happiness of an earlier time.

The country genre has been notable for spawning a number of highly successful male-female duet partnerships over the decades. Although the dynamics between such duos as Porter Wagoner and Dolly Parton, Conway Twitty and Loretta Lynn, and George Jones and Tammy Wynette differed considerably, close harmony male-female singing brings very different dynamics than the work of, say, the Everly Brothers or Simon and Garfunkel. For one thing, a song about a broken male-female relationship can seem to be coming to the listener from both sides. From a more technical basis, the vocal blend is also going to be quite different than that of same-gender duos. Although the relative newcomer Emmylou Harris sings harmony on several tracks on *Grievous*

Angel, the pairing of Harris and Parsons works particularly effectively on Boudleaux Bryant's 1960 composition "Love Hurts." The song itself fits in well on the album, in part because it offers similar sentiments as "Hearts on Fire." The pain of the broken relationship in the Bryant song seems to come at the listener from both sides, primarily because of the contrast between Harris's and Parsons's vocal tone colors. Parsons sings in an understated style that is noticeably closer to pop music than Harris's more folk/roots-oriented approach. This is not to imply that the two are like oil and water. Rather, the intonation of the duo matches well, and the pop-versus-roots approach is not so wide as to sound awkward. The effect is more like that of Parsons telling the listener of his heartache, while in a split frame Harris lets the listener know that Parsons is not the only one feeling the pain of the breakup.

Cowriters Parsons and Rick Grech turn to the darker side of Las Vegas in "Ooh Las Vegas." This up-tempo song, with a form that owes at least a little debt to country blues, can be heard as the flip side of the Elvis Presley hit "Viva Las Vegas." In "Viva Las Vegas," writers Doc Pomus and Mort Shuman have Presley extol the virtues of the women, the bright lights, and the thrill of possibly winning at games of chance while acknowledging that he may lose everything he has. In "Ooh Las Vegas" the gambling is acknowledged as an addiction, and Parsons expresses the knowledge that he knows he is going to lose, but he cannot help his need to let the "Crystal City" "Make a wreck outta me." Despite the debt to old-time country blues that can be heard in the harmonic progression and form of the song, James Burton's electric lead guitar ties "Ooh Las Vegas" to the rockabilly tradition that he had been a part of since his first recordings back in the 1950s.

Parsons collaborated with Emmylou Harris to write the album's final track, "In My Hour of Darkness." With its straightforward phrase structure, simple harmonies, and natural melodic rise and fall, the song calls to mind such early country songs as the Carter Family's "Worried Man Blues" and "There'll Be Joy, Joy, Joy." Although the structure of "In My Hour of Darkness" owes a debt to the country music of the 1920s and 1930s, the texture has a more contemporary feel and includes a backing vocal chorus of Parsons, Harris, guest vocalist Linda Ronstadt, and others. The instrumental arrangement includes fiddle and Dobro, so there is an old-time feel in that respect. Because of the fact that *Grievous Angel* was not issued until after Parsons's untimely death, the song's chorus, which asks the Lord to grant the singer "wisdom" and "speed" "in [his] hour of darkness" and "in [his] time of need," sounds eerily autobiographical. Add to that the fact that the verses also contain biographical and autobiographical details. For example, in the first verse, Parsons describes "a young man" who, "driving through the night," met his untimely death on "a deadly Denver bend," a reference to actor Brandon De Wilde, a friend of Parsons and Emmylou Harris who died in 1972 in an automobile accident outside of Denver, Colorado. In the second verse, Parsons describes "another young man" who "safely strums his silver-string guitar." This man who is viewed by some as "a star" is really at heart "a country boy" who is full of music. Although the verse could apply to any number of Parsons's contemporaries, it could just as well apply to Parsons himself. The "old man, kind and wise with age," whom Parsons encounters in the third verse is the embodiment of an elder who knows Parsons better than the singer knows himself. While one could probably have the proverbial field day speculating as to the identity of the inspiration for this character, it would probably turn out to be less interesting than the implications of the verse—that is, if one could positively identify the inspiration. Perhaps the more interesting feature of the verse is that it suggests that the singer's character does not show his real emotions and does not necessarily possess a fully formed self-knowledge or a high degree of self-esteem. Because Parsons died of a drug overdose before the album was released, these possible autobiographical references and possible insights into his inner self are particularly fascinating. Since more than 35 years have passed since the release of *Grievous Angel*, it is easy to miss another aspect of the significance of the third verse of "In My Hour of Darkness." Parsons sings with empathy for, connection with, and even love for the "old man." This aligns with the new appreciation of the older generation that coincided with the back-to-the-land movement of the early 1970s. This was the period in which folk and rock concerts began to include older blues, folk, and country artists, some of whom had made their earliest impact on American music as early as the 1920s. For example, Joan Baez brought Maybelle Carter, a member of the original Carter Family back in the 1920s, onstage at folk festivals that were attended primarily by young people. While the attitudes of young people may have differed from their elders with regard to the war in Vietnam, recreational drug usage, free love, and other issues, a sense of certain shared core values was recognized as extending across generational boundaries in the early 1970s as they often had not been acknowledged in the 1967–1968 period.

Grievous Angel was not a commercial success on the pop charts, nor was it a commercial success on the country charts. Its significance lies not so much, then, in how many people have experienced it since 1974 but instead in the way in which so-called outlaw country, the resurgence of interest in roots-style country, and the blurring of lines between the rock audience and the country audience and the development of alternative country are all anticipated on the album. Plus, Gram Parsons was a singer-songwriter whose lyrical imagery and engaging singing style stood well above the level of his public popularity, and most of the musical selections, arrangements, and performances of *Grievous Angel* hold up well, sounding fresh and vital even more than 35 years after the release of the album.

Notes

1. David Meyer, *Twenty Thousand Roads: The Ballad of Gram Parsons and His Cosmic American Music* (New York: Villard, 2007).

2. Edward Reilly, Maggie McManus, and William Chadwick, *The Monkees: A Manufactured Image* (Ann Arbor, MI: Pierian, 1987), 181.
3. The specifics of the authorship of the song are a matter of some dispute: Sylvia Sammons claims to have written most of the song in 1963. David W. Johnson, "Crediting 'Hickory Wind'," Folklinks, http://www.folklinks.com/hickory_wind .html.

3

John Denver

Back Home Again (1974)

James E. Perone

One of the most popular American musicians of the 1970s, John Denver strad-dled the worlds of folk, pop, and country music. Probably not by accident, Den-ver's greatest popularity as a singer-songwriter came during the first half of the decade. Since most of the material that Denver wrote and recorded—as well as his work as an activist—reflected optimism and traditional rural values, tem-pered with left-leaning politics and environmentalism, he at once offered relief from the social dissonance of the late Vietnam War era and affirmed the values of the period's back-to-the-land movement. Denver's optimism and his country/folk/pop hybrid style brought aspects of country music to a wide audience and to a nonstereotypically country audience. Generally, John Denver was a writer and performer of individual songs, as opposed to being a concept album artist. However, his 1974 album *Back Home Again*, which consists of songs written by Denver and members of his musical circle, can be heard as an album-length affirmation of the importance of home and family. *Back Home Again* contains some of Denver's best work and was named Album of the Year by the Academy of Country Music. The Country Music Association selected the album's title track as the 1975 Song of the Year. A commercially successful crossover album, *Back Home Again* hit No. 1 on *Billboard* magazine's country and pop charts, and four of the album's tracks that were issued as singles ("Annie's Song," "Thank God I'm a Country Boy," "Sweet Surrender," and "Back Home Again") were hits on various country, adult contemporary, and pop charts.

The album opens with its title track, one of the eight Denver-composed songs contained therein. Denver paints a picture of a rural scene in which a woman waits at home for her man, who is "ten days on the road." The simple humble home scene, the love that Denver expresses for his farm, and the love that binds the couple all reflect traditional values. Part of the beauty of this song—and this certainly is not the only John Denver composition for which this is true—is that it simultaneously can be heard as a universal statement and as an autobiographical one. While some of the details of the song do not jibe with John and Annie Denver's life at the time, the mention of "Sunshine," presumably Denver's song "Sunshine on My Shoulder," gives the text an autobiographical feel. The fact that Denver was spending a considerable amount of time on the road as a concert attraction at the time also lends an autobiographical-sounding touch to this expression of longing for home. At the same time, though, the autobiographical references are vague enough that they do not overwhelm the universal nature of the text.

Denver's musical setting in "Back Home Again" is also noteworthy. The melodic range at nearly an octave and a half is quite wide, as is the range within each phrase of the verse sections. This lends the song a melodic expansiveness that stood in relief to many of the pop and country songs of the era. Denver tempers the expansiveness of the melodic range with the use of repeated pitches at the beginning of each phrase of the verse sections. His use of musical form follows the pop song traditions of the prepsychedelic 1960s, with well-defined verse, chorus, and middle eight (or second bridge) sections. To the extent that the listener is familiar with older songs that use this form, Denver's setting can reflect nostalgia for a simpler time. And the traditional form, the balancing of wide melodic range with repeated pitches, and the rhythmic setting of the text all suggest a mastery of pop songwriting and a knowledge of American songwriting traditions. In short, it is a masterful country/pop/folk hybrid.

Denver's voice on "Back Home Again" and most of the other songs on the album achieves an intriguing balance. His controlled tenor and distinctively folkish vibrato generally could be characterized as sweet. In particular parts of his range, however, an edginess creeps into Denver's voice. This tends to make his ballads, such as "Back Home Again" and "Annie's Song"—even orchestrated as they are—sound less studied (and more authentically folklike) than the work of a pop crooner.

Of the 12 songs on *Back Home Again*, only "On the Road" was not a 1974 piece written by Denver or one of his close musical associates. Written by Denver's friend Carl Franzen, "On the Road" dates from 1970.[1] While it is easy to hear this piece as the least essential track on the album, the familiar focus of the lyrics fits in nicely within the overarching themes of *Back Home Again.*

"Grandma's Feather Bed," written by Denver's banjo player, Jim Connor, became a popular staple of Denver's live performances. A lighthearted, humorous reflection on the fun and innocence of childhood, the piece fits within the album's focus on home (in this case the home of the grandmother of Denver's character) and family. Connor's use of humor, his reflection on childhood, and the combination of folk revival and country styles might remind some listeners of songs such as Tom Paxton's "The Marvelous Toy."

The album's next track, Denver's composition "Matthew," is one of the more touching songs on *Back Home Again*. In this tribute to his father's youngest brother, Dean Deutschendorf,[2] Denver obscures some of the biographical detail. For example, based on a strict reading of the lyrics, the character Matthew would have to be the brother of Denver's character's mother. In any case, Denver reminisces about the uncle who came into his life and "became [his] friend." Interestingly, several of Denver's songs on *Back Home Again* seem to be linked melodically because of the way in which they emphasize a meandering descent from scale step five down to tonic in the verses. Although on the foreground level the tunes are quite different in shape, the longer-range descent from scale step five to scale step one links "Back Home Again" and "Matthew." "Matthew" is one of the more effective vocal performances on the album, particularly because of how Denver's soaring tenor on the refrain displays a touch of the grittiness that emerges in his voice from time to time. This enhances the bittersweet aspects of Matthew's life, as developed through the song, as well as the bittersweet nature of the relationship between Denver's character and his uncle—it is never stated explicitly, but the fact that Denver's character reminisces about his uncle can be understood to imply that his uncle has died.

Although John Denver wrote most of the hit songs for which he was known, "Thank God I'm a Country Boy" is one notable exception. Because one of Denver's musical associates, multi-instrumentalist John Sommers, wrote it and because the song fits Denver's rhetorical style so well, it is easy to assume that the piece came from Denver's pen. The piece contains the good-natured humor of "Grandma's Feather Bed" and finds Denver's character reflecting on the past but also singing about the simple pleasures of the present. As is the case throughout *Back Home Again*, home, family, and the simple pleasures of rural life are the focal points of the lyrics. The enjoyment of acoustic music is among these pleasures; the importance of music in the lifestyle of Denver and his fellow songwriters emerges in later songs on the album as well. As one might reasonably expect, the main focus of the performance is Denver's voice; however, "Thank God I'm a Country Boy" is an example of just how musically and technically proficient Denver's band was.

Denver connects love and music in his brief song "The Music Is You." The song consists of a single stanza of poetry, which is sung twice. On the repeat and during the coda section, Julie Connor provides vocal counterpoint to Denver. In the context of Denver's longer, more fully developed songs on the album, "The Music Is You" is a trifle and almost sounds like a chorus or refrain of an unfinished song.

The next track, "Annie's Song," remains one of John Denver's best-remembered compositions. Like "The Music Is You," this piece has very little text, especially compared with some of the multistanza songs on *Back Home Again*. However, it is the simple, concise statement of love in Denver's two stanzas of poetry that in part makes the song so successfully. As is the case with Denver's best compositions, too, the melody is easy to remember. Significantly, this musical setting is as simple as the lyrics: it is a short verse-refrain structure, similar to a hymn, as opposed to the more complex verse–chorus–middle eight structure of a song such as "Back Home Again."

Steve Weisberg's "It's Up to You" is a somewhat meandering song; however, it reinforces the image of the freedom and simplicity of rural family life. The next song, "Cool An' Green An' Shady," is a collaborative effort of Denver and Joe Henry. With images such as "easy afternoons," "lazy days," and "city ways make me want to hide," this song also reinforces the image of the carefree, relaxing life in a rural setting. The previous eight songs revolved so fully around the instrumental sounds of acoustic plucked and bowed strings—including the several songs that are sweetened by orchestral strings—that Buddy Collette's guest appearance on clarinet immediately stands out. Collette's obbligato provides the song with a feeling of nostalgia for early 20th-century life and might suggest to some listeners lazy New Orleans–style jazz. Nostalgia is part of several songs (e.g., "Grandma's Feather Bed," "Matthew," and "On the Road") on *Back Home Again*; however, this piece does not seem to fit as well, mostly because of the tendency for the clarinet to suggest a locale that is outside of the milieu of the album's other songs.

John Denver's concern about environmental degradation emerges in full force in "Eclipse." Here, he observes the "heavy smog between [him] and the mountains" and the contrast between the "serenity" of rural life and people "that work with their machines." The beauty of the song—aside from the folklike music and arrangement—is that although the piece can be heard as a lamentation about the destruction of the environment, it is as much about Denver's character's ruminations about life. In other words, it is a gentle topical "protest" song, one that uses the soft-sell approach to deliver its message.

"Annie's Song," "Thank God I'm a Country Boy," and "Back Home Again" were such major hits and received so much radio airplay back in the mid-1970s that it is easy to overlook "Sweet Surrender." It is not that the song is a lost album track: when issued as a single, "Sweet Surrender" was quite successful on the pop, adult contemporary, and country charts. It just was not as ubiquitous as the other three songs. Denver celebrates the possibilities of a future without plans and cares. With its length (more than five minutes) and orchestral and vocal arrangement, the piece becomes a near anthem to life on the road. The piece reflects the idealism and naïveté that pervades so much of the album. Could life on the open road or life on a working farm really be as easy and carefree as Denver and his fellow songwriters on *Back Home Again* paint it? Some listeners might hear many of these songs as pure escapism; however, this idealism provided an escape from very real national pain at the time: the pain of the Vietnam War, the Watergate Scandal, the Kent State Shootings, and so on. This was much-needed music at the time.

If some of John Denver's idealism and naïveté seems contrived, Denver lets the listener know that his music comes straight from the heart in the album's closer, "This Old Guitar." The autobiographical nature of the song is confirmed by the fact that the arrangement includes only Denver on acoustic guitar and voice. This pulls the earlier material into the era's introspective singer-songwriter genre. Concluding *Back Home Again* with this highly personal song was a masterful touch.

John Denver unquestionably was a singer-songwriter whose strongest gifts were found in his construction and interpretation of individual songs. *Back Home Again*, though, struck a proverbial chord with the public at a low point in U.S. history. Despite the fact that *Back Home Again* was an album that was so needed at the time, the best songs of the collection still ring true nearly four decades after their original release.

Notes

1. Liner notes to *Back Home Again*, CD reissue, RCA/Legacy 82876 68964 2, 2005. Note: The liner notes give the writer's name incorrectly as "Chris Franzen."
2. Timothy J. Kloberdanz, "Denver, John," in *Encyclopedia of the Great Plains*, edited by David J. Wishart (Lincoln, NE: Center for Great Plains Studies, 2004), 537.

4

Emmylou Harris

Pieces of the Sky (1975)

James E. Perone

After assisting country rock pioneer Gram Parsons as a vocalist and cowriter on Parsons' final album, Emmylou Harris emerged as a leading talent in the new country music of the second half of the 1970s. In fact, her career as a concert attraction, solo recording artist, and duet singer continues into the 21st century. As All Music Guide's critic Jason Ankeny writes, "Though other performers sold more records and earned greater fame, few left as profound an impact on contemporary music as Emmylou Harris."[1] As numerous critics and fans have noted, Harris followed the lead of Parsons in writing and recording in a highly individualistic way, refusing to follow trends. Harris's major label debut, *Pieces of the Sky*, was responsible in large part for establishing her as a major force in the music industry and remains perhaps Harris's most highly acclaimed album.

Pieces of the Sky begins with Rodney Crowell's "Bluebird Wine." It is an interesting love song in that it finds Harris singing that her "baby" gave her an entirely new outlook on life: now the couple enjoys staying at home, getting drunk on "Bluebird Wine." What the song really is about, though, is Harris's vocal performance style and the work of the band, which tend to explore the overlap between western swing, bluegrass, commercial country, and country rock. Throughout the album, Harris receives expert instrumental backup from a group that includes ties to the Eagles (Bernie Leadon on various guitars, banjo, and Dobro) and Elvis Presley's 1970s backup band (Glen D. Hardin on piano and James Burton on guitars and Dobro) and also included such expert progressive country instrumentals as Ricky Skaggs.

One of the Emmylou Harris trademarks that *Pieces of the Sky* introduces is her trend toward eclecticism with regard to repertoire. For example, the songs that make up this collection include old country standards, Bakersfield country rock, Appalachian-style folk, one of Dolly Parton's best-known compositions, a Beatles ballad, a Harris tribute to Gram Parsons, a song by author Shel Silverstein, and other pieces that do not necessarily seem at first glance to belong together. The strength of *Pieces of the Sky* is that there is a coherent stylistic approach throughout so that the repertoire selection—as slightly quirky as it might seem—somehow works.

The album's second track, Billy Sherill's "Too Far Gone," is the first song of heartbreak to appear. Harris's character continues to carry a torch for a former lover who now is with someone else. Because she is "too far gone" in love, she cannot give up the relationship, continuing to hope that should he break up with his current lover, he will return to Harris's character. With its light triple-meter feel, string arrangement, and connection to Sherill, this perhaps is the closest song on *Pieces of the Sky* to conventional commercial country music. However, one of the curious aspects of the arrangement that tends to make the recording stand out from the conventional can be found in the instrumental break. Here, producer/arranger Brian Ahern allows the listener's focus to fade between Glen D. Hardin's string arrangement, the pedal steel, the acoustic guitar, and the lead electric guitar in an almost impressionistic wash.

The Louvin Brothers' "If I Could Only Win Your Love" provides Harris and Herb Pederson an opportunity for the duet singing at which Harris has always excelled. That is not to say that she is not an effective soloist; it is just that ever since her work in the first half of the 1970s with Gram Parsons, Harris has proven herself to be one of the best harmony singers in pop music of any subgenre. When released as a single, "If I Could Only Win Your Love" made both the *Billboard* country and pop charts. Although the song fared significantly better on the country charts, the mere fact that it crossed over provides support to Harris's role as the logical successor to Parsons in fulfilling his vision of merging the various subgenres of Anglo-American popular music into one.

The next track, the Emmylou Harris and Bill Danoff song "Boulder to Birmingham," is a tribute to the aforementioned Parsons, the man who shortly before this recording had been Harris's mentor. Even if the listener does not hear the song as a direct reference to the recently deceased Parsons, it is still thoroughly effective as an ode to a lost (or deceased) lover or close friend. The intensity of loss is conveyed in various images throughout the song; however, the line in which Harris sings that she "would walk all the way from Boulder to Birmingham" if she thought that she could see the lost one's face once more is perhaps the most vivid image. The music and arrangement are engaging, making this an Emmylou Harris classic, perhaps the best song that she ever wrote or cowrote. Although the lyrics and musical setting could work effectively for many singers, the sense of somewhat detached resignation that permeates Harris's lead vocal contributes significantly to the strength of the recording.

The second stanza of the lyrics of the Danny Flowers song "Before Believing" provided the title of *Pieces of the Sky*. The lyrics can be read in a variety of ways. The "believing in you" can be heard as a religious reference; however, it can just as easily be heard in person-to-person human terms. Because of this, the piece works particularly well in the album's running order. Specifically, if heard as a religious piece, in which belief, or faith, carries the singer's character through the troubles of the world, then "Before Believing" can be heard as a reflection of what carries Harris's character through the loss that is at the heart of "Boulder to Birmingham." However, if heard in purely human terms, then the song might seem to further explain the relationship between the characters of the previous song. While the arrangement is absent the overdubbed strings of some of the tracks, there is a sense of expansiveness to the music. In large part, this is a result of the arrangement's use of extended instrumental sections in which acoustic guitars, fiddle, viola, piano, bass, and pedal steel all play individual accompanying roles: there is not really an instrumental solo per se. This suggests the introspective reflection of the lyrics. And it should be noted that the same sort of instrumental approach was a feature of the earlier track "Too Far Gone."

The Emmylou Harris rendition of Merle Haggard's "Bottle Let Me Down" (often given as "The Bottle Let Me Down") is one of the more curious tracks on *Pieces of the Sky*. Haggard's own recording had been around for nearly a decade and had found its way into the live repertoire of numerous country honky-tonk artists. In Haggard's original recording, the slightly drunken pedal steel lines and Haggard's vocal approach make the singer thoroughly believable as the man who has to keep drinking more and more in order to deaden the pain of having lost in love. Similarly, the rollicking 1981 version of the song by British rocker Elvis Costello is so over-the-top in tempo and in Steve Nieve's piano playing that one could easily imagine it being performed in a honky-tonk by a group of musicians who perhaps had a bit too much of a nip at the bottle before showtime. Emmylou Harris's approach is much more dispassionate. This can be heard throughout the recording but perhaps is easiest to detect as she flips the rhythm on the text "the bottle let me down." A lack of emotion can be a negative for a singer; however, the sense of emotional detachment and decidedly not-drunken approach that Harris takes is almost eerie. In fact, allowing the song to "sell" itself—as opposed to the singer selling the song by means of dramatizing the meaning—connects Harris more to the roots/folk tradition than to some of the commercial country music of the time.

The theme of lost or unrequited love that develops over the course of "Too Far Gone," "If Only I Could Win Your Love," "Boulder to Birmingham," and "Bottle Let Me Down" comes even more starkly into focus on "Sleepless Nights." Insofar as Harris has excelled as a harmony vocalist over the decades, her multitracked work on "Sleepless Nights" is interesting to consider. The track can be a bit of a disappointment but only because Harris tends to be a more interesting duet singer when she is paired with someone with a contrasting vocal timbre.

Because Dolly Parton became an enormously well-known entertainer and music business icon, it is easy to overlook her as an important songwriter. Certainly "Coat of Many Colors" is one of Parton's classic compositions. Harris and the other musicians give a sensitive folk-influenced performance. One of the distinguishing features of the Emmylou Harris vocal style is her tendency to crescendo on long notes. She does so on most of the slower songs on *Pieces of the Sky*, but the technique perhaps is most noticeable on "Coat of Many Colors."

An album track on the Beatles' *Revolver*, Paul McCartney's "For No One"[2] undergoes a substantial rhetorical change in the hands of Harris. Because of the singer's gender and the lyrical references to a woman who no longer needs her former lover, the song seems to come from the viewpoint of either the woman who was part of the relationship or a third party. While the McCartney performance can be heard in this second way, it perhaps is more logical to hear him as the man who will never be able to "forget her." Hearing Harris's interpretation as an expression from the woman who will not be forgotten provides an edge to the song. Because the woman to whom she refers is always referenced in the third person, the haunting emotional detachment that is present in other songs on the album also pervades this piece.

The original release of *Pieces of the Sky* concludes with Shel Silverstein's "Queen of the Silver Dollar." Here, Harris portrays a woman who rules the local bar, holding court on a barstool with a glass of cheap wine in her hand. Her relationships are transitory and tawdry and involve the other regulars at the bar. The dark humor of the piece is in the mold of such bar-based stories of what conventional society might call losers as Merle Haggard's "Swinging Doors." The piece was a brilliant choice for the conclusion of Harris's major label debut. First, Silverstein's lyrics move from a third-person observation of the "queen" to first person. This supports the feeling of detachment that permeates the album. Second, the narrative rounds out the album's subtheme of exploring alcohol: "Bluebird Wine" finds two lovers sharing wine for enjoyment, "Bottle Let Me Down" uses dark humor to explore the use of alcohol as escape from emotional pain, and "Queen of the Silver Dollar" explores bar regulars who are content to exist every night in a world in which they can rule.

In 2004 Rhino Records released *Pieces of the Sky* on CD and included as bonus tracks two Dallas Frazier songs: "Hank and Lefty" and "California Cottonfields." The two tracks were recorded at the same sessions as the songs that made it into the running order of the vinyl release of the album and, while not necessary tracks, support "Coat of Many Colors" as songs of growing up in poverty in the South.

Pieces of the Sky might not have contained any chart-topping hits, but it was an important album in bringing young people to country music. Gram Parsons may have had a vision for making a roots-based country music the music of America, of making it cool. However, it took Emmylou Harris to carry the torch through the second half of the 1970s and into the future to merge country, rock, and folk and to provide a hybrid form of country that appealed to an audience that was otherwise in age, politics, and geography removed from the stereotypical country audience. This album was an important stepping-stone along the way.

Notes

1. Jason Ankeny, "Biography: Emmylou Harris," All Music Guide, http://allmusic .com/cg/amg.dll?p = amg&searchlink = EMMYLOU|HARRIS&sql = 11:fifrxql5 ldse~T1.
2. The composition is credited to John Lennon and Paul McCartney; however, each member of the songwriting team tended to sing lead on songs for which they had been predominantly or solely responsible. On *Revolver*, McCartney is the only Beatle to perform on "For No One."

5

Joan Baez

Diamonds & Rust (1975)

James E. Perone

Joan Baez was a ubiquitous part of the folk revival and protest movement from the late 1950s to the end of the Vietnam War. As a performer, Baez perhaps was best known for her live appearances at rallies and music festivals, although she recorded numerous albums throughout the period. Additionally, she was best known in this period for her interpretations and adaptations of traditional folk music and compositions by her contemporaries. Her 1975 album *Diamonds & Rust* transformed Baez into an important figure in that era's singer-songwriter movement. Artists such as Joni Mitchell, John Prine, James Taylor, Jackson Browne, and Carole King wrote and sang deeply personal-sounding songs, often with largely acoustic and/or jazz-influenced arrangements. *Diamonds & Rust* found Baez including an unusually large number of her own compositions, most quite personal in nature, as well as covers of other singer-songwriters of the time. The musical settings are thoroughly contemporary sounding and include the contributions of some of the same rock and jazz musicians who appeared on recordings by other members of the singer-songwriter genre. With the possible exception of her 1960 self-titled debut album, *Diamonds & Rust* remains the crowning achievement of an important figure in American music whose performing and recording career encompasses the entire time period covered in *The Album*.

The album opens with perhaps the greatest and most personal song Joan Baez has ever written, the title track, "Diamonds & Rust." Baez acknowledges that the song concerns her love affair with Bob Dylan in the early 1960s. In fact, in her 2009 autobiography *And a Voice to Sing With*, Baez intersperses the song's lyrics with her recollections of her first encounters with Dylan, such that the imagery of "Diamonds & Rust" takes on a more concrete meaning.[1] One of the more interesting features of Baez's lyrics is her use of lines of varying length from verse to verse. In the context of her assertion that her former lover told her that her poetry was "lousy," the structural inconsistency from verse to verse might seem to confirm famed wordsmith Dylan's assessment; however, the structural inconsistency turns out, in fact, to be one of the great strengths of Baez's approach to lyrics in this piece: the lyrics seem to flow straight from the heart and are not subject to the conventions of pop song construction. Particularly effective is the use of the title imagery: diamonds, which Dylan bought for Baez and represent the hope, the promise, and the fulfillment of the relationship at its peak, and rust, which represents the disintegration of the relationship and the hurt that can never fully be healed.

"Diamonds & Rust" is in the key of F minor, and the melody is constructed from short sequential figures. Interestingly, Baez ends the verses on the tonic chord (F minor) but with the third of the chord (A flat) in the vocal line at the cadence. The mixture of the key F minor with its relative major (A flat) as the central pitch tends to give the piece a somewhat open, unresolved feel—in keeping with the lyrics in which Baez's former lover calls her years later on the telephone. The instrumental setting of acoustic guitar, electric guitar, electric piano, and synthesizers (along with electric bass and drums) might at first seem strange for a song by a long-standing member of the folk community; however, the instruments play an entirely subservient role to Baez's voice. The overall texture works beautifully for setting the story; it is appealing without venturing into the realm of trendy and overly commercial.

The next song, Jackson Browne's "Fountain of Sorrow," continues the theme of lost relationships. Here, a rediscovery of forgotten photographs reminds the singer of a former lover. However, even though the song is a suitable companion to "Diamonds & Rust" thematically, it is the performance that is most noteworthy. Much like Browne's own recording from the year before, Joan Baez's version of "Fountain of Sorrow" is more pop rock–oriented than what listeners might stereotypically think of when they think "Joan Baez." Although Baez maintains her usual clear soprano vocal tone color, her rhythmic approach and phrasing work beautifully within a rock-and-roll song, something that is not necessarily always the case when folksingers perform rock.

Baez's cover of Stevie Wonder and Syreeta Wright's "Never Dreamed You'd Leave in Summer," a song that Wonder included on his 1971 album *Where I'm Coming From*, is not quite as successful, particularly if one is familiar with the original. In particular, some listeners might sense a disconnection between the jazz-inspired torch song harmonies and structure of the song and Baez's vocal approach, which leans in the direction of folk and classical music. The vocal extemporization that helps to give Stevie Wonder's performance a feeling of spontaneity and expression gives way to an almost studied approach.

Baez's composition "Children and All That Jazz" is all about the two things that she includes in the title. The lyrics consist of statements that a parent might typically make to a child, so the piece becomes a celebration of parent-child relationships. Musically, the piece is an integration of the singer-songwriter style and jazz and includes blazing bluesy licks from pianist Hampton Hawes. The integration of jazz rhythms, harmony, and improvisation into the singer-songwriter genre was nothing new: Joni Mitchell (on several albums) and to a lesser extent Carole King (principally on the 1972 album, *Rhymes & Reasons*) had beaten Baez to the proverbial punch. The song is interesting for its over-all shape, especially in how Baez crafts the vocal arrangement and her multi-tracked performance. She begins by singing double-tracked in unison in the upper tessitura of her voice, almost in imitation of a young child's voice. As the piece develops, the vocal line moves into beautiful two-part harmony and finally into three-part harmony. Although some folk purists might cringe at the thought of such studio trickery on a Joan Baez recording, she is a near-perfect performer for singing harmony with herself, especially because of the control she has over vibrato and her strong sense of intonation.

Baez next turns to Bob Dylan's song "Simple Twist of Fate." Interestingly, Dylan's own recording of the piece was released at the time that *Diamonds & Rust* was being recorded,[2] so the cover is timely. The song's inclusion—and its message—might be interpreted as Baez's statement of forgiveness of Dylan for the disintegration of their relationship and does provide a workable coun-terpoint to "Diamonds & Rust." Part of the problem with Baez covering this particular Dylan song is that the melody is simple enough that it provides little opportunity for her to make full use of her voice. Perhaps sensing this, she adds a needed touch of humor to the performance when, starting at approximately the 2:18 mark, she imitates Dylan's distinctive *Sprechstimme* singing style.

A staple of the southern rock style, Dickey Betts's "Blue Sky" is most closely associated with the Allman Brothers Band, of which Betts was a member. Baez puts in a fine performance—she adapts to the southern rock style well, and the multitracked vocals successfully mirror the double lead guitar sound associated with the Allman Brothers Band. In fact, one of the highlights of the track is the twin lead guitar playing of Larry Carlton and Dean Parks. The choice of this particular cover also works well because the happiness of the lyrics provides a balance for some of the sad material from the opening of the album.

John Prine's song "Hello in There" is another well-chosen cover. An explo-ration of aging and the loneliness and alienation suffered by the aged, Prine's song benefits from a simple, easygoing arrangement in this recording. Baez sings the piece with little overt emotional expression: the dynamics are even-keeled, and there is little change of tone color. This supports the resignation and even the hopelessness that are expressed in Prine's lyrics.

Next, Baez turns to another singer-songwriter who perhaps is better appre-ciated by peers than by the general public: Janis Ian. The most haunting song of loss on *Diamonds & Rust*, "Jesse" also benefits from a resigned feel in Baez's voice. The piece again highlights the importance of the covers that Baez, coproducer David Kershenbaum, and executive producer Bernard Gelb selected for the album. The pauses in the chorus iterations of "Jesse" contrast so highly with the phrase structure of all of the other tracks that the song adds another dimension to the overall collection. Unfortunately, as sometimes is the case with 1970s' synthesizer performances, the synthesized horn solo that Baez plays at the end of the recording sounds somewhat dated—an acoustic horn, flute, or saxophone solo would have conveyed more personality and not had that dated tone color.

In her own composition "Winds of the Old Days," Baez uses somewhat impressionistic imagery—tempered with some very concrete references—to describe her world and the world of contemporaries such as Bob Dylan as being at a crossroads. The specter of the counterculture of the Vietnam War era remains; however, new and as-yet-undefined causes, challenges, and raisons d'être loom on the horizon. The musical setting is simple and folklike, with the melody constructed largely of short sequential phrases with a natural-sounding rise and fall. The arrangement, too, reflects the spirit of folk-country music. The entire gestalt of the piece is calm, which suggests the passing of the turbulence of the past 15 years and a resting period before what lies ahead.

Guest artists Joni Mitchell and Mitchell's backing band, Tom Scott and the L.A. Express, joined Baez for the song "Dida." Because the lyrics consist solely of numerous iterations of the title—with some "La, La, Las" thrown in—one might hear this as a jazz scat-like piece or even as an instrumental in which Baez's voice is the lead instrument. In the section that begins at approximately the 2:14 mark, Baez and Mitchell perform vocal call-and-response. The two singers have contrasting approaches to jazz vocalizing, with Joni Mitchell sounding more conventionally like what most listeners probably think a jazz singer would sound like (e.g., little vibrato, some ornamentation, small slides between pitches, and so on). The blend between the two singers is not as effective as that found on the earlier multitracked songs; however, purely as a jazz-pop composition, "Dida" is effective. One could almost imagine it as instrumental theme music for a mid-1970s' television program.

Diamonds & Rust concludes with a medley of what might at first seem to be an unlikely pairing of Stephen Foster's "I Dream of Jeannie" and the traditional Irish folk song "Danny Boy." Baez and her sole accompanist, pianist Larry Knechtel, take some liberties with the Foster song, adding some gospel touches to the harmony and to the vocal line. The sense behind the pairing comes when the listener considers the second stanza of "I Dream of Jeannie," in which the singer pictures Jeannie crying for her lost love (in this arrangement Baez changes the text slightly). That lost love could be the title character of "Danny Boy," the young man who goes off to war but does not return. It appears that Baez and her coproducers studiously avoided including overtly political material on this album. While this medley can be understood as an antiwar statement, it is more about the plight of soldiers and those left behind, a topic that was very much in the minds of Americans on either side of the Vietnam War issue at the conclusion of the war.

Diamonds & Rust found Joan Baez performing folk, rock and roll, jazz, folk-country, and various hybrids of all of the above, accompanied by some of the leading studio musicians of the day. The album exhibited her stylistic range as a performer and her talents as a songwriter better than perhaps any other album she has produced in a more than 50-year career. Despite the fact that one might not immediately think of Joan Baez as a leading figure of the 1970s' singer-songwriter movement, this album was highly successful at the time and wears well more than 35 years on.

Notes

1. Joan Baez, *And a Voice to Sing With* (New York: Simon and Schuster, 2009), 83–85.
2. Bernard Gelb, liner notes to *Diamonds & Rust*, CD reissue, A&M Records 75021 3233 2, 1988.

6

Patti Smith

Horses (1975)

Joe Tarr

In the summer of 1975, Patti Smith and her band—along with Smith's then-boyfriend Allen Lanier, guitarist for the Blue Oyster Cult—began recording their first record. Once again Smith selected Electric Ladyland Studios. She enlisted John Cale, former member of the Velvet Underground, to produce.

The recording process was contentious and combative, as Cale forced the band to do several takes of each song. "She struck me as someone with an incredibly volatile mouth who could handle any situation," Cale said. "She could also turn any situation around from a lethargic to an energetic one. But I think it was a very different experience for her going from being a band on-stage to working in the studio. It immediately throws you back on yourself. All her strength and instinct was there already, and I was trying to provide a context for it. It wasn't easy. It was confrontational and a lot like an immutable force meeting and immovable object. Still, something creative came out of it. There was push and pull."[1] Smith remembers long battles while making the record:

> I knew nothing about recording or being in the studio. We'd already done a single, but I didn't know anything. I was very, very suspicious, very guarded and hard to work with, because I was so conscious of how I perceived rock 'n' roll. It was becoming overproduced, overmerchandised and too glamorous. I was trying to fight against all of that. We had a big, hard battle. John did everything he could to fight our fight for us, even in his sleep. But I made it difficult for him to do some of the things he had to do.[2]

The tension, coupled with Smith's fiery desire and the energy of the time, produced remarkable results. Now regarded as one of the most important rock-and-roll records of all time, *Horses* endures as a powerful work of art. There isn't a weak song on the album, which holds up after repeated listenings, offering the listener new insights. It remains her best work because it captures the energy, excitement, and possibility of rock and roll in a way that few albums ever have. It broadened the landscape of what was possible.

The album is, in many ways, all about worshipping rock idols and being transformed by the music—or a tribute to how one fan was transformed by it. In these songs, Smith honors, rebukes, and becomes the avatars who inspired her. In a few of the songs she slips into various guises, sometimes taking on the identity of her heroes (at their darkest moments as they drift off into the abyss), at other times an omnipotent narrator, directing the whole thing from above. In between, we get touching narratives from her own life. Many of the songs are based on Smith's poems, as she mixed and matched what fit to the music.

Having studied and worshipped the likes of Bob Dylan, the Rolling Stones, Jim Morrison, Jimi Hendrix, and John Coltrane as well as earlier literary touchstones, Smith combined these personas to create one uniquely her own—post-modern rock and roll that showed a new world of possibility. The album is a tribute to excess, decadence, and liberty. It is a lusty homage to the masculine spirit that permeated rock music at the time, reflected back at the world from the eyes of a horny female fan, too proud and talented to settle for being a mere groupie. By paradoxically embracing rock's masculinity, Smith delivered a crushing blow against the tyranny of masculine rock.

The album has been written about and deconstructed extensively. Smith herself has explained the inspiration behind the songs in several interviews as well as in her lyrics compilation, *Patti Smith Complete, 1975–2006*. Several of the songs were interpreted in ways that Smith did not intend. This only adds to their power, as each takes on meanings beyond what the artist intended, with the listener becoming an active participant in the art. This is possible because the songs resonate with universal themes—loss, love, death, and sexual ecstasy—without becoming generic or bland. Smith created the landscape and vivid details yet never rigidly defined a meaning.

Horses begins on a soft note with Richard Sohl delicately opening with his keyboard on "Gloria (in Excelsis Deo)," but discord quickly follows as Smith drawls the album's most famous line: "Jesus died for somebody's sins, but not mine." The words are not necessarily, as they might seem, a rejection of God. Rather, they reject the need for salvation from "sins" of the world, because those sins offered their own salvation. In her Rimbaud view, Smith was proclaiming her earthly desires as good, pure, and completely hers. Jesus didn't need to die for her sins, because she was happy to commit them: "they belong to me," as she sings a few lines later. His blood wasn't on her hands. The song's title, "Gloria (in Excelsis Deo)," is a play on the Latin phrase "Glory to God in the Highest." It could be read as a blasphemous pun or as a praise of the God manifest in the world, in some hot young chick named Gloria, in the pleasures of sex, in the joys of being in love or being young.

In 1996 Smith said that she wasn't rejecting Christ with that line but instead was searching for freedom. "I happen to believe in Jesus. I never said he didn't exist. I only said that I didn't want him to take responsibility for my actions. Because I was young, I perceived myself as an artist, and the artist as a sort of cerebral criminal. I wanted the freedom to pursue all the things I imagined. Things within my art, not in life. In my art, I wanted the right to be misguided, misdirected, slightly criminal, utterly promiscuous, even a murderer. Within the realm of my work."[3] In 2007 she reiterated this sentiment:

> When I wrote "Gloria," it wasn't really anti-Christ—who I really admire— it was anti the idea that everything was set up for us and we had to fall into a certain behavior based on how things were organized for us. If I was going to do things wrong, I didn't want anyone having to die for my sins—I was going to take responsibility. It was really about personal and mental liberation. A writer called it a declaration of existence. To this day, I think that's the best description of that song, although I probably would not write the same lyric now because I've gone through a long process of evolution.[4]

Smith certainly was not the first to reject Christ in a rock song—John Lennon's "God" was the most famous (and more earnest) renunciation until the Sex Pistols' nihilistic "Anarchy in the UK" came along. Even so, rejecting God carried plenty of shock value in 1975 and continues to do so in pop culture. Smith herself later squirmed away from the sentiment, altering the lyrics in the late 1970s to "Jesus died for somebody's sins, why not mine?" In recent years, she has sung both lines in performances. The revised line feels like a prodigal daughter recanting. It also feels older (in the "My Back Pages" sense): the defiance of youth grows into an open question, uncertainty.

But in 1975, the original line captured the new defiance and rebellion that Smith was harnessing and that would soon erupt in the music world. The Jesus line introduced "Gloria," one of the great rock-and-roll songs, written by Van Morrison and originally performed with his group, Them. It is one of two rock standards that Smith uses on the album to reconnect with rock and roll's roots, tapping into the music's original energy and building her own music off of it, as if she had dusted off all the clutter and bombast it had accumulated to find what is really important.

The theme is that of countless rock songs—a sexy young woman whom the singer is in love with. What made the original so great was Van Morrison's lusty growl and innuendo—he's not just longing after this woman, he's nailed her, and she continues to thrill him as he brags of his love to the world. One of rock and roll's incomparable singers, Morrison brought to life not just ecstasy and desire but also the thrill of being young. The song was one of a handful that defined garage rock. Listening to it, you're easily transported to a drunken party.

Smith and her band picked these simple rock classics to merge with her poetry and give her a landscape to play in. According to Smith,

> "Jesus died for somebody's sins but not mine" is from a poem. I used to read this poem, but I wanted to go from it into something simplistic. I loved three-chord songs, and "Gloria" is the quintessential three-chord song. . . . We used to call it "fieldwork"—Lenny and Richard would give me three-chord fields. Even though I wrote the poem at the beginning of "Gloria" in 1970, it took all those years to evolve, to merge into "Gloria."[5]

As a singer, Smith is simply out of her league compared to Van Morrison—in her version of the song, she couldn't even manage to sing the chorus, "G-L-O-R-I-A," and instead just chants the letters, while her band sings backup. She cannot evoke the range of emotions with her voice that Morrison does. No matter. Her version works on the energy and audacity with which she declares her supreme right to be on the stage and sing this rock classic. In keeping with her philosophy of imagining the world however she saw fit, Smith sings the song the way a man would, with aggression and keeping all its phallic imagery, except that she is much more raunchy than the guys ever dared to be, seeing the woman "humping on a parking meter." There's no irony or shift in meaning. The song is about desire, and you're not left baffled by the song the way the Kinks (and, later, the Raincoats) left you on "Lola." Smith adds several lines, including a verse that puts her on the rock stage in a stadium with thousands of women groupies lusting after her.

It is not, as many assumed at the time (and continue to), a lesbian love song. Smith has confessed to having rather vanilla sexual tastes—even to being a bit bothered by gay male sex—and has said that she was merely imagining the world as a man desiring women:

> Sexually I'm really normal. I always enjoyed doing transgender songs. That's something I learnt from Joan Baez, who often sang songs that had a male point of view. No, my work does not reflect my sexual preferences, it reflects the fact that I feel total freedom as an artist. On *Horses*, that's why the sleevenote has that statement about being "beyond gender." By that, I meant that as an artist, I can take any position, any voice, that I want.[6]

That carefree abandon in choosing her voice had a staggering impact. From that opening song, Smith completely shattered old ideas of what a rock musician should be and forged a new model of cool. Musicians had been defining their own model of cool for decades, of course, but Smith pushed the boundaries further.

Smith follows "Gloria" with a very different kind of song, "Redondo Beach" (which also was interpreted as a lesbian love song by some, an easy leap with only the lyrics to go on). Intensely personal, it counterbalanced the role playing and hallucinatory narratives in Smith's other songs, presenting listeners with a life in all its precious fragility. Using a reggae beat that foreshadowed reggae's influence on punk, the song is about a quarrel that Smith had with her sister, Linda, who stormed off into the city. After several hours, Smith goes looking for her and comes across a young girl who killed herself on the beach, and a sense of foreboding about what might have become of her sister grows in her. "The hearse pulled away and the girl that had died it was you." It's a morbid fantasy but also a song of longing for something dear, something she may not ever touch again, something she knows will one day pass on. The song mourns not just the ephemeral nature of life but also the impossibility of controlling and containing the ones we love: our love cannot necessarily keep them from fighting us, from disappearing, or from killing themselves.

On the next song, "Birdland," Smith dives back deep into fantasy, inserting herself into the visions of Peter Reich, the son of renegade psychologist Wilhelm Reich. Smith has said that she was inspired by Peter Reich's *Book of Dreams*, in which he recounted seeing what he believed was a spaceship at a family gathering not long after his father's death. He at first thought that it was his father coming to take him away, but as he cried out to the spaceship, he realized that it was a flock of birds.[7]

Smith's "Birdland" is a hallucination, an extended poetic sequence. More than nine minutes long, the song is a close relative of Jim Morrison's poetic passages performed with the Doors, such as "The End," "When the Music's Over," and "Soft Parade" (except that Smith is the better poet, capable of subtlety and range that Morrison never managed). It's an intense moment to capture—the cataclysmic moment of mourning for a loved one, especially a parent. Smith nails it; in her delivery we can feel Peter writhing on the ground, screaming out to his father, "No daddy, don't leave me here alone."

There are no drums on the original recording of "Birdland," which breaks free of rock beat structure, allowing Smith to follow the rhythm of her verse. Lenny Kaye goes berserk on the electric guitar, fueling the celestial fantasy. But Smith has said that she felt most connected with Sohl while playing the song: "I can still picture Richard, his eyes like saucers, following, then staying in step, anticipating my next move." Part of the song's intensity is due to Cale, who "had me so nuts I wound up doing this nine-minute cut [of 'Birdland'] that transcended anything I ever did before."[8]

On "Free Money," Smith again indulged her outlaw fantasies, picturing herself as a thief bringing money to a loved one—but it's such a common fantasy that it feels completely genuine. Smith said that she wrote the song for her mother, who "always dreamed about winning the lottery. But she never bought a lottery ticket! She would just imagine if she won, make lists of things she would do with the money—a house by the sea for us kids, then all kinds of charitable things."[9] The specifics don't matter much; the song could just as easily be about a lover or a child.

Despite its implication of law breaking—"I know they're stolen but I don't feel bad"—the song feels completely righteous. Richard Sohl's tender piano intro seals it within a righteous sentiment. The money cannot be dirty if it goes to the narrator's love, which is pure and not of this world. But more than that, it's a working-class fantasy; increasing the tempo, Smith sings about how she imagines lying in bed each night in a pile of money. It's a fantasy that has been played out billions of times around the world, as dreamers picture a world where money, the magic elixir, is available to make things happen, ease burdens, and create opportunity. Smith tips her hat to such a fantasy, to anyone who ever bought a lottery ticket, and to those, like her mother, who dreamed of winning the lottery but never got around to buying a ticket. Much of Smith's art was inspired by artists of privilege—drawn to the New York art scene, she was always interested in transcending the banality of everyday existence and escaping the factories, dead-end jobs, suburbs, and closed minds. There is a loftiness to her work, and she has never been much of a working-class hero. But she remains connected to her working-class roots and understands what it means to work your ass off for a living. "Free Money" is perhaps the finest example of that righteous empathy at work. Once she had escaped Jersey she would never go back, but she also would never forget where she came from. "Free Money" remembers the feeling of wanting to escape where she'd come from.

"Kimberly" was also inspired by family, this time her younger sister. Based on a memory of when Kimberly was a baby and Smith was holding her while watching a storm roll in, the song describes the violence of the universe colliding with the innocence and vulnerability of a baby. But it all seems part of the grand scheme: "Little sister the fates are calling on you."

The album's final three songs revolve around rock stars, utilizing mythical imagery and grand sentiments about the struggle to make art, to live. The first is "Break It Up," written from a dream Smith had about Jim Morrison in which she saw him stretched on a marble slab. He was alive, with wings, and partly merged with the slab.[10] The song doesn't make much literal sense: it reads like Smith pleading with the gods to release some innocent boy from their clutches. There's a wonderment about where he went, how someone so precious and dear could have succumbed to the void, how such power could be suddenly silenced.

"Land: Horses/Land of a Thousand Dances/La Mer (De)" is an epic song that lasted 9 minutes and 25 seconds on *Horses*. In concert it often stretches to 20 minutes as Smith improvises new verses, inspired by whatever ghosts are possessing her. The song is riddled with allusion and symbolism, but to pull a single meaning out of it is futile; it works more as an intoxicating hallucination, with meaning clouded and beside the point. Obvious antecedents are, once again, Jim Morrison's extended poetic songs. There are also literary references: Arthur Rimbaud, William Blake, Walt Whitman, and the beat poets.

Smith has pointed to the character Johnny in William S. Burroughs's *The Wild Boys* as one ancestor of the song's main character, Johnny.[11]

The song begins with Johnny drinking a cup of "tea" as another boy creeps up on him in the hallway. Johnny sees the boy and is frightened but freezes. The rebel boy smashes him into a locker, laughing. It's a typical adolescent confrontation, one that boys both thrived on and were terrorized by and one that Smith must have fantasized about as she grew up idolizing and fixated by everything boyish. The fight progresses, as Johnny suddenly feels horses surrounding him, running around him. The horses might be a girl's sexual metaphor for force and power, but here they twist into formation, running to the classic rock-and-roll dance tune "Land of a Thousand Dances."

Smith's "Land of a Thousand Dances" is thick with homoerotic nuances. Sung by the too-cool sexy tomboy, the song allowed guys to feel safe to indulge in the fantasy. Smith could embody the masculine sexiness of Keith Richards, Mick Jagger, and Jim Morrison but retain a feminine allure, making it safe for both sexes to desire her. In this way, she liberated men to be completely passive fans, worshipping their idols. "Land of a Thousand Dances" evolves into male rape fantasy and violence. As Johnny lies in his sperm, Angel looks down and says, "Can't you show me nothing but surrender?" The encounter collapses into murder or suicide—the ultimate surrender or aggression—as Johnny picks up a knife and feels it harden against his throat, pushing it in. It's all about embracing your darkest fantasies about murder, rape, and suicide and feeling good about it, masturbating to it.

Sexual fantasies are largely about power, either the surrendering of your power or seizing power over others. "Land of a Thousand Dances" is remarkable in that it takes both perspectives simultaneously, as Smith puts the listener in the heads of rape victim and rapist, murderer and corpse, both of whom are thrilled to be there. The fantasy is, of course, not literal. It is a means of getting off, of feeling alive—enjoying the thrill of committing a thought crime.

For me the climax of the song comes when Smith screams "When they built that Tower of Babel they knew what they were after," another thought crime against God. For if there's a point to the song, it is the celebration of people's attempts—in all their miserable limitations and pathetic fragility—to climb out of the grit and grime of life, of people's struggle to transcend death, heartbreak, and hunger in order to become something larger than life and create a thing of beauty. In building the Tower of Babel, the humans of the Bible were simply emulating God and trying to be like Him. They wanted the heavens, and who can blame them?

The attempt, however noble, is doomed to failure. The song closes with Johnny alone, screaming a cry that no one hears, his pituitary glands spitting out of his throat. In the final moments, however, as his world unravels, he sees Gloria humping a parking meter, hears a Fender guitar, and sees the dancing of a simple rock song. Smith has said that the Johnny who dies at the end of the song is Jimi Hendrix, who died vomiting in his sleep.[12] It's a comforting thought to imagine such a brilliant talent experiencing a moment of affirmation as his life was fading away.

Horses ends with a tribute to Hendrix, "Elegie," borrowing lines from the late musician's song "1983 (a Merman I Should Turn to Be)": "Well it's too bad that our friends can't be with us today." It was recorded on September 18, 1975, the anniversary of Hendrix's death.[13] In recent years, the song has become something of a requiem for the fallen angels of Smith's generation. Often, she gives a roll call of the casualties, as she did on the night that the nightclub CBGB closed.

Accompanying this startling music on *Horses* was a distinctive cover, which has been written about as much as the music has. The black-and-white photograph was shot by Smith's old friend Robert Mapplethorpe and is regarded as one of the greatest rock album covers ever. It shows Smith leaning against a white wall, on which she casts a slight shadow. She's dressed in black pants and a white shirt, open slightly at the collar and sleeves, which are frayed. Suspenders wrap over the shirt. Draped over her left shoulder is a suit jacket. Pinned to its lapel is a small pin of a horse, which is upside down to the viewer. Her hands touch slightly across her chest, her left one holding the jacket in place. Her coal black hair stretches down to her shirt collar. The right side of her face is partly in shadow as she stares out at the camera. There is no smile—not a mean look exactly, but it's cocksure, intimidating, as though she is the Johnny in "Land" saying "Come and get me man."

Smith later wrote that she had overslept on the day of the photo shoot and simply tossed on her usual clothes, which she wore both onstage and in the streets. As Mapplethorpe was shooting, the light that he liked began to fade, and he asked her to take off her jacket to highlight her white shirt. "I tossed the jacket over my shoulder Sinatra-style, hopefully capturing some of his casual defiance," she said.[14] In another interview, she said of her attire that "I liked to dress like Baudelaire."[15]

Her pose is reminiscent of not just Frank Sinatra but also many other poses—Keith Richards is there, Bob Dylan, James Dean. It is distinctively male and impossible to look at without thinking about men. Smith absorbed all the sexy masculinity of her heroes and reflected it back in a style that was even sexier. She certainly wasn't the first tough female rock star, but she was the first to look tough, haggard. She made masculinity feminine, merging the genders in pop culture. When the album was released, Smith suddenly found herself an icon, irresistible and unique.

The critics—many of whom knew Smith and Kaye from their rock critic days—understandably gushed. "For some of us, Patti Smith is the girl of our rock-and-roll dreams. As a performer she doesn't merely flirt with danger, she seduces it, trying at the same time to be both audacious and ingratiating, to challenge an audience and win it over," wrote Mitchell Cohen.[16]

"Each song builds with an inexorable seethe, a penchant for lust and risk that shakes you and never lets you forget you're listening to real rock 'n' roll again at last. Meanwhile, every song contains moments that go beyond raunchy into emotional realms that can give you chills," Lester Bangs wrote in *Creem*. "Patti's music in its ultimate moments touches deep wellsprings of emotion that extremely few artists in rock or anywhere else are capable of reaching."[17]

In *New Musical Express*, Charles Shaar Murray called Smith's album better than the first albums of Dylan, the Beatles, the Rolling Stones, and Roxy Music. "It's hard to think of any other rock artist of recent years who arrived in the studios to make their first major recordings with their work developed to such a depth and level of maturity," Murray wrote.[18]

In retrospect, it can be hard to measure the impact that *Horses* had on the culture. Smith said not long after the album appeared and throughout her career that she and the band were on a mission to shake things up with *Horses*.

> We were on a mission. But we were also making it up as we went along. I mean, I was never a singer, I can't play any instruments, I had no training. Plus, I was brought up in a time when all the great rock stars were male. I didn't have any template for what I was doing. I did what I did out of frustration and concern. I felt like rock 'n' roll was disintegrating. We'd lost Jimi Hendrix, Jim Morrison, Bob Dylan was in a motorcycle accident, the Rolling Stones were shifting into a new phase. I was concerned about what was going to happen to rock 'n' roll. I had no ambition to make records, nor even thought that I had the ability, or even deserved, to do so.[19]

In another interview, she said that "The reason why I came to rock was 'cause I saw the art was in a bad position. I felt that for a long time I had depended on rock 'n' roll for my life's blood, and it was about time that I started payin' it back. I owe much more than I could ever hope to give."[20]

The altruism is a bit hard to buy and feels like self-mythologizing. Personal desire, ambition, and an artist's urge to create surely had more to do with this fiery music than a desire to save rock and roll. Still, her disgust with the state of music undoubtedly nudged her forward and gave her confidence to make rock the way she knew it should sound.

Smith was the first CBGB band to release an album, but many others soon followed suit: Television, the Ramones, and Blondie. This New York scene didn't yield huge commercial successes but raked in critical plaudits and, more important, influenced hundreds of bands in both America and Europe. For serious rock fans, the music began to thrill again. "Patti Smith was, and is, pure experience," guitarist Thurston Moore wrote for *Bomb* magazine in 1996. "Her reign in the '70s as a street-hot rock 'n' roll messiah seemed to exist from a void. No past, no future—'the future is here,' she'd sing. I'd hear tales of romance, the girl with the blackest hair hanging out at recording session writing poetry. But I didn't know her. I could only embrace the identity I perceived. I was impressionable and she came on like an alien."[21] Michael Stipe remembers getting *Horses* after it came out when he was 15 years old. "It pretty much tore my limbs off and put them back on in a different way. . . . It was like the first time you went into the ocean and got knocked down by a wave. It killed. It was so completely liberating."[22]

Many consider *Horses* to be the first punk rock album; today, Smith is often described as the godmother of punk. There are some similarities, evidence that the group was in tune with the times. Smith's music utilizes a simple chord structure—"field work," as her band called it—which was a defining element of punk rock. But Smith's music used the structure as a means toward improvisation, a launching point to go places both lyrically and musically, a tendency that was less evident in punk. Many punk groups scorned straying outside the simple three-chord structure and extended guitar solos.

There's also a tone of reverence toward the past in Smith's work, a reclaiming of the revolution that rock once promised, whereas many punk rock groups (especially in Britain), despite their emphasis on basic rock-and-roll structure, scorned the past as corrupt. "Phony Beatle Mania has bitten the dust," the Clash famously declared in "London Calling."

If anything, the Patti Smith Group played a transitional role. Lenny Kaye has said that "Sometimes I think of us as the last of the Sixties bands. We liked those long rambling songs, we liked 20 minutes of improvisation. . . . We had a lot of that revolutionary 'kick out the jams, motherfucker' fervor."[23] The group was an essential bridge between the two eras, distilling the more powerful elements of the 1960s and foreshadowing the later movement.

Others, such as her former lover and sporadic collaborator Tom Verlaine, saw her influence in punk. Talking about the English punk rock bands, Verlaine told a journalist that "They all sounded the same to me. The sound was copped from the Ramones and the lyrics, the attitude, were taken from Patti Smith. Not the manic side, but the 'fuck off' side. I know what her style was like at the time she first toured there. I think a lot of people were struck by her attitude—especially bands."[24]

The Patti Smith Group was certainly a kindred spirit to the punk movement, looking to get back to basics and inspire daring actions. By deliberately trying to shake things up, trying to create a sound that felt dangerous and exciting, the group helped create a space where punk could flourish. The group fits squarely on a continuum of primitivist rock bands: from 1950s' rockabilly to the British Invasion to 1960s' garage rock to the urban rock of Velvet Underground, MC5, the New York Dolls, the Modern Lovers, and the Stooges. After Smith and the Ramones came the landslide of punk rock in Europe and America, with far too many bands to mention.

Smith often came off as a mentor and mother figure to the punk rockers. "Well, I love the Clash, and I really love the Sex Pistols. I think Johnny Rotten's great, I have a real crush on him. See, all those kids were my friends before they had bands, so it's real gratifying to me to see them up there."[25] When the punks became more vitriolic toward their predecessors, Smith lectured, "Part of the style of these kids is to dump on the heads of anybody over 19. Sometimes I get real mad and want to give Johnny Rotten a spanking . . . but I understand them, I think it's cool."[26]

In 2005 on the 30th anniversary of the release of *Horses*, Patti Smith and her band performed the album in its entirety at the Royal Festival Hall in London. The concert was released as a CD, coupled with the original recordings. After 30 years, the songs continue to thrill with the idea of possibility. Listening to Smith sing, it's striking how she seems to have lost none of her fire. As with all anniversary celebrations, there's a whiff of nostalgia for the memories that the songs evoke, both in musicians and the fans, but this is not what gives the music its power. The album still feels daring, and Smith hasn't lost her conviction, her belief in rock and roll, despite the genre's obvious failures and disappointments. Eminent rock critic Sasha Frere-Jones called Smith's performance of *Horses* in 2005 "one of the most viscerally affecting things I have ever seen. Her enthusiasm as a performer is never mere crowd-pleasing, and her lack of cynicism is never empty cheer."[27]

In concert Smith is prone to improvising, tweaking each song to make it contemporary or following whatever whims inspire her. She has honed this talent over 30 years. "I'll never do a number in which I don't have to put myself on the line. By that I mean that I'll always enjoy putting myself on the spot, always enjoy playing with fire. That's what 'Land of a Thousand Dances' is for; that's the one where I always hallucinate a long story at the end. And sometimes it's really frightening, it's like boxing: go crazy or go down."[28] These moments can be powerful as the song is reinvented. Occasionally they fall flat. In the 2005 live recording, Smith somehow turned "Land of a Thousand Dances" into a rant against technology and parents who don't speak to their children: Would Johnny have been spared some measure of pain if his parents had talked to him more? Didn't he really want it, after all?

More often than not, Smith finds fertile ground in her live musings. Her recent performances of "Elegie" are always touching as she recites a list of the dead. The 2005 performance of "My Generation" (which was recorded during the *Horses* sessions—with Cale on bass—and released as a B-side to "Gloria")—ends with a condemnation of Smith's own generation: "my generation . . . created George Bush. New generations, rise up, rise up."

Smith has always felt proud of *Horses* and her place in rock-and-roll history. Ultimately, however, she understood that she is part of a long tradition and hoped that the tradition—of scraggly young people making rebellious, sexy art—would continue.

Notes

1. Lucy O'Brien, "John Cale and Patti Smith: How We Met," *Independent on Sunday*, August 25, 1996, http://www.independent.co.uk/arts-entertainment/how-we-met-1311486.html.

2. Ibid.
3. Ben Edmonds, "The Rebel," *Mojo*, August 1996.
4. Jessica Robertson, "Patti Smith Q&A," AOL Music, http://spinner.aol.com/rockhall/patti-smith-2007-inductee/interview.
5. David Fricke, "Exclusive Q&A: The Final Word from Patti Smith on CBGB," *Rolling Stone* online, October 17, 2006, http://www.rollingstone.com/music/news/exclusive-q-a-the-final-word-from-patti-smith-on-cbgb-20061017.
6. Simon Reynolds, "Patti Smith: Even as a Child I Felt Like an Alien," *Guardian Observer Music Monthly*, May 22, 2005.
7. Patti Smith, *Patti Smith Complete, 1975–2006* (New York: Harper Perennial, 2006), 32; Reynolds, "Patti Smith"; Tony Hiss and David McClelland, "Gonna Be So Big, Gonna Be a Start, Watch Me Now!" *New York Times Magazine*, December 21, 1975.
8. Dave Marsh, "Her Horses Got Wings, They Can Fly," *Rolling Stone*, January 1, 1976.
9. Reynolds, "Patti Smith."
10. Smith, *Patti Smith Complete*, 44.
11. Ibid., 48.
12. Reynolds, "Patti Smith."
13. Ibid.
14. Smith, *Patti Smith Complete*, 25.
15. Jenny Turner, "Patti Smith and Richard Hell: Two Punks Don't Make a Summer," *New Statesman*, July 5, 1996.
16. Mitchell Cohen, "Patti Smith: Avery Fisher Hall, NYC," *Phonograph Record*, May 1976.
17. Lester Bangs, "Stagger Lee Was a Woman," *Creem*, February 1976.
18. Charles Shaar Murray, "Weird Scenes Inside the Gasoline Alley," *New Musical Express*, November 1975.
19. Sean O'Hagen, "American Icon," *Observer*, June 15, 2003.
20. Bruce Berman, "The Queen of Acid Punk Rock," *Acid Rock*, November 1977.
21. Thurston Moore, "Patti Smith," *Bomb*, no. 54 (Winter 1996).
22. Ben Edmonds, "Michael Stipe on Patti," *Mojo*, August 1996.
23. Reynolds, "Patti Smith."
24. Dave Schulps, "Tom Verlaine: In Search of Adventure," *Trouser Press*, May 1978.
25. Steve Simels, "Patti Smith," *Stereo Review*, August 1978.
26. Lisa Robinson, "Patti Smith's Intuitive Mania," *Hit Parader*, March 1978.
27. Sasha Frere-Jones, "Ring in the Old," *New Yorker*, December 25, 2006–January 1, 2007, 28.
28. Nick Tosches, "A Baby Wolf with Neon Bones," *Penthouse*, April 1976.

7

Janis Ian

Between the Lines (1975)

James E. Perone

By 1975, the introspective singer-songwriter movement had enjoyed approximately a half decade of widespread popularity, and female artists in the genre, such as Carly Simon, Joni Mitchell, and Carole King, had written and recorded songs that incorporated stylistic elements of jazz and lyrics that explored the real-life wide range of emotions experienced by millions and millions of women. Janis Ian's 1975 album *Between the Lines* was the right work in the right style at the right time. Ian's explorations of emotions and situations resonated for listeners, as evidenced by the fact that the album made it to or near No. 1 on major pop and adult contemporary record charts, and its best-remembered Grammy-winning single "At Seventeen" remains an iconic song into the 21st century. The mixture of jazz and coffeehouse folksinger style is more restrained than some of the jazz and folk hybrids of Ian's bigger-name contemporaries, which tends to give her songs a more authentic, less commercially motivated feel.

Between the Lines consists entirely of Ian's own compositions, the first of which is "When the Party's Over." The piece can be interpreted in a variety of ways. On the surface, Ian seems to invite a potential lover whom she meets at a party to fall in love with her. One might hear Ian's reference to her "song and dance routine" as a metaphor for flirtation. Because of the straightforward could-be-performed-live nature of the vocal and instrumental arrangements throughout the album, it is also possible to hear this as a song about a listener's love of and for a musician. In this interpretation, Ian invites the listener at her performance (her "party" in the text of the song) to understand and love her because of her music.

The second song on the album, "At Seventeen," was Janis Ian's biggest hit ever for good reason. Her recollections of the meanness, the pettiness, and the emphasis on popularity and physical beauty in high school resonate with anyone who went through similar situations and with anyone who knows someone who was similarly victimized in high school. But "At Seventeen" is also one of the better integrations of mood, lyrics, and music of the 1970s. The low-register narrow-range melody of the opening of the verses is built upon one principal motive. After the initial statement of the motive, it rises and then eventually falls to its original range. With Ian's understated singing and the restraint of the instrumental backing arrangement, it is easy to hear these verses as a musical expression of the sense of resignation that Ian must have felt 7 years before, when she was 17. The repetitious nature of the verse melody suggests the endlessness of the taunts, the shunning, and the other forms of exclusion about which Ian sings. Later in the song when the melody rises higher in Ian's range, she sings with more intensity, suggesting the anger that also came from feeling that she was an outcast. The real genius of Ian's setting is that the syncopation in the melody and the tempo of the performance allow just enough of a lilt to be heard so as to eliminate any feeling of self-pity that might have emerged for a slower performance of a less-syncopated tune. Clearly, Ian's character felt hurt, pain, anger, frustration, and lack of self-confidence and self-respect. She may still feel pain and hurt but has developed a self-knowledge and a sense of self-worth that allow her to recall the past with an objectivity that never would have been possible had she simply pitied herself. So ultimately, "At Seventeen" is at once about the shallow values of some high schoolers and about the struggle to attain the sense of self-worth to try to overcome the shallowness and the mean-spiritedness of others.

In "From Me to You," Ian addresses "a friend" with whom she apparently has been staying to help her or him[1] build some self-esteem and self-reliance. Ian's writing here tends to be somewhat metaphoric and open to interpretation. In the context of its time and probable audience, however, "From Me to You" can be heard as a feminist statement. Some of the lines (e.g., "Those people who surround you only want to see you weak enough to crawl") are especially easy to hear as references to sexism. Still, Ian's lyrics are oblique enough that a wide range of listeners can project a variety of their own life experiences into the song. Ian continues the motivic style of melodic construction of "At Seventeen." In "From Me to You," however, it is the rhythmic motive of the opening phrase of the melody that carries through into other phrases of each verse, even though the pitch contours change. In this song, as in "At Seventeen," the motivic nature of Ian's melodic construction tends to allow the listener to focus on the lyrics, an important attribute in the introspective singer-songwriter genre.

In "Bright Lights and Promises," Ian explores the form and style of mid-20th-century jazz ballads. Revisiting "When the Party's Over," Ian sings of the world of club musicians; however, here her musical setting and her lyrical references to "bar rails and cocktails" and her performance attire of "gold lamé and diamonds" place her in a nightclub. Like the album's opening track, "Bright Lights and Promises" can also be understood on a metaphorical level. In this interpretation, the woman who tries to please the "sucker at the bar" with a musical come-on might be understood as the prostitute who tries to lure a potential customer or as the woman who is forced to use her charms to attract a husband for the proverbial good life. The "gold lamé and diamonds" can be understood as a front for the dull reality of life for the nightclub singer, just as the trappings of wealth can be understood as an ultimately cheap compensation for an otherwise unfulfilled life in affluent suburbia.

"In the Winter," the shortest song on *Between the Lines*, adds another stylistic dimension to the album. Here, a string section is added to the guitars, bass, drums, and piano of the accompanying ensemble. In the verse sections of the song, the string writing includes chords in a rhythmic ostinato, one note accentuating each beat of each measure; however, in the first verse, individual solo strings play little two-note descending sigh-like figures. The opening verse is also notable for the dramatic drum figures at the end of some of the phrases. All of this accompanies Ian's lyrics, which speak to a former lover about meeting the former lover's new female "friend." Inwardly, Ian's character reflects on the loneliness she feels day after day. For example, she calls Dial-a-Prayer, calls Time and Temperature, and listens to the radio just to hear human voices. Despite her apparent utter hopelessness and isolation, she puts on a front for her former lover. Perhaps because of the pulsating strings and the picture of utter loneliness that Ian paints, the song can be heard as a companion to the Beatles' 1966 song "Eleanor Rigby," except from the viewpoint of the Beatles' title character.

The five-minute-long "Water Colors" is more complex and more specific. Ian's character and her male lover end their relationship after making love for the last time. He is jealous of her "stage hand lovers," another reference to the real-life Janis Ian's work as a musician. Her former lover, too, speaks as though he does her a favor by making love to her, while her character feels used. Even more to the point is that Ian raises the issue of fundamental (although some listeners may hear them as stereotypical) differences between men and women. For example, Ian's character relates to watercolor-like photographs from the better days of the past, which can be interpreted as representative of the emotional side of human nature. Her lover's references tend throughout the song to be more physical and less impressionistic. The lovers' impasse can be heard simply as the state of being of one now dysfunctional relationship between two people, or it can be understood as representative of the viewpoint that men and women view the world in fundamentally different ways. Ian offers nothing concrete to suggest the wider interpretation; however, as one listens to the tracks on *Between the Lines*, it becomes pretty clear that Ian's female characters are fairly consistent in their experiences, feelings, and struggles, and her male characters generally stand apart with fundamentally different motivations.

The musical setting of "Water Colors" is also notable. Ian uses her customary technique of building verse-length melodies from small motives. In this song, as opposed to, say, "At Seventeen," she allows for more space, more pauses between the lines. This allows the listener to digest each phrase and, I believe, tends to allow the listener—to quote the title of the album—to read between the lines, in this case possibly to extrapolate the experiences of the two characters into the broader context of the basic differences between men and women.

One of the more notable musical features of *Between the Lines* is the way in which Ian blurs the lines between jazz, singer-songwriter, folk, pop, and classic Tin Pan Alley torch song. Her song "The Come On," like Leon Russell's 1970 composition "A Song for You," with which it shares some motivic similarities, brings the style of earlier 20th-century torch song tradition into the 1970s. The lack of self-respect and emotional detachment that can be heard in other songs emerges perhaps even more strongly in this piece. Ian sings to a potential lover that she has not "been loved by a man in quite a while." Throughout the song, her character expresses the need to believe that she is loved and tells her potential lover that she would be happy even if he "faked" his feelings and desire for her. The lyrics can be understood on a variety of levels. Perhaps the fact that Ian's character is "difficult to please" can be heard as an expression of a lack of desire for men. She intimates that her friends all have "a man on a string" and suggests that she is somehow inadequate for not following suit. Perhaps ultimately she really suffers from a lack of self-identity and self-understanding. Since Janis Ian began openly discussing her homosexuality in the 1990s,[2] her character's grapplings with her feelings and identity can be understood as the autobiographical search for self-knowledge of Ian's sexuality. Even if the listener does not read the search for sexual self-identity into "The Come On," Ian's character stands in opposition to social norms and the lives of her more conventional friends and has questions about her place in the world. The touches of the earlier torch song tradition in Ian's musical setting work effectively in conveying the emotional pain, the questions, and the need for self-understanding of the lyrics.

Throughout *Between the Lines*, there is an ebb and flow to the emotional states and the moves between questioning one's identity and affirming one's self-worth and self-identity. Such is the case as Ian moves between the emotional damage of "The Come On" to the more musically and lyrically conventional—and more optimistic—song "Light a Light." Here, Ian's character addresses her "lover" (gender not defined) and optimistically reflects on the ability to put aside past differences. Although she sings the question "Lover, am I comin' home again," the implication is that, indeed, she is returning to a renewed relationship. Ian's musical setting is entirely consistent with the work of the most commercially successful proponents of the singer-songwriter style, such as James Taylor. This track is also notable for the emphasis on vocal harmony work. Curiously, there are places in which the phrase cutoffs are imprecise, and the balance between the voices seems to be a bit inconsistent. Production quirks aside, this is one of Ian's most immediately engaging works. The relief from the angst of the preceding songs is particularly refreshing as one listens to *Between the Lines* in its original running order.

The album's penultimate track, "Tea & Sympathy," is also its slowest. This introspective ballad finds Ian's character lying next to her lover, finally accepting the realities of life. She bids farewell to the "good old days," which, given what the listener has learned in the album's earlier songs, were hardly "good" at all. It is as if the pain, the isolation, the uncertainties, and the lack of self-knowledge and self-confidence have finally subsided. This is a classic tale of love conquers all. Ian's music and the arrangement support the mood. The setting suggests the relaxed sigh as Ian's character realizes fully who she is and what her place is in the world. The musical setting itself is not her most memorable work on the album, but it sets a fully appropriate mood for the lyrics.

Ian's *Between the Lines* concludes with "Lover's Lullaby," another slow love ballad. Ian allows the listener to interpret the song in two distinctive ways: as either a lullaby to a male lover or as a lullaby from a mother to a young son. Curiously, she refers to the hearer of her song as "mama's boy," but she tells him that she sings a "lover's lullaby." In either case, however, Ian's overarching message is consistent with that of her song "Tea & Sympathy." Here, she acknowledges the dreams and the promise of the past but observes that "all the leaves are gone brown," suggesting the passage of time and possibly the lack of fulfillment of the past's dreams. Incidentally, Ian's introduction of this temporal element also lends support to the understanding of this "lullaby" as a song that consoles an adult lover. Perhaps the most important feature of the lyrics, however, is the mere fact that it is Ian's character who has come to terms with the past and now consoles her lover: the stronger female character consoles the weaker male character. Ian created a more complex musical setting for the album's finale than for any of the other more conventionally structured songs of *Between the Lines*. The metrical changes in this song recall the tempo changes of Ian's early hit single "Society's Child." In the context of the album, the effect is of a slow and, even in its quietness, powerful move to self-realization and strength.

Janis Ian's *Between the Lines* was a significant commercial and critical success in its day. Although the American society of the 21st century has changed from that of 1975, the songs of *Between the Lines* can still resonate lyrically. The understated instrumental and harmony vocal arrangements also hold up well, particularly because they tend not to scream out "1970s" to listeners the way that some other recordings of the period do. And, Ian's pleasant and clear voice remains a joy to listen to, especially in the digitally remastered versions of the album that are available today. All of these aspects of the recording support Ian's characters' struggles against obstacles imposed by a patriarchal society, by narcissistic high school bullies, and by thoughtless former lovers. Ultimately her characters achieve self-knowledge and a quiet strength that is borne out by the musical settings.

Notes

1. Ian is gender-neutral in her references in the song.
2. "Janis Ian: Press Kit," Janis Ian official website, http://www.janisian.com/presskit .php.

8

Bruce Springsteen

Born to Run (1975)

Rob Kirkpatrick

The long-awaited album *Born to Run* was released on September 1, 1975. Advance sales had already put the album on the charts a week earlier. It shot into the Top 10 within the first month of its release, and by the end of October it had gone gold. It would go on to become the first album ever to earn platinum (million-selling) status. Bruce Springsteen's career would never be the same again.

As with *Greetings* and *Wild*, Springsteen's third album is ridden with Catholic/Christian imagery. There are references to ghosts, visions, and visionaries; crosses, churches, and prayers in the dark; original sin and at least one savior offering redemption; Mary, angels, wings, and heaven; soul crusaders and forced confessions; holy silence and holy nights; and faith and the Promised Land. Yet any redemptive virtues that might be found within are tempered by darker images of an apocalyptic landscape: burned-out cars, a tattered graduation gown, chromed invaders, abandoned beach houses, suicide machines, kids huddled in the mist, dying in the streets, broken heroes, lovers in the cold, wasted and stranded midnight boys, empty homes, stolen sisters, and a death waltz. And while the album represents a height in rock romanticism—due in no small part to the contributions of newcomer Roy Bittan's melodies—the album's lyrics are more gritty than romantic, more city noir than teen beach romance. In the course of *Born to Run*'s eight songs, we meet "a killer in the sun," a faithless "tramp of hearts," a distinctly femme fatale angel who tells "desperate lies," two would-be hoods and a tough guy who doesn't dance, knife-fight victims, and a gang member dying (or dead) from gunshot wounds. These characters warn each other that no one rides for free. They make "secret pacts" and then curse each other for betrayals. Rather than ascending to love, they "surrender" to it.

While the Springsteen of *Born to Run* still retains moments of youthful romanticism, from the first stanza of "Thunder Road" (with Mary fearing that "we ain't that young anymore") to the street toughs of "Jungleland" who end up "wounded / Not even dead," this Springsteen paints a landscape of lost youth. "It was the album where I left behind my adolescent definitions of love and freedom. . . . [It] was the dividing line," he later reflected.[1]

The characters of *Born to Run* still display the same sense of rootlessness as the characters of Springsteen's earlier work, yet they are more grounded; facing the loss of their youth, and with it the dreams of youth, they are tied more closely to Earth. The album's opening track, "Thunder Road," has the singer telling Mary (named Angelina or Chrissie in earlier versions) that they should "trade in these wings for some wheels." As Springsteen described in his *Storytellers* performance on VH-1, "Thunder Road" was an "invitation" to an "earthly journey."

Springsteen originally intended the track sequence of *Born to Run* to add up to a concept album that collectively follows its character throughout the course of a day, and the finished album still conveys that sort of feel. (In his review of the album, Lester Bangs noted that *Born to Run* "could almost be a concept album.")[2] Originally, "Thunder Road" was to appear in two versions—an acoustic one to open the album and then the full-band version to close it. But the song works intrinsically as an opener, not a closer. Marsh reports that Springsteen wrote "Thunder Road" in "a morning mood" and that he even played with the idea of beginning the song with "a clock radio clicking on and blaring Orbison's 'Only the Lonely.'"[3] (The fourth and fifth lines of the song allude to a radio playing this song.) The uncharacteristically imagistic opening lines—"Screen door slams / Mary's dress waives"—initiate the action at daybreak. Then, as Marsh observes,

> The record moves through a series of encounters, some of which are flashbacks—"Tenth Avenue Freeze-Out," "Night," "She's the One"—but all of which are harrowingly current in their emotions. "Backstreets" ends Side One evoking the heat of the afternoon; "Born to Run" begins the second side with the early evening mist. By the time "Jungleland" is over, we have reached dawn of the next day. Much has happened, here in Nowhere, but nothing is finished. There is the feeling that these characters may be condemned to repeat such days forever.[4]

"Thunder Road" is "Rosalita" rewritten from the perspective of a less innocent, more realistic perspective. Again, the singer sits in his car in front of his girlfriend's house, calling for her to come out and drive away with him. But whereas "Rosalita" depicts a rock-and-roll savior, the singer of "Thunder Road" warns that he isn't a savior and that he offers no redemption except the chance to drive away. What's more, his invitation is distinctly unromantic: he tells Mary that she "ain't a beauty" but she's "all right," and he warns her that the ride he's offering her "ain't free." The last two lines of the song—"It's a town full of losers / And I'm pulling out of here to win"—could very well have been sung by the singer of "Rosalita," but the singer of "Thunder Road" seems more realistic about where he's headed.

"Backstreets," a painful organ-drenched saga of a broken summertime romance and friendship, can be seen as Springsteen's answer to Dylan's "Idiot Wind." While the singer of "Backstreets" twice describes the departed girl, Terry, as a friend and never once as a lover, there's no mistaking the passion involved. Sung in retrospect, the song is about a relationship that was doomed to end. The lovers meet during a "soft infested summer." Marked by Original Sin (the "fire we was born in"), they were doomed to betrayal and expulsion. In the end Terry has been stolen away by another man, and the singer is left to recall their pledge of "forever" and the image of her lying on his chest. He recasts Terry in hindsight as "Just another tramp of hearts / Crying tears of faithlessness." When it comes to songs about romance won and lost, Springsteen would never write a more powerful one or one more bittersweet.

Although the object of desire in "She's the One" goes unnamed, she could just as well be Terry. In fact, an early version of the song included the line "I hated you when you went away," which was moved into the final version of "Backstreets." (Meanwhile, the references to French cream and French kisses in "Santa Ana" reappear here.) The girl of "She's the One" is also a liar; she has an "angel in her lies / That tells such desperate lies / And all you want to do is believe her." Musically, with its roller-rink piano and Buddy Holly rhythms, it hearkens back to rock-and-roll past, as does the song "Tenth Avenue Freeze-Out," the one and only song on the album with a distinct R&B feel. Although "E Street Shuffle" contains the band's name in the title, "Tenth Avenue Freeze-Out" (which refers in title to a Belmar Avenue that intersects E Street) became the band's signature number. Even though the song is perhaps the least interesting of the eight songs, it lyrically calls out Clarence Clemons ("the Big Man joined the band") while musically announcing the arrival of Steve Van Zandt, who arranged the song's soulful horn section.

Two other songs, "Night" and "Born to Run," dip back into classic car culture. "Night" is a feverishly up-tempo track, sung in second person, of an Average Joe hot-rodder who endures his nine-to-five job until he can go out at night to drag race against "chromed invaders" on the circuit and can search for his as-of-yet unfound love waiting for him somehow, somewhere.

A similar story is told in the album's title track. Again, the narrator works a dreary job by day, sweating out the "runaway American dream," while at night he joins a "chrome-wheeled fuel-injected" community. Of all the album's songs, "Born to Run" most embodies adolescent romanticism. The singer's car becomes a sexual metaphor around which he invites the girl, Wendy, to wrap her legs and strap her hands. Wendy's name renders the singer a rock-and-roll

MALE DUOS

In the late 1950s, Phil and Don Everly, known collectively as the Everly Brothers, took the traditional country vocal harmony of such groups as the Louvin Brothers and put a rockabilly/pop spin on it. The Everly Brothers' close vocal harmony style brought them widespread success, and in the 1959–1962 period the Everly Brothers enjoyed a number of Top 10 pop hits, including "Bye Bye Love," "Wake Up Little Susie," "All I Have to Do Is Dream," and "Cathy's Clown." The often-parallel harmony of Phil and Don Everly also influenced the Beatles' John Lennon and Paul McCartney, Paul Simon and Art Garfunkel, and others. Perhaps just as importantly, however, the Everly Brothers established the male duo as an important force in pop music. The surf duo of Jan (Berry) and Dean (Torrence) enjoyed considerable popularity, especially in 1963 and 1964, with such songs as "The Little Old Lady from Pasadena," "Surf City," and "Dead Man's Curve." Unlike the work of most of the successful male duos, however, Jan and Dean's recordings featured extensively multitracked vocals. Simon and Garfunkel took the Everly Brothers style of two-part harmony into the arena of folk rock and became one of the leading groups of the period 1964–1970, on the strength of Paul Simon compositions such as "The Sound of Silence," "Homeward Bound," "Mrs. Robinson," and "Bridge over Troubled Water." Although they worked together on and off from the early 1960s into the early 21st century, the duo of Bill Medley and Bobby Hatfield, known professionally as the Righteous Brothers, made virtually all of their chart impact in 1965 and 1966. However, blue-eyed soul Righteous Brothers hits such as "You've Lost That Lovin' Feelin'," "Unchained Melody," and "(You're My) Soul and Inspiration" continue to be staples of oldies radio and film and television soundtracks. In fact, the Phil Spector–produced "You've Lost That Lovin' Feelin'" is widely acknowledged as the biggest radio hit of all time. In the 1970s, male duos included Loggins and Messina ("House at Pooh Corner" and "Your Mama Don't Dance") and Seals and Crofts ("Summer Breeze," "Diamond Girl," and "Get Closer"). After the chart and radio dominance of Simon and Garfunkel in the 1960s, however, the next major dominant male duo was Hall and Oates. Daryl Hall and John Oates enjoyed hits such as "Maneater," "Rich Girl," "Kiss on My List," "Private Eyes," and others, with their work combining blue-eyed soul and rock influences. By 1984, Hall and Oates had dominated the pop charts to the extent that they were acknowledged as the most commercially successful duo act (of any gender) in the history of the recording industry. Because the male duo as a commercial force on the American pop music charts came out of the Everly Brothers' adaptation of the work of country duos, perhaps it is fitting that in the 1990s into the early 21st century the dominant male duo was the country act Brooks & Dunn. In fact, in the genre of country music, so dominant were Kix Brooks and Ronnie Dunn that the duo won numerous awards from the Country Music Association and two Grammy Awards and produced some of the biggest-selling country albums of the 1990s.

version of Peter Pan, calling to her to run away with him. He wants Wendy to help him discover if his youthful notions of love are real, and in the best tradition of adolescent overstatement, he pledges his desire to die with her in the street, locked in an "everlasting kiss," and to love her "with all the madness in my soul."

"Born to Run" would become Springsteen's signature song, an accessible anthem that most compactly captured the themes of the sympathetic loser yearning for romance and escape. The characters of "Born to Run"—the title itself invoking the 1970s' punk motto "born to lose"—are "tramps." Their lives, we're told, are marked by "sadness," and although the singer promises Wendy that they will one day reach a romantic promised land, he can't tell her when. As in "Night," the theme of escape in "Born to Run" is undercut by a feeling of desperation.

Two songs after the tramps of "Born to Run," we move to the two-bit hoods of "Meeting across the River." The unnamed singer plans an unnamed illegal deal with his partner in crime, Eddie. (The song's original title, "The Heist," and the thousands of dollars promised to the singer imply grand larceny.) The song's plot and Randy Breckner's slick trumpet line imply the world of film noir, but these are not big-time characters. The singer warns Eddie that they can't "blow this one" and says that the word is out: this is their "last chance." The singer's instructions for Eddie to stuff something in his pocket to make it look like he's concealing a gun and to change his shirt to convey the style they usually don't have further convey the desperate acts of losers. The singer even warns Eddie to play it cool or else; if their job falls through, they'll be looking for Eddie, too.

Again, Springsteen renders his loser sympathetic. The singer of "Meeting" is trying to salvage his relationship with his girlfriend, who has threatened to leave him. We can assume that she realizes she's with a loser—especially since he's just hocked her radio for cash—and the planned heist is his last chance to impress her. He dreams of returning with the $2,000 payment he's been promised and—more importantly—throwing it on the bed for her to see. "She'll see this time I wasn't talking / Then I'm gonna go out walking," he vows, convincing himself more than he convinces us. Given the song's title, the reference to "the tunnel," and the fact that Springsteen was still writing from a New Jersey perspective (he wrote most of the songs on *Born to Run* while living in West Long Branch), we emerge with the image of hoods from the New Jersey suburbs headed for a job in New York, a town too big for them. (Remember, New York is where Kitty ran off to when she was lured by her big-city lover.) If we had to take a guess, it would be that the singer and Eddie meet their end on the other side of the Hudson.

As Brian Hiatt reflects, "the song's tale of a Jersey guy risking it all for a big score in the city hit close to home." "By that time we'd been counted out, and it probably had something to do with that—a feeling I had about myself," Springsteen remembers. "It was that New York/New Jersey, big-time/small-time thing."[5]

"Meeting across the River" serves as a prelude to the album's closing song, "Jungleland," which plants us firmly on that other side of the Hudson. It's hard not to notice similarities between the song and the one that closed *Wild*, "New York City Serenade." Both songs are extended opuses—grand finales set amid the urban jungle. But whereas "Serenade" was more mood piece than narrative, this street-urchin story of "Jungleland" more closely resembles "Incident on 57th Street" and "Zero and Blind Terry," though it's superior to either song.

Roy Bittan's piano is the driving force of the song, as it is throughout much of *Born to Run*. "Jungleland" is introduced by Suki Lahav's bittersweet violin, accompanied by Bittan on piano. Lahav provides a classical element that helps create the sacred-within-the-profane motif that Springsteen had explored throughout his albums to date. Then Lahav gives way to Bittan, who explores note sequences within a single chord. Only then does Springsteen enter to tell the story of the Magic Rat, a gang member who drives in from Jersey and flees the cops in Harlem with his unnamed "barefoot girl." After an organ rings out to underscore the holy silence found "From the churches to the jails" (again, juxtaposing the sacred and the profane), the band kicks in with its rock components of guitar and drums. As the gang members gather on the street at midnight, Springsteen again summons a theatrical sensibility: "Man there's an opera out on the turnpike / There's a ballet being fought out in the alley."

Bittan pounds out a fervent chord progression at the song's midpoint, and after the lovers disappear for the moment, Clemons's sax provides a soulful bridge to the song's conclusion. It's a stirring solo and one that Springsteen took great care in working on with Clemons. Mike Appel remembers Springsteen "literally going through [singing] every note" for 16 hours with Clemons in the studio. Clemons describes it as "the most intricate solo" in all his years with the E Street Band.[6]

After Clemons's solo, the Rat and the barefoot girl are reduced to two hearts beating beneath the city. Her "whispers of soft refusal" give way to "surrender." It's unclear whether she is conceding to passion or, as with Spanish Johnny and Maria in "Incident," his leaving (or both). In the end he does leave her to return to the streets and is gunned down. He is carried away in an ambulance as she unknowingly turns off her bedroom light and goes to bed. (Unlike Spanish Johnny and Puerto Rican Jane, these lovers won't be meeting later on Lover's Lane.) Beneath a "wordless howl" that Springsteen improvised at the last minute,[7] Bittan delivers an ascendant chord progression to a resolution—the first and only in the song's nearly 10 minutes—bringing song and album to a transcendent ending.

Quite simply, *Born to Run* is a masterpiece. Its vocals don't soar as melodically as Roy Orbison's, its lyrics are more Leonard Bernstein than Bob Dylan, and its musical core is derived from piano lines, not guitar riffs. But the record's elements were a recipe for a breakthrough blockbuster. The album not only gave Springsteen his first hit record but also transformed 1970s' rock music while pushing the boundaries of what a singer-songwriter could achieve within the rock genre. Hilburn writes that

> *Born to Run* breathed with the same kind of discovery that made Elvis Presley's *Sun Sessions* and Bob Dylan's *Highway 61 Revisited*, the two most important rock albums before it. Listening to all three works, you feel present at the forging of a major artistic vision. You sense the artist's excitement at finding something within himself that he hadn't known was there until it burst forth in the studio.[8]

Born to Run made such a splash that both *Newsweek* and then *Time* came calling for feature stories. Appel had a rule of allowing interviews only to magazines that promised cover stories. Surprisingly—and unknowingly—both magazines agreed, and Springsteen appeared on the cover of the October 27 issue of both *Time* and *Newsweek*. While Appel had achieved an unprecedented publicity coup, to many the dual covers smacked of yet more media hype.

To make matters worse, the *Newsweek* feature focused more on Springsteen as hype than it did on Springsteen as artist. The agenda of the piece, penned by Maureen Orth, with researchers Janet Huck and Peter S. Greenberg, is easily seen in the title of the piece, "Making of a Rock Star." For Orth and her colleagues, Springsteen was more media creation than rock-and-roll salvation. The article focused on Columbia's promotional efforts and also cited a piece that Henry Edwards wrote for the *New York Times* in October titled "If There Hadn't Been a Bruce Springsteen, Then the Critics Would Have Made Him Up." In his transparently cynical article, Edwards dubbed Springsteen's lyrics an "effusive jumble," his melodies "second-hand or undistinguished," and his performance "tedious" and cited "vigorous promotion" as the secret to the album's success.[9] The *Newsweek* piece reported that "some people are asking whether Bruce Springsteen will be the biggest superstar or the biggest hype of the '70s," and while stating that "most of the country . . . isn't even aware of Springsteen yet," in the same breath it mentioned a "back-lash" against Springsteen. "Women think he's sexy and it's likely he'll end up with a movie contract," said Orth. She quoted an envious Warner Bros. executive who described Springsteen as being merely "a kid with a beard in his 20s from New Jersey who happens to sing songs" and who lacked the stage presence of Elton John, couldn't sing any "sweeter" than James Taylor, and couldn't write lyrics any "heavier" than Dylan's. "Hypes," the article concluded, "are as American as Coca-Cola so perhaps—in one way or another—Bruce Springsteen *is* the Real Thing."[10]

Jay Cocks's piece in *Time*, "Rock's New Sensation," considered Springsteen with less cynicism and gave more space to a discussion of the artist's work.

> His music is primal, directly in touch with all the impulses of wild humor and glancing melancholy, street tragedy and punk anarchy that have

made rock the distinctive voice of a generation. . . . Casting Springsteen as a rebel in a motorcycle jacket is easy enough . . . but it ignores a whole other side of his importance and of his music. . . . The sound is layered over with the kind of driving instrumental cushioning that characterized the sides Phil Spector produced in the late '50s and '60s. The lyrics burst with nighthawk poetry.[11]

Famed rock journalist Lester Bangs profiled Springsteen in the November 1975 issue of *Creem* with a brilliant article titled "Hot Rod Rumble in the Promised Land." Writing from the Midwest, where Springsteen (he noted) had yet to even tour, Bangs observed that "you can smell the backlash crisp as burnt rubber in the air." Yet Bangs seems to have understood what Orth did not, arguing that Springsteen would "withstand the reactionaries" because "street-punk image, bardic posture and all, Bruce Springsteen is an American archetype, and BORN TO RUN will probably be the finest record released this year."[12]

Although Bangs felt that Springsteen was not an "innovator," he noted that Springsteen's genius lies in the way in which he "rethought traditional sounds and stances" of early rock, teen rebel movies, and beat poetry. And although Bangs acknowledged a friend's criticism that Springsteen's depictions of New York City were more romanticized than realistic, he argued that perhaps that was the point behind Springsteen's rock vision: "Springsteen's landscapes of urban desolation are all heightened, on fire, alive. His characters act in symbolic gestures, bigger than life [and his] music is majestic and passionate with no apologies." For Bangs, *Born to Run* was the work of a "gifted urchin cruising at the peak of his powers and feeling his oats as he gets it right, that chord, and the last word ever on a hoodlum's nirvana."[13]

In mid-October, Springsteen and the E Street Band touched off the West Coast wing of the tour with four dates at the Roxy in Los Angeles. That first night, celebrities abounded: Jack Nicholson, Jackson Browne, Wolfman Jack, and Robert De Niro. At one of the dates, while playing "Quarter to Three" in the encore, Springsteen playfully taunted the audience, asking, "Are you talking to me?" According to some sources (including Eric Alter-man in *It Ain't No Sin to Be Glad You're Alive*), this bit of audience interplay became the inspiration for De Niro's famously improvised mirror soliloquy ("Are you talkin' ta me?") in the film he was shooting at the time, Martin Scorsese's *Taxi Driver*.[14]

The following month, the band brought their act across the Atlantic for the first time. London's Hammersmith Odeon was the site of their European debut on November 18. The skeptical English critics were measured in their reception, but the British fans went home happy. Covering the event for *Creem*, Simon Frith wrote that "He arrived as the most hyped-up American act in ages. . . . The audience clapped and cheered a lot but the critics were cagey."[15] According to the E Street Band members, Springsteen was angered by the hype for the event and was disappointed at the end of the night, apparently thinking that he had bombed in his first English performance. But after one-night stands in Sweden and Holland, they returned a week later to the Hammersmith Odeon on November 24 for an encore performance that, by most reports, blew the first one away. Then they brought it all back home to the United States, where the *Born to Run* tour concluded in Philadelphia on New Year's Eve.

The popular and critical acclaim for *Born to Run* would not be fleeting. Rankings of the all-time best popular music albums often place it in the Top 10. In 2003, a Zagat Survey poll named it the best all-around CD recording in history.

It is hard to evaluate the breakthrough that *Born to Run* was without being colored by hindsight. It unquestionably announced Bruce Springsteen's arrival. But it did not make his career. In the years that followed, Springsteen would encounter struggles within his own camp. And by the time he released his next record, his writing had evolved, delving deeper into the runaway American Dream that he first began to explore on *Born to Run*. From this point on, the writer of "Rosalita," "Thunder Road," and "Born to Run" would begin to explore what his characters were running from, what they were running to, and if they had anything to run to.

Notes

1. Robert Hilburn, *Springsteen* (New York: Scribner, 1985), 47.
2. Lester Bangs, quoted in June Skinner Sawyers, ed., *Racing in the Street: A Bruce Springsteen Reader* (New York: Penguin, 2004), 76.
3. Dave Marsh, *Bruce Springsteen: Two Hearts; The Definitive Biography, 1972–2003* (New York: Routledge, 2004), 142.
4. Ibid.
5. Brian Hiatt, "Bruce Gets 'Born' Again," RollingStone.com, November 11, 2005, http://www.rollingstone.com/news/story/8789518/bruce_gets_born_again.
6. *Wings for Wheels* (DVD), directed by Thom Zimny, *Born to Run: 30th Anniversary Edition* (box set), Columbia Records, 2005.
7. Hiatt, "Bruce Gets 'Born' Again."
8. Hilburn, *Springsteen*, 68.
9. Henry Edwards, "If There Hadn't Been a Bruce Springsteen, Then the Critics Would Have Made Him Up," *New York Times*, October 5, 1975.
10. Maureen Orth, et al., quoted in Sawyers, *Racing in the Street*, 53–63.
11. Jay Cocks, quoted in Sawyers, *Racing in the Street*, 64–73.
12. Bangs, quoted in Sawyers, *Racing in the Street*, 75–77.
13. Ibid.
14. Eric Alterman, *It Ain't No Sin to Be Glad You're Alive: The Promise of Bruce Springsteen* (Boston: Back Bay, 2001), 176.
15. Simon Frith, "Casing the Promised Land: Bruce Springsteen at Hammersmith Odeon," *Creem,* March 1976, 26. www.rocksbackpages.com/article.html?Article ID = 362. Note: rockbackpages.com misdates this as a 1975 article.

9

Queen

A Night at the Opera (1975)

James E. Perone

The first half of the 1970s found a number of rock styles hitting the radio airwaves and enjoying strong album and single sales, including pop, hard rock, progressive rock, heavy metal, and glam rock. The British band Queen managed to incorporate aspects of all of these styles into their work but within the context of elaborate vocal harmony arrangements that hearkened back to the best work of late 1960s' pop (e.g., the Beatles' *Abbey Road*). Along with these styles, though, Queen was never hesitant to include the influence of barbershop harmony and the early 20th-century British music hall. Queen's 1975 album *A Night at the Opera* arguably is the group's best album, track by track. It also contained one of the greatest singles of the rock era: "Bohemian Rhapsody." The album is packed with intricate arrangements, spectacular lead and harmony vocals, and the kind of stylistic shifts and diversity that perhaps only Elton John, Queen, and Led Zeppelin could pull off at the time. The songs of *A Night at the Opera*, however, also represent spectacular excess, from the operatic setting of "Bohemian Rhapsody" to the near self-parody of Queen's arrangement of "God Save the Queen" and the are-they-serious-or-are-they-joking love ode to an inanimate object "I'm in Love with My Car." Some of the songs, such as the aforementioned "I'm in Love with My Car," sound almost like outtakes from the 1984 spoof film *This Is Spinal Tap*. What makes *A Night at the Opera* such an effective album is that the mock seriousness, the clear silliness, and all of the flamboyant excess come together to form something that clearly is meant to entertain. By not taking themselves too seriously, Queen produced something that is a thoroughly enjoyable and always entertaining work of art. Furthermore, listeners who are attuned to the technical demands of the voice, guitar, piano, and drums may notice that just when *A Night at the Opera* is on the verge of getting too silly or too obviously campy, superb musicianship flashes into the arrangements and shows just how superb a studio band Queen was. And *A Night at the Opera* is no doubt all about the recording studio—while Queen was a popular concert attraction at the time, the production and extensive overdubs on *A Night at the Opera* resulted in a collection of songs that truly exist at their best only on the studio album.

A Night at the Opera opens with one of the most engaging musical settings of some of the nastiest lyrics possible in the prepunk half of the 1970s, Freddie Mercury's "Death on Two Legs (Dedicated to . . .")[1] This song, purported to be "dedicated" to a former Queen manager who Mercury believed had mistreated the band is filled with invective, with Mercury ultimately telling the dedicatee that he can "kiss [his] ass." The song includes elaborate instrumental and vocal arrangements that shift from hard-hitting heavy metal to pop vocal harmony. The result is that what might have come off as a self-serving putdown somehow comes off as balanced.

A Night at the Opera tends to ping-pong emotionally and stylistically, an effect that is heightened by the numerous direct segues from song to song. The album's second track, Mercury's very brief "Lazing on a Sunday Afternoon," sounds pretty much as though it comes out of the 1920s' and early 1930s' music hall/Tin Pan Alley style. The lead and harmony vocals are processed so as to sound like they are coming from a vaudeville singer's megaphone (in the manner of Rudy Vallee). It is quite a shock to hear Mercury singing the praises of "lazing on a Sunday afternoon" supported by Brian May's jazz-influenced guitar work after the invective of the album's opening track.

"Lazing on a Sunday Afternoon" itself makes a direct segue into Roger Taylor's "I'm in Love with My Car." Taylor anthropomorphizes his car and sings that he prefers it over women because cars "don't talk back." This is a curious song, because it teeters on the edge of being a self-parody—a joke—and a serious exploration of the virtues of Taylor's favorite car. Taylor is not heard as lead singer on Queen recordings nearly as frequently as Mercury or Brian May; however, on "I'm in Love with My Car," a moderately light example of heavy metal, Taylor displays a thoroughly workable metal voice.

Bassist John Deacon continues the theme of love and friendship in his song "You're My Best Friend." Mercury takes the lead vocal, and Deacon contributes a prominent overdubbed electric piano part. Deacon's lyrics are perhaps the most straightforward on the entire album: they are a simple expression of love. The musical style on "You're My Best Friend" moves completely in the direction of Top 40–style pop music. Because the song is so similar in style to pop music by other bands—there are not a great deal of conventionally Queen-ish touches to make it stand out like some of the songs on the album—it tends to get lost in the shuffle somewhat. What does stand out about the song somewhat, though, is the lack of section-length repetitions in it. It is not entirely through-composed sounding but is less predictable structurally than most Top 40–ish pop rock songs.

Mercury was such an iconic part of Queen as the band's front man and as the writer of Queen's most iconic songs (e.g., "Bohemian Rhapsody," "We Are the Champions," and "Crazy Little Thing Called Love") that it is easy to forget just how democratic Queen really was throughout the group's lengthy career, especially in the area of compositional representation. The first four songs on *A Night at the Opera* include two by Mercury and one each written by Deacon and Taylor. The next track, "'39," is a folkish ballad composed and sung by guitarist Brian May. As the song progresses, it becomes increasingly clear that the "ship that sailed away" in 1939 was a spaceship on an exploratory mission; however, the listener can easily extrapolate May's tale as a more generalized story of exploration. Some listeners might be tempted to read the text as a reference to the start of World War II in 1939. The ship's multiyear voyage can be understood as a metaphor for the soldiers who went off to war in Europe in 1939, only to return possibly years late; however, the references to the discovery of a new world that promises a new and better life for future generations seems contradictory to the state of Europe in the aftermath of the war. The upshot of the story is that the homecoming and the reports of "the Voyagers" is bittersweet for May's character. On one hand, he gladly welcomes his beloved; however, he realizes that he has grown so old while the spaceship was gone that he will never be able to visit the land of promise about which he hears. The song "'39" is a curious one in the context of Queen's style. Individually, the themes of space fantasy and almost Renaissance period–style waiting for a returning ship fit with the progressive rock style of the late 1960s and early 1970s. However, they seem somewhat incompatible, especially given the decidedly non–Space Age almost Moody Blues–type (e.g., "For My Lady") musical setting. That being the case, the song and May's vocal performance are haunting.

The next song, May's "Sweet Lady," presents a portrait of a dysfunctional relationship, with lead vocals by Mercury. First, Mercury portrays the male character and complains to his "sweet lady" about how she mistreats him verbally and through her actions. Then, he portrays the "sweet lady" and delivers a similar string of complaints to her male counterpart. The real essence of the song, however, comes from the instrumental arrangement and performance. Here, May, Taylor, and Deacon put on a prototypical heavy metal performance filled with instrumental virtuosity, implied metrical changes, and typical metal tone colors, such as May's heavily compressed electric guitar tone. It is probably safe to say that even if the vocal tracks were completely removed, the listener would still feel the mood and message of the piece solely from the instrumental setting.

Following the pattern that they established on the album's opening two tracks, Queen abruptly shifts mood and relieves the emotional tension with a Mercury-composed 1920s-style music hall number: "Seaside Rendezvous."

Also following the pattern of the music hall–style songs on *A Night at the Opera*—and other Queen albums before and after—"Seaside Rendezvous" is at once a tribute to the music hall and a humorous send-up of the style. The lighthearted mood and the portrait of an earlier more innocent time in Britain are so integral to the piece that it might be easy to miss the technical stuff of the recording. In the middle section, Mercury and Taylor's voices are electronically processed and overdubbed so as to imitate a woodwind and brass section in a pre–swing-era jazz or music hall band. It is no wonder that *A Night at the Opera* was widely rumored at the time of its release to have been the most expensive-to-produce album to date, when one considers that what might be heard as a two-minute trifle was given such care (and presumably such time) in the studio.

At nearly eight and a half minutes long, Brian May's composition "The Prophet's Song" easily is the longest song on the album. The message of the piece is fairly typical of the heavy metal genre. The prophet of the song's title warns of disastrous consequences if the people's warring ways are not replaced by peace—a sort of divine retribution. The people, however, cannot give him heed, and by the end of the song "the prophet" is viewed as "the madman." In retrospect, "The Prophet" is a curious track. It is not as unrelenting instrumentally or vocally as, say, the heavy metal style of Black Sabbath on similarly themed songs (e.g., "War Pigs"). Typically nonmetal effects such as Queen breaking into vocal harmony unexpectedly give the arrangement a sense of freshness; however, some listeners might find that these effects tend to diminish the impact of the message of the lyrics.

Mercury's gentle, classically oriented ballad "Love of My Life" is the next track on the album. Whether intentionally or perhaps because Mercury had certain melodic, harmonic, and piano-playing formulae that were just a standard part of his songwriting vocabulary, there are vocal and piano motives in "Love of My Life" that anticipate the yet-to-appear album track "Bohemian Rhapsody." Because "Bohemian Rhapsody" is so widely known, the subtle stylistic and melodic connections between it and "Love of My Life" tend to give the album a feeling of structural coherence that somewhat balances the wide stylistic and mood changes between some of the pairs of songs. Mercury's piano part includes rubato (slight tempo changes characteristic of European piano compositions of the 19th century) as well as classical period–style trills (rapid oscillations between two adjacent pitches). Brian May adds an additional classical-style touch with his occasional harp arpeggios. "Love of My Life" stands apart from the rest of the songs on *A Night at the Opera* because it is simply a straightforward love song, absent the explorations of the fantasy world or the deliberately mixed messages of other tracks. The song may present some challenges to some listeners. Most importantly, while Mercury was one of the most talented and most versatile singers in the history of rock music and while he uses classical restraint on "Love of My Life," the fast, quivery vibrato represents less classical vocal technique than perhaps a not entirely successful attempt at classical technique. For listeners who do not focus on technique or the alignment of the piano technique with the vocal technique, the song can be heard for what it is: a simple, honest expression of love and devotion.

One of the interesting structural features of *A Night at the Opera,* particularly because of the way coproducers Roy Thomas Baker and Queen sequenced the tracks, is how Freddie Mercury and Brian May play a sort of musical game of good cop/bad cop well into the second half of the album. Mercury's compositions tend to be either bright and happy or tender; May's deal with such subjects as impending doom for humanity ("The Prophet"), dysfunctional relationships ("Sweet Lady"), and the frustrations of the aged ("'39"). The pattern continues as the simple expression of love embodied by Mercury's "Love of My Life" gives way to May's "Good Company." The piece opens innocuously enough with May's character sitting on his father's knee receiving life advice. His father tells him that the secret to a happy, successful life is to "keep good company." After growing up, falling in love, and marrying, May's character finds himself working long hours to try to build a still-better life for himself and his family. His character's time away from home becomes too much for the relationship to bear, and his wife leaves him. At the end of the song, May's character finds himself in the same position his father was in at the start of the song: he gives the same advice to the next generation. The theme of members of each generation failing to heed the advice of their elders not to get wrapped up in pursuit of money and material goods was found in other songs in the mid-1970s (e.g., Harry Chapin's "Cats in the Cradle"). May's musical setting of this theme, though, stands out from those of others: May uses Freddie Mercury–style 1920s' music hall/jazz. And, interestingly, this seems to bring Queen's two most prolific songwriters back together both lyrically and rhetorically. The disarming musical setting might be construed to suggest at least the possibility of hope that the next generation might finally break the cycle of materialism and focus on relationships. The song also allows May to exhibit his jazz guitar sensibilities, as he imitates a music hall clarinet solo on electric guitar.

The opening two lines in the introduction of Mercury's "Bohemian Rhapsody" truly set the stage for one of the most celebrated and one of the most parodied songs of the rock era. Mercury asks the rhetorical question "Is this the real life? Is this just fantasy?" What follows, especially in its operatic excess and abrupt shifts between classical, pop, and heavy metal styles, suggests a dream/nightmare fantasy about the last days and hours of a "poor boy" condemned to die for murder. However, the piece could also be taken as the ravings of a madman for whom "nothing really matters." Part of the appeal of "Bohemian Rhapsody" is that it can be interpreted in either of these ways or even as a metaphor for the feelings brought on by a complete lack of hope. It really is a song with which one can live for multiple hearings as one puts together a mental image of all of the possible meanings. However, what is perhaps most striking about the song is the complex, highly eclectic musical setting. After the introduction, the piece contains two verses. Instead of a chorus section, which generally follows the first two verses, "Bohemian Rhapsody" next features its famous operatic section. The operatic section is followed by another contrasting heavy metal–style section and then a reprise of part of the introduction as a coda. The instrumental interludes focus heavily on the work of Brian May, Roger Taylor, and John Deacon; however, Freddie Mercury's classical piano is also prominent in the introduction, the first two verses, and the coda. The interweaving lines are so complex—yet so completely integrated—that "Bohemian Rhapsody" is one of the greatest examples of the use of the multitrack recording studio ever.

The album concludes with Queen's arrangement of the traditional British patriotic piece "God Save the Queen." As might be expected, the piece, an instrumental dominated by Brian May's multilayered guitars, has a double meaning, given the name of the band. However, just like a fair number of the songs on *A Night at the Opera*, it is difficult to determine to what extent the piece is meant to be a joke and to what extent it is meant as a statement of British patriotism.

Queen's *A Night at the Opera* can be taken as a study in lyrical and musical contradictions or as a study in musical eclecticism. However, perhaps the album is more of a study in the making of state-of-the-art rock music in an era of disco and just prior to the era of punk rock. The album includes integrations of progressive rock, pop, and heavy metal with barbershop quartet-style harmonies as well as songs that are at once deconstructions of and tributes to the old British music hall and vaudeville traditions. The complexity of the vocal and instrumental arrangements—particularly Freddie Mercury's vocal work and Brian May's multitrack guitar parts—alone would have made *A Night at the Opera* one of the important albums of the rock era. However, the pop hooks are so strong, the writing is so good, and the raising of questions and the creation of various moods through combinations of music and lyrics are so interesting—even with repeated hearings—that *A Night at the Opera* goes beyond just important; it is one of the greatest album-length achievements of the rock era.

Note

1. The title is presented in this open-ended form, without the expected closing parenthesis.

10

Gordon Lightfoot

Summertime Dream (1976)

James E. Perone

The Canadian singer-songwriter-guitarist Gordon Lightfoot emerged as a star just as the introspective singer-songwriter style came into prominence at the dawn the 1970s. However, Lightfoot (b. 1938) was somewhat older than most of the other emerging artists of the time and, in fact, bridged the gap between the folk revival of the early 1960s and the 1970s' singer-songwriter era. Lightfoot's baritone voice was instantly recognizable among the numerous synthesizers of acoustic folk and pop of the era. Lightfoot's music also tended to include musical references to American country music more frequently than the work of others of the singer-songwriter cadre of the 1970s. In short, there were plenty of features of Lightfoot's music that made it stand out.

Lightfoot was, more than anything else, a writer and performer of songs, as opposed to albums. Despite this, his 1976 album *Summertime Dream* perhaps is the best single-disc collection of his career. If nothing else, *Summertime Dream* contains Lightfoot's iconic, notable, and (in some circles) notorious song "The Wreck of the Edmund Fitzgerald" as well as more conventional songs about one-on-one human relationships. The album opens with "Race among the Ruins." In this song, Lightfoot deals somewhat impressionistically with the need to pick oneself up after a loss, presumably of a friend or a lover. In fact, part of the appeal of the song—and others like it—is that the lyrics are so nonspecific to any particular situation that many different listeners who have suffered different kinds of losses can understand the text as an encouragement. Generally, though, Lightfoot perhaps is not as notable for his lyrics per se as much as for his engaging song settings. His tunes tend to be memorable, often with clearly defined melodic shapes in the phrases. The melody of "Race among the Ruins" is no exception. Lightfoot begins each verse with an emphasis on scale step five. The emphasis through the first several measures on the dominant is followed by motion down to the third scale step and then finally to tonic at the end of the verse. Therefore, Lightfoot provides a long-range melodic shape to each verse in addition to the more foreground-level shape to each phrase within the verse. The chorus is somewhat more meandering and is reminiscent of mid-1960s' pop rock. I mention this because part of what made Lightfoot stand out during the 1972–1977 period was his musical ties to the prepsychedelic 1960s.

There is a long Anglo-American/Anglo-Canadian folk tradition of documenting significant events in song. The most common way of doing so is by means of strophic songs, settings in which the same music is used for each stanza of text, a form not all that common in commercial pop songs.[1] Lightfoot turns to this folk song–inspired strophic form in his documentation of the highly publicized wreck of the Great Lakes ore carrier *Edmund Fitzgerald*. In fact, the folk song/chantey-like nature of the piece also is confirmed by Lightfoot's use of the Dorian mode for his melody and harmony and by basing the entire melody of each stanza on the same short, basic melodic phrase.

"The Wreck of the Edmund Fitzgerald," probably because it is in the style of a folk ballad (or story song), contains some curious, if not awkward, lines and rhymes. Lightfoot set the story with a triple-meter feel and, as mentioned before, based the entire melody of each stanza on a single, simple phrase. Conventional wisdom might suggest that these attributes as well as the fact that the story is quite grim—all 29 crew members perished in the shipwreck—would mean that this song would be a rather anonymous album track. In fact, "The Wreck of the Edmund Fitzgerald" came within a hairbreadth of making it all the way to No. 1 on the pop singles charts. Still, it seems to be remembered as a song that listeners either loved or hated. It received much radio airplay, despite the single's nearly six-minute length (the album version clocks in at six and a half minutes), and arguably has caused the subject of Great Lakes shipping disasters to be better remembered within the shared American and Canadian culture perhaps more than any other work in any popular medium. However, humorist Dave Barry included "The Wreck of the Edmund Fitzgerald" in his list of the worst songs of all time, writing that playing the recording is a sure way to break up a party.[2] No matter where the listener falls in their reaction to "The Wreck of the Edmund Fitzgerald," this remains one of the most iconic songs of the 1970s.

In "I'm Not Supposed to Care," Lightfoot sings a farewell to a soon to be former lover. His character puts on a brave face but suffers an underlying sense of loss and remains in love with the one who is about to leave him. In other words, even though he is "not supposed to care," he clearly does. The lyrical sentiments fall squarely within the introspective singer-songwriter style that was popular at the time. In fact, in its triple meter and general melodic shapes, the verses bear a slight resemblance to Jim Croce's 1973 song "Time in a Bottle." Curiously, the melody in the chorus of "I'm Not Supposed to Care" bears an even closer resemblance to that of the 1960s' Procol Harum song "A Whiter Shade of Pale," itself written in the melodic and harmonic style of Baroque-period composer Johann Sebastian Bach.

In his song "I'd Do It Again," Lightfoot provides a profile of the proverbial musician on the road. Although the lyrics contain references to specific events in the musician's life, he can be understood as a universal character. Like most of Lightfoot's songs, the melody and performance are engaging. Perhaps the most noteworthy part of the recording is the fuzz-tone electric guitar work of Lightfoot's longtime band member Terry Clements. Clements and drummer Barry Keane provide a rock feel that extends the musical range of the album.

The next track, "Never Too Close," moves firmly in the direction of country rock. And as one listens to *Summertime Dream*, it is interesting to note how seamlessly Lightfoot and his band move between country rock, country, folk, pop, and various combinations of these genres. It is also interesting to note the shifts in rhetorical voice and song forms from track to track. The glue that holds all of the songs together is Lightfoot's distinctive and somewhat plaintive baritone voice.

A tribute to soldiers past and present, "Protocol" is a particularly moving song in the context of its time and in the context of the release of *Summertime Dream* in the United States. In the wake of the highly controversial Vietnam War and revelations about atrocities committed on both sides, public regard for soldiers in the United States had fallen considerably since the storming of Normandy during World War II. Lightfoot places the veteran of the Vietnam War alongside the veterans of World War II and earlier conflicts. The song is not, however, an endorsement of the failed war in Southeast Asia. There is, in fact, a feeling of sadness in this slow, understated ballad that suggests the sense of loss and emptiness that follows the death of soldiers. Be that as it may, "Protocol" ties the soldiers of history and the present together, with the unspoken implication being that the Vietnam War veterans deserve the respect that they found difficult to obtain in the mid-1970s.

In the next song, "The House That You Live In," Lightfoot turns again to triple meter and strophic form. His lyrics provide advice about a variety of possible life situations; however, each stanza concludes by reminding listeners that their house will always remain standing if they "pity the stranger who stands at your gate" or "door," depending on the stanza. The prominent acoustic guitar and steel guitar suggest the influence of country music, but the melodic structure and strophic form reflect folk leanings.

At two and a half minutes in length, the album's title track is its shortest. Much like several of John Denver's highly popular songs of the early 1970s, the lyrics of "Summertime Dream" recount the simple pleasures of nature on a rural summer day. It probably is a matter of personal preference, but some listeners might find that Lightfoot's resonant baritone voice is not as well suited to this type of song as Denver's more overtly emotional voice—Lightfoot is better suited to introspection and melancholy.

"Spanish Moss" turns to territory more suited to Lightfood's style. Here, his character is "driving north," away from the woman he loves after the breakup of their relationship. In his mind, the woman and the image of Spanish moss growing on southern trees are and forever will be linked. Interestingly, Lightfoot's harmonic progression and the chromatic voice leading in the electric guitar are reminiscent of the song "There's a Kind of Hush," a 1967 hit for Herman's Hermits. Listeners might also note that John Lennon used a variant on the same kind of chromatic inner-voice leading and harmonic motion in his 1980 song "(Just Like) Starting Over." What is even more intriguing is that "There's a Kind of Hush" concerns the start of a romance, "Spanish Moss" concerns the end of a relationship, and "(Just Like) Starting Over" concerns the rekindling of a relationship. The overarching story line of the three songs in sequence aside, it is interesting to note that similar harmonic and voice-leading materials were used successfully in three different decades for three very different phases of relationships.

Summertime Dream concludes with "Too Many Clues in This Room." In this piece, Lightfoot turns to the psychedelic imagery of the 1960s. The lyrics are especially widely open to a variety of interpretations and contain widely flung references to the sea, space exploration, and the plight of soldiers, just to name a few. The musical setting of the verses and the chorus feature different metrical feels and different tempi, which again suggest the psychedelic music of, say, 1967. However, the texture fits squarely within the musically clear singer-songwriter style. It is the kind of song that tempts one to listen to it over and over, if just to try to sort it all out, but it is not among the most memorable songs of the album. With its scattered images, which run the range of all of the other songs on *Summertime Dream*, "Too Many Clues in This Room" plays the role of the summation of everything that preceded it. In an undefinable way, it tends to pull all of the other songs together. The piece is so psychedelic in its imagery that it is not entirely successful in doing so. Ultimately, though, this does not work to the detriment of the album so long as the listener experiences Lightfoot as a writer and singer of individual songs.

Back in the singer-songwriter era of the first half of the 1970s, introspection and exploration of the "me" seemed to be all the rage. Gordon Lightfoot, with his background in 1960s' pop, folk, and classical music, provided something just different enough that his work on *Summertime Dream* stood out from the work of others of the genre, and the album's second track, "The Wreck of the Edmund Fitzgerald," clunky as some of the rhyming couplets may be, continues to stand as one of the greatest 1970s' representatives of the centuries-old folk ballad tradition.

Notes

1. Pop songs more frequently will have clearly defined verse, chorus, and bridge (sometimes called middle eight) sections.
2. Dave Barry, *Dave Barry's Book of Bad Songs* (Kansas City, MO: Andrews McMeel, 2000), 42.

11

Harry Chapin

Greatest Stories Live (1976)

James E. Perone

The introspective singer-songwriter movement of the early 1970s perhaps is best remembered for the work of James Taylor, Joni Mitchell, Carole King, and several other performers. Some of the lesser-known names, such as Harry Chapin, nonetheless developed strong, yet smaller, fan bases. Chapin was notable for his live appearances. They were not glitzy. Chapin himself might even be found in the lobby at intermission signing autographs, perhaps in support of UNICEF or World Hunger Year, one of his favorite causes, and Chapin's fans felt that he was telling his stories straight from the heart. It often has been suggested, and I can attest to the fact from personal experience, that Chapin was more effective live than on his studio recordings. The 1976 album *Greatest Stories Live* captured Chapin perhaps at the height of his popularity and included his best-known songs, and yes, the purity of the sound, the spontaneity, and even the rough edges speak with an honesty that was not possible in the recording studio.

The album begins with Chapin's "Dreams Go By." Perhaps in order to drive home the live nature of the album and perhaps to reinforce the strong connection that Chapin enjoyed with his audience, the song begins with the audience providing a group count off. Chapin then interrupts the instrumental introduction, remarking that it sounds like something that would come from the soundtrack of *The Godfather II*. Once the piece begins for real, it establishes a theme that runs through much of *Greatest Stories Live* and indeed through most of Chapin's work: that of loss. Chapin sings of dreams for the future that a couple has at various points in their relationship. None of these dreams, however, are ever realized: the realities of day-to-day late 20th-century life always get in the way. Chapin set his tale of sadly unrealized dreams to perky postragtime music hall–style music. Although the intentional disconnection between the sadness of the lyrics and the happiness of the bouncy music does not reach the level of, say, Country Joe McDonald's "I-Feel-Like-I'm-Fixin'-to-Die Rag" or Phil Ochs's "Outside of a Small Circle of Friends," both of which date from the mid-1960s, the sense of irony cannot be missed, even by listeners who are not particularly familiar with Chapin's work. More so than on his studio albums, Chapin's voice here is not particularly pretty in the commercial sense. The rough-hewn vocal quality, however, tends to make him sound more believable: he becomes the character who has seen time pass him by and now reflects on what might have been.

Chapin portrays a long-standing radio disc jockey in "W.O.L.D." He travels from job to job, at some point earlier in his life he left his wife and children, and now he has taken a position at an FM station back in the town where his wife lives. The song is written from the perspective of the DJ talking, probably on the telephone, with his ex-wife, recounting his career from the time he left her to the present. Chapin's brother, Tom, the keyboardist and backing singer in Chapin's band at the time,[1] sings the middle eight section. Here, the DJ tells his wife of his recent success as a guest MC at "high school sock hops" and how well he gets along with the kids at these gigs. The unspoken irony is that he left his own children and now considers himself to be a success with young people because of how well they accept him in his role in the music business. In the stanza that follows the middle eight, Harry Chapin returns as lead vocalist. Here, he asks his ex-wife to take him back again. Although we only hear one side of the conversation, we learn that she turns him down. He tells her that it is alright, because he is the happiest man in the world. The presumption that the listener makes, however, is that his self-professed happiness is only a smokescreen for a deep sense of loneliness that the DJ feels: he has no roots, he has burned his bridges as he moved from town to town, and he has real workable plans for the future. And, naturally, the refrain, with its statement "I am the morning DJ on WOLD," reinforces the fact that the character is aging—the call letters that Chapin selected clearly are not an accident—and, like the lead character of "Dreams Go By," reflects on what might have been had some of his earlier choices been different. "W.O.L.D." was one of the few Harry Chapin songs that ever made it on to Top 40 radio and one of the few that achieved success as a single in its original studio version. Although Chapin was part of the folk-oriented introspective singer-songwriter movement and although a fair number of his songs might stereotypically be labeled as reflections of depressed people who lead depressing lives, the music of "W.O.L.D.," "Cat's in the Cradle," and "Taxi" as well as some of his lesser-known compositions contain strong pop music hooks. The refrain of "W.O.L.D.," in particular, is catchy, and Chapin's heavy use of syncopated rhythms and a major-key melody stand in sharp relief to the pain that the DJ probably really feels beneath the surface.

It seems likely that several factors probably went into the decision to include two of Tom Chapin's songs on *Greatest Stories Live*. These were staples of Harry Chapin's live show in the mid-1970s, a show that included significant contributions from Harry's brothers Tom and Steve Chapin; Tom Chapin sang with a more conventionally commercial-sounding vocal timbre, thus providing a contrast to Harry's lead vocals; and Tom Chapin's songs tended to come from a contrasting rhetorical voice. For example, in "Saturday Morning," Tom Chapin sings about his desire to return to a lost love. While the feeling of loss would seem on the surface to link the song to "Dreams Go By" and "W.O.L.D.," it is more thoroughly universal than the story songs of brother Harry. Whereas Harry Chapin focused in on specifics in creating vivid characters and then developed the sources of their sense of loss, Tom Chapin's "Saturday Morning" dwells on the emotions themselves. Another stark contrast between this song and the previous two on the album is that the sense of irony that the listener hears in the intentional dissonance between emotion and musical style in Harry's work is missing in Tom's work: the music of "Saturday Morning" is as introspective, low-key, and sad as the lyrical sentiments.

In "I Wanna Learn a Love Song," Harry Chapin takes on the persona of a young nearly starving guitar player and teacher who teaches lessons in his students' homes, each one for "a crisp ten dollar bill." One of his students, a married financially well-off woman, wants to "learn a love song." Not only does she want to learn to play and sing, she wants to hear Chapin's character play and sing. The implication is that this is the only love song she hears, both literally and metaphorically. The unspoken subtext is that while she may be financially well off, there is little emotional connection within her marriage. Eventually the woman and her guitar teacher become sexually involved, she splits from her husband, and she and the itinerant guitar player become a couple. In fact, this tale is largely the story of Harry Chapin and his wife, Sandy. The meat of this five-minute song is not so much in the story itself, which can be summed up in a sentence or two, but in the emotional shifts that take place during the tale. It is also, in the context of *Greatest Stories Live*, the first time in which depressed people living depressing lives actually find a way out of their predicament.

At Chapin concerts throughout the 1970s, audiences were treated to the vocal talents of bass player John Wallace in an obbligato he sang in Chapin's "Mr. Tanner." Chapin's story concerns Tanner, a baritone-voiced dry cleaner from Dayton, Ohio, who sings to himself while he is working. Chapin, in one of his rare third-person songs, sings that "music was his life, it was not his livelihood," and tells the listener of the joy that Tanner feels from singing classical music. Eventually Tanner begins singing at shows in the area and then, at the urging of his friends, books a formal professional debut recital in New York's Town Hall. After Chapin describes the concert, he changes the chorus to tell the listener that this time when Tanner sang, he was only aware of the flaws in his performance. A New York music critic pans Tanner's concert in a four-line review, and Tanner returns to Dayton only to sing "very late at night" when there is no one around to hear him. It would seem that while Tanner can still find some solace in his music, his attempt to become a professional musician, to make music his livelihood, nearly destroyed music's earlier role as "his life." Like many of Chapin's melodies, "Mr. Tanner" is filled with syncopation. It is a more meandering and therefore less immediately commercial-sounding melody than those of the songs with which Chapin achieved his greatest sales success. The sense of melancholy and impending doom that the listener might sense as Tanner moves further and further away from treating music as "his life" and ever closer to trying to turn it into a profession pervades the musical setting.

In his introduction to "A Better Place to Be," Chapin explains to the concert audience that he was inspired to write the song by a story he heard in Watertown, New York. On the surface, Chapin's introduction simply serves to put the story into a context; however, it also lets the listener know that while one might want to read Chapin's work as autobiographical—and that was very much the way that original material by 1970s' singer-songwriters was understood by audiences—the basis for his work tended to be his creative extensions of stories that he learned from various sources. In "A Better Place to Be," Chapin tells the tale of a night watchman and a waitress, both of whom seem to suffer from low self-esteem, who find fulfillment in each other. It is a bittersweet story but provides more hopefulness than most of Chapin's other songs on *Greatest Stories Live*.

The album's next track, Tom Chapin's "Let Time Go Lightly," is a loving tribute to music from the viewpoint of a working musician. As such, it is the most obviously autobiographical-sounding song on *Greatest Stories Live*. Although a good example of the kind of introspective, almost confessional kind of material that exemplified the early 1970s' singer-songwriter movement, the piece seems out of place in the context of the story songs. The same cannot be said for the next track, "Cat's in the Cradle," one of Chapin's best-remembered story songs and certainly his most commercially successful single in its original studio release. A collaboration of Harry and Sandy Chapin, "Cat's in the Cradle" tells the story of a father who has little time to build a strong relationship with his son as the boy grows up. Eventually the boy becomes a man, marries, has a son of his own, and finds that he grew up to be just like his father, a mistake he had hoped never to make. There is a certain melancholy quality to Chapin's music, despite his usual use of syncopation in the melody. The bittersweet nature of the music largely comes from the interaction of this melody with harmony that, although technically in a major key, includes the subtonic (VII) chord, the minor dominant (v), and a chord based on the lowered (minor) third above tonic. This mix of a major tonic chord and chords that are drawn from the Mixolydian mode and from the tonic minor scale tend to obscure the "majorness" (to coin a term) of the piece.

Next, Chapin turns to his well-known 1972 song "Taxi." He takes on the persona of a San Francisco taxicab driver who picks up his final fare for the night. As he drives the well-heeled woman to "16 Parkside Lane," she looks at his license and he looks in his rearview mirror. It is then that the two recognize each other as high school lovers. As the woman, Sue, leaves the cab, she and Harry agree that they will have to get together sometime, although Chapin's text makes it clear that they never will. Sue hands Harry a $20 bill "for a $2.50 fare," and he, without showing shame, "stuffed the bill in [his] shirt." "Taxi" perhaps is the quintessential Harry Chapin composition: Chapin's character and the situation are based in part on fact, Chapin's character ends up failing to live out his dreams, and Chapin bases the disconnection between the male and female characters in part on social and economical class differences. In this performance, as on the 1972 studio recording, John Wallace sings several lines from what is widely purported to be a Sylvia Plath poem—one about dying, naturally—and the entire recording, from Chapin's and Wallace's singing to the instrumental backing, the record production, and the audience response, works well. In fact, one could argue that the entire "Taxi" package on *Greatest Stories Live* is superior to the original recording.

The song "Circle" includes vocal contributions from all three Chapin brothers and bassist Wallace. The work itself concerns the unpredictable, twisting nature of life. In concert—as is clearly discernable in the recording included on *Greatest Stories Live*—it is an ideal closer. The second stanza, sung here by Steve Chapin, references the musicians' intent to return to town again, which is greeted by applause.

The concert portion of *Greatest Stories Live* concludes with "30,000 Pounds of Bananas." While this 11-plus-minute tale of a banana-laden semitruck that overturned on a twisty downhill coming out of Scranton, Pennsylvania, is rather long for an encore,[2] this is the role that it plays on the album. Because the piece relies on humor—what seriousness there is tends to be mock serious—it tends to soften the overall concert experience. In fact, it is really the only out-and-out levity on this album. It is as though Chapin's philosophy was to tug at the hearts and souls of listeners, providing them with flashbacks into the bittersweet moments of their own lives and forcing them to confront some of the world's social issues but then to make sure they left the auditorium in an upbeat mood.

The album concludes with its sole studio recording of Chapin's song "The Shortest Story." This austere slow-paced piece comes from the viewpoint of a newborn baby who enters a world of hunger and absolute deprivation—his mother's breast "has nothing to provide." In the third and final stanza, Chapin sings in a parched, weak voice that now, in his 20th day of life, all he is aware of is complete loneliness, that a bird is circling overhead, and that all he now can do is die. This is followed by the tolling of a bell, signifying the death of the child. "The Shortest Story" is easily the most gut-wrenchingly depressing song that Harry Chapin ever wrote and recorded. It came at the time that he was most active in working to alleviate world hunger, and while it is difficult to listen to, it still can touch listeners decades after Chapin's untimely death in an automobile accident in 1981.

Harry Chapin's *Greatest Stories Live* only made it to No. 48 on the *Billboard* album charts; however, that made it Chapin's second–highest-charting album, after the 1974 *Verities & Balderdash*, which hit No. 4. More important than its chart standing, though, is the way in which it captures an often-underappreciated member of the 1970s' singer-songwriter movement interacting with his fans and particularly the way in which that artist-fan interaction resulted in a live album that accomplishes what the sterility and the gimmickry of the recording studio cannot accomplish. The human bond was an essential part of the singer-songwriter movement, and *Greatest Stories Live* captures it particularly well.

Notes

1. Tom Chapin achieved success in his own right as a singer-songwriter, particularly in his work in children's music.
2. The original 1974 studio version of "30,000 Pounds of Bananas" was less than six minutes in duration.

12

Stevie Wonder

Songs in the Key of Life (1976)

James E. Perone

Curiously, only two Stevie Wonder albums ever made it all the way to No. 1 on both the *Billboard* R&B and pop charts. That *Fullfillingness' First Finale* (1974) did so can probably be attributed more to the fact that Wonder had developed a huge fan base with his 1972 and 1973 work and that the album marked his return from a nearly fatal automobile accident. That *Songs in the Key of Life* was his second album to hit No. 1 on both charts can be attributed to the strength, breadth, and depth of the material: there literally is something for everyone in the massive package. Indeed, this double album—plus an extended-play bonus disc—is in many respects Stevie Wonder's greatest achievement as an artist. If *Talking Book*, *Innervisions*, and *Fulfillingness' First Finale* proved that Wonder was one of the most important singer-songwriter-instrumentalists of the 1970s, then *Songs in the Key of Life* put him in an entirely different class from any of his contemporaries. Even though this album had none of the structural unity of *Innervisions* and is a denser and sometimes less immediately accessible package than *Talking Book*, this 1976 collection was by far Stevie Wonder's most exuberant album—his greatest display of keyboard, harmonica, percussion, and vocal performances as well as possibly his best work as an arranger willing to bring in guest artists to play important musical roles. But a package like this one can be a double-edged sword. It certainly was for Wonder, for no album he would record afterward would ever meet with the broad commercial and critic appeal of *Songs in the Key of Life*. Likewise, this outpouring of creativity, particularly as a multitalented artist without peer, would be followed by several years of musical silence. When that silence was broken in 1979 by Wonder's film soundtrack for *Journey through the Secret Life of Plants*, it was broken by music that was very different in character and style from *Songs in the Key of Life*. It almost seemed that Stevie Wonder himself knew that he had done the performance of his life as a jazz-based R&B/pop songwriter, singer, and instrumentalist at the ripe old age of 26.

Songs in the Key of Life opens with "Love's in Need of Love Today." Wonder's lyrics speak of the need for love in the turbulent world of the mid-1970s. In fact, it is more timeless than that: Wonder performed the song to great effect on the *America: A Tribute to Heroes* telethon shortly after the September 11, 2001, terrorist attacks. This message that love will overcome all evil is one to which Wonder has turned many times since he began writing his own lyrics in the early 1970s. The anthem-like song of more than seven minutes' duration has a sparser accompaniment than many of Wonder's arrangements on *Songs in the Key of Life*, which places the listener's attention squarely on the lyrics. Musically, "Love's in Need of Love Today" is an easygoing R&B ballad. Wonder's melody incorporates some interesting contrasts from phrase to phrase, involving the use of an upward leap in the first antecedent phrase of each stanza, a leap that is contrasted with a more consistently downward stepwise motion in the consequent phrases. The harmony of the oft-repeated chorus includes some jazz-oriented added-note chords and some meandering harmonic motion. These features paint the song as somewhat impressionistic, although they also can make it challenging for the casual listener to instantly relate to the musical subtleties of the song.

The next track, "Have a Talk with God," is a mildly funky short collaboration of Wonder and his brother, Calvin Hardaway. The lyrics suggest that prayer to "the only free psychiatrist that's known throughout the world" can help one through any problem. Although musically "Have a Talk with God" contrasts with the album's first track, lyrically it continues what will become established as one of the primary themes of *Songs in the Key of Life*: the need for love in its many manifestations.

If the first two songs on the album did not establish the fact that Wonder the composer, arranger, and producer would be using extreme stylistic contrasts from song to song in order to hold the listener's attention, then the next couple of tracks certainly would make this attribute of *Songs in the Key of Life* crystal clear. "Village Ghetto Land" finds Wonder and collaborator Gary Byrd exploring the late 18th-century European classical court musical style aligned with graphic lyrics describing the harshness of life in the late 20th-century American ghetto. This creates an eerie, haunting mood that is as effective as the well-known "Living for the City" but framed in a musical world that is about as far away from the funk of "Living for the City" as possible. Wonder accompanies his voice solely by orchestral string parts that he plays on the synthesizer. Fortunately, synthesizer technology had advanced enough by 1976 that the sound is very natural. In fact, there is little difference in arrangement of timbre between Wonder's *Songs in the Key of Life* recording of "Village Ghetto Land" and the performance of the song on the 1995 *Natural Wonder* album, on which

Wonder is accompanied by the strings of the Tokyo Philharmonic Orchestra in an orchestration by conductor Dr. Henry Panion III.

Given Stevie Wonder's excellent credentials as an instrumentalist and his use of jazz harmonic and rhythmic styles in his songs, it is unfortunate that he has recorded so little straight-ahead instrumental jazz. "Contusion" is an example of such a work. Filled with metrical changes and tight ensemble work from Wonder, lead guitarist Mike Sembello, and members of Wonderlove (Raymond Pounds, drums; Nathan Watts, bass; Ben Bridges, rhythm guitar; and Gregory Phillinganes, keyboards), "Contusion" is representative of the type of rock/jazz fusion that was quite popular in the mid-1970s. The problem, however, with a piece like this—and possibly the reason that Stevie Wonder generally refrained from recording jazz instrumentals—is that absent Wonder's voice (or his trademark harmonica), it sounds fairly generic: good straight-ahead jazz fusion that could have come from any one of several artists of the era.

By the early 1980s, Stevie Wonder had written and recorded a few tribute songs, exemplified especially well by *Hotter Than July*'s Bob Marley tribute "Master Blaster (Jammin')." The first of these songs, however, was "Sir Duke," a tribute to Wonder's musical heroes of the big band swing era, "Basie, Miller, Satchimo [*sic*], and the king of all Sir Duke [Ellington]." Unlike Wonder's 1980 tribute to reggae pioneer Marley, "Sir Duke" does not actually incorporate the style of the subject of the tribute. Sure, there is the superficially big-band sound of a horn section that supplements Wonder's backing band, Wonderlove, but the musical style of "Sir Duke" owes more to R&B, a tinge of funk, reggae, and disco than it does to 1930s' and 1940s' swing. This is particularly apparent in the overall rhythmic feel and in the use of unison horn lines. Although it is not as obvious as in some of the other songs on the album, "Sir Duke" carries on the album's theme of spirituality and love conquering all obstacles. The difference is that here it is nostalgic, innocent, rhythmic dance music that effects a positive psychological change on humankind. When Motown issued the song as a single in the spring of 1977, it hit No. 1 on both the *Billboard* R&B and pop charts.

The next track on *Songs in the Key of Life*, "I Wish," similarly was a No. 1 R&B and pop single. Musically, the song is in a direct continuum from "Sir Duke," although with the funk/disco quotient ratcheted up a couple of notches. It is a thoroughly danceable song, but the real analytical interest lies in its lyrics. Throughout his lyrics-writing career—essentially from the early 1970s on—Stevie Wonder has rarely been overtly and obviously autobiographical. In fact, it could be argued that by retaining the moniker "Stevie Wonder" instead of his given name, Stevland Morris has maintained a healthy distance in other ways. The song "I Wish," however, contains much autobiographical insight into not only Wonder but also into the young Stevland Morris.

On one level, the song seems to be a simple paean to the composer's childhood—the days before Stevland Morris became Stevie Wonder. It is important to remember that Wonder was a child star from the age of 12 onward;

ALBUMS ON TAPE

The use of magnetic audio tape originally came out of the military during World War II; prior to that time, magnetic tape had not been used for the recording or reproduction of sound. By the end of the 1940s, tape was a viable commercial medium for recording companies, and its use undoubtedly played a role in making possible the long-playing vinyl album. For individual consumers, however, the vinyl album, plastic 45-rpm single, and shellac 78-rpm single remained the primary media for home listening through the 1950s. In the early 1960s, however, two inventions—the eight-track tape and the compact cassette tape—fundamentally changed the way and the locations in which consumers could listen to music. The eight-track tape was developed by a consortium of Bill Lear (of Learjet aviation fame), Ampex, RCA, Motorala, General Motors, and Ford Motor Company. From 1964 through the 1970s, millions of commercially produced eight-track versions of albums were sold and probably more often than not were used in automobiles, recreational watercraft, and so on. The cassette tape was developed by Philips Corporation in the early 1960s. Although at first the eight-track offered superior audio fidelity, by the 1970s improvements in the audio quality and its small size helped the audio cassette to become more popular than the eight-track. Portability in music went one step further when Sony Corporation introduced the Walkman personal cassette player in 1979. Although cassettes and eight-tracks increasingly are only relegated to antique malls and flea markets, they played important roles in furthering the portability of music from the mid-1960s to the end of the 20th century.

therefore, he did not have the opportunity to grow up as a normal teenager. And that is not even considering the differences between growing up sighted versus growing up unsighted. Wonder includes one particular turn of phrase that raises questions of a somewhat complex nature. This comes at the start of the song when he sets up the time frame of his reminiscences by singing "Thinking back to when I was a little nappy-headed boy." At first hearing, the lines seem simply meant to place the time as childhood. But why does Wonder define himself as a "nappy-headed boy"? In the 1990s, a noted African American children's author, Carolivia Herron, ran into problems by using the word "nappy" in the title of her book *Nappy Hair* because it was viewed as a derogatory term. Although the term did not necessarily generate the same level of consternation in the mid-1970s, it was still used to define a particular physical trait of blacks. Could Wonder's use of the term have come from the desire to paint Stevland Morris as just another anonymous black youth facing an uncertain future in a world in which American blacks had considerable difficulty surviving, let alone getting ahead? Perhaps. Could Wonder's use of the term have come from his personal experience of texture, as a person without the sense of sight—that is, someone who could relate better to texture through the sense of touch than to color? Perhaps. The point is, no matter what Stevie Wonder's intentions were in using a somewhat loaded turn of phrase, it lends itself to multiple interpretations and can cause the listener to ask questions pertaining to racism in particular and social conditions in general. Opening up his lyrics to a variety of possibilities and multiple understandings—whether by design or by fortunate accident—enriches the overall effect of the song.

One of the notable features of some of Wonder's compositions and recordings is his ability to play roles, much like an actor. Certainly, a song such as the early 1980s' piece "Front Line," in which songwriter-singer Wonder portrays a returned Vietnam War veteran, relies completely on Wonder's ability to suspend the listener's sense of reality in a convincing way. In part it is because of his frequent use of role playing that the autobiographical feel in "I Wish" tends to stand out. Sighted individuals might find the picture that Wonder paints of his youth to be quite different from what they expect. By all accounts, however, Stevland Morris really did get in trouble for playing doctor with a neighborhood girl, and he really did climb trees, run and jump, and hang around with the young neighborhood hoodlums writing profanities on the walls of buildings, just as Morris's alter ego, Stevie Wonder, documents in "I Wish."

As Wonder sings that he wishes those days of childhood mischief and innocence had not passed so quickly and, indeed, that they could return again, one cannot help but hear the song as an expression of the plight of the child star. That Wonder speaks so little of his own childhood in his songs and in interviews adds to the importance of "I Wish" as a documentary of his prefame days. It is simultaneously one of his funkiest and most touching compositions. "I Wish" gives the listener a reason to consider just how much childhood the musician had to leave behind when he became a star at such an early age; however, it also causes one to consider just how different Stevie Wonder the public adult is from some of the considerably more tragic child stars of the past and some of the idiosyncratic former child stars (including one who at one time recorded for the same record label as Wonder) who came along after Wonder first enjoyed fame.

Given the thematic focus on spirituality and love on *Songs in the Key of Life*, one can question how a song that essentially praises childhood mischief could possibly fit on the album. The best way to explain what might be behind the song is to quote some lines from *Northern Exposure*, a television program of the early 1990s, spoken by the character Chris Stevens. When the disc jockey/preacher/biker Stevens is caught stealing radios, he explains his behavior to his discoverer, Ed Chigliak, as follows:

> Wildness, Ed. We're running out of it. Even up here in Alaska. People need to be reminded that the world is unsafe and unpredictable. And at moment's notice, they could lose everything. Like that.

I do it to remind them that chaos is always out there, lurking beyond the horizon. That plus, sometimes, Ed, sometimes you have to do something bad—just to know you're alive.[1]

I think it is this belief that one needs to participate occasionally in innocent mischief in order to feel alive that drives "I Wish." In the background of Wonder's explorations of love in various forms (romantic, platonic, etc.) and spirituality on *Songs in the Key of Life* is the even more overarching theme of healing. What Wonder does in "I Wish" is to place that badness into the mix because of its healing power, its ability to make one feel, as the *Northern Exposure* character Chris Stevens puts it, "alive."

Fortunately, Stevie Wonder the record producer and arranger recognized the need for a real bass player and horn section on "I Wish." One of the minor musical problems that plagued his otherwise-superb work of late 1972 through 1974 was the fact that the bass sound that Wonder achieved on the synthesizer just did not capture the timbre or the spontaneity and power of a real electric bass player. Part of the problem resulted from the somewhat pedestrian bass lines in some of the funkier early 1970s' pieces. Even in pieces in which Wonder obviously tried to create a feeling of improvisatory spontaneity, such as "Jesus Children of America," however, the timbre of the synthesizer sounds today like a dated imitation of the electric bass. In a very real sense, it was not entirely Wonder's fault but instead can be blamed on the technology of the day. His goal seemed to be to have total control of his product not just as writer, arranger, singer, and producer but also as a one-man band, so he was forced to rely on a technology that was near its infancy. But percussion is another thing altogether—Wonder had recorded as a drummer since he was barely into his teens. As the 1970s moved into the 1980s, some Stevie Wonder recordings relied on studio drummers and others on drum machines, neither of which were as inventive as Wonder himself. On "I Wish," however, drummer Raymond Pounds plays with the kind of improvisatory inventiveness heard in the best of Wonder's own drum playing from the first half of the 1970s.

The album's next track, "Knocks Me Off My Feet," is a gentle moderate-tempo love ballad. Wonder, who wrote both music and words for this song—as well as playing all the instruments and providing all the vocal parts—does a nice job capturing the spirit of the great Motown love songs of the 1960s. A large part of the secret to the song's success lies in Wonder's text painting. He sets the lines "There's sumptin 'bout your love, that makes me weak and knocks me off my feet" with a deliberate rhythmic stumble during the phrase "knocks me off my feet." As the song progresses, Wonder the drummer also adds a tom-tom roll to capture the spirit of the fall. The melodic hook is also strong in the tradition of earlier Motown hits.

"Pastime Paradise" explores an entirely different subject and an entirely different musical style. Wonder's lyrics speak of the way in which some people waste their lives living in the past, dedicated to the "evils of the world," when they should be living for "the future paradise" of a world of peace. He sets these lyrics to an interesting mixture of Latin dance and Spanish classical sounds. The synthesized, classically oriented strings recall the album's earlier track, "Village Ghetto Land." The text, too, deals with similar issues, especially with a focus on how improving race relations and equality can help to bring about "the peace of the world." Wonder's somewhat stark minor-key melody is haunting and is well supported by the repeated percussion and synthesized string figures. The repetitive nature of the string writing anticipates further steps that Wonder would take in exploring the contemporary classical technique of minimalism at the end of the 1970s in his soundtrack for *Journey through the Secret Life of Plants*. Although "Pastime Paradise" was not necessarily the best-known or best-remembered song from *Songs in the Key of Life*, it was to reemerge in the form of rapper Coolio's version "Gansta's Paradise," which hit the top of the charts in 1995.

"Summer Soft" is, as the title suggests, an ode to summer. Here, we find Wonder discovering a kind of spirituality in nature, thereby complementing the album's pieces about finding spirituality in God, in music, and in romantic and platonic love. Both "Summer Soft," which turns into a rock jam by its end, and "Ordinary Pain" suggest the style of Wonder's song just before his career as an independent artist really broke out with the 1972 album *Talking Book*. Musically, the two share a rhythmic feel, the use of chromatic voice leading with jazz-based harmonic motion, and the spirit of instrumental jamming that pervaded much of the 1970–1972 albums *Music of My Mind*, *Where I'm Coming From*, and even a little of *Signed, Sealed & Delivered*. The end result is that a song such as "Ordinary Pain," which is not the most profound lyrical piece Wonder had written or the best music he had written, stands as a fully workable and pleasant pop song but not much more.

For some strange reason, the song that begins side three of *Songs in the Key of Life*, "Isn't She Lovely," was never released as a single. I say "strange" because the song rivaled "Sir Duke" as the best-known track on the album. It still receives airplay in the 21st century on oldies radio stations. The highlight of the six-and-a-half-minute song, which is a tribute to Wonder's young daughter, Aisha (who can be heard in the background of the recording), is Wonder's uncharacteristically extended harmonica solo. Throughout this improvisation, Wonder references the main melody of the song but remains constantly inventive. In fact, there is a discernable chorus-to-chorus shape and connection and an overall shape to the entire solo. Maybe this is not quite the same sort of overall shaping of an extended improvised jazz solo for which saxophonist Sonny Rollins became famous in the 1950s and 1960s, but Wonder does exhibit attention to motivic development and shaping beyond the level of the phrase and even beyond the level of the chorus. In doing so, he places himself well beyond the level of most pop stars as an instrumentalist. The song's relatively simple and goal-oriented harmonic scheme lends itself to the kind of improvisation treatment that Wonder gives it. And although the lyrics of "Isn't

She Lovely" consist of three short stanzas of poetry, they serve an important purpose in relation to the focus of *Songs in the Key of Life*. By including this song on the album, Wonder expands the spirituality that he finds in love to include love of and love within a family, especially when it involves the miracle of children. Those who are musicians or aficionados of instrumental improvisations might find the sounds of Aisha and Wonder playing with Aisha to be an intrusion, but this documentation of intergenerational interplay fits right in with the overarching theme of the album.

"Isn't She Lovely" is followed by the six-and-a-half-minute ballad "Joy inside My Tears." Unlike the similarly anthem-like "Love's in Need of Love Today," this song unfortunately seems like it might be as long as it is because *Songs in the Key of Life* is a double album and there was time to fill. It is not one of Wonder's more interesting compositions, nor is it one of his most distinctive vocal performances.

The same criticism cannot be leveled at "Black Man." Here, Stevie Wonder sounds like a man who truly stands committed to everything about which he sings. His lyrics work through history, providing a chronicle of human achievements and attributing each to the person of a particular race who made the discovery, pioneered the procedure, or created the invention. His point is that all of humanity is creative and fully worthy of equal treatment. The one very obvious downside to Wonder and collaborator Gary Byrd's historical choices is that they are not nearly as gender-inclusive as they are racially inclusive: Sacagawea's assistance to Lewis and Clark is the sole example that the songwriters cite of a woman, at least until the mention of Harriet Tubman in the fade-out. Musically, "Black Man" is up-tempo funk, and it features Wonder playing all the instruments except the horns.

Wonder maintains the multicultural theme in the album's next song, "Ngiculela—Es Una Historia—I Am Singing." Through these lyrics, Wonder is singing of love, of tomorrow, and from his heart. He sings in English, Spanish, and Zulu, and his musical setting manages to suggest both African and Hispanic pop music styles.

"If It's Magic" presents Wonder in a most unusual texture: voice, harp, and just a touch of harmonica. Although he never actually uses the word "love," it seems that the "it" to which he refers is love. Wonder's lyrics question why we do not act as carefully as we might and "make it everlasting," "if it's special" and "if it's magic." Despite the classical nature of the voice and harp setting, harmonically and melodically, the song resembles the Tin Pan Alley/jazz ballad style of Wonder's earlier composition "All in Love Is Fair."

Like "Contusion," "As" fits right into the contemporary popular jazz idiom of the mid-1970s. However, unlike the harder-edged jazz rock fusion style of the earlier track with its tight unison lines and Mahavishnu Orchestra–like metrical changes, "As" suggests the lighter CTI jazz of Hubert Laws, George Benson, and others. In fact, the song, with its ostinato groove, was later covered by a number of jazz musicians, including trumpeter Blue Mitchell on his 1977 album *African Violet* and jazz rock fusion violinist Jean Luc Ponty on his 1982 album *Mystical Adventures*.

Songs in the Key of Life proper concludes with "Another Star," an up-tempo song of unrequited love. As a fast energetic song about Wonder's character having been wronged in love, it resembles some of the material he had recorded back in the mid and late 1960s. Musically, however, this is a thoroughly contemporary jazz-pop-disco song. In fact, the pop-jazz sound is confirmed by the presence of guest artists Bobbi Humphrey on flute and George Benson on guitar and backing vocals. The eight-and-a-half-minute song has excellent potential as a disco dance track but somehow does not seem to fit the overall theme of the album: that love conquers all. In fact, this is part of the problem with *Songs in the Key of Life* as a concept album: there is simply too much material and in too many different styles for it to hold together as a unified artistic statement in the same way *Innervisions* does.

The songs on the bonus disc originally issued with *Songs in the Key of Life* (they are included as tracks 8–11 on disc two of Motown's 2000 double CD reissue of the album) similarly are not necessarily focused on the album's apparent theme, at least as it was developed fairly clearly over the first three sides. For example, "Saturn," while a musically grand and thoroughly engaging collaboration between Wonder and Mike Sembello—recalling if anything the space-themed anthems of the Canadian studio band Klaatu—finds Wonder escaping from the problems of Earth by "going to Saturn where the rings all glow." Throughout the bulk of *Songs in the Key of Life*, Wonder the lyricist deals head-on with personal, political, and social issues, so the escapism of "Saturn" seems incongruous. "Ebony Eyes" is a gospel-influenced tribute to "Miss Black Supreme," the "pretty girl with ebony eyes," while "All Day Sucker," with its funkiness, synthesizer effects, and oft-repeated lyrical expression of being a "sucker for your love," recalls the music of *Music of My Mind* and *Where I'm Coming From*, two of Wonder's less accessible albums. The bonus record concludes with the instrumental track "Easy Goin' Evening (My Mama's Call)." This piece is slow and features Wonder playing a nostalgic melody on the harmonica. The tune features short, sequential motives within a fairly narrow range, which suggests Wonder's vocal compositions. The nostalgic nature of the music and the tune's title suggest an alternative view of Stevland Morris's childhood that complements the funky "I Wish."

Containing elements of nostalgia, social consciousness, spirituality, and a wide range of musical styles and textures, *Songs in the Key of Life* captured the American public's imagination: it was highly successful on the R&B and pop charts, and it spawned two successful singles ("Sir Duke" and "I Wish"). As a fully developed artistic statement, however, there was just too much material and too much variety in style, arrangement, and production to match the cohesiveness of Wonder's work of a few years before. But if viewed as a collection of individual songs, *Songs in the Key of Life* was a formidable achievement and continues to stand as one of the greatest albums of the rock era. This is not entirely because of the compositional strengths of the songs but can also be attributed to the tightness of the instrumental ensemble work, both in tracks that were recorded entirely by Wonder and in those in which he was accompanied by Wonderlove and other assisting musicians.

Note

1. Louis Chunovic, ed., *Chris-in-the-Morning: Love, Life, and the Whole Karmic Enchilada* (Chicago: Contemporary Books, 1993), 33.

13

The Eagles

Hotel California (1976)

James E. Perone

Between 1972 and 1975, the Eagles in many respects came to epitomize the laid-back California folk–country pop hybrid that had been developing several years earlier in the work of the Byrds (during Gram Parsons's brief tenure in the group), Poco, and the Flying Burrito Brothers, not to mention Rick Nelson, Linda Ronstadt, and Michael Nesmith. What the Eagles did not excel at was playing hard-rocking music. That ended, however, when the band's original lead guitarist, Bernie Leadon, left and was replaced by Joe Walsh. Walsh's first album as an Eagle, *Hotel California*, was perhaps this long-standing band's greatest achievement. All five Eagles—Don Henley, Randy Meisner, Glenn Frey, Don Felder, and Joe Walsh—along with noted songwriter J. D. Souther and percussionist Joe Vitale played a role in writing the album's eight songs.[1] Most of these songs either overtly or metaphorically explore the darker side of the California lifestyle and its emphasis on commercialism, vanity, consumerism, and instant gratification.

The album begins with its title track. "Hotel California," a product of Felder, Henley, and Frey, frames the seductive nature of the California lifestyle around the metaphor of a hotel—a nightmarish hotel from which "you can check out any time you like, but you can never leave." While this image can be understood on more than one level, as the listener moves through the album to its culmination on "The Last Resort," it tends to sink in that perhaps the most plausible meaning is that one can "check out" by means of a drug-taking, partying lifestyle; relentless pursuit of wealth and material goods; and so on. While the lyrics are impressionistic, there are enough specific references to the era's consumerism and partying lifestyle (the Mercedes Benz automobile that one character drives and the "pretty, pretty boys" who deem to be a constant part of the disco scene as some of them "dance to remember" and others "dance to forget") that in the context of the entire album, "Hotel California" serves as an introduction to some of the specific topics that later are developed with more focus. Both Felder and Walsh provide electric guitar solos, and the extended fade-out section features interplay between the two. Despite the generally accepted notion that Walsh's presence on lead guitar is one of the important factors that took the band from the status of country rock favorites to arena rock megastars, it is interesting to note that it is not just his playing that changes the overall sound of the Eagles beginning with *Hotel California*—he seems to spur Felder on as a solidly rock-oriented guitarist as well.

"New Kid in Town," written by Souther, Henley, and Frey, is the most overtly country-leaning song on *Hotel California*. In contrast to the country signifiers of previous popular Eagles recordings—such as the imitation of the sound of pedal steel guitar in "Peaceful, Easy Feeling" and the banjo in "Take It Easy," both significantly played by Leadon—here the country influences are heard more in Frey's vocals, Walsh's electric piano playing, and Frey and Felder's guitar playing. Insofar as the banjo and the direct imitation of pedal steel guitar are more stereotypically a signifier of the influence of country music than the electric piano, the country portion of the Eagles' style is muted in comparison to their earlier output.

More important, though, than the fact that "New Kid in Town" shows the Eagles moving closer to what today is called classic rock than in their earlier albums is what the song tells the listener lyrically. Actually, the song can be interpreted several different ways. On the surface, it would seem that the singer was once the proverbial "new kid in town," who made a big splash and found what he thought were lasting friendships and lasting love. Now, however, there's another newcomer, and that newcomer threatens the singer's position. In fact, it would seem that the fact that the singer's friends are flocking to the newcomer proves the true superficiality of their "friendship." Given Walsh's new position in the Eagles, some listeners might read him into the song. One weakness with that interpretation, though, is the fact that Walsh, while new to the Eagles, was a well-established guitarist, singer, and songwriter as well as an established part of the Laurel Canyon community of musicians that included members of the Eagles as well as Linda Ronstadt, Carole King, and a host of others. Because the bookends of *Hotel California*—the title track and "The Last Resort"—paint the reality of California life as pretty much the polar opposite of the sunny California dream, one can hear "New Kid in Town" as being more about superficiality, popularity, and the pursuit of transitory pleasure than about one particular character.

While the title track might be the best-remembered song from *Hotel California*, "Life in the Fast Lane" is still heard on oldies and classic rock radio in the 21st century. Since this is the highest-energy rock song on the album, it is also the song on which Bill Szymczyk's punchy production perhaps is most notable.

In fact, a large part of the song's success is because of the power not only in the vocal and instrumental performance but also in the solid way in which Szymczyk puts it all together in the mix. Songwriters Frey, Henley, and Walsh tell a tale about the long cocaine and other drug-fueled parties for which the Los Angeles area was known at the time. It is not a glorification of drug abuse and a focus on instant gratification, however. As the Eagles note about the aftermath of a night of partying by one couple, "he was too tired to make it; she was too tired to fight about it."

The next song, "Wasted Time," is a study in the classic story of a broken relationship. This slow ballad, though, could have come from just about any time and any place in America from the 1950s through the time of *Hotel California*. In other words, the hope that each member of the former couple can get beyond the hurt of the breakup and ultimately realize that the relationship was not just "wasted time" is not unique to the social scene that is explored throughout most of the album.

The focus on the dark side of the California experience returns on the next track, "Victim of Love." While the lyrics do not actually place the story in California, it is easy to connect the tale with the dark experiences of the women who populate some of the album's other songs—songs that do place the action in California. The lead character of "Victim of Love" is found partying in a "room full of dangerous boys." Apparently, she has claimed to the singer that she is over her feelings for another male character; however, she apparently is still engaged with the other man sexually ("you still have his gun in your hand"). Ultimately, the singer invites the woman to be a victim of his love. Set to a fairly hard (although not particularly fast) rock style, the song highlights codependency and superficial sexual couplings that marked this pre-AIDS disco era. Musically, the song is notable for the high degree of stylistic contrast between the verses and the chorus, particularly in the electric guitar parts.

Although they could not be more different musically, the next track, "Pretty Maids All in a Row," is a fitting lyrical follow-up to "Victim of Love." In "Pretty Maids All in a Row," Walsh sings about the loss of innocence, perhaps characterized best by lines such as "why must we grow up so fast?" and "the storybook comes to a close; gone are the ribbons and bows." In a different setting—or if considered as a stand-alone song—"Pretty Maids All in a Row" is a 12/8-meter slightly gospel-inflected song about the loss of childhood innocence. In the context of such songs as "Victim of Love," "Hotel California," and "The Last Resort," though, it appears that this yearning for the innocence of youth results from the realization that the indulgent, hedonistic lifestyle of some members of the Eagles' circle of friends and acquaintances has taken a heavy psychic and physical toll.

Meisner's "Try and Love Again" features the twin lead guitar texture associated with southern rock bands such as Lynyrd Skynyrd and the Charlie Daniels Band. The melody, harmony, and lyrics tend to be the closest in style to the Eagles' pre–*Hotel California* work. In fact, "Try and Love Again" sounds so much like a product of the early 1970s' folk–country pop scene that it could be mistaken for a product of the British-American trio America.

Aside from the album's title track, the most important song on *Hotel California* perhaps is the final track, "The Last Resort." Songwriters Henley and Frey tie all the previous songs together in this final reflection on the dark side of California life. For example, when Henley sings of a woman who went west from Providence (like her father a generation before had done when he set sail for America from Europe), the natural connection is with one of the album's tragic female characters. The implication is that she set out for California to live out a dream, only to find that the dream was a nightmare. Not just the tale of one particular character, though, the song presents the broader dialectic between the California dream and the harsh reality that lies beneath and behind the glamour. The lyrics contrast the natural beauty of the California desert with the "a bunch of ugly boxes" (look-alike suburban houses) and a love of the "red man's ways" with present-day hedonistic pursuits ("the town got high"). Gradually the lyrics come to focus in on the concept of manifest destiny, the idea that originally justified and continued to propel the westward expansion of the United States. Perhaps the most telling phrase—both lyrically and musically—in this assessment of what this unbridled expansion led to is when Henley sings the text "They call it paradise; I don't know why." The melodic falloff at the end of the phrase and the resignation in his voice sums up the entire album. The anthem-like size and grandeur of the musical production on this song is similar to that in the Beatles' 1968 ballad "Hey Jude" and mid-1980s' hits by Foreigner ("I Want to Know What Love Is") and Prince ("Purple Rain").

Although both "Pretty Maids All in a Row" and "The Last Resort" both contain somewhat dated-sounding synthesizer scoring, it is perhaps more noticeable on the album's closing song. Certainly, orchestral strings were employed on Jim Ed Norman's fantasy on "Wasted Time," so one must question why "Pretty Maids All in a Row" and "The Last Resort" use synthesized strings. Since sound synthesis technology later improved to the extent that the imitation orchestral strings later sounded more like the real thing, the artificial nature of the synthesized strings on *Hotel California* probably is more apparent in the 21st century than it was when the album first was released. Still, the use of synthesized strings was a minor weakness of the album and especially of "The Last Resort" even back in the mid-1970s, primarily because the very nature of synthesized sound stands in such sharp contrast to the real sounding tone colors of the instruments with which the Eagles are most closely associated. Still, the grandeur of the arrangement and the gradual crescendo of the piece up to the extended fade-out suggest the grandeur of the desert, mountain, and seaside landscape of a California long lost. It also might be heard by some listeners as a sign of hope that the old ways and the old dreams might someday return.

In 2003, *Rolling Stone* ranked *Hotel California* at No. 37 on its list of the 500 greatest albums ever recorded.[2] The individual songs "Hotel California,"

"The New Kid in Town," and "Life in the Fast Lane" were commercially successful singles. While the Eagles continued to enjoy a sizable following as a concert attraction, the promise that *Hotel California* provided for them as a harder-edged and more socially conscious rock band in the studio largely was unfulfilled. The Eagles' next studio album did not appear until 1979, and after that the band has only produced two additional studio albums, one in 1994 and one in 2007. So, what looked like a new direction for a highly popular band ultimately turned out to be a career climax, followed by relative silence. As a document of the California scene and perhaps more specifically the Los Angeles Laurel Canyon scene of the mid-1970s, *Hotel California* continues to paint a near-definitive picture of the time and the place.

Notes

1. A brief orchestral fantasy on "Wasted Time," written by arranger/conductor Jim Ed Norman, immediately follows the song proper.
2. "500 Greatest Albums of All Time," *Rolling Stone* online edition, 2003, http://www.rollingstone.com/news/story/5938174/the_rs_500_greatest_albums_of_all_time.

14

David Bowie

"Heroes" (1977)

James E. Perone

David Bowie's 1977 album *"Heroes"* continues the overall feel of *Low*, his previous album from the same year—that is, a mixture of songs that largely focuses on social outcasts and experimental instrumental pieces. Generally, though, *"Heroes"* is a more accessible package, mostly because it contained one megahit song ("Heroes") and because the instrumental pieces feature more acoustic instruments and fewer hazy, impressionistic washes of ambient sound. Still, there is a darkness that pervades *"Heroes,"* which is part of what makes this album both fascinating and challenging. The cover art, which shows Bowie in stark black and white in a highly stylized, almost kabuki-like gesture (dressed in leathers), hints at the stark contrasts that the songs and instrumental pieces present. This becomes the overarching theme of *"Heroes."*

The album's first song, "Beauty and the Beast," bears a superficial resemblance to the title track of Bowie's *Station to Station*. This can be heard especially well in the opening accompaniment figures. Once Bowie's vocal melody begins, though, the resemblance to "Station to Station" is forgotten. "Beauty and the Beast" is a particularly interesting melody in terms of Bowie's use of short motivic figures to construct a longer-range melody. Although this may be an overgeneralization of his compositional style, Bowie typically writes melodies that feature a high degree of melodic contrast between the verse and chorus sections. "Beauty and the Beast" contains contrast between the sections, but there is one phrase in the chorus that clearly is based on the opening melodic motive of the verse. This gives the piece a greater feeling of structural integrity than would be provided by a lack of motivic sharing between verse and chorus.

"Beauty and the Beast" is one of those David Bowie songs with lyrics that can leave the listener scratching his or her heard and wondering just what they mean. Bowie establishes a basic feeling of evil in the air through his impressionistic and nonlinear lyrics. His references allow the listener to read the Beauty and the Beast characters two possible ways: as two entities or perhaps two sides of the same entity. In either case, the fact remains that the dark side—which Bowie paints as unavoidable—rules the situation that he constructs. The listener must keep in mind that Bowie has created images based on the good-evil dialectic throughout his career: it is not unique to "Beauty and the Beast." However, it is interesting to consider the possible influence of his living in Berlin at the time. Certainly, the East Berlin–West Berlin and communism-democracy dialectics can fit conveniently in the listener's possible understanding of the song.

The second track on *"Heroes,"* the song "Joe the Lion," paints the picture of a man—the title character—who morphs from one personality type to another after "a couple of drinks." Joe the Lion is emboldened by drink. Insofar as David Bowie has turned time and time again to depicting various social outcasts who fit in only within their own subculture, this character is somewhat atypical. Joe seems to fit in with the regulars at the local bar, at least after he has enjoyed his drinks. There is nothing to suggest, however, that he cannot fit into the world at large or some other subculture when he is fully sober. His almost Jekyll and Hyde personality represents a concrete manifestation of the rather more abstract portrayal of bipolarity of the song "Beauty and the Beast." It is with "Joe the Lion" that the theme of the entire album revolving around the good-evil, Jekyll-Hyde dialectic starts to become clear. It is not always as easy to hear as in these first two songs, but there is always a sort of black and white contrast lurking below the surface throughout *"Heroes."*

Bowie's music for "Joe the Lion" is closely connected to his work on *Station to Station* and *Low*. In particular, he uses ample dissonance in the harmonies and harsh electric guitar timbre but balances this with tuneful melodic hooks. He also balances the avant-garde tendencies and thick texture of the introduction and verses with a middle eight section that features a thinner texture and rounder tone colors, both in Bowie's voice and in the instrumental accompaniment. One of the more interesting features of the song from a musical standpoint is Bowie's use of an easy-to-remember three-note descending stepwise figure in the lead guitar, which contrasts sharply with the meandering *Sprechstimme*-like melody of the vocal line.[1] All in all, Bowie balances his avant-garde and pop sensibilities throughout the album, sometimes falling more clearly on one side of the fence than the other. In the case of "Joe the Lion," the balance favors the avant-garde. This makes the song's middle eight section stand out in fairly sharp relief. The more avant-garde nature of "Joe the Lion" also makes the track that follows seem even more accessible, since it falls more squarely on the other side of the musical fence.

The album's title track is easily the best-known song on *"Heroes."* In a 2004 issue, *Rolling Stone* magazine placed "Heroes" at No. 46 on its list of the 500 greatest songs of all time.[2] In order to fully appreciate the song, the listener must keep in mind that "Heroes" was a product of the end of the Cold War, when today's Germany was still divided into East Germany and West Germany and the infamous Berlin Wall was still standing. During his extended stay in Berlin, Bowie happened to see a couple rendezvous near the wall and kiss. The song "Heroes" represents his view of what could be behind the couple's rendezvous and its symbolic defiance of the political state of Europe at the time. And like "Beauty and the Beast" and "Joe the Lion," "Heroes" has at its core a conflict between two opposing forces. In this case the dialectic is formed by the sense of separation caused by the Berlin Wall, on one hand, and the couple's dedication to each other, on the other.

The text of "Heroes" is written from the viewpoint of the male member of the couple and stresses first the unity of the couple (verse one) and then their unconditional love and acceptance of each other (verse two). After those first two verses, the concept of

THE DISCO ERA

The 1970s were known for, among other things, the popularity of disco music, primarily in the second half of the decade. This genre was characterized by a danceable beat, elaborate music arrangements and productions, and the entire cultural scene that developed around the discos. Disco and its culture were noted for racial integration as well as for the integration of sexual orientations. Stars such as Gloria Gaynor, the Bee Gees, K. C. and the Sunshine Band, Van McCoy, Chic, the Village People, and Donna Summer sold records in droves. They were among the artists whose recordings were most frequently programmed by disc jockeys in discos and for a period seemed to rule the radio airwaves as well. Disco albums tended to include longer tracks, since longer mixes were preferred in dance clubs. Singles too changed as a result of the demands of the dance club, and some of the most popular disc singles were issued in extended mixes on 45-rpm 12-inch vinyl records, as opposed to the standard 45-rpm 7-inch plastic record. Commentators have suggested that part of the appeal of punk rock was that it was viewed as the polar opposite of the glitz of disco; however, by the 1980s, some new wave rock was a virtual hybrid of disco and punk.

being heroes seems only to mean that they will be unconditionally supportive of each other; at this point there is no other overly political message. The instrumental interlude that follows features a synthesized-sounding solo that more than anything else calls to mind Keith Emerson's Moog synthesizer solo in Emerson, Lake and Palmer's "Lucky Man," that band's famous 1970 song of chivalry. The third verse of "Heroes" finds Bowie's character moving away from the almost naive clarity of the song's opening and wishing that his lover could "swim, like dolphins can swim." This lyrical shift, which is bookended by instrumental interludes, gives the listener the sense of a long transition and suggests perhaps a more significant shift in the nature of the story. The fourth verse, which Bowie sings an octave higher and in a near scream, is a restatement of the first verse. In the song's next verse, Bowie's character recalls the couple standing and kissing by "the Wall," in open defiance of the bullets flying overhead. At this instant, it becomes clear that the characters' love can overcome anything. And at this point the meaning of his desire to see his beloved able "to swim, like dolphins can swim" takes on a hidden political meaning. Dolphins swim as they wish; they are free. Bowie's character's lover does not enjoy that degree of freedom. It is clear that the heroism described at the end of each verse—"we can be heroes"—goes well beyond anything the listener might have anticipated at the start of the piece. Bowie's narrative technique, in which he presents a fairly generic picture at the start and then sharply and quickly focuses the scene and its background meaning in the conclusion, works exceptionally well.

The other obvious strength of "Heroes" is that the song is so full of vocal melody and accompaniment hooks that it is a great example of contemporary pop music. This is balanced by the early 1970s' progressive-rock nature of the synthesizer interlude and the avant-garde tone color manipulations of Brian Eno. One might reasonably assume that a song with a near-ideal mix of pop and experimental sensibilities and a story line that both reflects the times and contains a timeless message of love could not help but be a commercial success as a single. Curiously, Bowie's highest-ranked song on *Rolling Stone*'s list of the 500 greatest songs of all time did not even make it into the *Billboard* pop Top 40. Why? The answer might at least in part lie in the way in which the single version was chopped up to make it fit commercial radio. The single version omits the first two verses, thereby degrading the entire pacing of the song and the tension that Bowie's album version creates by sharply contrasting the deliberately vapid sentimentality of the first two verses with the emotional defiance of the Cold War battle lines at the song's conclusion. For one thing, this makes "Heroes" more one-dimensional. For another, the song does not make as much sense or have nearly as much impact if it starts with the impressionistic image of dolphins swimming. The long and the short of it is that the artistic integrity of an exceptionally strong pop song was severely compromised in an attempt to place the record on more radio playlists. It seems curious that this happened, because the full album version of "Heroes" weighs in at just over six minutes, shorter than a number of highly successful earlier singles of the rock era (The Beatles' "Hey Jude," for example).

The next song on *"Heroes,"* "Sons of the Silent Age," is one of those Bowie songs that probably raises more questions than answers. For example, the listener never learns definitively just who these men are, the ones with "blank looks and no books." These characters could be members of just about any marginalized group. They could be citizens of East Berlin or East Germany, those faceless victims of communism whose access to literature or outside news ("books") was inhibited by a repressive regime. Insofar as *"Heroes"* is a product of Bowie's stay in Berlin, this would seem to be a workable interpretation, but it is by no means a necessary interpretation: he does not give the listener enough clues to nail down the identity of the characters in any definitive way. The fleeting reference to the sons of the silent age listening to "tracks by Sam Therapy and King Dice" raises the specter of a fictional rock band on the order of Ziggy Stardust and the Spiders from Mars. It also, however, suggests a kernel of reference to *"Heroes"* guitarist Robert Fripp's famous band King Crimson. The chorus section of "Sons of the Silent Age" sounds like a lover's plea for forgiveness after some unspecified transgression but does not necessarily relate to the verses in a linear fashion. But it is important to note that Bowie has used the technique of juxtaposing seemingly contradictory or seemingly unrelated images in numerous songs. He has also used the technique of placing abstract or highly impressionistic images right next to concrete images in numerous songs before *"Heroes"* and since. As he customarily does when he presents highly contrasting lyrical images and reference points, Bowie also writes highly contrasting music in "Sons of the Silent Age": the verses use speech-like rhythms and a low portion of Bowie's vocal range, while the chorus is more pop song–like and in a higher range.

Even more than its predecessors on *"Heroes,"* "Blackout" is a mood piece replete with disconnected images. The mood is that of desperation, and Bowie plays it out in both his words (written in free verse) and his music. Significantly, coproducers Bowie and Tony Visconti treat Bowie's vocal lines with more than a little artificial reverberation. This renders some of the lyrics nearly incomprehensible (although they are printed on the album's inner sleeve) and really leaves the listener with only impressions of the atmosphere surrounding Bowie's character's desperation. The song is harrowing and is easily the least immediately accessible piece on the album. In that regard, it sets the stage of the challenging experimental songs of Bowie's next album, *Lodger.*

After five songs, Bowie turns to instrumental composition for the next four tracks on the *"Heroes"* album. The first, "V-2 Schneider," is the closest of these instrumentals to traditional pop song structure and feel. Once the tonality is established, approximately 20 seconds into the piece, a rhythmic groove is established. Following that, Bowie basically alternates between an R&B-style saxophone section (Bowie multitracked) figure and a melody performed by electronically processed voice that uses the rhythm of the phrase "V-2 Schneider." Since the piece has a clear tonal center, uses conventional symmetrical phrase structure, and contains melodic hooks, it is the one part of the four-composition instrumental suite to most closely resemble pop music. Because of this nature, the song provides a nice transition into the more experimental instrumental works that follow.

Bowie's "Sense of Doubt" is an entirely synthesizer-based composition. It begins with a dramatic, ominous, low-register descending four-note figure: C, B, B flat, A. This helps to establish the key of A minor as the tonal center.

Ultimately there are hints of major tonality, but the vast majority of the nearly four-minute composition maintains the minor-key slightly ominous feel. The slow pace of the piece and its minimalistic static feel paint it as an example of the Brian Eno–inspired ambient music that Bowie had first included on the second half of *Low*. The pacing, however, is better in "Sense of Doubt" than in the quicker developing electronic pieces of *Low*. Most importantly, Bowie takes his time developing the material and allows for more stasis than in his slightly earlier electronic compositions. In "Sense of Doubt," he sounds more like a composer of electronic ambient music and less like a pop song composer experimenting in ambient music.

Bowie certainly is not best known for his work as a multi-instrumentalist. In fact, aside from the album *Diamond Dogs*, on which he is the only credited guitarist, and on the recordings throughout his career on which he plays saxophone, Bowie's instrumental contributions are easy to overlook. Such is not the case on the Bowie and Eno collaboration "Moss Garden." Here, Bowie performs on koto. The solo passages that he plays on this Japanese stringed instrument are consistent with the faux-Asian atmosphere of the piece. Bowie and Eno develop their material to a lesser extent than on the Bowie-penned "Sense of Doubt." "Moss Garden" becomes, then, truly an ambient composition that captures a single static, Zen-like state of being. Because it is the only such instrumental piece on the album—all of the others contain more thematic contrast and are more clearly sectionalized works—it seems not to fit quite as well. However, Bowie and Eno deserve credit for sticking to their guns and maintaining that Zen-like state of being, since it is entirely consistent with the style of Asian music they are trying to create.

"Neuköl," another collaboration of Bowie and Eno, features a slow-moving ambient texture with a melody based on a three-note descending motive. What really sets the piece apart from the electronic compositions of *Low* and the electronic compositions of *"Heroes"* is Bowie's tenor saxophone improvisation. He plays the instrument with the intensity of American avant-garde saxophonist John Zorn and members of the Dutch avant-garde school of saxophone playing, and Bowie's playing combines elements of avant-garde jazz and blues, along with a couple of passing references to a Middle Eastern musical scale. The Middle Eastern reference effectively connects this piece with the song "The Secret Life of Arabia." In fact, it is Bowie's careful use of transitions ("V-2 Schneider" to link the opening songs with the experimental instrumental pieces and the Middle Eastern scalar material to link the last of the instrumental compositions to "The Secret Life of Arabia") that gives *"Heroes"* a much more thoroughly integrated composite sound and progression than *Low*.

The last piece on the album, "The Secret Life of Arabia," is another mood piece. Here, writers Bowie, Eno, and Carlos Alomar combine faux Middle Eastern music with funk. There are even a few rhythmic references to the earlier Bowie song "Golden Years," probably the best-known song on the album *Station to Station*. This is most evident in the background hand-clapping part (a two-measure pattern, with claps on beats two and four in the first measure and on beats two, three, and four in the second measure). The lyrics suggest images or impressions from watching a film with an Arab theme. Since the other vocal compositions on *"Heroes"* feature contrast between opposing forces as their theme and "The Secret Life of Arabia" does not, it stands somewhat apart. The song also does not fit in with the explicit and implicit German references in songs such as "Heroes" and "Sons of the Silent Age." In fact, thematically and musically "The Secret Life of Arabia" points the way to Bowie's next album, *Lodger*, a work in which Bowie explores around-the-world references.

That a song such as "The Secret Life of Arabia" seems perhaps more to belong with Bowie's next album is significant. *Low*, *"Heroes,"* and *Lodger* all come from Bowie's Berlin period and seem to have an overarching shape that shows Bowie growing into new musical styles and integrating pop and avant-garde tendencies. Taken alone, though, *"Heroes"* feels like a unified whole, in part because the album begins and ends with vocal pieces, tends to focus on a good-evil dialectic, and includes stylistic transitions from songs to instrumental pieces and back to the final song. While *"Heroes"* might not be David Bowie's most commercially successful work, it is a significant artistic statement, particularly in what it represents as a late Cold War document and for the way in which it finds Bowie collaborating with Brian Eno, Robert Fripp, and Tony Visconti to merge pop and avant-garde aesthetics.

Notes

1. *Sprechstimme* (German for "speech-song") was a singing style associated with the early 20th-century composer Arnold Schoenberg and Alban Berg, who were known for their expressionistic and 12-tone work. In this style, the singer would consciously slide between pitches in what might be called a melodically heightened version of speech.
2. *"Rolling Stone* 500 Greatest Songs of All Time: David Bowie—'Heroes,'" *Rolling Stone*, no. 963 (December 9, 2004): 102.

15

The Ramones

Rocket to Russia (1977)

Karen Fournier

Rocket to Russia was the third studio album by the Ramones, who launched their careers with the eponymous album *Ramones* (released on April 23, 1976), followed soon after with the album *Leave Home* (released on January 10, 1977). Enormously prolific, the Ramones released *Rocket to Russia* on November 4, 1977, on the Sire label. The record featured the original lineup of the band, with Joey Ramones on vocals, Johnny Ramone on guitar, Dee Dee Ramone on bass guitar (and vocals), and Tommy Ramone on drums. The album was produced by Tony Bongiovi, who had previously worked with Gloria Gaynor and Jimi Hendrix, and Tommy "Ramone" Erdelyi.

Part of the impact of the Ramones on the budding punk movement of the time lay in the stark contradiction between their pop music sensibilities and the grunge image of the band. On the one hand, many of their songs parody American Top 40 hits, with strong superficial musical connections to such 1960s' genres as bubblegum pop (typified in the music of the Partridge Family) and surfer pop (such as the Beach Boys) or the girl group and blue-eyed soul hits produced by Phil Spector (with whom they later worked on their 1980 album, *End of the Century*). Their music is replete with references to high school dances, surfing parties, and young love, albeit seemingly driven at a dizzying tempo by what appears to be an amphetamine-induced energy. Moreover, like the musical antecedents that it imitates, the Ramones' music is relatively simple, typically with a conventional verse-chorus song structure that is often supported by a simple recurring three- or four-chord pattern. The I-IV-V (or, in some cases, I-II-V) chord progression that forms the harmonic foundation of many of their songs also hearkens back to early rock and roll. On the other hand, however, the image of the band and the performance aesthetic that they adopted bore no resemblance whatsoever to the musical sources from which they drew, and the band's social commentary upon American suburbia and middle-class values arises from the stark contrast between their musical sound and their visual appearance. Typically sporting torn stovepipe jeans, biker jackets, T-shirts, and beat-up sneakers, the Ramones looked less like 1950s' rockers or California surfers and more like sun-deprived anorexic heroin addicts in desperate need of haircuts. Furthermore, unlike the kinds of staged performances that document their musical precursors, the Ramones' concerts were marked with energetic, unruly, and aggressive playing.

Like the two albums that preceded it, *Rocket to Russia* comprises a set of short tracks, ranging in duration from 1 minute and 38 seconds ("I Don't Care") to 2 minutes and 47 seconds (the ballad "Here Today, Gone Tomorrow"), many of which express their ideas in a few sentences that repeat for the duration of the song. On this album, few individual songs exhibit a clear and running narrative; rather, most of the songs can be described as minimalist in content, contributing an idea or two to the larger message of teenage alienation that is articulated as the theme of the entire album.

Rocket to Russia consists of 12 original songs, written by various members of the band, that are contextualized by the two covers that appear on the album. These covers provide a web of historical and cultural associations through which the remaining songs on the album can be read and as such are the lynchpins that hold the rest of the album together. For example, the Ramones' rendition of "Do You Wanna Dance?" aligns the band with such American pop artists as Bobby Freeman, who wrote the song in 1958; Del Shannon, who charted with the song in 1964; and the Beach Boys, whose 1965 cover is likely the most familiar to those who know the song. A further historical reference is provided by the penultimate track on the album, where the Ramones' cover of "Surfin' Bird," itself an amalgamation of two doo-wop hits by the Rivingtons ("Papa-Oom-Mow-Mow" and "The Bird's the Word"), reference the Trashmen's 1963 surfer hit. *Rocket to Russia* is not unique in its use of covers as a means to associate the band with a particular slice of the history of American pop, and the first two albums reference such artists as Chris Montez (whose 1963 hit "Let's Dance" was covered by the Ramones on their eponymous debut album), the Rivieras, and the Crickets (the Rivieras and the Crickets both recorded the song "California Sun" in 1964, which was covered by the Ramones on their second album, *Leave Home*). The thematic conventionality of these originals, which were designed to reflect the mores of the American suburban middle class, sets the stage for the parodies of American culture that are represented in the remaining songs, written by the Ramones in the style of 1960s' pop but with an obvious twist.

Within an established framework of 1960s' pop, the original songs on *Rocket to Russia* can be grouped into two broad categories: songs that critique American popular culture from within through their parody of 1960s' pop

---

PUNK ROCK AND PUNK ATTITUDE

Punk rock was an antiestablishment genre that developed primarily in the United States and the United Kingdom in the mid-1970s. The roots of this fast-paced, high-energy, antiestablishment garage band type can be found in such early 1960s' classics as the Kinks "You Really Got Me" and the Who's "I Can't Explain"; however, later garage bands, the MC5, Patti Smith, Iggy Pop, the New York Dolls, and other artists of the late 1960s and early 1970s also influenced the style. In the United States, punk rock centered around New York City's famous CBGB nightclub, a venue noted for performances by the Patti Smith Group, Television, the Ramones, and other artists of punk's first wave. Some of the American punk musicians included social and political commentary in their songs, although the Ramones are best remembered for lighter-hearted material, such as "Sheena Is a Punk Rocker," "Rockaway Beach," and "Blitzkrieg Bop." In the United Kingdom, London-based bands such as the Damned, the Clash, and the Sex Pistols reflected a general hatred of the establishment as well as a distrust of the British government and the monarchy. In both countries and elsewhere, punk rock resonated with young people during this politically and economically uncertain time period. In addition to humorous updates of 1960s' surf style (the Ramones), lyrics that generally reflected alienation from mainstream society, and social and political commentary (particularly from the Clash and the Sex Pistols), punk rock was associated with loud heavily distorted electric guitars, screamed vocals, and on-stage violence. Another artist of the time, Elvis Costello (b. 1954), was categorized together with the punks by some listeners and critics, largely as a result of the bitterness and sense of alienation reflected in his lyrics. However, Costello's musical style was more closely associated with British pub rock and later grew in eclecticism to include jazz, classical, torch song, psychedelic, and other influences. Costello has been acknowledged as one of the leading songwriters of his generation, and his work continues to evolve from its punkish roots.

genres ("Cretin Hop," "Rockaway Beach," "Sheena," and "Ramona") and songs designed as social commentary from without through lyrical content designed to take an objective view on the American middle class ("I Don't Care," "We're a Happy Family," "I Wanna Be Well," "I Can't Give You Anything," and "Why Is It Always This Way?").

The Ramones' social critique from within involves the composition of songs as they might have been produced for a suburban 1960s' audience. Songs such as "Cretin Hop," "Rockaway Beach," "Sheena Is a Punk Rocker," "Locket Love," and "Ramona" fall into this category as songs that make clear reference to earlier pop music genres without any overt commentary embedded within the lyrics. Rather, the critique arises from the stark juxtaposition of a familiar musical landscape and a set of images that seem out of place within that landscape.

With very limited text, "Cretin Hop," the first song of the album, provides an example. The musical content of the song invites its listener into a high school dance but manages to parody the image with its reference to those "cretins" who presumably participate in sock hops. (The song begins with the lyric "There's no stoppin' the cretins from hoppin'!") "Rockaway Beach," a clear takeoff on the California surfer genre, ridicules that genre with its suggestion that New Yorkers might "hitch a ride to Rockaway Beach," a locale in the working-class neighborhood whose beach bears little resemblance to the terrain described by the Beach Boys. Similarly, "Sheena Is a Punk Rocker" uses surfer music and references to "surf boards" and the "discotheque a go go" to stress the difference between mainstream kids, whose interests lie there, and Sheena, a punk rocker who needs to "break away." More sinister, "Locket Love" appeals to bubblegum pop to reframe the image of the locket from a benign token of affection, into which a young teenager might put the photograph of her boyfriend, to a chain that can be used to hang its recipient ("Hang on, you're a goner"), so that the musical innocence of the song is harshly contracted by the reinterpretation of its central image.

In contrast to this group of songs, the Ramones' critique from without involves songs that depend on their lyrical content to construct messages of social alienation. These songs may or may not invoke references to earlier musical genres and therefore do not necessarily depend on the juxtaposition of familiar music against unfamiliar themes to construct their messages. On *Rocket to Russia*, the songs that fall into this category include "I Don't Care," "We're a Happy Family," "Teenage Lobotomy," "I Wanna Be Well," "I Can't Give You Anything," and "Why Is It Always This Way?"

In true minimalist fashion, the song "I Don't Care," which is ostensibly about social alienation expressed in as few words as possible by what would seem to be a sullen teenager, provides a very brief laundry list of items about which the protagonist doesn't care ("I don't care about this world, I don't care about that girl"). Seen from the outside by the backup singer, the vocalist's isolation is reiterated by the observation "he don't care." To underscore the simplicity of the song, the harmonic structure comprises a repetitive pattern of three chords that move from a focus on A through F to G and then return to A for the next iteration of the pattern. "We're a Happy Family" is darker still, with a complex narrative that strips away the veneer behind which suburban families are said to exist. Exposing the underbelly of the American family, the Ramones reveal that "Daddy's tellin' lies, Baby's eating flies, Mommy's on pills, Baby's got the chills" and, more damningly at that time, "Daddy likes men." The complexity of the lyrics is reflected in an equally complex harmonic progression, relative to the songs that have appeared thus far, that focuses on E, with diversions to G, A, and D. "Teenage Lobotomy" and the minimalist "I Wanna Be Well" comment on drug use with such lines as "DDT did a job on me" or "LSD, golly gee, DDT, wow-ee!" and "My future's bleak, ain't it neat?" The latter of the two songs invokes vocabulary reminiscent of the 1950s, and its lyrics can be seen as a send-up of sanitized language that a listener might find in hits such as Jerry Lee Lewis's "Great Balls of Fire" ("goodness gracious!"). Coupled with the drug theme, however, exclamations such as "golly gee" and "wow-ee" seem all the more ridiculous. "I Can't Give you Anything," a minimalist rock song based on the progression G, F, to C, paints a realistic picture of teenaged love, where the lack of money—rarely discussed in the teenage ballads of the 1960s—becomes an obstacle to a more lasting kind of commitment. Finally, the song "Why Is It Always This Way?" ends the album on a bleak note, with a parting comment about a by-product of social alienation. With references to surfer bands, the song begins with a rather flip "ooo" and "hey" before launching into a narrative that describes teenage suicide ("Now she's lying in a bottle of formaldehyde"). A driving guitar lick, which runs from B through C sharp to F sharp, propels the song to the conclusion, where the band simply asks why it has to end this way (perhaps in a fitting end to the album itself).

To this listener, the most curious song on the album, and the one song that fits neither of the categories drawn here, is the ballad "Here Today, Gone Tomorrow." Heartfelt, slow, and mournful, the song describes the end of a relationship in terms that are neither derisive nor mocking, thereby distinguishing the ballad from a song such as "I Wanna Be Well." Nor does the ballad track the kind of overt musical reference to historical pop genres that can be discerned in songs such as "Sheena Is a Punk Rocker" or "Rockaway Beach." Rather, "Here Today, Gone Tomorrow" appears to be the most sincere on the album, and its distinctive tone might therefore highlight even further the ironic representations of American culture that mark the remainder of the album.

16

Sex Pistols

Never Mind the Bollocks Here's the Sex Pistols (1977)

Karen Fournier

The story goes that in searching for a title for their debut (and only) studio album, the Sex Pistols could not have cared less. More interested in creating social commentary than in providing a title for their work, they simply invoked the familiar phrase "Never Mind the Bollocks." Production of the album itself also has a storied history. The Sex Pistols were signed to their first recording contract on October 8, 1976, with EMI, which hired Chris Thomas (formerly the producer of Pink Floyd and Roxy Music) to record the single "Anarchy in the UK." This song was released into the British market on November 26, and although, as an angry and aggressive political manifesto, the song represents a turning point in the history of British popular music and came to define punk for those bands that would follow in the Sex Pistols' footsteps, this single was not the first punk recording to hit the marketplace. That honor goes to the Damned's "New Rose," which was released almost a month earlier, on October 22. In mid-November the Sex Pistols' debut single reached 38th on the UK singles charts and stayed in that position for three weeks, but despite this success, their contract with EMI was to be short-lived. On December 1, 1976, the group appeared in a live interview on Bill Grundy's *Today* (a UK television program, not to be confused with the U.S. *Today Show*) and, sparring with a clearly drunk host, issued a torrent of profanities the likes of which had never been experienced on television. After British newspapers ran such headlines as "The Filth and the Fury!" and record packers refused to handle the single for distribution, EMI rescinded their contract. Undeterred, the Sex Pistols signed to another contract on March 10, 1977, this time in front of cameras at Buckingham Palace, but this union with A&M was annulled a week later after members of the band issued death threats to a friend of one of the company's directors. In the end, the band signed with Richard Branson's Virgin label in May 1977, which almost immediately released the Sex Pistols' most famous single, "God Save the Queen," on May 27. The release party, which took place on a private boat hired by Branson to sail past the Houses of Parliament, was carefully choreographed to coincide with celebrations of the Queen's Silver Jubilee. The audacity of this move had the intended effect of generating enormous press for the album, although the members of the band were arrested and hounded by those who perceived the Sex Pistols' alternative anthem as treasonous or, at the very least, as an offense to civil British society.

The Sex Pistols released *Never Mind the Bollocks Here's the Sex Pistols* in the United Kingdom on October 27, 1977, on the Virgin label. In its original pressing the album comprised 11 tracks, but the Sex Pistols changed their minds shortly after the original release, deciding to include the song "Submission" as a 12th track in the subsequent pressing of the album, which was released in November 1977. Needless to say, the 11-track album is extremely collectible. Musicians on the album(s) included Paul Cook (drums), Steve Jones (guitar), Glen Matlock (bass), and John "Johnny Rotten" Lydon (vocals), and despite the fact that Matlock had quit the band in February 1977, he returned as a session musician when it became apparent that his successor, Sid Vicious, was unable to play the instrument. Furthermore, while Lydon has been credited with writing the lyrics for each of the songs on *Never Mind the Bollocks Here's the Sex Pistols*, Matlock has been identified by Cook as the musical author of most of the songs on the album.

The Sex Pistols' music is characterized by simple chorus-verse song structures, conventional chord progressions, and a propensity for rhythmically reiterated chords. Perhaps the most notable aspect of the music, beyond its lyrical content, is its idiosyncratic vocals, provided by Lydon. Eschewing the Mid-Atlantic accent that was more common in popular music of the time, Lydon's diction is identifiably British working class, with rolled consonants and elongated vowels that seem intended to mock upper-class British pronunciations. The songs that appear on *Never Mind the Bollocks* can be said to fall into two broad categories: political songs that are intended as critiques of British society and personal songs that appear to comment on romantic relationships (although an alternate reading of these will be presented below).

Three of the Sex Pistols' political songs were released as singles prior to their appearance on *Never Mind the Bollocks* and include "Anarchy in the U.K.," "God Save the Queen," and "Holidays in the Sun" (released on October 14, 1977). A fourth, "Bodies," was never released as a single and appears only on the album. To frame the messages inherent in each of these, I would like to discuss them as a group, even though this requires that I take each song out of its ordering on the album.

The A side of *Never Mind the Bollocks* features two politically motivated songs, and the album kicks off with the sound of marching footsteps, punctuated by four distorted guitar chords on D that frame a quadruple meter. A drum roll initiates a descending bass line, which marches down by step from C to G, returns to C, and repeats a pattern that later becomes the harmonic foundation of each subsequent chorus. Once the militaristic tone has been established, Lydon intones the phrase "cheap holiday in other people's misery!" (rolling his "r" and emphasizing the final vowel in the final word). Originally released as a single with a sleeve that depicts a comic strip family whose characters speak various lines from the song as they tour Europe on vacation, "Holidays in the Sun" became the first track on the album and sets a decidedly political tone with its militaristic imagery and its references to the Belsen concentration camp, the Berlin Wall, and the "communist call." This imagery is built into the music of the song, as Lydon's chorus is accompanied by an insistent reiteration of the word "Rea-son! Rea-son!" that barely conceals its reference to the famous Nazi salute "Sieg Heil!" However, these signifiers are meant to refer less to the repressive policies of Nazi Germany than they are intended to point an accusatory finger at British society and its unstated policy of segregation by class and ethnicity. The song draws the parallel between a then-divided Germany and what it characterizes as the "claustrophobic" class divisions in England, and Lydon, in a passionate and hysterical ending to the song, issues a cry for freedom when he says, "I gotta go over the Berlin Wall, I don't understand this thing at all."

"God Save the Queen," which appears as the fourth track on the A side of the album, is similarly pointed in its social critique and is perhaps the song that gained its performers the greatest notoriety. Rising to the position of No. 1 on the *New Musical Express* charts, the song is likely most famous for its scathing commentary on the Royal monarch, described variously as a "figurehead" who "ain't no human being" and who exists only because "tourists are money." In the chorus of the song, Lydon warns the listener that in a society that is as rigidly class-structured as Britain, there is "no future for you!" Extremely simple in its harmonic construction, the verses center around an A chord, with the choruses moving to the dominant of E. The outro, a reiteration of the "no future" messages heard in the chorus, underscores the hopelessness expressed by these final lyrics with a descending scalar passage from D through A.

Released as their first single on EMI and later appearing as the second track on the B side of *Never Mind the Bollocks*, "Anarchy in the U.K." is a testament to the anger and social alienation felt by many working-class youths in Britain during the economic hardships of the mid-1970s. Characterizing himself as the "anti-Christ" and as an "anarchist," Lydon suggests that the only way to "get what you want" is to "get pissed, destroy!" The underlying chord structure, which moves from D through G to A, repeats incessantly throughout the song, interrupted only by the insertion of a B minor chord in the chorus to emphasis the word "anarchy."

"Bodies," which appears as the third track on the B side of the album, is likely the most shocking song on an album that is replete with challenges to its listener. Tackling the taboo issues of mental illness and abortion, the Sex Pistols describe the life of Pauline, reputed to be a fan of the band who had been raped by a male nurse in the mental institution where she was a patient and who decided to abort her baby upon discovery of her pregnancy.

The songs "Liar," "No Feelings," and "Problems" can be read as negative portrayals of interpersonal relationships. "Liar" comments on betrayal from the first-person perspective of the singer, "No Feelings" is a statement of solitude and self-absorption, and "Problems" describes a partnership in which one party seems reasonable while the other seems irrational. Read in the context of Lydon's troubled relationship with the manager of the band, Malcolm McLaren (whom Lydon later sued for unpaid revenues and contract rights), the songs can be said to signify different aspects of McLaren's personality, as perceived by Lydon, in his role as songwriter.

The second track on the A side of *Never Mind the Bollocks*, "Liar," can be read as an accusatory barrage of anger that challenges McLaren's trustworthiness in several lines in the opening verses. The song conforms to a conventional verse-chorus structure and is harmonically straightforward; however, the emotions of the song lie in its presentation, where the verse of the song simply reiterates the word "lie" on D, which is repeated frenetically as the song builds toward the chorus, where Lydon spews the phrase "you're in suspension, you're a liar!" supported by the chord progression A, B, G, D.

The next track on the A side, "No Feelings," is more harmonically complex, with an intro that sets the stage for the piece with a four-chord pattern (F, G, B flat, C) that recurs throughout the song. In the verse, Lydon can be said to mock and imitate McLaren with such lines as "I'm in love with myself, myself, my beautiful self," while in the chorus Lydon steps away from the object of his ridicule and suggests that "You never realize I take the piss out of you."

"Problems," which ends the A side, can be seen as a portent of the legal wrangling to come, as Lydon sets up the song with the verse "Too many problems, oh why am I here? I need to be me, 'cause you're all too clear." In hindsight, the lyric appears to refer to Lydon's legal quest to regain his identity and his control of the songs that he wrote. In a later verse he uses some clever wordplay to reject instructing orders, on the basis of the lack of order in his life. This again suggests his desire to break free from the control of those such as McLaren who attempted to manage Lydon's life. The verses are set to a simple and repetitive harmonic progression that moves downwards from D through C to A. The direction of the progression changes in the chorus, as Lydon intones "problem, problem, problem, the problem is you" to a descending progression that moves upward by step from A to D, at which point the chorus resumes its repetitive progression.

The final two tracks on the B side of the original release include "New York" and "EMI," both of which serve as a send-up of the recording industry. "New York" unceremoniously critiques the New York Dolls, an American proto-punk band upon which McLaren attempted to fashion the Sex Pistols. Similarly, the recording company EMI becomes the topic of ridicule in a song that chronicles their difficult relationship with the label in particular and with the recording industry in general.

In its original UK release, *Never Mind the Bollocks* comprised only 11 songs; however, the band decided to include a 12th song, "Submission," in a rerelease of the album in November 1977. "Submission" was placed as the third track on the B side of the album, with "Bodies" moved to the third track of the A side. Likely the most accessible song on the album, "Submission" is based on a familiar chord progression borrowed from the Who's "I Can't Explain." McLaren intended this final song to focus on sexual submission, perhaps as a reflection of his growing interest in leathers and bondage wear; however, Lydon, now disenchanted with what he perceived to be the artsy pretense of his manager, wrote a novelty song about underwater submersion.

17

Jackson Browne

Running on Empty (1977)

James E. Perone

Various artists have recorded live albums over the years; in 1977, Jackson Browne broke new ground by recording *Running on Empty*, an album about musicians' lives on the road, recorded on the road in concerts, backstage, and in hotel rooms. The concept worked well at the time and continues to hold up into the 21st century. While some of the individual tracks are not particularly well remembered, the title track and the cover of the Zodiacs' "Stay" continue to be heard on oldies radio programs today.

The album begins with Browne's composition "Running on Empty." The song sets the stage for the entire album, as Browne sings about his life on the road. He links the road and travel as a form of escape with his present life as a traveling rock musician. His reasons for living on the road have changed from the me-centered escapism of youth to a focus on the audience (at least in part). Still, although Browne expresses a desire to get the audience "to smile" in the bridge section, in the final stanza of the song he acknowledges that he does not "even know what [he is] hoping to find" in his life on the road. It is the very real conflict of emotions, the tug-of-war between restlessness and the desire to someday find a home, that drives the piece.

Musically, "Running on Empty" is a classic pop rock song. The melodic and lyrical hook of the chorus is instantly identifiable and memorable. Perhaps more important for the lasting emotional impact of the song, however, the melody of the verses is built of short narrow-range phrases that lie low in Browne's vocal range. There is a general descent from the beginning to the end of each phrase, which suggests the resignation that Browne (or his character) feels about remaining on the road. Browne also separates each of the lines with brief instrumental interludes that suggest the ongoing travel, the time spent moving through life without a firm goal or vision for the future.

From up-tempo high-energy rock, Browne turns to the acoustic folk style for Danny O'Keefe's song "The Road." O'Keefe's text focuses on the transitory nature of relationships for musicians on the road, about the idleness between shows, and so on. If the listener expects to hear about the glamorous life of the rock star, he or she will be disappointed: "The Road" is about loneliness, lack of direction, and the transitory. The slow tempo and acoustic setting at the start of the piece emphasize the immediacy and the straight-from-the-singer-songwriter's-heart nature of the piece. Interestingly, "The Road" is the grafting together of two separate recordings. The beginning was recorded in a hotel room in Columbia, Maryland, and the end of the song was recorded in concert at the Garden State Arts Center in Holmdale, New Jersey.[1]

Cowriters Browne and tour production manager Donald Miller examine the relationship between a groupie and a band and its sound and stage crew in "Rosie." In this song, the title character shows up at a preconcert sound check, and the sound engineer gives her a pass so that she can come to the show. As he drinks a beer with the young woman and tries to make small talk, the technician sees that she is really "looking for a star"; eventually she leaves with the band's drummer. The technician supposes that his heart will be broken as it has been in the past by women who are more concerned with "who you look like" than with "who you are"; however, in the chorus we learn that Rosie and the technician eventually do end up together. The piece was recorded backstage in a rehearsal room, with Browne on lead vocals and piano. Doug Haywood and tour photographer Joel Bernstein provide background vocal harmony. The music itself is vintage Jackson Browne, with simple melodic shapes and a tendency to turn to the minor-quality submediant (vi) chord to lend a sense of poignancy and bittersweet resignation.[2]

In his composition "You Love the Thunder," Browne explores a relationship between a couple that is not so much built on love as it is on mutual desire and need. The connection to the musician-on-the-road theme of the album becomes clear only near the end of the song in which Browne tells the woman "I got your number if it's still the same." This suggests that he is passing through town and that the two might resume, for one night, their transitory relationship. Musically, "You Love the Thunder" is conventional mid-1970s' country rock, in the manner of the Eagles. Browne draws his harmonies largely from the three principal chords (I, IV, and V) of the key. This makes the deceptive cadences that are part of the song stand out in sharp relief. The melody is based on expansions of simple motives, much like the verses of "Running on Empty." Throughout the album, the listener might be struck at the extent to which slide guitar solos predominate. In comparison to most of the rest of the live concert tracks, however, in "You Love the Thunder" it is clear that this sound is coming from a lap steel guitar played through effects pedals. In some respects, the sound of David Lindley playing lap steel—traditionally a country instrument—in a rock context is part of what defined the Jackson Browne sound during this era, the era of Browne's greatest popularity.

The first side of the original vinyl release of *Running on Empty* concludes with Reverend Gary Davis's song "Cocaine," which includes additional lyrics by Browne and Glenn Frey (of the Eagles). The song deals with addiction to and the physical ravages caused by the drug. While the copyright date for the original song is 1968, it probably was even more of a timely song in the mid-1970s, since there were numerous tales of rock, soul, R&B, and country stars who were addicted to "blow" at the time. The presence of cocaine in the period's wealthy, hip circles was so widely known that one of the most memorable and funniest scenes in Woody Allen's 1977 film *Annie Hall* was the one in which Allen's character accidentally sneezes and sends a cloud of cocaine into the air. The recording is of an informal hotel room session during the tour. Timeliness of the subject matter notwithstanding, it is interesting to note that Browne and his band chose to jam on a song written by Reverend Gary Davis, the blind acoustic blues singer-guitarist-songwriter who was a favorite inspiration to the early 1960s' folk crowd, as well as to the Grateful Dead and Bob Dylan. The song's inclusion links Browne to that acoustic folk tradition.

Guitarist Danny Kortchmar's song "Shaky Town" leads off the second side of *Running on Empty*. According to the album's liner notes, this recording was made in the same hotel room as "Cocaine";[3] however, the instrumentation includes electric guitars, electric piano, and drums, unlike the other hotel room recordings. In any case, Kortchmar does not deal with the feelings of road musicians to the extent that Browne does in his songs on the album. This is more observational, so that the emphasis is on what the musician sees and hears, not on what he feels. In this respect, it balances some of the more inward-reflecting sentiments of the other songs.

The next track, the Lowell George, Valerie Carter, and Jackson Browne composition "Love Needs a Heart," is the one song on *Running on Empty* that contains no obvious connections to the theme of the life of a traveling rock musician. True, the piece does find Browne singing about the pain he has suffered since he left behind the woman to whom he sings. And true, the mention of "vacancy signs" suggests that his character lives a life on the road; however, the lyrics are not career specific in the manner of the rest of the songs. The lyrics and the musical setting are pretty much standard 1970s' singer-songwriter fare. For example, the introspection can be found in the work of Carole King, James Taylor, and Joni Mitchell, and short melodic phrases, extensive use of syncopation in ending phrases, and the largely acoustic setting are also all representative not only of some of Jackson Browne's work but also of his confessional singer-songwriter contemporaries.

Perhaps the most curious recording venue for any of the songs on *Running on Empty* can be found in the next track, "Nothing but Time," which was recorded on the tour bus. Cowriters Browne and tour manager Howard Burke describe life aboard the tour bus as a series of bottles of wine, listening to recordings, watching movies, trying to sleep on a "rolling hotel," and simply killing time. Mostly, though, the piece is a jam. The musical style is more stripped down than most of Browne's other compositions and somewhat reflects the swamp blues rock of Creedence Clearwater Revival. While it may be interesting as a document of the tour, it is not an essential track.

To a large extent, the bookends of *Running on Empty*, the title track at the beginning and "The Load-Out" and "Stay" at the end, are what today's audiences remember and will perhaps continue to remember long after the concept behind *Running on Empty* is forgotten. For one thing, these were the commercially successful singles from the album and are about the only tracks heard on oldies radio today. Jackson Browne and Bryan Garofalo collaborated on "The Load-Out," a tribute to the roadies who do all of the grunt work on a rock-and-roll tour. In part, though, the song also recaps all of the rest of the themes of the album: the transitory nature of life and relationships on the road, the passing of countless hours of time, and so on. Browne sings and accompanies himself on the piano, with minimal accompaniment from the rest of his band. The melody includes some of Browne's signatures, including the quick syncopated ends of phrases in which the last syllable tends to anticipate the downbeat and the use of short melodic motives. Browne also includes a nice contrasting touch as his voice soars upward in some of the phrases. This combination of disparate melodic approaches matches the yin-yang, almost bipolar, extremes of resignation/boredom and triumph that is a concert tour. "The Load-Out," combined by Browne's cover of the old Maurice Williams song "Stay," work exceptionally well as an encore set, particularly in the context of concerts that include songs about concert tours.

"Stay" had been a hit for the Zodiacs back in the pre–British Invasion early 1960s. While the lyrics might not literally be true—surely the union would mind if the show ran late and the union workers were not paid overtime—the sentiments really bring the entire concert tour experience into focus for Browne and his audience. He, as a performer, would undoubtedly want his audience to believe that everyone involved in the concert—musicians, roadies, sound technicians, and so on—are there for them, the fans. The song also sweetens (in a good sense) the bittersweet focus of most of the rest of the songs, which tend to lean more toward the bitter than the sweet. Aside from its structural importance—telling the audience that everyone is happy to sing one more song for them and that the audience is why everyone on the tour endures what they endure—the song is notable for fiddle and lap steel player David Lindley's falsetto singing, which instantly takes the entire scene back to the days of pre–Watergate Scandal, pre–Vietnam War innocence.

As mentioned previously, the best-remembered tracks on *Running on Empty* come at the album's opening and closing. Be that as it may, the entire album provides a portrait of the life of musicians, promoters, roadies, drivers, and technicians on the road that stands in stark relief to the public's overly glamorized assumptions about the life of a touring rock-and-roll entourage. The album stands as a document of a life that very few people live but a life that leads to the music that affects many.

Notes

1. Liner notes for *Running on Empty*, LP, Asylum Records 6E-113, 1977.
2. Browne includes deceptive cadences on minor chords in "Running on Empty" and other songs in which his character or other characters find themselves in bitter-sweet situations.
3. Liner notes for *Running on Empty*, LP, Asylum Records 6E-113, 1977.

18

Elvis Costello

My Aim Is True (1977)

James E. Perone

Pigeon-toed, sporting 1950s-style black-rimmed Buddy Holly prescription eyeglasses and holding an old-school Fender Jazzmaster electric guitar, Elvis Costello (real name Declan Patrick MacManus) seemed to be an unlikely character to burst onto the musical scene as one of the leading angry young men of the late 1970s. Although grouped with British punk rock performers of the time, Costello's music reflected mainstream rock and roll but included his soon-to-be-famous biting, ironic, bitter, insightful, and sometimes inciteful lyrics. Costello's 1977 debut album, *My Aim Is True*, found the singer-songwriter-guitarist backed by producer Nick Lowe, John McFee, Johnny Ciambotti, Andrew Bodnar, Mickey Shine, Steve Goulding, and other musicians who generally were associated with other contemporary groups; Costello's backing trio, the Attractions, were not yet organized.[1] The album features Costello's compositions, most of which include his later better-known punk-like lyrical bite but with a musical style that would not have been entirely out of place in the prepsychedelic 1960s. *My Aim Is True*, like some of the British and American punk recordings of the time, provided a clear alternative to the disco, glam, and arena rock that had characterized the earlier part of the 1970s.

Costello's debut opens with "Welcome to the Working Week," a brief song that itself begins with one of Costello's classic lines, "Now that your picture's in the paper being rhythmically admired." Aside from the fact that such a direct implication of masturbation is uncommon in pop songs, the imagery provides a hint of Costello's playful use of language in his lyrics. In the era of angry young punk rockers, Costello did not admit to a knowledge of—let alone the possible influence of—great pop songwriters of the earlier 1970s (e.g., Randy

Newman and John Prine), not to mention Tin Pan Alley sophisticates such as Cole Porter. Within a few years of Costello's debut, critics and fans would talk about him in the same terms as the songwriters of earlier generations. It was Costello's lyrical imagery and propensity for the unusual, thought-providing turn of phrase—perhaps more than anything else—that caused him to be included in discussions of the best of the pop songwriters of the second half of the 20th century.

While some of the details of "Welcome to the Working Week" are not entirely clear, Costello seems to be addressing a young woman—possibly a socialite—who is outside of his working-class world. The theme of class distinction and its effects on society at large, as well as its effects on relationships, is not unique here: it would become part of the Elvis Costello canon.

Today's listeners—and even listeners back in 1977—cannot help but notice Nick Lowe's decidedly low-tech production not just on "Welcome to the Working Week" but throughout *My Aim Is True*. None of the songs on *My Aim Is True* truly reflects the punk rock style of the era, especially because of the avoidance of heavy guitar distortion and the screaming out of inflammatory lyrics. The low-fidelity production and the bitterness of the autobiographical-sounding characters whom Costello created (flavored though it is with richer lyrical imagery than what one might find in the run-of-the-mill British punk song of the time) made Costello's early work at least a spiritual cousin of British punk.

While "Welcome to the Working Week" contains at least one classic Elvis Costello image (the woman whose picture is "rhythmically admired"), the album's second track, "Miracle Man," is more substantial and more fully developed lyrically and musically. In this song, Costello's character expresses frustration and bitterness with the codependent relationship in which he finds himself. He tries everything he can to please his mate, only to hear her tell him about the other men she knows "who can do it better than I can." As was the case with "Welcome to the Working Week," "Miracle Man" uses conventional rock-and-roll melodic, rhythmic, and harmonic materials. In fact, there is little from a musical standpoint that would be out of place in a 1965 or 1966 song. This, though, was part of the attraction of the punk/new wave/pub rock of the late 1970s: musically it was retro feeling, but lyrically it spoke to the psychological hang-ups, angst, and frustrations of the young people (particularly males) of its time.

If one aspect of *My Aim Is True* does not age particularly well, it may be the at times almost single-minded focus on dysfunctional relationships. The subject rears its head on the album's third track, "No Dancing." Costello effectively varies the narrative, however, by playing the role of observer. Once again, it is the male character who is controlled and "made a fool of" by the female character. With a few more albums under his belt, Costello would be more gender inclusive in his observations of society and the various mental games of control that individuals play with each other. Keeping in mind that the Elvis Costello of the mid to late 1970s was a male singer-songwriter looking at the world of the characters he created to tell the story of the frustrations of 20-something males, a fair number of the songs on his first few albums lean in the direction of blaming everything on women. Whether or not they truly are misogynistic might be open to the interpretation of the listener; however, this was an accusation that found its way into reactions to Costello's early work at the time of its release.

The focus shifts abruptly as Costello launches into "Blame It on Cain." In this song, his character seems to have formed an alliance with a young woman, probably his character's girlfriend or wife, based on the implications of the lyrics. The objects of his character's scorn are the tax collectors ("government burglars") and unscrupulous businessmen ("the man with the ticker tape") that have little regard for his character's (and others of his social and economic class) need for whatever money he might have. Costello explains his plight by singing "Blame it on Cain, but don't blame it on me," suggesting that his character was predestined to a life of living from meal to meal. Costello references a Roman Catholic sense of predestination elsewhere in his early works, most famously in the pun "There's no such thing as an original sin" in "I'm Not Angry." In "Blame It on Cain," however, there is little sense of the irony or sarcastic playfulness that might be heard in "I'm Not Angry." Here, the biblical Cain plays the role of universal scapegoat, the reason behind the otherwise unexplainable problems in life.

The album's sole ballad, "Alison," includes the oft-repeated line that became the title of this album. More than that, however, the song at once demonstrates Costello's commercial potential, his ability even early in his career to create a pithy turn of phrase, his affinity for R&B and soul, and his underrated ability as a vocalist. Costello's character addresses the title character, a former lover, who now is married to someone else. The mixture of lingering love and bitter resentment is captured in the phrase "my aim is true" in its multiple meanings (e.g., his love is true and his aim, as in with a gun, is accurate). More than some of the more single-emotion songs on the album, "Alison" captures the complexities of human emotions among the jilted. The added-note chords and largely pentatonic melody suggest R&B and Motown ballads of the early 1960s. A particular highlight of the performance is Costello's multitracked vocal work in the chorus sections.

The next track, "Sneaky Feelings," finds Costello somewhat obliquely exploring the idea of lust from afar. It can be inferred that his character is married but lusts after another woman. While "Sneaky Feeling" is not the most memorable song on the album, perhaps the most interesting part of the piece is Costello's Randy Newman–esque vocal tone color.

It probably is safe to suggest that had Costello written and recorded nothing other than "Watching the Detectives," he would have been ensured a place in pop culture history. Ironically, this track, which is used as the theme music for the PBS series *History Detectives* into the second decade of the 21st century, was not included on the original UK release of *My Aim Is True*. On the U.S. release, it is a strong finisher to side one.[2] The oft-told story is that Costello based the song on his wife's casual watching of a detective thriller on television ("She's filing her nails while they're dragging the lake") and contacted producer Nick Lowe to arrange a hastily prepared recording session while the song was still fresh in his mind.

Costello explored the possibilities of putting mid-20th-century film noir into song several times later in his career, but the somewhat free reggae feel of "Watching the Detectives" and the distinctive James Bond–esque lead guitar line help this song to remain his best-remembered example. Because of the musical style, the richness of the images he recounts and creates (e.g., "red dogs under illegal legs" to describe a femme fatale wearing red shoes as well as the abrupt "cut to" scenes he describes) from the televised drama, and the stark contrast between the drama and the casual coolness of his coviewer, "Watching the Detectives" adds significantly to the richness of *My Aim Is True*. The 1993 Rykodisc CD reissue places the song after the 12 tracks that constitute the original British running order of the album; however, the placement of "Watching the Detectives" at the conclusion of the first half of *My Aim Is True* gives the entire album a stronger overall shape.

The second half of *My Aim Is True* opens with "(The Angels Wanna Wear My) Red Shoes," perhaps the best sleeper track on the album. I suspect that longtime Elvis Costello fans cannot help but remember "Watching the Detectives," "Less Than Zero," "Mystery Dance," "Alison," and "Welcome to the Working Week." "Red Shoes" has some of the richness of those songs but is an easy piece to overlook. Once again Costello allows his Roman Catholic upbringing to flow into his lyrical imagery: his character achieves salvation not through grace but instead through what he barters with the angels.

The next song, "Less Than Zero," is one of Costello's most famous. The work opens with a reference to Sir Oswald Mosley, a British politician perhaps best remembered for his fascist, protectionist, and racist politics. Costello mocks Mosley and his political stances but only by giving the politician's first name. American listeners assumed that Costello's reference to "Oswald" meant Lee Harvey Oswald, the assassin of U.S. president John F. Kennedy. The basic gist of Costello's text is that in the face of the officially sanctioned racism and fascism of political leaders such as Mosley, everything seems to "mean less than zero." The moderately slow, hypnotic, vaguely Latin rock feel of the piece is unique on *My Aim Is True* and helps the piece retain its lasting quality, even if the lyrical references are not entirely understood by the listener.

Costello next turns to extremely up-tempo 12-bar–blues-based 1950s-style rock and roll for his exploration of sexual dysfunction: "Mystery Dance." A brief track, weighing in at just over one and a half minutes, the piece includes references to a would-be Romeo who is unable to satisfy his Juliet, a teenaged boy looking at pornographic pictures under the covers, not quite sure about how to experiment with masturbation, and so on. Aside from the way in which Costello deals with these topics metaphorically, a large part of the attraction of the track comes from the powerful rocking performance. Arguably, Costello would rock out even more powerfully with his post–*My Aim Is True* band, the Attractions, but "Mystery Dance" remains one of the classic late 1970s' rock songs.

The song "Pay It Back" includes references to retribution and the sort of yin-yang concept that everything that goes around, comes around. It confirms the sense of salvation being earned of "(The Angels Wanna Wear My) Red Shoes" and also suggests the inevitability of bad things happening to Costello's characters of "Blame It on Cain." "Pay It Back," however, is more oblique than those earlier tracks. Costello's move to a catchy shuffle rhythmic feel and a memorable almost sing-along chorus melody tend to make the music stand out, even if some of the impressionist phrases of the lyrics might be difficult for some listeners to connect.

"I'm Not Angry" can be heard as an exercise in contradiction. Just as the Beatles' single version of the song "Revolution" found John Lennon's text and the style of the arrangement and performance at odds with each other, Costello sings "I'm not angry anymore" in response to being jilted in love, to being left in sexual and emotional frustration; however, he sneers through the lyrics in this up-tempo high-energy setting in such a way that suggests that he is about as angry as he possibly could be. Among the more interesting phrases is "there's no such thing as an original sin," a punning reference to the Catholic concept of original sin, mixed with the suggestion that every wrong that one person can do to another already has been done before.

The various forms of frustration, resignation, and anger tempered by a biting sarcastic humor that runs through nearly every previous song on *My Aim Is True* comes to a head in "Waiting for the End of the World." Costello creates a wild Frederico Fellini–like succession of images that his character experiences and observes on a ride on the London Underground (subway). He references the ultimate hopelessness of a doomed marriage, the fears that one might feel when trapped in a subway tunnel, and the nihilism of a dropout from society, and in each case the specific fears are extrapolated to an overarching fear of the coming apocalypse. Although it is the case with most of the louder harder-rocking tracks on *My Aim Is True*, it is perhaps easiest to experience Nick Lowe's slightly distorted, sonically overloaded production style on "Waiting for the End of the World." The low-tech do-it-yourself quality helps Costello's *My Aim Is True* match the homemade aesthetics of punk rock, without being a work from the punk rock musical genre.

The independent label Stiff Records originally released *My Aim Is True* in the United Kingdom. While the U.S. release came from the major label, Columbia, this album is typical of the renegade approach taken by Stiff during its existence. Punk rock, pub rock, ska, and other contemporary styles recorded by Stiff artists such as Graham Parker and the Rumour, Nick Lowe, Elvis Costello, Wreckless Eric, the Damned, and Ian Drury and the Blockheads largely was quirky and nerdy, sometimes humorous, sometimes angry. By and large, the

Stiff artists just did not seem to fit into the definition of what it was to be a cool pop music star. They seemed to ignore the conventional wisdom about what it took to make it in the world of commercial pop music from the standpoint of production, lyrical subject matter, the way they dressed, and so on. However, this quirky group of artists was fashionable for a short period of time in the late 1970s, and Elvis Costello became a major significant singer-songwriter with a rabid cadre of fans. Although Costello later broadened his work with references to psychedelia, torch song, Beatles-esque pop, Tin Pan Alley, folk, and jazz, the roots of his exceptional talents as a writer and as a convincing-sounding singer can be heard on every track on *My Aim Is True*.

Notes

1. Information on the backing musicians from the liner notes to *My Aim Is True*, CD reissue, Rykodisc RCD 20271, 1993; the original vinyl release contains no musician credits.
2. U.S. listeners should note that the various digital reissues of *My Aim Is True* present slightly different track orderings. The 1993 Rykodisc reissue, for example, follows the UK running list and places "Watching the Detectives" after "Waiting for the End of the World."

19

Billy Joel

The Stranger (1977)

Ken Bielen

The Stranger (1977) is the album that reenergized Billy Joel's music career. He had a hit single with "Piano Man" in 1974, but he received little airplay on the releases from his following two albums. The hit singles and FM airplay of tracks from *The Stranger* catapulted Joel into a high level of popularity, where he has remained since. Joel explained to David Fricke that *The Stranger* album was birthed in a period of "self-exploration."[1] Joel saw the differing personalities in himself and others, so he wrote about the varied facets and moods of people. The immediacy of the album's instrumental performances is a result of the band playing full takes together to get down the basic tracks.[2] Before deciding on who would produce the album, Joel sat down for exploratory talks with Beatles producer George Martin. The Englishman, however, did not want to use Joel's band in the studio, so that was the end of the discussion. As noted earlier, producer Phil Ramone was impressed with the road band and wanted them to retain their live energy in the studio.

The boxing gloves hanging on the wall on the cover of *The Stranger*, Anthony as the subject of the opening title, and songs about Catholic girls and an Italian restaurant all dovetail with the spirit of the year 1977, a time when Sylvester Stallone's boxing character Rocky Balboa was introduced to the American movie audience. When John Mellencamp was inducted into the Rock and Roll Hall of Fame in March 2008, his inductor, Billy Joel, told a story about being invited by Mellencamp to participate in the first Farm Aid concert in 1985. Joel was concerned that he would not be accepted in the Midwest (the concert was in Champaign, Illinois) because of his Jewish heritage. At the induction ceremony, Mellencamp responded that Joel had not needed to worry. Mellencamp told the audience that everyone in the Midwest thought Joel was Italian. This image was created by *The Stranger* album.

"Movin' Out (Anthony's Song)" creates a vignette centered on ethnic groups in Manhattan. One character—Mr. Cacciatore—is named after an Italian chicken dish. Another character—Mama Leone—is named after a popular Italian restaurant in Manhattan. Sergeant O'Leary represents another ethnic stereotype (the Irish cop) in Joel's tale. Geographic references in the song include Hackensack and Sullivan Street. Sullivan Street is located in lower Manhattan, not far from the streets where Joel's characters live. Even though there are many ethnic groups residing in the city of Hackensack, across the river in Bergen County, New Jersey, the municipality represents an escape to a better lifestyle from the urban ethnic neighborhoods of lower Manhattan, such as the Little Italy section. Joel's protagonist Anthony wonders, though, whether it is worth working so hard to go someplace where he will get less housing at a higher cost. He asks, "Is that all you get for your money?"

The lyrics question the notion of working to move away from everything a person is familiar with for the express purpose of bettering oneself. Do you really need to move to what some people think is a nicer neighborhood or have a fancier car? And why risk your health in the process? As the production draws to a close with a piano break, underneath is the sound effect of a motor vehicle, engine roaring and tires squealing, as Anthony attempts to escape the cycle of madness of working hard for something that does not seem important or worthwhile. The lyrics present the wanderlust of urban dwellers who desire something more for themselves and their families.

As Joel's generation approached the age of 30, many wanted to find the right location to settle down and raise a family. Moving up meant not only changing your neighborhood but also spending more on luxury items. One character in the song turns in his Chevrolet for a Cadillac. There was a growing consciousness of materialism and having the best. A similar theme was presented in "I've Loved These Days" in the story of the couple who borrowed more than they could afford and lost it all.

The horn line throughout "Movin' Out (Anthony's Song)" sounds like it is being played by a group of street musicians, emphasizing the lower Manhattan setting of the composition. The track contains some Beatles-style touches too, including a guitar line reminiscent of George Harrison and Beatles-style background vocals. The performance was the first single release from the album. Airplay was sluggish, however, and radio programmers started paying attention to another track on the album. Their interest forced Columbia to release "Just the Way You Are" as a single only six weeks after the initial release of "Movin' Out (Anthony's Song)." Later, the recording was rereleased and became a hit as well.

"Just the Way You Are" became Joel's biggest best seller to date. The recording garnered AM radio airplay and perked up the ears of the easy listening/ adult contemporary crowd. Released in the midst of the disco craze, Joel offered a pleasant melody with electric piano, acoustic guitar, and mellow saxophone backing. Producer Phil Ramone suggested the use of the Brazilian *baion* rhythm for the song.[3] The production was a throwback to the soft rock of the group Bread and the duo Seals and Crofts. The wordless background vocal chorus was even reminiscent of Karen and Richard Carpenter's soft productions. The gentle, romantic lyrics (each verse a greeting card sentiment) soothed an audience wrapped up in the unrelenting bass notes of disco or the coarse guitar chords and vocals of British hard rock bands. The song was a harbinger for later adult contemporary music (e.g., Kenny G's saxophone instrumentals). Also, the basic premise of the lyrics, which has the male saying to the female that she does not have to change for him, resonated with the emerging independent woman movement. Joel wrote the song for his wife and manager Elizabeth Joel as a gift for her birthday.[4]

With the setting in an old favorite bistro, Joel and his female companion reminisce about the old days in "Scenes from an Italian Restaurant." The couple is seated at a romantic window table, where the only one you notice in the eatery is the person across from you (and the activity going on out on the street). Conversely, passersby on the street view the two persons on the other side of the plate glass in an intimate conversation. Joel begins the song with a lazy vocal delivery over a piano ballad foundation. The mood is tender. The listener can imagine candlelight softly illuminating the faces of a couple who had passion in their history together but who now respect each other as friends. An accordion enters and adds to the ethnic eatery ambiance.

After the second verse, shimmering cymbals lead into a quiet fire saxophone solo that is soon enriched by strings. The third and fourth verses are a bit more up-tempo as the narrator talks about his family and his work and thinks back to the old days in the neighborhood.

Joel tells his friend that he is married and has children. He admits that he did not think his old flame would look as good as she does today. He speaks nostalgically of being with friends at the village square[5] and playing the hit single "New Orleans" by rhythm and blues singer Gary U.S. Bonds on the jukebox. After singing the verse that ends with the "sweet, romantic, teenage nights" phrase, the band plays a few bars of Dixieland jazz, featuring the clarinet in the instrumental break. This seems out of place. Although the music references the city in the song on the jukebox, the genre is not the growing-up soundtrack of the couple at the restaurant. The couple appears to have been in their late teenage years sometime between the mid-1950s and the mid-1960s.

And then, like two souped-up cars peeling out when the stoplight turns green on Long Island's Sunrise Highway, the tempo accelerates into high gear. The narration moves from the first person to the third person. Joel tells the story of Brenda and Eddie, the high school couple whom their classmates figured would get married and live happily ever after. Joel wrote this fast-tempo section of the song first. Originally it was titled "Ballad of Brenda and Eddie" and dealt with "people who peaked too early in life."[6] Royalty at the prom, the couple cruised in a convertible with the car radio turned up, blasting rock and roll for everyone to hear. But Brenda and Eddie did not get married right out of high school. In their mid-20s they were still dating. Their friends realized that this was not a match made in heaven, but one summer night they decided to tie the knot. The newlyweds rented a place with new carpet, purchased a waterbed, and bought artwork from a mass-market retailer. They were living the Long Island suburban dream. However, they could not make ends meet financially, and that spelled disaster for the couple's relationship. The late 1970s witnessed the end of many first marriages as the baby boom generation decided that the lifelong commitment of for better or worse was for their parents and earlier generations, not for them. Divorce rates increased as young couples became disillusioned.

After a saxophone solo, Joel announces that Brenda and Eddie divorced. He notes that the couple tried to go back to the hangout of their youth, but the feeling and the place they were looking for was no longer there; it vanished because they could not turn the clock back to the good old days. Joel is optimistic that the couple will end up on its feet again. And for all we know as listeners, the couple having its reunion in the little restaurant may indeed be Brenda and Eddie. A horn line with strings returns the song to its languorous tempo and the old friends sitting at the window table in the bistro.

Joel felt that he had to give "Ballad of Brenda and Eddie" some context. So, he took an idea from the Beatles' *Abbey Road* album. Side two of *Abbey Road* is made up of a series of song fragments pieced together by producer George Martin. Joel had a piece of a song (the slow-tempo portion that opens and closes the production, which had the working title "The Italian Restaurant Song") that was not blossoming into a fully realized composition. Another partially realized work in progress, "Things Are Okay in Oyster Bay," was employed for the transitional third and fourth verses of the final recording. Joel placed "The Italian Restaurant Song" at the front and back portion of the story of Brenda and Eddie and gave the couple's story a framework.[7]

The final verse of "Scenes from an Italian Restaurant" is a repeat of the second verse with a couple of almost imperceptible but important changes. Instead of singing about red wine and white wine, Joel sings "a bottle of reds, a bottle of whites." As Joel's generation faced the challenges of finding work and settling down in the late 1970s, many attempted to make themselves feel better not with wine but instead with pills, prescription and otherwise. A romantically slow saxophone solo accompanied by shimmering cymbals closes out the long, ambitious production.

The saxophone solos in the later live versions (especially *2000 Years: The Millennium Concert*) are reminiscent of Clarence Clemons's performances with the *Born to Run*–era Bruce Springsteen and the E Street Band. Even in the original studio version of "Scenes from an Italian Restaurant," Joel and his band quote the phrase from "Born to Run" (just before Springsteen counts off four beats and begins the "highway's jammed with broken heroes" verse) in the transition back to the slow-tempo portion of the song. This is highlighted more so in the live versions in which the saxophone is more prominent. Other saxophone parts in the live versions of the song sound like Clemons's work on Springsteen's "Jungleland." The 1977 Carnegie Hall performance of the song is dedicated specifically to the setting for the narrative, Christiano's Italian Restaurant in Syosset on Long Island.

"Only the Good Die Young" is a Hammond B-3 organ- and saxophone-fueled raucous and raunchy rocking conflagration of religion and sex. The theme is Joel's plea to seduce a virgin Catholic girl who just happens to be named Virginia. The title phrase suggests that those who do not live a "good" life (in the eyes of the church) live an exciting life. In the first verse, Joel notes that Catholic girls postpone having sex until later than other girls in their age group. He argues that the deed will eventually be done, so she may as well give up her virginity to him now.

Each of the remaining verses has at least one religious image in the lyrics. The second verse mentions the statues that are prevalent in Roman Catholic Church sanctuaries. In Catholic practice adherents pray before the statues, so Joel mentions prayer in the same line. In the next line, Joel says that the teachings of the church erected a temple for her. This alludes to the Christian teaching of the human body as a temple of the Holy Spirit, not to be violated by some guy who just wants to seduce the young woman. He continues by noting that the church "locked (her) away." The precepts of the church became, as it were, a chastity belt for the object of the singer's desire.

Joel's gang is cut from the same cloth as the wild bunch who hung out with Brenda and Eddie at the village gathering place in the song set at the Italian restaurant. These boys could only give girls bad reputations, in the view of their Catholic parents. The stained-glass windows of the church are described as "stained-glass curtain(s)" that not only prevent light from entering but also block out the fun. Virginia takes refuge behind the curtains away from the temptations of the rough crowd in the square.

The sacrament of confirmation is the Catholic rite most related to the age of sexual awakening. Joel addresses the religious rite of passage and the tradition that accompanies the event. The girl to be confirmed wears virginal white. Family and friends gather for the festive occasion. The young woman receives a necklace from which a gold cross hangs. Joel has a sharp eye for the Roman Catholic religious tradition. He mentions the rosary and the counting of beads as Hail Marys and Our Fathers that are repeated by adherents to the Catholic faith. Joel details his philosophy. It is better to have the rewards of the flesh now than to wait for the reward of heaven. He will have more fun with sinners than he will with saints, and he is busy convincing the object of his plea of seduction to do the same. Virginia's mother does not like him, but he wonders if she petitions the Lord in prayer for him to change his attitude. Joel and his band experimented with a reggae-flavored version of the song when they were shaping its form. Guest musician Richard Tee's organ line spices up the reggae flavor of the demo (which is found on the *My Lives* anthology). The authorized live versions replace the six-note organ riff that punctuates the verses with a full horn line blowing the riff.

"She's Always a Woman" is a midtempo ballad anchored with Joel's piano and tender fingerpicked acoustic guitar lines. Joel wrote the song as a folk song and plays the piano in the same manner as he would strum a guitar.[8] The McCartney-like bridge introduces woodwinds to the mix. The portions of the song where Joel hums wordlessly were placed there to illustrate the pensive mood that he enters when he thinks lovingly about his woman.[9] Joel's woman is a study in contrasts. She can be kind and then turn around and be cruel, she can be a child or a lady, and her smile can be deadly. Joel sings of how she will love him and then leave. Her personality also draws out the best and the worst in him, but he will continue to persevere in the relationship if only for the fact that "she's always a woman to (him)." Joel states that the song was misunderstood as being "sexist" and "chauvinistic." He was saying in the lyrics that the woman was "just as good as (him), if not better."[10] The lyric is one that takes on a more genuine cast of wisdom almost 30 years later when Joel sings it in front of a Manhattan audience (who know every word) for the *12 Gardens Live* set.

The many facades that we put forth in our romantic relationships is the subject of "The Stranger," the album's title track. The production opens with almost a minute of a slow, jazzy instrumental with piano, cymbal taps, and one person whistling. Joel explains that the whistling was suggested by producer Phil Ramone.[11] While composing the song, Joel whistled the melody for Ramone to get an idea of what instrument could be used to play the melody. Ramone recommended Joel's whistling as the most powerful way to get across the feeling that Joel wanted in the song. Joel adds that while whistling he visualized "Humphrey Bogart with his raincoat over his shoulder walking down a rain-soaked street in France."[12] Immediately after the slow-tempo introduction, the song changes to a fast-paced electric guitar–charged number as the foundation for Joel's lyrics.

In the bridge, Joel encourages his listener to try to love again. She was burned by someone who was not who she thought he was. However, there have been occasions when she has been just as adept at showing multiple faces. The bridge (which appears after the second verse and is repeated after the fourth verse) adds an acoustic guitar, which aids in giving the section an air of the Beatles' *Rubber Soul* era. The fourth verse and the second bridge lyrically duplicate the second verse and the first bridge, respectively. At the close of the song, the guitar-energized mix fades into a reprise of the opening piano, whistling, and cymbal. Although we all wear masks and are aware of the ones we employ, we are enticed by the masks of others in our search for love.

"Vienna" is a plodding ballad with a continental flavor contributed primarily by an accordion solo in the bridge. Joel wanted the music to have the "decadent" flavor found in the music of German composer Kurt Weill.[13] The ambiance is reminiscent of the group Supertramp, which was popular at the time. The lyrics are directed to a young protégé who does not want to wait to reach a goal. And Joel lets the aspiring artist in on a little secret: creative people are never satisfied. And furthermore, although we aim for a number of goals, we do not attain all of them. The birth of ideas and the lack of their realization is all part of the artistic process. But the person is impatient, and Joel chides the subject to wait. Vienna is the setting because of its history as an Old World hub of classical music. The city is a place where artists long to perform. Reaching a Vienna stage is a pinnacle in the artist's career.

According to Joel, "Vienna" is a metaphor for a passage into the elderly years of one's life. At a question-and-answer session on the campus of Princeton University in 1994, Joel was asked why he chose the city of Vienna as the locale for the lyrics. He spoke of a trip he made while in his 20s to the city to reunite with his father, whom he had not seen since he was a young child. While there Joel saw a very old woman working. He learned that older citizens in the region were valued and not put out to pasture for their senior years, as Joel had observed in the United States. He also thought of Vienna as a "crossroads" between the Eastern bloc and Western bloc of nations during the Cold War period.[14] So for these reasons, the city is pictured as the intersection where we turn to a new chapter in our lives.

"Get It Right the First Time" is an upbeat track with a Caribbean feel. Tasty work on the high-hat cymbals, flutes, and Joel's "la, la, la's" between verses give the production a happy bounce. In the lyrics, Joel knows that he has to give it his best shot in the opening round of meeting a woman he wants to get to know better. If the relationship is going to go long term, he instructs his male listeners to start out on the right foot. This is not a sad song of unrequited love. The island feel of the tune contributes a carefree sense to the recording.

"Everybody Has a Dream (Stranger Reprise)" is a feel-good inspirational gospel-influenced ballad. The gospel chords on the piano and the organ accompaniment remind the listener of a Sunday night hymn sing in the church sanctuary. Joel encourages everyone to follow his or her dream. Although he told the protagonist of "Vienna" that one cannot realize each aspiration that comes to mind, we can still seize a vision and passionately pursue it until it becomes a reality. Sometimes the dream will not be realized, but its embrace still gives a purpose to life.

As Joel has noted in other songs, he tires of the road and of being away from his roots. His personal dream is to be home with the one he loves. Although he is separated from her, Joel can get lost in "palaces of sand" and "fantasies" to while away the "empty hours" until he is reunited with her again. The actualization of a vision does not happen overnight.

Joel offers a soulful vocal in the manner of Eddie Brigati or Felix Cavaliere in the late 1960s' era of the Young Rascals' recordings. The background vocals (contributed by Phoebe Snow, Lani Groves, Gwen Guthrie, and Patti Austin) cement the gospel mood. After the upbeat atmosphere of the track, "Everybody Has a Dream" fades and segues into the melancholy piano and whistling voice section that appears at the beginning and end of the album's title track. A string ensemble contributes a sad atmosphere to the coda. The closing measures are a jarring transition and close the collection on a glum note. Hope is tempered by reality.

The Stranger was the first Joel album produced by Phil Ramone. The producer had the vision to base Joel's song arrangements around Joel's band rather than solely around the piano.[15] Ramone would go on to produce every Joel studio recording through *The Bridge* in 1986.

Notes

1. David Fricke, liner notes for *The Stranger* (30th Anniversary Legacy Edition), Columbia/Legacy 88697-22581-2, 2008.
2. Ibid.
3. Phil Ramone, commentary, *The Making of The Stranger,* bonus DVD included with The Stranger (30th Anniversary Legacy Edition), Columbia/Legacy 88697-22581-2, 2008.
4. Dave Marsh, "Billy Joel: The Miracle of 52nd Street," *Rolling Stone*, December 14, 1978, 74.
5. The village square location is based on the Parkway Green located in Joel's hometown, Hicksville. Hank Bordowitz, *Billy Joel: The Life and Times of an Angry Young Man* (New York: Billboard, 2005), 12.
6. Billy Joel, "An Evening of Questions and Answers . . . and Perhaps a Few Songs," *A Voyage on the River of Dreams*, Columbia 478091-2, 1994.
7. Ibid.
8. Billy Joel, commentary, *The Making of The Stranger.*
9. Ibid.
10. David Sheff and Victoria Sheff, "Playboy Interview: Billy Joel," *Playboy*, May 1982, 90.
11. David Fricke, liner notes for *The Stranger* (30th Anniversary Legacy Edition), Columbia/Legacy 88697-22581-2, 2008.
12. Debbie Geller and Tom Hibbert, *Billy Joel: An Illustrated Biography* (New York: McGraw-Hill, 1985), 60.
13. Joel, "An Evening of Questions and Answers . . . and Perhaps a Few Songs."
14. Ibid.
15. Stephen Holden, "Billy Joel Bites the Big Apple," *Rolling Stone*, December 14, 1978, 83.

20

Elvis Costello

This Year's Model (1978)

James E. Perone

There is nothing on the packaging or on the sticker in the center of the original U.S. release of the vinyl album itself to indicate as much, but the 1978 album *This Year's Model* marked the start of Elvis Costello and the Attractions as a recording force. Even though Costello provided all of the vocals, wrote all of the songs, and had his photograph prominently placed on the cover of the album, Steve Nieve (keyboards), Pete Thomas (drums), and Bruce Thomas (electric bass) contributed so much to the overall sound that *This Year's Model* should have been credited to Elvis Costello and the Attractions. On this album, Costello focused the anger of *My Aim Is True* and ratcheted up his wordsmithing abilities. At the time, he was thought of as an angry young man who, at least in intensity of his lyrics, fit in with the British punk rock movement. The thing is, the sound of Costello on rhythm guitar, Nieve on organ and piano, Bruce Thomas on bass, and Pete Thomas on drums, not to mention the overdubbed Costello backing vocals, was much, much closer to the music of the prepsychedelic 1960s than to the music of the Damned, the Sex Pistols, and so on. And the do-it-yourself techniqueless musical approach of punk bore absolutely no resemblance to the technical proficiency and range of musical knowledge of these four musicians or to Elvis Costello as a musical and lyrical craftsman.

Nick Lowe's production on Elvis Costello's debut album was decidedly low-tech. Some of the sound was muffled, and the drums seemed at times to have overloaded the recording and/or mixing equipment to the point of distortion. Lowe completely changed his approach on *This Year's Model*, with all but one of the tracks ("Pump It Up" features the murkier texture of Lowe's earlier production) exuding clarity. This allowed all of the individual instrumental and vocal lines to come through in the final mix with precision. And this was a crucial change that added significantly to the impact of Costello's new band and the group texture that it achieved. In particular, Bruce Thomas's virtuosic bass lines and Steve Nieve's piercing pinpoint organ lines, as well as Costello's underrated work as a minimalistic (in a good sense) electric guitarist, come together to create a counterpoint more complex and interesting than what was heard from many late 1970s' bands.

The album opens with Costello quietly intoning the words "I don't wanna kiss you, I don't wanna touch." The band then breaks in at full volume into the rest of the first verse of "No Action." The sneer in Costello's voice and the dynamic contrast at the opening of *This Year's Model* made for one of the most striking kickoffs to any album in the 1970s. As the piece develops, the listener learns that Costello's character is a jilted lover (a common character in early Costello songs) who stalks his former lover using the telephone. He makes frequent hang-up calls, both for revenge and for excitement. He seems to derive special delight from making hang-up calls when his former lover is with her new man. As the song progresses, it also becomes clearer that the telephone is both the instrument that Costello's character uses to torment the one who jilted him and a metaphor for the woman herself; the Bakelite of the telephone receiver essentially becomes the woman's skin. The lyrics contain an element of Costellian wordplay in which he leaves the listener with a double (or triple) meaning. Costello's character tells his victim that every time he calls her "I just wanna put you down," which can be understood as an expression of the desire to administer verbal abuse, the desire literally to put down the telephone receiver, or on an even more sinister level to put down—as in to kill—the former lover.

Compositionally, one of the more notable features of "No Action" is Costello's use of varying numbers of repetitions of a short, simple, arch-shaped melodic motive to build the second part of each verse section. Like Bob Dylan in some of his folk revival–era protest songs and like Bruce Springsteen in the 1980s on the motivically based song "Born in the U.S.A.," Costello varies the number of repetitions of the motive from stanza to stanza. As the song progresses, the spinning out of lyrical vitriol on successive repetitions of the melodic figure is so insistent as to illustrate the high degree of obsession that rules the life of Costello's character.

The next track, "This Year's Girl," turns more in the direction of conventional mid-1960s–style pop, at least from the musical standpoint. Costello's lyrics are a bit hazier in this song; however, he creates images that suggest the superficiality of fashion and glitz and the tendency of men to fantasize about inaccessible celebrity women.

A number of singer-songwriters of the 1970s defied the usual—or stereotypical—conventions of rock song structure, Elvis Costello among them. In "The Beat," for example, Costello blurred the lines between verse, chorus, and bridge (sometimes called the middle eight). The song has distinct sections, which are defined by contrasting melodic phrase length and melodic contours; however, these sections move so quickly and smoothly from one into the next that the overall structure of "The Beat" sounds as though it falls between pop song structure and that of folk songs that alternate stanzas and refrain. While this description might suggest the phrase-to-phrase flow of the song, what probably is most interesting about the recording is its overall feel. This is one of the strengths of *This Year's Model* over *My Aim Is True* and is due in large part to the clarity of Nick Lowe's production and the weave of the instrumental and vocal lines.

The next song, "Pump It Up," is far more musically aggressive. Like the rest of the fast songs on *This Year's Model*, though, the melody and the instrumental lines are filled with pop-like hooks. In "Pump It Up," however, the main melodic feature is Costello's use of short minimalistic melodic motives to spit out the clipped phrases of the verses. Despite the fact that most of these lines are filled with frustration and downright invective, the verses of "Pump It Up" are filled with some of Costello's most scattered and cryptic references. However, in the third stanza Costello more clearly deals with the frustrations with which he sees male-female relations being fraught. In fact, the overall message of the songs seems to be about the contrast between frustrations and loud rock-and-roll music. It's interesting to consider "Pump It Up" as a sort of "School Days" (the 1957 Chuck Berry song) for the edgier punk-spirited late 1970s.

Next comes "Little Triggers," the album's sole slow ballad. Even though Costello's musical composition suggests 12/8-meter rock going back through the Beatles' "Oh! Darling," back to the Beach Boys' "In My Room," and all the way back to the late 1950s and early 1960s, what really tells the listener immediately that this is a product of the late 1970s is the bitterness in Costello's lyrics. The "little triggers" of the song's title are pulled by the tongue of Costello's character's nemesis: presumably, his lover. Again, Costello touches on the deep hurt that comes in intense relationships. In doing so and in articulating the hidden thoughts that might have gone through the minds of his audience members, Costello filled an important need at the time. However, the topics with which he deals in most of the songs on *This Year's Model* are so universal that the songs continue to resonate.

The first side of the original vinyl release of *This Year's Model* ends with "You Belong to Me," a musical and spiritual descendant of the 1965 Rolling Stones song "The Last Time." In fact, the opening phrases of the vocal melody sound and the instrumental riff that runs throughout the song as though they could have been deliberated based on the Mick Jagger and Keith Richards song of 13 years before. While Costello included several oblique references in his lyrics, he also provided sufficient hints to suggest that the situation about which he sings revolves around teen pregnancies, abortions, and the desire not to be forced into a marriage because of pregnancy.

While the first half of *This Year's Model* ended with a near remake of a 1965 Rolling Stones song, the atmospheric guitar feedback and backwards vocals that open the second half of the album suggest the influence of 1966–1967 psychedelic music, perhaps in the form of the work of the Beatles. The lyrics of "Hand in Hand" also contain touches of the impressionistic images of the songs of alienation of the Beatles' John Lennon, particularly in the 1968–1969 period. Costello deals with the basic inability of a man and a woman to communicate and to agree to acknowledge the desires of the other. In fact, the broader theme of calling people out for inconsistencies and for being two-faced runs through most of the songs on this album, despite the fact that specifics of the situations change.

While "Hand in Hand" is somewhat brief and not particularly memorable, as least as compared with Elvis Costello's best compositions, the same cannot be said for the next track, "Lip Service." Here, Costello and the Attractions pull out all the stops in the area of accessibility and pop hooks. The lyrics, although somewhat oblique, still manage to touch on Costello's favorite themes of sexual frustration, the insincerity that he observes all around him, and dismissal of a would-be lover who leaves him frustrated and whom he believes to be insincere. This, though, really is a song that works because of the musical feel and because of the prominent placement of several key lines of text that just do not sound like lines that you would expect to hear from any other pop songwriter of the time.

Costello and the Attractions next turn to the Latin-tinged "Living in Paradise." In this song, Costello deals with the topics of jealousy, sexual frustration, and sexual fantasy. The most interesting thing about the piece—in part because the lyrical themes were nothing new for Costello, even at this early stage of his career—is the tightness of the ensemble, the virtuosic bass lines of Bruce Thomas, and Costello's raked chords that help to drive the rhythm of the piece.

Again, the familiar themes of insincerity, insecurity, and frustration in love come to the fore in "Lipstick Vogue." The things that allowed Costello to explore a limited number of themes from song are the key little quirky phrases that he threw into every song (these tend to stick in the listener's mind more than the sameness of the larger lyrical themes), wink-wink-nudge-nudge double entendres, and the contrasting styles and textures from song to song. "Lipstick Vogue," for example, opens with a drum solo and includes several instrumental breaks that are more expansive feeling than those on any other track on *This Year's Model*. Likewise, "Lipstick Vogue" stands apart from other songs in which Costello explores similar lyric themes because it is a rare (on this album) minor-key song and the piece with the greatest amount of textural contrast from section to section.

This Year's Model is filled with Elvis Costello and the Attractions doing what they did best: performing songs about frustration and the vagaries and vulgarities of human beings. The material is consistently strong; however, if the album contains one pièce de résistance, it is the final track: "Radio Radio." The song itself gained notoriety after Costello and the Attractions' performance of it on NBC's *Saturday Night Live* at a December 1977 appearance at which they were scheduled to perform "Less Than Zero." Be that as it may, "Radio Radio" proves the power of Elvis Costello and the Attractions as a rock band, and Costello's lyrics that protest the conservative stance of commercial radio and media manipulation of the population ring true in 21st-century America nearly as much as they did in the Britain of the 1970s.

Over the decades, Elvis Costello has recorded far more ambitious albums, explored an even wider range of musical styles, and broadened his lyrical content. All of the seeds of his future projects were sown and in clear evidence on *This Year's Model*, one of the greatest sophomore efforts of any singer-songwriter ever. And the album marked the debut of one of the strongest four-piece rock outfits to emerge in the late 1970s. The musical styles and the lyrical themes resonated strongly at the end of that decade; however, they are universal enough that the album has lost little of its vitality in the second decade of the 21st century.

21

Patti Smith

Easter (1978)

Joe Tarr

The 1976 tour for the album *Radio Ethiopia* found Patti Smith and the press pushing against each other. It was apparently a grueling schedule, so much so that Smith's good friend, Richard Sohl, quit the European tour, which certainly must have taken a toll on her. Complaining about Sohl's departure, Smith told a London press conference at which she compared herself to Jesus Christ, "Like, I don't know if you guys are aware of this but rock and roll is like very hard work. Like being on the road is like really [fucking] hard work. It's like worse than being in the army. You have to be an athlete. You have to be an army guy. And it's, like, really rigorous. And you know, like, the pain and the physical exhaustion of touring was too much for [Sohl], because he's a very sensitive guy."[1]

Back in the United States, Smith was banned from New York's WNEW, an alternative rock station, because of her belligerence during this period. The program's host, singer-songwriter Harry Chapin, had told Smith before an interview on November 29, 1976, not to use any profanity. Smith responded with a rant against the station, during which she used the word "fuck" or "the people's slang." "I want to know how alternative this radio is. The first thing that happens when I walk in is that you tell me you don't have a bleep machine and to watch what I say—that's no alternative, that's the same old stuff."[2]

Smith later wrote a manifesto about her experience, which was printed in the March–April 1977 issue of *Yipster Times*: "We believe in the total freedom of communication and we will not be compromised. The censorship of words is as meaningless as the censorship of musical notes; we cannot tolerate either. Freedom means exactly that: no limits, no boundaries . . . rock and roll is not a colonial power to be exploited, told what to say and how to say it. This is the spirit in which our music began and the flame in which it must be continued."[3]

In this increasingly combative and hyperbolic atmosphere, Smith literally took a dramatic tumble. On January 26, 1977, in Tampa, Florida, Smith played a show at the Curtis Hixen Hall, a sports arena that seated 6,000 people, opening for Bob Seger and the Silver Bullet Band, a pairing that made some aesthetic sense, given both performers' working-class roots, but in reality bridged two vastly different audiences. It was the largest arena she had played in up to that point.[4] The show reportedly was not going well, with an unresponsive audience. While the band was playing "Ain't It Strange" and Smith was doing her usual dance routine, she tripped over a sound monitor and fell off the stage, 15 feet to the ground. Her brother, Todd, who was heading her stage crew, tried to catch her but failed. Smith hit her head on some two-by-fours and then on the ground.[5]

Smith broke two vertebrae in her neck. It could have been much worse. "I'm so lucky. The doctors can't believe it! [And] I feel just like the Field Marshall, down in the line of duty. I know I'll be standin' soon, and in the meantime, just tell the troops to keep fightin'," Smith said shortly after the accident.[6] She romanticized the accident to the press:

I feel like I've done it. I've seen the Angel of Death, and wrestled with it. Maybe the other guys wrestled and lost and I won. . . . [I]t happened when I was spinning like a dervish—you've seen me do that—and just as I stopped spinning, I reached for the mike, and just went off the stage. It was the most amazing thing that's happened to me. I'm like the kind of performer that courts risk, I court death, but the way I kept it together was totally relaxed. I saw, like a spiral tunnel of light, and I felt my consciousness draining through it. I felt myself going and I said—GET BACK HERE! I gripped my consciousness by the throat. . . . [T]he biggest battle was in my head, and I won.[7]

A year later, the Angel of Death had mutated into God:

When I perform, I always opt for communication with God, and in pursuit of communicating with God, you can enter some very dangerous territory. I also have come to realize that total communication with God is physical death. The part of the song that I fell in was on "Ain't It Strange": "Go, go on, go like a dervish / Come on, God, make me move." I was opting for communication with my Creator, and it led me down the most nondisciplined path I've ever taken. Disintegrating and going into a black tube, that's what I felt like. I was losing consciousness, and then I was in a tunnel of light, a classic Jungian dreamspace. I felt like I was being pulled and it was not at all unpleasurable. But it was a leap out of this state of being, which I happen to be very fond of, so I made a conscious decision not to pursue that kind of communication while in performance.[8]

Others speculated that she was simply drunk or high and lost her balance when the accident happened. But Smith has consistently denied that. The band had to play in front of Bob Seger's equipment, and this left little room for Smith to move around and dance, which has always been a trademark of her performance. "Y'know, people said all kinds of things. They said I was totally stoned and fell off the stage, and all these things are, y'know, a total lie. It had nothing to do with that. If I, if I was in any special state, it was more of a, y'know, we would really drive ourselves to some kind of fever pitch or spiritual state in that particular song, and, as a band, we were in the top of our form."[9]

"It was an accident," Smith said 25 years later. "I wasn't drunk or fucked up, no matter what anyone says. . . . It was an accident on a practical level, but on a spiritual level it was time for me to assess what I was doing and where I was going. Which I did. I was laid up for four or five months."[10]

Her injury was serious and caused blurred vision (her eyesight was permanently damaged),[11] and one doctor warned that she might not regain full use of her legs. After doctors gave her conflicting recommendations—one called for spinal surgery, another for extensive physical therapy—Smith chose the latter, which was a more grueling treatment.[12] She also fractured her jaw and eventually lost two of her teeth from the fall.[13]

Such an accident would have been traumatic for anyone. But for a fledgling rock star obsessed with fallen rock idols, the injury must have given Smith pause to wonder whether she would soon be another rock-and-roll casualty (comments about wrestling with and beating the Angel of Death notwithstanding). For the time being Smith was out of commission, which turned out to be a blessing for her. She spent much of the next year wearing a neck brace and in physical therapy, which was paid for by Sam Wagstaff, a friend of Robert Mapplethorpe.[14] She used the time off to collect herself and write.

"Probably it was the best thing that ever happened to me. I was in a period of constant motion and it forced me to stop. I was just moving, ya know, just going. I had no direction. My period of immobility gave me the time to reassess myself. I've reaccepted certain responsibilities. We really care about kids, we care about rock and roll, we care about the future and we work as hard as we can. We aren't always great, but our motivations are clear, and they've never altered."[15]

Fighting the Good Fight

While recovering from the injury and the pitfalls of stardom, Smith's thoughts turned toward recovery and redemption, as she became more focused on what she wanted rock and roll to be. Again, she sought inspiration from both God and art. She reread the New Testament and watched Pier Paolo Pasolini's film *The Gospel According to St. Matthew*, which accentuated the Marxist and revolutionary aspects of Christ's life. She worked on her third book of poetry, *Babel* (with the assistance of Andi Ostrowe, who took dictation, an arrangement that was mocked in the music press), and her third album, appropriately titled *Easter*. The religious metaphors continued to run through her music.

As the music scene began to explode and burst with new energy, Smith yearned to be back in the game. "The following months of recovery and rehabilitation were a difficult time for the band. But we stuck it out together. In this period off I was able to resume my studies, reclaim my relationship with language. . . . It was in this period that the punk movement came to the forefront," Smith wrote in *Patti Smith Complete, 1975–2006*, and, returning to the battlefield metaphor, added, "It seemed to me that rock and roll was back on the streets, in the hands of the people. I trained, we regrouped and we joined them. And our bywords we gleaned from the scriptures, 'Fight the good fight.'"[16]

With a flare for myth making and a keen sense of when to be in the spotlight and when to bow out, Smith made a dramatic return to the stage of CBGB on Easter Sunday 1977, playing a string of shows dubbed "Out of Traction/Back in Action" or "La Resurrection." The shows turned out to be not just a return to form; they were therapy for Smith. "It's like a very ecstatic, mutual kind of vampirism that you have to have with the people. Sometimes, I need their energy, and especially after my injury, when I was first trying to learn how to be on the stage again, I was not only afraid, but my energy . . . I couldn't really move around so much," she told William S. Burroughs. "I hadn't been out of bed for a few months, and I was addicted to pills, or whatever, and had to be carried on to the stage. . . . I remember getting on the stage and I was thinking, 'This was crazy, to do this show. I can't even walk, I'll have to sit.' And I had them put a chair on the stage and I thought, 'Well, they won't mind if I sit on the chair.' Their energy, their psychic and spiritual, as well as physical energy, lifted me up."[17]

She credited the shows with her eventual recovery, and they inspired her to call her next album *Easter*.

> Everybody was a Christ figure that night . . . or at least Mary Magdalene, and there was just so much energy, and for the first minute. . . . It was like being shot up by 500 people or something, it was so fantastic. We did this show and it was so great, I felt cured of something. 'Course I had to go right back to bed . . . but it was like after that my . . . my recuperation. It was almost instantaneous. It was such a breakthrough and I was filled with so much energy and I got a lot of confidence that it got me up ten times faster. Doctors, nobody could believe it, they couldn't believe that I did it, and it was very symbolic to me. You know, Easter's a great time, so that's what [the record is] going to be called.[18]

The accident didn't appear to inhibit Smith's manic stage performances: "I thought I would be more conservative after my fall, but I think I'm crazier than ever. I have some fear, but it just doesn't outweigh my desire to be a maniac."[19]

Easter was released in March 1978. The album found her more confident and was generally well received. With Jimmy Iovine as producer, it sounded more polished and commercial, though it was a far stretch from being a sell-out, as some claimed. But the understated experiments were scrapped, and the listener could once again understand the words that Smith was singing. It was straightforward rock and roll, with a recognizable language—which meant you could sing along or tap your foot to it, without having to put much effort into it. On the album cover was the quote "I have fought a good fight, I have finished my course" from the second book of Timothy, suggesting that Smith felt she had been through some divine trial and saw her music as part of some ultimate battle of good against evil.

Easter opened with both combative and religious notes with "Till Victory," on which she begged God, "Do not seize me please, Till victory." The song also suggested, from God's point of view at least and presumably also Smith's and that of anyone else who had been involved in the good fight, that the trials were over: "The nail. The grail. That's all behind thee." It was as though the time that Smith had dreamed about and was fighting for had finally arrived, and the world was being remade, with the people rising up to reclaim rock and roll, the lost tongue.

The following song, "Space Monkey" (cowritten with Television's Tom Verlaine), is much more opaque. Is it about monkeys being blasted into space? Despite the title, the song's meaning is hazy. "Space Monkey" begins by evoking images of madness and bloodshed on television news, but hope is on the way in the form of a "space monkey" wandering up 9th Avenue, promising transcendence: "I'll never do dishes again." Is that what the good fight was all about, freedom from doing dishes? You could read this as a feminist rally against women's work or perhaps against the drudgery of any work, but it is such a small part of the song and probably was not all that carefully considered. The song also takes on elements of Revelation, with an Antichrist coming to make sense of the anarchy or perhaps Christ returning to shatter that peace and bring justice. The only clue to an interpretation comes when she drops the name of Pierre Clementi, "snot full of cocaine." The Italian actor had been arrested in 1977 on drug charges and began a hunger strike in jail. But pulling strands of meaning from the song is difficult. Overall the song seems absurd, especially when the band starts making monkey noises toward the close. Fortunately, it has a nice melody and doesn't need to be taken all that seriously. Even the monkey noises start to sound catchy after a couple of listens. (Later live versions of the song were dedicated to Michael Stipe, who later became a good friend and who, with his band R.E.M., was legendary early in their career for his incoherent mumbling and obtuse lyrics.)[20]

Much more straightforward was *Easter*'s hit single "Because the Night," which was cowritten by Bruce Springsteen and climbed as high as No. 13 on the *Billboard* charts, giving Smith her first taste of real rock stardom. Another darling of the American music press at the time, Springsteen had much in common with Smith: both grew up in working-class Jersey, and both were consciously searching for the heart of rock and roll, for simplicity and authenticity. The two did not write the song together—Springsteen wrote the music and the song's title and passed it on to Smith, through Jimmy Iovine, telling her to do with it as she pleased.

> Bruce wrote the music, and I always think of myself as the translator. He gave me the music, and it had some mumbling on it, and Bruce is a genius mumbler, like the sexiest mumbler I ever heard. I just listened to it, and the words just tumbled out of me. I wrote it alone, but it was a very direct thing. I got the tape, I immediately wrote the lyrics, he wrote the tag "Because the night belongs to lovers," which was in between the mumbling, he'd say that every once in a while. He said I didn't have to keep that bit, but I thought it was really nice—I always write the lyrics to my own songs, unless they're covers, but I respected his lyrics, and I thought it was a very nice sentiment, so I built the rest of the lyrics, which are obviously mine, around his sentiment.[21]

Springsteen later recorded a version of the song—complete with Smith's lyrics—on his live album *Live 1975–1985*. His version is more muscular (thanks to the beefy E Street Band and the stadium where they performed it) and retains a sexual edge but lacks some of Smith's tenderness, the clichéd woman's touch, which was demonstrated in her single. But you can hear echoes of "Because the Night" in Springsteen's own "Candy's Room" and "Human Touch."

Others have reported that Smith wrote the lyrics while waiting for a phone call from her love interest at the time, Fred "Sonic" Smith, whom she would later marry.[22] The song is so evocative that it is easy to believe that she had a real-life lover in mind when she penned it. She says she had good feelings about the song:

> I knew it was going to be a hit. . . . Not because Bruce Springsteen wrote it, 'cos Bruce Springsteen hasn't written a hit lately. It's not that he churns hits out, it's not like Smokey Robinson or Holland-Dozier came to me with music that was formula hit music, it was just that it had something special. There was a certain heart and energy that I knew would make it a hit. And I was right—sometimes I go to horse races or greyhound races and I know a horse or a dog's going to come in. I knew this song was going to come in, and it was done by the band in that spirit—a very up, chemical, frontal, fast-action song.[23]

It's a great single, one of the greatest in rock history, and it gave you a taste for what Smith was capable of, given the right material. It begins with Bruce Brody (Sohl's replacement) playing a soft serenade on piano. Smith sings "Take me now baby, here as I am / Pull me close try and understand." Her voice is sexy, a pleading lover's whisper in the middle of the night. The song is soon punctuated by the band joining in. Daugherty's drums thump the tune along, giving it urgency and rhythm. It's a great tune, because it is filled with the desperation that is at the heart of lust. This comes mostly from Smith's sensual yet powerful delivery; wanting her man badly, she moans "Take me now." The song is very much an urban love song, defined as much by what is outside those bedroom walls as by what is happening inside them. Thematically, it is a whiter, raunchier (and sexier) version of the Drifters' "Up on the Roof" (which was written by another female maverick, Carole King). The implied forces that are caving in on the couple are what give the song power. The world is out there: the hard mean streets, the grind of the rat race, the pressures to survive doing backbreaking work. The world churns on, but not tonight—in my arms, dear, you're safe—until that alarm clock rings and you've got to be back at work. The song drew added punch from Smith's explicit sexual desires: she wants to be commanded and dominated by her lover, and you can hear that in her delivery—something the more tepid cover version by Natalie Merchant never came close to. Smith is a tough rock-and-roll chick bursting with sex and desire who uses all her ragged edginess to full effect. The song fits in the album because it is also a tribute to sacred places—the home, the bed of lovers, a refuge, a place not to be disturbed, places to be defended, places where people are reborn and rejuvenated.

The next song on the album dives further into sacred territory, aiming for a tribal feel with the prayer-like "Ghost Dance." On *Easter*'s liner notes, Smith explains that the song was inspired by Native American dances that evoked the spirits that had passed: "the beauty of the dance was the call to convene. communication w/past and future through the sounds and rhythms of the present."[24] This is of course at the heart of what Smith was aiming for with her music, trying to connect to the spirits not just of rock and roll's past but of art's: Jimi Hendrix, Jim Morrison, Arthur Rimbaud, Jack Kerouac, Pablo Picasso, and others. Smith aimed to find a way to continue the tradition and imbue future generations with her heroes' values and talents. The song's refrain is "We shall live again."

"We Three" is a mournful song about a lover's triangle, being wanted by someone when you want another: "You say you want me / I want another." Smith gives us both sides of desire at once, unrequited love and the spurned lover. It's depressing, and you don't quite know whom to root for.

Another of Smith's torch songs is "25th Floor," written for her new lover, Fred Smith. The song is about wandering around the top of a building in Detroit, making out in the men's room, and generally getting lost. But within this love song is an ode to rock and humanity's hopeless pursuit of transforming waste. The end drifts off into a long meditation about playing guitar, the aptly titled "High on Rebellion," which also could be read as about sex: "What I feel when I'm playing guitar is completely cold and crazy." Smith rambles on in her meditation about riding the wave of notes, and it's one of the most successful and evocative free-form rock-poetry songs she's created, no doubt in part because it was inspired by love. But it's not just a love song about Fred Smith, it's a love song to rock and roll and to the guitar noise that he was so brilliant at creating.

The album closes with the title track, which although technically a tribute to rebirth is a mournful lament yet one imbued with hope. The pain and death that lead to the rebirth are obviously present: "the thorn the veil the face of grace." But the song celebrates the death that leads to the rebirth, embracing the fall for what comes afterward. It is nostalgic but in a twisted way that remembers a long-ago funeral with fondness (and who is to say that funerals cannot be remembered with fondness?). The song and album clash to a close with church bells.

Left off the original LP but included on a CD reissue was "Godspeed," which had Smith singing in a frenzy. In this song she is much more successful at her improvisational rants than in the ones she included on her records—suggesting that she is not, perhaps, the best judge of her own material.

Easter was generally praised by many critics as a return to form after the disappointing *Radio Ethiopia*. Nick Tosches called her "the greatest broad poet that ever was" in *Creem* magazine.[25] In *Rolling Stone*, Dave Marsh wrote that "*Easter* makes good on Patti Smith's biggest boast—that she is one of the great figures of Seventies rock & roll. . . . More importantly perhaps, it focuses her mystical and musical visions in a way that makes her the most profoundly religious American popular performer since Jim Morrison."[26]

But even the favorable reviews noted that there were problems. Inspired much more by ego than love was the album's most controversial song, a landmine buried in the middle of an otherwise great rock album.

Careless Words

White Reflections on the Word "Nigger"

- In Lenny Bruce's famous routine on the word "nigger"—dramatically reenacted in Julian Barry's *Lenny*, the movie version of which starred Dustin Hoffman (which is where I first heard of Bruce and which I refer to here because it is how Bruce's sentiment lives on in pop culture)—the comedian began by asking whether there were any niggers in the audience and then pointing them out. After gratuitously throwing the word about—usually by singling out the African Americans in the audience, increasing the tension as much as possible—Bruce would then make his point: "Dig: if President Kennedy would just go on television, and say, 'I would like to introduce you to all the niggers in my cabinet,' and if he'd just say 'nigger nigger nigger nigger nigger' to every nigger he saw, 'boogie boogie boogie boogie boogie,' 'nigger nigger nigger nigger nigger' 'til nigger didn't mean anything anymore, then you could never make some 6-year-old black kid cry because somebody called him a nigger at school."

- It's summer. I'm maybe 12 or 13 years old, sitting at dinner with my family in Erie, Pennsylvania. The windows are open, letting in a cool breeze through the screens. My dad, revived after work by a couple of manhattans, is telling a story and uses the word "nigger." A protest or two from his kids, raised in a more polite world, prompts a mild lecture from him on how the world is. "There is a difference between 'niggers' and 'black people,'" he said. The hardworking family who lived down the block—and whose son was my friend—were black people, my dad explained. Niggers were something else, but his exact definition escapes me now.

- During the O. J. Simpson trial in 1995, the word "nigger" suddenly found itself prominently on the front page of newspapers, as one of the police investigators was alleged to have used it—which, if true, would bias his testimony and investigation against Simpson. But many newspapers of the day squirmed about whether to use the epithet. Some, like a midsized daily where a friend of mine worked, substituted "N-word" for nigger in print. Several reporters protested this softening of it, the African Americans among them leading the charge. "Apart from the fact that 'N-word' looks unbelievably stupid in a headline, we felt that not using the actual word ended up protecting the person alleged to have said it (Mark Furman, in that case), because it wasn't really forcing people to confront the full force of what he said," my friend said. The paper's managing editor heard the reporters' concerns, but "he didn't want readers to have to sit down to breakfast in the morning and be confronted by that word. He thought it would upset them, and he didn't want to upset them. . . . The paper printed 'N-word' in every story. But at least we got an honest answer about what was being protected: We were trying to keep readers, in some small way, from having to deal with the real world."

Smith has always declared herself free to do whatever she pleases within the realm of her art, which includes using words such as "nigger." While that's a fair approach to take as an artist, it has sometimes produced ridiculous results. The most controversial song of Smith's career is "Rock n Roll Nigger"—although "controversy" might be too strong an adjective, given that she was generally mocked for her choice of words and sentiment rather than attacked as a racist.

The song does rock, and "nigger" has a rhythmic ring to it as a chant. On the album, the song is preceded by "Babelogue," a fierce minute-and-a-half spoken-word piece that works as an introduction and artist's statement. Audience clapping—it's unclear whether it has been dubbed in or whether the track was recorded live—provides an intense, uneven beat that Smith plays off of. Her delivery shows just how masterful of a performer she has become—the way she accentuates lines by chuckling or stuttering, using the rhythm of the piece and the moment to full advantage. "I seek pleasure," she declares. The piece builds, joined by a steady drumbeat, and as Smith yells, "I have not sold myself to God," the band erupts into "Rock n Roll Nigger."

The song is an ode to being "outside society," which, in Smith's romantic notions of outlaw artistry, is the highest place to be. She declares herself a "nigger," a notion that is clearly romantic and noble to her. Then she lists other so-called niggers: Jimi Hendrix, Jesus Christ, Jackson Pollock, and grandma (perhaps in case there was any question of why she used the word or maybe because it fit the melody or maybe she ran out of people to bestow the title on). "Outside society they're waiting for me."

It is easy to get swept away by this audacious rock anthem. Some of the best rock and roll is a hammer smacking you on the head, making little sense. On *Easter*'s liner notes, Smith wrote that the word must be redefined—"any man who extends beyond the classic form is a nigger." But when you start to think about what she's really saying in "Rock n Roll Nigger," the song falls apart. It doesn't hold up to scrutiny the way great art does. You feel a little stupid for buying into such a simplistic, dopey notion—and that's what it is.

Smith's intentions might start off admirably enough. Ostensibly, she's sticking up for those who have been kicked around by history because of their skin color yet from another perspective were the coolest ones of all, victims who created brilliant art despite being oppressed, art that continues to inspire, and who generally pushed society along a path to bettering itself. She is also engaging in some Lenny Bruce–style redefining of ugly words, trying to strip them of their negative connotations. In other words, she wants to turn an insult into a badge of honor, but an honor that anyone can earn. In her world, a nigger isn't someone who is black—it refers to someone who is a renegade, doing what he or she sees fit despite society's rules. Unfortunately, many people who tried living in American society were murdered, enslaved, or otherwise destroyed because of the color of their skin. Many black people weren't rebels but were law-abiding people who acquiesced but still died as niggers at the hands of cruel men. Smith dreams of joining the ranks of "niggers . . . outside of society," but were she to get her wish, she would find no freedom waiting for her. The word "nigger" doesn't mean someone who lives outside of society. Instead, niggers were people enslaved and imprisoned by society. Society stripped them of their humanity. The term "nigger" was a construct and creation of society—one of the ugliest things society was capable of: systematic and organized repression.

Smith has divorced herself from the true meaning of these words—who used them, who they applied to, the violent power that the word gave some people over others. It is irresponsible for a white person to do that, given how much white America (which includes Smith) profited from slavery and racism. It is upsetting to see someone for whom words—and history—are so important savage their meanings and neglect that history. Her use of the term is especially galling when you consider her critique of Native American culture as racist (on *Easter*'s liner note explanation of "Ghost Dance") for excluding non–Native American souls from their spiritual rituals. "The failure of the dance was its racial aspect," she wrote. "No souls—living or transcending—were welcome if not American Indian."

Early in her career Smith was fond of using offensive words, tossing them around not just to get a rise but also to collect a bit of contrarian cool. In early interviews, she often floated the word "nigger" around, defending it as justifiable slang. "If I wanna say pussy, I'll say pussy. If I wanna say nigger, I'll say nigger. If somebody wants to call me a cracker bitch, that's cool. It's all part of being American. But all these tight-assed movements are fucking up our slang, and that eats it."[27] But some of the people "fucking up" her slang were people who had suffered from the violence of that slang.

On the liner notes for *Radio Ethiopia*, she called Satan the "first absolute artist—the first true nigger." She also used the word in a 1974 review of a Velvet Underground live recording. The review is mostly incomprehensible. She drops the names of her heroes and experiments with language, explaining the music surrealistically but doing little to enlighten the reader as to what is happening in the music. It reflected the style of the times, a bad imitation of masters such as Lester Bangs and Richard Meltzer. But this line in particular jumps out: "And I love the way Lou talks like a warm nigger or slow bastard from Philly that THING that reeks of old records like golden oldies."[28] I have no idea what a "warm nigger" is supposed to be—friendly, hot, southern? As an adjective, it sounds like parody. She seems to use the word as a way of claiming some renegade cool, which is as distasteful a use of it as any. Despite her patronizing use of the word, it is clearly meant as a compliment. She frequently called her idol, Mick Jagger, a nigger. At least at first, Jagger did not return Smith's admiration—however oddly expressed—and famously dissed her in an interview: "I think she's so awful. . . . She's full of rubbish, she's full of words and crap. I mean, she's a poseur of the worst kind, intellectual bullshit, trying to be a street girl when she doesn't seem to me to be one, I mean, everything. . . . A useless guitar player, a bad singer, not attractive. . . . I was always very attractive, much better singer, much better with words, and I wasn't an intellectual poseur. She's got her heart in the right place but she's such a POSER! She's not really together musically, she's . . . all right."[29]

In concert, Smith has declared herself a nigger too.[30] In an exchange with a reporter captured by *Rolling Stone* magazine, Smith said that

> Ya think black people are better than white people or sumpthin'? I was raised with black people. It's like, I can walk down the street and say to a kid, "Hey nigger." I don't have any kind of super-respect or fear of that kind of stuff. When I say statements like that, they're not supposed to be analyzed, because they're more like off-the-cuff humorous statements. I

do have a sense of humor, ya know, which is sumpthin' that most people completely wash over when they deal with me. I never read anything where anybody talked about my sense of humor. It's like, a lot of the stuff I say is true, but it's supposed to be funny.[31]

But her excuse of humor is a hard sell, given how ferociously she attempted to wield her power through language.

Ultimately, any well-meaning attempt by white people to redefine the word "nigger" is doomed to fail. When white people, after using the word for centuries to dehumanize and belittle people of color, ease their guilty conscience, and justify their exploitation, suddenly declare with smug righteousness that the word now has a positive meaning, it remains dehumanizing and patronizing. A few years later, African American hip-hop artists would begin redefining the term in pop culture, giving it new nuances of meaning (both negative and positive), tossing the word back on itself. Unlike Smith, though, they could claim ownership of it without having to apologize for or acknowledge its violent legacy because they were victims of it, not perpetrators or benefactors.

Critics at the time roundly dismissed "Rock n Roll Nigger" in generally favorable reviews of the album. Lester Bangs mocked Smith not for being racist but instead for her arrogance:

She's got this song on her new album *Easter* (talk about justice! I could even accept that Jesus was a woman, but from New Jersey?), called "Rock 'n' Roll Nigger," wherein her and coconspirator/cabalist Lenny Kaye (who used to be a real fun guy) go on about living "outside of society" (On Fifth Ave., to be precise), and cite "Jackson Pollock was a nigger, Jimi Hendrix was a nigger," etc. Well, guess I'll have to admit it: I am not a nigger. I'm a pawn of the imperialist power structure, which I guess puts me more in the line of sucker.[32]

Nick Tosches wrote that "the concept of artist as nigger is silly and trite,"[33] while Dave Marsh stated that "Though Smith's contention that Jackson Pollock was a 'nigger' (presumably in his dealings with wealthy art patrons) is amusing, her attempt to make the word respectable is foredoomed. 'Rock n Roll Nigger' is an unpalatable chant because Smith doesn't understand the word's connotation, which is not outlawry but a particularly vicious kind of subjugation and humiliation that's antithetical to her motive."[34]

Notes

1. Allan Jones, "Meet the Press," *Melody Maker*, October 30, 1976.
2. Smith's interview is documented in Victor Bockris and Roberta Bayley, *Patti Smith: An Unauthorized Biography* (New York: Simon and Schuster, 1999), 168–170; and Charles Young, "Patti Smith Catches Fire," *Rolling Stone*, March 1977.

3. Page from *Yipster Times* reproduced in Patti Smith, *Patti Smith Complete, 1975–2006* (New York: Harper Perennial, 2006), 65.

4. Bockris and Bayley, *Patti Smith*, 174–176.

5. Ibid., 175.

6. Vivien Goldman, "Patti Cracks Noggin, Raps on Regardless," *Sounds*, February 5, 1977.

7. Ibid.

8. Charles Young, "Patti Smith Catches Fire," *Rolling Stone*, March 1977.

9. Terry Gross, interview on *Fresh Air, National Public Radio*, June 24, 1996.

10. Sharon Delano, "The Torch Singer," *New Yorker*, March 11, 2002, 59.

11. Thurston Moore, "Patti Smith," *Bomb*, no. 54 (Winter 1996), http://bombsite.com/issues/54/articles/1928.

12. Bockris and Bayley, *Patti Smith*, 176.

13. Young, "Patti Smith Catches Fire."

14. Delano, "The Torch Singer," 59.

15. Young, "Patti Smith Catches Fire."

16. Smith, *Patti Smith Complete*, 88.

17. William S. Burroughs, "When Patti Rocked," *Spin*, April 1988.

18. John Tobler, "High on Rebellion: Patti Smith Speaks, Part 2," *ZigZag*, June 1978.

19. Lisa Robinson, "Patti Smith's Intuitive Mania," *Hit Parader*, March 1978.

20. David Fricke, "Patti Smith, Flea Bid Farewell to Iconic Punk Club," *Rolling Stone* online, October 16, 2006, http://www.rollingstone.com/news/story/12045842/patti_smith_rocks_final_cbgb_show.

21. John Tobler, "15 Minutes with Patti Smith," *ZigZag*, October 1978.

22. Bockris and Bayley, *Patti Smith*, 184.

23. Tobler, "15 Minutes."

24. Smith, *Easter*, liner notes.

25. Nick Tosches, "Easter," *Creem*, June 1978.

26. Dave Marsh, "Can Patti Smith Walk on Water?," *Rolling Stone*, April 10, 1978.

27. Nick Tosches, "A Baby Wolf with Neon Bones," *Penthouse*, April 1976.

28. Patti Smith, review of Velvet Underground's 1969 live record, *Creem*, September 1974.

29. Sandy Robertson, "Mick Jagger," *Sounds*, October 29, 1977.

30. Paul Rambali, "Breaking the Shackles of Original Sin," *New Musical Express*, September 16, 1978.

31. Young, "Patti Smith Catches Fire."

32. Lester Bangs, "Dear Patti, Start the Revolution without Me," *Phonograph Record*, May 1978.

33. Tosches, "Easter."

34. Marsh, "Can Patti Smith Walk on Water?"

22

Warren Zevon

Excitable Boy (1978)

James E. Perone

In the 1960s and 1970s, a number of singer-songwriters emerged who, while they enjoyed some commercial success, produced higher-quality work and were more highly critically acclaimed and influential than commercial measures alone might suggest. Harry Nilsson, Laura Nyro, Randy Newman, and Warren Zevon, among others, fit into this category to varying degrees at the time. Zevon's 1978 album *Excitable Boy* included one cult hit, "Werewolves of London," but was packed with quirky songs that explored the fringes of society, the macabre, and vivid imaginary characters, all with catchy melodies and the instrumental skills of Zevon on keyboards, supported by a virtual who's who of prominent studio musicians and guest artists.

The album opens with the Zevon composition "Johnny Strikes Up the Band." Lyrically the most conventional song on *Excitable Boy*, "Johnny Strikes Up the Band" is a tribute to the title character and his keyboard music's ability to leave listeners "rocking in the projects" and "along the strand." What is perhaps most unexpected about this song is that while Zevon informs the listener that Johnny's music brings happiness that cuts across demographical and geographical lines, he does so in verses that are set in a minor tonality. In a stand-alone song, this might seem confusing or awkward to the listener; however, in the context of songs about loss in love, werewolves, headless Thompson gunners, mercenary soldiers engaging in clandestine operations, rapists and murderers, prison, and all of the ironic associations that Zevon makes about these topics, "Johnny Strikes Up the Band" serves as an effective overture to *Excitable Boy*.

The Zevon–David Lindell song "Roland the Headless Thompson Gunner" concerns the exploits of the title character, a Norwegian mercenary soldier. After fighting in Biafra and the Congo in the 1960s, Roland is murdered by one of his comrades who acted as an agent of the CIA. Subsequently, Roland's headless ghost hunted down his killer. In the final verse, Zevon sings that Roland's headless ghost still wanders wherever there is armed conflict, "in Ireland, in Lebanon, in Palestine, and Berkeley." He concludes by name-checking heiress/kidnap victim/bank robber Patty Hearst (who subsequently had her sentence commuted by President Jimmy Carter and later received a pardon from President Bill Clinton). The minor-key musical setting features a natural rise and fall to the melodic line, akin to what might be found in a folk ballad. This gives the music something of a timeless feel. The song itself, however, does not age as well as other Zevon works because of the lyrical references to events that are not particularly well remembered 30–40 years after they transpired.

Zevon collaborated with LeRoy P. Marinell in writing the album's title track. The "Excitable Boy" of whom Zevon sings moves from playing with his food in childhood to biting a movie usherette on the leg to raping and murdering his prom date. When the murderer is released from "the Home" 10 years later, he "dug up the grave" and "built a cage with her bones." The lyrics reflect Warren Zevon's fascination with the macabre and his macabre sense of humor, something to which he turned time and time again throughout his career. However, on a more serious level, the lyrics also suggest the state of denial in which those around the "Excitable Boy" live. In the Marinell/Zevon tale, the proverbial emperor has no clothes, but he does have the means to rape and murder.

"Excitable Boy" features disarming music, cast in the prevailing pop style of 1970s' singer-songwriters such as Jackson Browne, with whom Zevon worked during the period and who coproduced the album with Waddy Wachtel. Jim Horn's tenor saxophone solo and the backing chorus of Linda Rondstadt, Jennifer Warnes, and Wachtel reflect the aesthetics of easygoing 1950s' rock and roll. This combination of a macabre story with disarming rock and roll enjoyed a certain degree of popularity around at the time: the 1976 copyright of "Excitable Boy" places the song right between the 1975 film *The Rocky Horror Picture Show* and Nick Lowe's 1977 pop song "Marie Provost."

The songwriting team of Zevon and Marinell was joined by Wachtel for "Werewolves of London," the best-known song of Zevon's career. In the first verse, Zevon tells of a werewolf that his character saw walking through London's Soho. The werewolf carried a menu from a Chinese restaurant and was looking to buy "a big dish of beef chow mein." In the subsequent verses, Zevon warns those who might hear the werewolf not to allow him into their homes because of violent crimes that have been attributed to him. Zevon and his cowriters then describe seeing horror film legends Lon Chaney and Lon Chaney Jr. "walking with the Queen, doing the Werewolves of London." For some listeners, this might suggest that the image of a werewolf preying on the unsuspecting at night is replaced by the image of film stars, perhaps dressed in werewolf costume, doing a new dance fad with the queen of England as they walk the streets of London. Even with the morbid humor of "Werewolves of London," Zevon hints at a more serious side, with some subtle social commentary. In the final verse, he uses more clever wordplay to construct observations that suggest that the werewolves may metaphorically represent well-heeled, well-groomed individuals who metaphorically dismember their victims.

Zevon and his collaborators set the tale of the "Werewolves of London" to engaging music that has at its core a simple ostinato V-IV-I-I chord progression. The same progression is used in both the verses and the chorus. The harmonic simplicity and the up-front placement of the vocals in the recording's mix tend to place the listener's focus squarely on Zevon's vocals. It should be noted that Fleetwood Mac members Mick Fleetwood (drums) and John McVie (bass) join guitarist Waddy Wachtel and pianist Zevon as the instrumentalists on the track. The emphasis on the vocals, repetitive harmonic pattern, and Wachtel's electric slide guitar solo combine to suggest the popular style of the time of Jackson Browne.

The next track, Zevon's "Accidentally Like a Martyr," turns in the direction of a pop country ballad. The lyrics concern a loss in love. Although this is a familiar theme in country pop, Zevon moves beyond the ordinary by applying the title line in reference to how the physicality of the relationship started and to how the relationship ended. The next piece, "Nighttime in the Switching Yard," a collaboration of Zevon, Wachtel, David Lindell, and Jorge Calderón, is a funk-style piece. Because of its minimalistic lyrics, the piece is more about the musical groove than about the lyrics—the only such song on *Excitable Boy*. Still, Zevon's description of the passing of the trains in the switching yard might be taken as the observations of a vagrant rider of the rails—a hobo. The lyrics contain no direct references to the nature of the character; however, the only activity in which he is engaged is listening to the sound of the passing trains. To the extent that the listener understands Zevon's character to be an outsider from society, then he fits in with the social outcasts of some of the other songs on the album.

Zevon collaborated with Jorge Calderón for "Veracruz." This song takes the listener back to the April 1914 U.S. naval blockade of the port of Veracruz, Mexico. Zevon portrays a resident of the city who vows to return after the withdrawal of U.S. troops. His character thereby confirms the reputation of Veracruz as a historically important and proud city and its designation as a "Heroic City" in the face of attacks from Spain, the United States, and France in the 19th and early 20th centuries. The minor mode setting and the story itself are poignant. Also poignant is Zevon and Jackson Browne's song "Tenderness on the Block." In this song, Zevon addresses the parents of a young woman who is growing up quickly before their eyes. Specifically, the woman/girl is now of dating age, and the parents now must deal with balancing their concerns with the need to give their daughter the freedom to grow and learn about love on her own. The musical setting reflects the style of cowriter Jackson Browne, with perhaps a touch of the style of the Eagles. This is important to note, because the musical style and Zevon's age at the time (31 years) suggest that he plays the role of an observer who is somewhere between the daughter and her parents age-wise. It is, in fact, easy to hear the song as the expression of a man who perhaps now has a young daughter and sees his family's future in the family he observes.

Excitable Boy concludes with a more conventionally Warren Zevon song, "Lawyers, Guns and Money." In this piece, composed solely by the singer, Zevon sings about various misadventures and the proverbial hot water in which these have landed him. Specifically, the waitress he picks up turns out to be a Russian spy, and a gambling risk he takes in Havana turns sour. The upshot of the tale is that he is now "hiding in Honduras," and he asks his father to help him out of his jam by sending "lawyers, guns, and money." While the song can be understood on the surface as an example of black humor, like many of Zevon's songs there are some deeper issues that can be heard as well. His character's misadventures involve foreign countries, two of which have histories of adversarial relationships with the United States. The character's request supports the view that Americans believe that the legal system, money, and military might can win any battle.

Excitable Boy barely made it into the Top 10 on the album charts, but the album was Warren Zevon's most commercially successful of his career. Zevon continued to perform the album cuts "Lawyers, Guns and Money," "Roland the Headless Thompson Gunner," "Excitable Boy," and "Werewolves of London" for years, reaching large television audiences, particularly with his numerous appearances on *The Late Show with David Letterman*. While it is convenient to think of Zevon as a cult figure—someone with fewer fans than some pop musicians of his generation but with more rabidly faithful fans—the engaging musical settings and Zevon's rich vocal style on *Excitable Boy* remain effective at pulling the listener into his sometimes bizarre, macabre, humorous take on life. To the extent that the 1970s were the heyday of the singer-songwriter genre, Zevon's *Excitable Boy* presents the listener with a side of the movement that is not captured by the likes of Jackson Browne, Carole King, Gordon Lightfoot, Joni Mitchell, and James Taylor, a side that deserves to be better known.

23

The Clash

London Calling (1979)

Karen Fournier

In 1976, Joe Strummer (née John Mellor) and Mick Jones began to collaborate as songwriters for a new band, the Clash. One of their efforts, a song titled "1977," came to typify not only their songwriting style but also the proclaimed beginning of an era of music where there would be "no Elvis, Beatles, or the Rolling Stones, in 1977." The song was recorded for the Clash's eponymous debut album, released in the United Kingdom on the CBS label on April 8, 1977, featuring Strummer and Jones on vocals and guitars, Paul Simonon on bass, and Terry Chimes (billed as "Tory Crimes") on guitar. Intensely political, *The Clash* comprised commentaries on racial tensions, class disparity, economic hopelessness, and the Americanization of Britain, and the extent of their political awareness led the band to be touted as "Thinking Man's Yobs" on the cover of the April 7, 1977, issue of *New Musical Express*. To promote the album, the band immediately launched their "White Riot" tour of the United Kingdom through May 1977, joined on the road by such early punk acts as the Buzzcocks, the Jam, the Slits, and Subway Sect. The album reached No. 12 on the UK music charts and received positive reviews from critics, but despite its success at home, *The Clash* was not released into the U.S. markets because it was feared that the album's British themes would not resonate with an American audience who was assumed to have little understanding of the British social system. Musically speaking, The Clash's debut album was a reflection of the diverse musical tastes of the members of the band and drew its influences variously from Jamaican reggae and dub to Latin American music and early American rock and roll. These musical sources would continue to inform the band until its demise in 1986.

The Clash's second album, *Give 'Em Enough Rope*, was released on November 10, 1978, with Nicky "Topper" Headon on drums. Headon had been enlisted to replace Chimes, who is purported to have quit the band after a particularly violent gig at which he was almost hit by a flying wine bottle, and joined the band before they launched the White Riot tour. (Chimes would rejoin the band in 1982 but also worked with Johnny Thunders and the Heartbreakers, Generation X, Hanoi Rocks, and Black Sabbath.) Sandy Pearlman, who had gained fame as the manager and producer of the American psychedelic rock back Blue Öyster Cult, was hired to produce the album, which soared to second position on the UK charts. Like the first album, *Give 'Em Enough Rope* was highly political and featured comments on global terrorism ("Guns on the Roof"), hijacking ("Tommy Gun"), and the state of politics in Britain ("English Civil War"). However, despite its British perspective on contemporary domestic and foreign issues, the album reached the 128th position on the American *Billboard* charts, and this success inspired the U.S. release of the band's first album, *The Clash*, on July 26, 1979 (albeit with modifications to the original lineup of songs to suit what was perceived to be the interests of an American audience). The release of *Give 'Em Enough Rope* coincided with the band's Sort It Out tour through England and Western Europe, which began on October 13, 1978, and lasted until the end of November. During the tour, the band parted ways with their manager, Bernie Rhodes, whom they blamed for his role in negotiating a poorly financed recording contract for the band with CBS. The band was subsequently managed by Blackhill Enterprises, which oversaw the production of the next album and the tours that preceded and followed. In February 1979, Blackhill arranged the Pearl Harbour tour, where The Clash was heard live by Canadian and American audiences for the first time. With Bo Diddley in tow, the band sold out every show and received rave reviews from critics across North America. As a result, the promised release of their third album, *London Calling*, at the end of 1979 was widely anticipated by audiences on both sides of the Atlantic. Produced by Guy Stevens, who had previously worked with such bands as Procul Harem and Mott the Hoople, the album was completed and released in the United Kingdom on December 14, 1979, and entered the British music charts at No. 9. In the United States, it was released on January 5, 1980, and charted at No. 27 on the *Billboard* charts. *London Calling* was released as a double-album set that originally featured 18 songs (with a 19th, "Train in Vain," added to the end of the second album after the cover had gone to print). Perhaps in recognition of the financial hardships suffered by many of their fans, the Clash opted to sell the album at a price that was only slightly higher than that of a single album. The iconic cover, which features Paul Simonon smashing his bass guitar in concert, presents the name of the album along the left and lower margins in pink and green typeface as a takeoff of Elvis Presley's debut album, where the artist's name appears in similar typeface and location on the cover. This visual reference to Elvis extends to the musical content of the album, where the influence of rock and roll is felt alongside that of reggae, ska, jazz, soul, and pop.

Like the earlier albums, *London Calling* captured the zeitgeist of its time with references to various domestic and international news items that had captured the attention of Strummer or Jones as they composed the songs. Many tracks seek to represent the state of Britain in the late 1970s, where an inflation rate of 25 percent and high unemployment fueled anger at the government and sparked attacks on minorities who were blamed for taking jobs that might otherwise have employed Britons. Also notable was the election of Margaret Thatcher on May 3, 1979, which began a period of conservative fiscal and social policies that would endure through the 1980s, many of which increased the financial hardships faced by the working class in the short-term. As a response to its time, *London Calling* tackles such issues as racial disharmony, police brutality, unemployment, drug and alcohol abuse, and the sense of alienation felt by many working-class youths and contextualized these social ills in a broader international frame with references to similar political and social crises in Spain, the Caribbean, and the Middle East.

London Calling begins with the title track, released as a single in the United Kingdom a week before the final release of the album. Likely the most famous song on the album and perhaps one of the most memorable songs of the punk period, "London Calling" is a pastiche of references to various historical and contemporary events, all of which are set to a reggae bass line. The title of the song and its opening lyrics borrow from the wartime BBC international broadcasts that began with the phrase "this is London calling," and the song itself stands as a commentary on social conditions in the United Kingdom in the wake of World War II. In a sense, the song seems to suggest that the war solved little and that the threats that the listener currently faces (the police, drug dealers, and potential nuclear accidents) are perhaps less easy to overcome than those of the past. The helplessness of the song is underscored by the concluding line, "I never felt so much a-like, a-like," drawn from Guy Mitchell's hit song "Singing the Blues" (1957) and set over a recurring Morse code radio distress signal that brings the song back to the historical period of its opening line. The lyrical content of the song sets the tone for the rest of the album, which meanders through a variety of international and domestic topics that will be the focus of this discussion.

The issue of the racial tensions that plagued the United Kingdom in the 1970s is raised in a number of songs on the album, many of which combine jazz or reggae musical influences, used to signify the oppressed and disenfranchised black minority who lived in such areas of London as Brixton and Notting Hill, with a punk vocal aesthetic. Songs that focus on this political topic include "Jimmy Jazz," "Rudie Can't Fail," and "Wrong 'em Boyo" (written by Jones and Strummer) and "Guns of Brixton" (by Simonon), each of which I will discuss in the sequence in which it appears on the two albums.

The third song on the first album, "Jimmy Jazz," traces its musical references to jazz, particularly in its use of saxophone and brass instruments, and reggae, in its allusions to steel drums, and describes a police search for an elusive "Jimmy Jazz" (also described as "Jimmy Dread," in reference to dreadlocks). The song begins with a distant whistling, presumably by someone who is minding his own business, but then proceeds with a series of verses that are interrupted by instrumental solos and then repeated in increasingly shortened lengths. The topic of racism is reiterated in the fifth song, "Rudie Can't Fail," where Strummer invokes the Jamaican slang "rude boy" to describe the life of a juvenile delinquent who begins his day "drinking brew for breakfast" and then proceeds to look unsuccessfully for work. Like "Jimmy Jazz," this song references reggae explicitly in its use of horns and off-beat metric accents. The first album concludes with "Guns of Brixton," the first song to be written by Simonon and to feature him as the lead vocalist. The song predates but seems to presage the Brixton race riots of 1981, during which Metropolitan police clashed with the African Caribbean community over the sus laws that allowed police to detain suspicious individuals with no obvious cause. The sense of us-versus-them that was felt toward the police by minority groups who lived in Brixton in the late 1970s is captured in particular by the chorus, which asks its listener, "When the law break in, how you gonna go? Shot down on the pavement or waiting on death row?" Released as a single in July 1990, the song charted at No. 57 in the United Kingdom. The second album continues the theme of racial tension with a version of the "Stagger Lee" ballad (originally published in 1911 and recorded widely as a folk song in the United States) that draws a parallel between the murder of William "Billy" Lyons by "Stagger" Lee Shelton in St. Louis on Christmas Eve 1895 and the racial problems in the United Kingdom in the 1970s. Sympathetic toward the convicted black murderer Stagger Lee, the song "Wrong 'em Boyo" suggests that Billy lied and cheated at a game of dice and thereby goaded his attacker into action. By extrapolation, the song suggests that while visible minorities were often criticized in British society for their apparent roles in raising the level of racial tensions in the country, these tensions were more often the product of actions taken by the predominantly white police force. To represent the two sides in the racial narrative, "Wrong 'em Boyo" begins with a rockabilly rendition of the first verse, to signify Billy Lyons, but switches to ska at the moment that the Clash expose their sympathies for the accused.

Another domestic topic that is explored on *London Calling* is the problem of class and poverty in Britain in the 1970s, which is discussed in a handful of songs that make less obvious allusions to reggae and ska but tend to project a pop sensibility. These songs include "Hateful," "Lost in the Supermarket," "Clampdown," and "Koka Kola," all of which were written by Jones and Strummer.

"Hateful," which appears as the fourth song on the first album, compares the problem of drug addiction to the growing addiction to spending and depicts the relationship between the protagonist, in the guise of a drug addict, and his junkie, who "gives me what I need . . . I need it all so badly." The urgency to spend and the emptiness of its reward is also a theme explored in "Lost in the Supermarket," the eighth track on the first album, which describes the quest for "a guaranteed personality" that can be artificially constructed from material goods available at the shops. This song is decidedly slower than the other songs on the album, and its tempo gives the quirky and seemingly superficial lyrics a sense of self-reflection and seriousness. The price to be paid by those from the working class who manufacture the goods that are sold to the British consumer is described in "Clampdown," the ninth track on the album, which cautions its listener against the allure of meaningless and directionless employment and draws a parallel between unskilled labor and prison (where, in both cases, "you start wearing the blue and brown"). Originally conceived as an instrumental track titled "Working and Waiting," the song is often misunderstood as a comment on the Nazi regime, mostly because of the reference to Jews in the first verse, its suggestion of the "blue-eyed" Aryan race, and the allusion to the brownshirts in the phrase quoted above. This is a common misreading of punk, which often used Nazi imagery to represent the oppression of the British class system. Despite these clear sympathies for the working class, the life of the white-collar worker was also subject to critique in the song "Koka Kola," the third track on the second album. Here, the Clash comment on the pursuit of wealth, whose emptiness can only be mitigated by the use of recreational drugs. In a twist on a familiar advertising campaign, the chorus of the song proclaims that "Koke adds life where there isn't any," but in the absence of any meaningful purpose to life, the song warns that after awhile "you're leaping from the windows saying don't give me none of this." More broadly, the British economic crisis of the 1970s, during which few could engage in the kind of spending critiqued by the Clash in the songs described here, is represented in the rock-and-roll–inspired song "I'm Not Down," which appears as the seventh track on the second album. On its surface, the song appears to urge the poor to fight against their financial hardships, with a chorus that assumes a working-class perspective that states "I've been beat up, I've been thrown out, but I'm not down." A more reflective reading might interpret the song as a reference to the ups and downs of Britain itself, particularly in its allusions to a "depression" followed by "skyscrapers rising up floor by floor" and the closing verse, which disparages those who hold to the myth of the British Empire and who think that they are "the toughest in the world, the whole wide world, But you're streets away from where it gets the roughest." The British tendency to "keep calm and carry on" in the face of crisis is also critiqued in "The Right Profile," a song that is rich with signifiers and can be interpreted as an allegory for the British denial of the economic climate of the 1970s. The song, appearing as the seventh track on the first album, chronicles Montgomery Clift's 1956 car accident, which left him permanently scarred and addicted to painkillers and alcohol. Like the media spin put on the various social crises experienced in Britain in the 1970s, the damage done to Clift's face was hidden from view by filmmakers who focused on "The Right Profile." (Given its reggae setting, the song might also serve as a commentary on race, suggesting that the "right" British profile is the "white" profile.)

As the purported "Thinking Man's Yobs," the Clash tended to contextualize British domestic crises in wider international terms, drawing parallels between tensions of race and class in the United Kingdom and political situations elsewhere. While all of their songs mark a keen interest in and understanding of global history and geopolitics, this is particularly evident in tracks that make direct reference to world events, such as "Spanish Bombs" and "London Calling." Written as an analysis of the Spanish Civil War (1936–1939), "Spanish Bombs" glorifies the efforts of the Republicans to resist the Fascists and was particularly timely in the wake of the election of Margaret Thatcher in May 1979. With its allusions to such key places and figures as Andalucia, the Costa Brava, and Federico Garcia Lorca, the song seems to advocate for a similar working-class revolution in Britain (a theme that is echoed later in the album in the novelty song "Revolution Rock").

24

The B-52's

The B-52's (1979)

James E. Perone

In the punk and new wave era of the late 1970s and early 1980s, some artists turned the clock backwards and recaptured the spirit of the prepsychedelic 1960s. For example, the British band the Jam created a 1970s' version of the mod style of the Who. The Athens, Georgia, band the B-52's[1] had little previous musical experience but put together a 1979 debut album that captured, celebrated, and exaggerated the kitschy and campy side of early 1960s' American popular culture. This self-titled album included one truly strange cover of the Petula Clark hit "Downtown" but was mostly populated by original songs that managed to capture some of the spirit of an earlier more innocent time while including more contemporary musical references (e.g., the influence of Yoko Ono's singing style and minimalism) and lyrics that are humorous, mysterious, sometimes silly and sometimes seductive, fantasy-oriented, and occasionally haunting. *The B-52's* also exhibits the do-it-yourself nature of what would later be labeled alternative music to a greater and more successful degree than any other album of the era.

The album begins with "Planet Claire," a collaborative work by B-52's vocalist Fred Schneider and drummer Keith Strickland.[2] Schneider half sings and half speaks the lyrics, lyrics that speak of a woman from "Planet Claire" who "drives a Plymouth Satellite faster than the speed of light." It may be silly, but in an era in which David Byrne of Talking Heads was as well known for his spasmodic dancing and grossly oversized suit as for his writing, guitar playing, and singing, the quirky humor fits right in. While to a large extent the B-52's stand apart from all of the other groups of the late 1970s (mostly because of the extreme to which they took the kitsch retro style), it should be noted that several features

NEW WAVE ROCK

In the wake of the formal, harmonic, and melodic minimalism and rough intensity of punk rock, some musicians sought a somewhat more commercially appealing return to the musical aesthetics of pre-psychedelic rock. New wave rock groups differed widely in their approaches and included the humorous party band the B52's as well as the sometimes more serious Talking Heads. When the Police moved away from their prefame punk roots and integrated ska and reggae into their style, they added another dimension to new wave rock. As the 1970s moved into the 1980s, synthesizer-based new wave bands, such as the Human League and others, continued the style's move away from its beginning as an offshoot of punk rock.

of "Planet Claire" were very much in the air with other progressive artists of the late 1970s and early 1980s. In particular, the lengthy instrumental introduction includes additive compositional technique. This might be known to some listeners from some artists of the period—notably Elvis Costello and Laurie Anderson—as building lyrical phrases through repetitions in which one new word is added each time, using homonyms to produce a meaning that changes as the context gradually becomes clear. In "Planet Claire," additive techniques can be heard as the number of repeated, almost beep-like, tones, which are doubled by wordless female voice, increases by one, moving from one to five repeated tones. This happens twice, first at the 1:39 mark and again at the 2:16 mark, concluding just before Fred Schneider enters with his lead vocals.

One of the hallmarks of new wave music is its clarity and outward simplicity. Certainly, the B-52's with their minimalistic approach to keyboards, drums, percussion, and electric guitar, and with Chris Blackwell's production style, represent that aspect of the genre. On "Planet Claire" and some other songs on the album, however, producer Blackwell and the band include longer-range structural activity that gives those songs a greater overall complexity than what the surface level might suggest. Specifically, in "Planet Claire" the introduction and larger part of the song proper includes a gradual crescendo. Therefore, while the surface level is dominated by repetition of short motifs, the work has a longer-range large-scale shape that is driven by a gradual change of dynamics.

Throughout *The B-52's* there are clear references to the late 1950s and early 1960s. In "Planet Claire," the clearest example of this can be found in Ricky Wilson's electric guitar riff, which bears a striking resemblance to the accompaniment riff in Henry Mancini's theme music for the 1958–1961 *Peter Gunn* television series. Throughout the album, Wilson uses a de-tuned electric guitar—the lowest open string is a major third lower than in standard tuning—that produces a tone color similar to the electric baritone guitar that was used in some surf music right around 1960.

The next piece, "52 Girls," a collaboration of Ricky Wilson and Joe Ayers, comes in at a faster, more danceable tempo. Here, Cindy Wilson and Kate Pierson sing in unison a text that largely consists of 24 (not 52 as the song's title suggests) girls' names. Notably, some of these (e.g., Mabel, Madge, and Hazel) are names that were more common in an earlier era, and some (e.g., Tina Louise—which is given in the song as a single name—and Jackie O.) reference celebrities from the 1960s. The singers' names, Cindy and Kate, are part of the list, as are names that might most be associated with singers of the late 1950s and early 1960s, such as Brenda (Lee) and Ronnie (Spector). In addition to the fast-paced rock-and-roll rhythm of the piece, the most notable musical components are Ricky Wilson's use of harmonies that change around a static melody note (heard in the text "These are the girls" on the world "girls") and the snaky at-first-listen unpredictable melody line.

One of the textural attributes of the recordings of the B-52's that continues to set the band apart from most groups of the rock era is the interplay between lead vocal lines sung by Fred Schneider, Cindy Wilson, and Kate Pierson in some of their songs. "Dance This Mess Around" is one such song. The instrumental accompaniment, largely limited to minimalistic electric guitar, Pierson's electronic organ, and drums, is particularly sparse. Thus, the focus is on the musical feel and the interplay between the vocalists. The song opens with Wilson singing "Remember, when you held my hand," a line that calls to mind the 1964 Shangri-Las hit "Remember (Walking in the Sand)." Wilson severs the connection to the Brill Building girl-group style when later she screams, "Why won't you dance with me," telling her would-be dance companion that she is "not no limburger." Following that is a litany of mostly fictional popular dance styles, including "the Shy Tuna" and the "Hip-o-crit." Then Wilson implores Fred Schneider to dance; he joins the vocal mix, and lines are tossed back and forth between the two.

The next track, "Rock Lobster," was the first hit single released by the B-52's and, despite the greater commercial success of "Love Shack," still defines the band in the minds of some fans. The album version of "Rock Lobster" is nearly seven minutes long, approximately two minutes longer than the single version. Because of the progression of textures, the album version is the more interesting of the two.

"Rock Lobster" begins with Ricky Wilson's C minor electric guitar riff, to which is added Strickland's drums and Schneider's impassioned beating of a cowbell on each quarter note of the measure. In the first verse, Schneider, coauthor of the piece with Wilson, sings an absurdist tale of a man at a beach party whose earlobe falls into the water. When he tries to retrieve it, he pulls out the crustacean of the song's title. In the second verse, Schneider sings about a party at which "everyone had matching towels." One partygoer ventured "under a dock" and picked up what the person thought was a rock; however, "it was a rock lobster." In the third stanza, the lyrics become even more abstract and describe a fantasy world under the waves. At approximately the 4:50

mark the texture of Ricky Wilson's electric guitar accompaniment changes, and Cindy Wilson emits a Yoko Ono–inspired wail, which includes the avant-garde artist's characteristically exaggerated vibrato. Approximately 22 seconds later the guitar riff changes again, setting up Schneider's final stanza, which itself is followed by Scheider, Pierson, and Cindy Wilson trading off names of real and imaginary sea animals with vocal sound effects associated with them. The final 23 seconds of the recording feature counterpoint between Pierson and Schneider, each singing the song's title but with different melodies and different rhythms. Generally, then, the song is broken into two longer-range sections: approximately 4 minutes and 50 seconds, in which traditional surf/ British Invasion rock structure prevails, and the second section of approximately 2 minutes, in which there are several major texture shifts. Therefore, the listener might get the sense that the pace of change dramatically speeds up at the end or at least to the last 23 seconds, which function as a conventional coda section. The dramatic quickening of the pace of texture changes is missing from the shorter single version.

The ocean scene, Ricky Wilson's surf-style guitar, and Strickland's use of the go-go drum pattern[3] in the chorus (first heard beginning approximately 21 seconds into the song) all combine to suggest 1964.[4] And "Rock Lobster" is fun in the manner of some surf songs of the early 1960s. It is, however, not so much a re-creation or an imitation of surf music as a deconstruction of it. The absurdist lyrics suggest postmodernism. While some of the imagery is imaginary (e.g., some of the sea animals, not to mention the first scene in which a beachgoer's earlobe falls "in the deep"), some of it simply glorifies pop culture and the trivial (e.g., lines such as "pass the tanning butter"). The mix of common images, silly images, and truly bizarre images leaves the listener guessing about the seriousness of the song. Ultimately, though, it is a classic in its mix of tribute, parody, old and new, and pure party band rock-and-roll energy.

The next song, the group-composed "Lava," is somewhat sexually seductive, particularly because of Cindy Wilson's vocals. The hot volcanic love about which Wilson—supported by Schneider and Pierson—sings is more conventional pop/rock material than that of most of the songs on the album. There are, however, a few quirks, including a reference to "Krakatoa, east of Java." In actuality, Krakatoa is west of Java; however, the reference may be related to the 1969 Bernard Kowalski–directed film *Krakatoa, East of Java*.

The absurdist nature of the B-52's reemerges in "There's a Moon in the Sky (Called the Moon)." This piece incorporates vocals from all three singers, with most of the solo focus on Fred Schneider. The lyrics concern various objects and phenomena in outer space; however, they also suggest human travel through them all. While not necessarily the best example of the group's wit or retro musical deconstruction, "There's a Moon in the Sky" is especially notable for the two Wilsons' minimalistic, hypnotic electric guitar riffs.

The next song, "Hero Worship," came from the pens of Ricky Wilson and Robert Waldrop. It is a dark song that finds Cindy Wilson singing what is surely one of the most tortuous lead vocal lines of the rock era. The melodic contour abruptly moves from stepwise to jagged and requires a large range. Wilson sings with intensity, sometimes including full-throated screams. She portrays a groupie who obsesses over a hero. The groupie is not content, however, merely to be "down on [her] knees" trying "to please" him, implicitly through fellatio—she also implores God to "give me his soul." The groupie's obsession is disturbing, particularly through Wilson's performance and because of the stark instrumental setting.

The next track, "6060-842," is credited to all of the members of the band except Cindy Wilson. Here, the good-natured humor that is at the heart of much of the group's most popular work returns. Fred Schneider sings the tale of "Tina," who in the "Lady's room" sees a telephone number "written on the wall." She also finds the promise of a "very good time" to anyone who dials the number. Eventually Tina puts a dime in the payphone, dials the number, and is told by the operator that the number has been disconnected. The song ends with Schneider and the operator alternating between the lines "Hello?" and "I'm sorry." The situation, therefore, is left unresolved. And, this is one of the unifying factors that runs throughout *The B-52's*: the album includes many songs that allow—or force—the listener to use his or her imagination. In the case of "6060-842," the listener never discovers why Tina felt the need to call the number or what her reaction is to the fact that the number is no longer in service—that is for the listener to fill in.

Like all of the B-52's–composed songs on their debut album, "6060-842" utilizes a minimal amount of harmonic material, in this case the tonic (I), subtonic (VII), and supertonic (ii) chords. The musical interest in this piece—and the others—lies in rhythm, texture, sound effects, and engaging melodic material. It should be noted that in "6060-842," Ricky Wilson changes harmonies around static melodic tones, which links the song back to "52 Girls."

Cindy Wilson's lead vocal performance on the B-52's' cover of the 1960s' Petula Clark hit "Downtown" falls squarely into the realm of postmodern deconstruction. The affected British accent, the *Sprechstimme* approach to pitch, and the tonal edginess—not to mention the minimalistic accompaniment, Fred Schneider's background shout that he wants a beer, and the fake party noise in the background—all combine to call into question the very essence of Petula Clark's version. If the Clark recording, produced by the song's author, Tony Hatch, was the essence of Top 40 pop music, then the version here is antipop. This type of deconstruction of 1960s' popular music was not new. For example, the 1977 Ramones' release "Rockaway Beach" is basically a deconstruction of surf music and the California surf scene of the early 1960s. What is most striking about "Downtown" is that it is at once a funny (if one knows the Petula Clark recording) and brutal deconstruction of the aesthetics of the early 1960s.

The B-52's was one of the most unusual-sounding albums of its era because of the counterpoint between Fred Schneider, Cindy Wilson, and Kate Pierson, along with the minimalistic accompaniment of guitarist Ricky Wilson, drummer Keith Strickland, and the singers on various keyboard, percussion, and occasional second guitar parts; the frequent use of humor; and a balance of reverence for and deconstruction of early 1960s' pop culture. Interestingly, 1960s' retro is again part of American popular culture in the 21st century, and this helps to keep the debut album by one of the greatest American party bands ever relevant and fun even 30 years after its release.

Notes

1. The band subsequently changed its name to the more grammatically correct moniker the B-52s.
2. After the 1985 death of guitarist Ricky Wilson, Strickland switched to guitar.
3. This percussion pattern, in which the drummer plays the snare drum on beat two, on the "and" of beat two, and on beat four was a staple of some surf music and British Invasion rock in 1964.
4. Kate Pierson's minimalistic electronic organ lines call to mind the 1966 hit single "96 Tears" by Question Mark and the Mysterians.

25

Neil Young

Rust Never Sleeps (1979)

Ken Bielen

While Neil Young was mining the country rock vein and dabbling with Crazy Horse and the Stray Gators, the punk scene was emerging in the late 1970s, with British bands the Sex Pistols and the Clash and American bands such as X and the Ramones. Punk threatened the rock music establishment that still embraced a 1960s' aesthetic and was making the earlier music its canon. Punk questioned the old school. It was the first time that rock performers were on the defensive. Young and Crazy Horse reacted to the young defiant sounds on side two of *Rust Never Sleeps*. This must be the album that a young Eddie Vedder, the singer and songwriter of Seattle's Pearl Jam, and the late Kurt Cobain of Nirvana took to heart. *Rust Never Sleeps* is at the core of the mantle bestowed on Young as the godfather of grunge.

Rust Never Sleeps is a schizophrenic record. Side one is acoustic and seems like an extension of his previous release, *Comes a Time*. The side one ensemble includes Nicolette Larson, Joe Osborne, and Karl Himmel. Side two is electric and is performed only by Young and Crazy Horse. The album is book-ended by two versions of the same song. "My My, Hey Hey (Out of the Blue)" is given a folk ballad treatment by Young. In the lyric he mentions Johnny Rotten, lead singer of the Sex Pistols, the archetypal purveyors of punk rock. Young sings "the king is gone," a reference to the passing of Elvis Presley two years earlier, and comments negatively on the closing years of Presley's career. Young sings "It's better to burn out than it is to rust," suggesting that it would have been better not to witness the decline of Presley. Recording artists who die when they are young (Buddy Holly, Ritchie Valens, Sam Cooke, Otis Redding, Jimi

Hendrix, Janis Joplin) never "rust." They are remembered as they were. They did not sell out on a casino stage.

"Thrasher" is a long story-song like "Last Trip to Tulsa" and contains a narrative that is difficult to comprehend. But "Thrasher" has a more pleasant melody and aesthetic to it. Young sings alone backed by one or two acoustic guitars and his harmonica. The song is nostalgic, there are rural images, and there is the sense that things change for the worse. Young acknowledged to Bill Flanagan that the song was partially about breaking away from Crosby, Stills, and Nash.[1] "Ride My Llama," too, has a tale that is hard to follow. The lyrics evoke frontiers such as when he calls the listener to "Remember the Alamo" or when he names the planet "Mars," but they do not seem to have a central place in the story. It is an account of moving on and traveling on.

"Pocahontas" is a classic piece of music in Young's body of work. He opens with a wonderful lyric image that makes you feel the cold breeze whistling by. He sings "Aurora borealis, the icy sky at night, paddles cut the water." It is easy to visualize a canoe in an earlier era cutting through a stream. The song is about the plight of Native Americans. He brings forth images of escaping the "white man," "women" murdered, and the killing off of the "buffalo." He portrays a harrowing scene of motherless "babies cryin' on the ground." The narrator wishes that he could go back to a purer time before the European invasion of North America. In the last verse, Young mentions Marlon Brando and Hollywood. This may seem out of place, but here Young makes reference to the 1973 Academy Awards ceremony, which the nominated Brando refused to attend. He sent a Native American actress, Sacheen Littlefeather, in his place. When he was selected as Best Actor for his portrayal of *The Godfather*, she mounted the stage, refused the award, and explained Brando's distaste for the way Native Americans were portrayed in film.[2]

Rust Never Sleeps, like the album before it, was a Top 10 hit. It reached No. 8 on the *Billboard* charts in the summer of 1979. Side one ends with a pretty song called "Sail Away" that features a dobro line. Nicolette Larson contributes a pleasing harmony in the chorus. The song is about how things will be fine as long as the couple can escape from the hassles of life when they need to.

On side two Young answered the punk rockers by experimenting with highly distorted fuzz-tone notes on his guitar. This is particularly evident in the closing track, "Hey Hey, My My (Into the Black)," the electric version of the album's opening tune. The electric notes are almost a white noise. When Young sings "rock and roll will never die," he expresses hope. His optimism stems from the fact that the punk rockers are challenging Young's complacent musical peers. Nirvana's Kurt Cobain listened carefully to these lyrics. He included the line about it being "better to burn out 'cause rust never sleeps" in his suicide note in 1994. The opening and closing tracks on the album were both recorded live. The ambient sounds of the audience at the venue are evident on the two tracks. None of the other cuts on the album are live performances.

The second side opens with "Powderfinger," a song from the Young catalog that has remained in high regard over the decades. Like a film noir, the youthful narrator is already dead and gone as he begins to unfold the story of his untimely demise. In the first verse, a hostile military vessel approaches a rural homestead. The theme of the song is the tragic and wasteful loss of youth to the conflicts between countries and their leaders. The 22-year-old protagonist realizes that it is his responsibility to defend his family's outlying land against the invader. But the firepower of "Daddy's rifle" is no match for the vessel with "numbers on the side." Gruesomely, the young guardian elucidates his demise ("my face splashed in the sky"). Sorrowfully, he "fade(s) away . . . with so much left undone."

The production of "Welfare Mothers" is a rambunctious wall of sound stirred up in a messy mix. The members of Crazy Horse loudly chant "Welfare mothers make better lovers" after every line delivered by Young, adding an off-balance quality to the track. It is one of those blowing-off-steam tracks like "Bite the Bullet" and "Motorcycle Mama" from previous albums. The lyrical premise is tongue-in-cheek or sarcastic. The lyrics suggest that low-income women are easier sexually. Part of the setting is a "Laundromat," suggesting a lower-income environment. Each verse ends with a one-word line as the vocalists extend out the word "Divorcee," suggesting that these women at the center of the song are experienced in the ways of love.

"Sedan Delivery" is characterized by its varying rhythms. The track starts off at a sprint and alternatively slows down and speeds up through its course. Each verse presents a different scene. The narrator may be a drug runner, because the only time he actually delivers something it is a package of "chemicals and sacred roots." We view him at a "pool hall," at a dentist's office for tooth extractions, and "sleepin' in a hallway." Young's lyrics often only create an atmosphere rather than unfold a linear narrative. He adds a verse about watching a film of "Caesar and Cleo," and unlike them he was able to "get away." Another verse is set in a "lab" where an "old man" (a mad scientist) wears "white clothes."

Notes

1. Bill Flanagan, *Written in My Soul: Conversations with Rock's Great Songwriters* (Chicago: Contemporary, 1987), 123.
2. Sacheen Littlefeather biography, Internet Movie Database, http://www.imdb .com/name/nm0514693/.

26

Billy Joel

Glass Houses (1980)

Ken Bielen

With success, Billy Joel and his band began to play larger venues, including the big arenas in major cities. The impetus for the songs that he composed for *Glass Houses* was the desire to have material in his repertoire that he and his fellow musicians could effectively deliver to the large audiences.[1] Joel also added another guitarist, David Brown, to his band to create a fuller sound.

"You May Be Right," the opening track on the *Glass Houses* album (issued in 1980), begins with the sound of breaking glass. The sound effect complements the theme of the record album cover. Joel stands outside the large windowed wall of his Long Island home looking ready to heave a rock through one of the frames (following the phrase "people in glass houses shouldn't throw stones"). He states that the cover idea was to shatter the image of him as just a samba-playing pianist.[2] The guitar line has a British rock aesthetic to it. It is a cross between George Harrison of the Beatles and Gerry Rafferty of Stealer's Wheel.

The broken glass sound effect also relates to this tale of a guy on the edge who is portrayed in "You May Be Right." He is unstable and capable of doing crazy things, such as throwing a stone through the glass wall of a luxury home on Long Island or riding a motorbike on rain-soaked roads. Joel's character has wide mood swings. One night he is rude at a party, and the next day he is apologetic. He puts himself at risk. He sings about walking alone through the Bedford Stuyvesant area of Brooklyn. Bedford Stuyvesant (or Bed Stuy, as it is known in the New York area), was a poor neighborhood with a large minority population. In the 1970s, the district had a reputation as a rough and dangerous place. Joel's character shows his recklessness and instability by going to the area by himself. In the chorus, Joel admits that he does not know whether or not he is a lunatic. Whatever he is, he still feels that he is the best choice for the woman to whom he addresses the song, the person whom he suggests has driven him to the edge.

Joel has toured several times with Elton John. The *My Lives* box set includes Joel and John performing a duet of Joel's "You May Be Right." Recorded at Giants Stadium in East Rutherford, New Jersey, in the summer of 1994, Joel and John barrel through a fast-paced, exuberant reading of the song. The performance opens with the sound effect of breaking glass in the same way that the *Glass Houses* album opens. Joel delivers the vocal in a gruff, deep voice. Crystal Taliefero adds high harmonies to the vocals. Smoking guitars propel the rocker along. The Australian release of *A Voyage on the River of Dreams* includes Joel's version of John's "Goodbye, Yellow Brick Road" from the same concert. During the introduction, Joel mentions that he chose to sing the song because John did not plan on performing the tune as part of John's set.

Many of Joel's vocals are founded in a musical theater aesthetic. However, "Sometimes a Fantasy" was one of the first popular tracks by Joel that demonstrated a more strapping vocal delivery. The hard-rocking song is Joel's ode to phone sex. It joins the ranks of songs that refer to autoeroticism, such as the Who's "Pictures of Lily" or the Vapors' "Turning Japanese." The subject nods to the increasingly prevalent culture of anonymous, impersonal sex at the time. The track opens with the sound effect of dialing a touch-tone phone. Joel is separated from his woman but wakes up with erotic desires. He needs satisfaction and insists that it can come only from calling her and not from an anonymous female voice on the phone line for which Joel's love has provided the number. In either case, the stimulation is located at a distance, and therein lies the rub. Whether his phone sex episode is with his woman or an anonymous service employee, it is still just an illusion or fantasy. The live version on *Kohuept* ends with a short, scorching guitar solo.

In front of strumming acoustic guitars, Joel affects a Paul McCartney–influenced vocal in "Don't Ask Me Why." A theme of the song is taking a leap into the unknown. Joel suggests that there does not have to be a reason to take actions. The words seem to be addressed to someone who has grown accustomed to a life of luxury, although the person is "no stranger to the street." Just as the lyrics contain a montage of unrelated images that do not make sense when streamed together, Joel promotes the idea of living life in a similar random manner in his pleasant midtempo composition. Adding to the odd lyrical juxtapositions is an unusual musical combination in which Joel adds a Latin music–drenched piano break in the midst of the production.

Joel's opinion of the music scene at the beginning of the 1980s is summarized in "It's Still Rock and Roll to Me." He cites "hot funk," "cool punk," and "new wave" as the new rock and roll. Joel is making the point that the cycle of music popularity and appreciation repeats itself. A hot new band or sound emerges. A new set of fans takes to the music. Magazines oriented to young record buyers proclaim the new music. Joel is critical of the importance of fashion in the image of the new music. In the end it is the sound that matters, but as an entertainer, Joel should be keenly aware that image is an integral component of the rock music scene, whether it is the clothes the recording artist wears or the automobile she or he drives. He notes that artists spend vast sums of money to dress in clothes that look inexpensive. Joel makes reference to the Miracle Mile, a shopping area in Manhasset in the northern part of Nassau County, Long Island, where Joel grew up. He references the age-old ritual of young people driving up and down the strip (in this case, Northern Boulevard), with guys looking for gals and gals looking for guys.

The production opens with repetitive low guitar notes that set the midtempo beat that leads into a shuffle. Joel's voice is enveloped in heavy echo as he opines. The instrumentation is relatively sparse, evoking the lean sound of 1950s' rock and roll, 1970s' punk, and the emerging new wave music. Joel calls out to his saxophone player to do a solo in the break, which gives the track a live-in-the-studio feel. The instrumentalists all come together at the end, bringing the song to a close in a 1960s-style flourish. In the live version included on *2000 Years: The Millennium Concert*, male background voices perform in a call-and-response fashion to Joel's lead vocals. They sing the second and fourth lines of each of the verses.

"All for Leyna" follows in a long line of popular music lyrics about unrequited love. The keyboard-based track is heavy on the beat and dangerously close to being bombastic. Rapid and repetitive piano chords punctuate the verses. After a one-night stand, Leyna has moved on. But Joel's narrator (a young man still in school and living at his parents' home), who is not mature enough to discern the fickleness of short-term summer relationships, continues to pursue and pine for the woman. The first verse sets the scene in the New York area, as there is a reference to the electrified third rail found in the subway systems of New York City and other cities. In the coda, Joel repeats a variation of the title phrase over and over again. The narrator will not give up.

Joel delivers a casual yet emotional vocal in "I Don't Want to Be Alone." The production reflects the late 1970s' British rock aesthetic. The guitar line is reminiscent of the guitar in Joe Jackson's "Is She Really Going Out with Him?" The guitar dominates the backing track, although an incongruous placid saxophone solo is tossed into the bridge. The setting is midtown Manhattan as Joel waits for his date at the tony Plaza Hotel near the corner of Fifth Avenue and Central Park South. He follows his date's instructions and dresses up for the occasion. The two had a past relationship. She was hurt, but she is forgiving and willing to initiate something new. On this night, they come together for a romantic tryst that may or may not lead to more time together.

"Sleeping with the Television On" continues in the vein of late 1970s' rock from the British Isles. The recording is a tight three-minute rock performance. The production opens with the sound of the closing bars of "The Star Spangled Banner" coming through the low-fidelity speaker of a television set; it is the signal of a television broadcast station signing off for the night. Following the portion of the national anthem are a few seconds of the high-pitched droning tone that accompanies the test pattern graphic broadcast by a TV station just about to go off the air. The television is turned on, but nothing of any substance is on the screen.

The lyrics are about a hard-to-connect-with woman named Diane. She is a superhero of sorts, shooting down guy after guy who tries to get close to her. She opts for the "white noise" of a television set tuned to a station without a broadcast signal over the overtures of fellows who desire to be close to her, albeit for some only a one-night stand. Diane may be waiting for someone who does not exist (a "solid" guy). The narrator suggests that even though she has been hurt in love before, Diane needs to take a risk because her fantasy guy is not a reality.

Joel's character would like to get to know Diane better. If he was not a "thinking man" but rather a "fool who's not afraid of rejection," he would have the gumption to approach her. Alas he does not, so he too sleeps alone with the television on. Joel flips from her attitude in the first bridge to his attitude in the second bridge. In the first bridge, her stance is that he will get no further whatever he says to her. In the second bridge, his position is that whatever he does will not help the relationship with Diane to blossom. Joel adds a brief Farfisa organ solo before the last chorus, reflecting the mid-1960s' rock productions of the Sir Douglas Quintet ("She's about a Mover"), ? (Question Mark) and the Mysterians ("96 Tears"), Sam the Sham and the Pharaohs ("Wooly Bully"), and the Swingin' Medallions ("Double Shot [Of My Baby's Love]"). The male background vocals add to the rock ensemble sound of the track, giving the take more of a group sound than a performance spotlighting a solo artist.

"C'Etait Toi (You Were the One)" is a tribute to the Paul McCartney–composed "Michelle," as recorded by the Beatles in 1965. Like McCartney, Joel sings a portion of his composition in French, and Joel's vocal delivery on the performance is reminiscent of the McCartney sound. The harpsichord and accordion on the instrumental track give the production a continental flair. A cheesy electric piano tosses in a few scattered notes that do not fit with the European instrumentation. Joel pines for a woman who he once had but who is no longer interested. He knows that he should look to others to soothe his lonely soul, but the woman to whom he addresses the lyrics is the only important one in his life. Twenty-five years later Joel admitted that he should never have recorded the song.[3]

Joel spews a barrage of slurred words in the guitar-based rocker "Close to the Borderline." His affected vocal performance acknowledges the new wave and power pop of the era. The setting is an urban summer. Fifteen years earlier, John Sebastian of the Lovin' Spoonful described it as "hot town, summer in the city." Joel's vision is grittier. There are electric blackouts, murders, and a young woman desiring to commit suicide facing an eager media egging her on below. The city's soundtrack consists of young men marching to the sounds of their boom boxes.

Joel references the energy crisis of the mid-1970s, when it was difficult to get gas for the car. At the time, the federal government instituted a national mandatory speed limit of 55 miles per hour. So, even if you could fill up the tank, "you can't drive fast anymore on the parkways." He expands his energy concerns to the threat of a nuclear disaster. Joel names the No Nukes concerts that took place at Madison Square Garden in the autumn of 1979 to raise awareness of the issues related to nuclear power plants. A year earlier, a serious accident occurred at the Three Mile Island nuclear plant near Harrisburg, Pennsylvania. Joel evinces a fatalistic attitude. A possible nuclear tragedy is just part of the menace of life in the city. Later in the verse, Joel adds, "I'd start a revolution but I don't have time." He has seen many causes come and go, and he is wary of attaching his name to any of them (whether for an individual or for the environment). Is it because he has become comfortable and complacent? Is his attitude a facade? The narrator is not sure. He is drifting "close to the borderline." He may be in for a change in his worldview. It is not easy to walk your talk if your public stance is radically different from your private lifestyle.

The album closer is a solemn Beatles-like ballad titled "Through the Long Night." Joel's double-tracked vocal is reminiscent of the 1960s' vocal duets of John Lennon and Paul McCartney. The composition itself is similar to a McCartney song in nature. The piano, acoustic guitar, and single horn on the instrumental track point to the *Revolver*-era Beatles. Joel's narrator attempts to comfort the person he addresses in the lyrics. Joel will stay and embrace the one who combats the nightmares of the past that prevent peaceful and quiet nights. The curtain is quietly drawn on the mostly rocking *Glass Houses*.

Notes

1. Anthony DeCurtis, "Billy Joel: The Rolling Stone Interview," *Rolling Stone*, November 6, 1986, 80.
2. David Sheff and Victoria Sheff, "Playboy Interview: Billy Joel," *Playboy*, May 1982, 77.
3. Austin Scaggs, "Q and A: The Piano Man Hates to Love Britney's 'Toxic,' Dug the Cream Reunion and Wishes He Never Sang in French," *Rolling Stone*, December 15, 2005, 42.

27

The Police

Zenyatta Mondatta (1980)

James E. Perone

The Police was a band that came out of the British punk rock movement but became famous as part of the postpunk new wave music scene. Although the band enjoyed a run of substantial album and single hits, the 1980 album *Zenyatta Mondatta* arguably captures the Police at the height of their creativity, this despite the fact that the Police reached the height of their popularity in 1983 with the release of *Synchronicity* and the megahit single "Every Breath You Take." However, song for song and as a complete package, *Zenyatta Mondatta* probably is the group's finest work. In fact, All Music Guide critic Greg Prato writes that "*Zenyatta Mondatta* remains one of the finest rock albums of all time."[1] Despite the Police's trademark infectious reggae-influenced pop rock musical style, the album contains surprisingly dark lyrics and dark subject matter. This gives *Zenyatta Mondatta* a depth that has helped it to remain a vibrant and thought-provoking album into the 21st century.

Zenyatta Mondatta opens with its most iconic hit single track, "Don't Stand So Close to Me." Sting—bassist, lead singer, and the band's principal songwriter—sings a tale about a young male schoolteacher who apparently gives in to the charms of one of his female students who has a crush on him. Sting allows the listener to fill in some of the gaps in the story; he never definitively divulges if the two consummate their relationship or if the teacher's feeling of guilt in the last stanza is entirely because of his illicit thoughts and desires. Sting does, however, hint at the teacher's guilt in his reference to "that book by Nabokov," an only partially oblique reference to *Lolita*.

The music and the arrangement of "Don't Stand So Close to Me" are typical of what made the Police so popular in the early 1980s. The melody is strong in the hook department, is singable, and is built in short motives. The main vocal melody and the instrumental tracks feature a significant amount of syncopation and bear the mark of the influence of reggae. The melody of the verses is in the upper part of Sting's distinctive vocal range, and the guitar lines of Andy Summers feature a distinctive electronic processing. While all of these traits are not shared by every piece on *Zenyatta Mondatta*, they are found in abundance on nearly all of the Police's most popular singles.

In "Driven to Tears," Sting presents a picture of hopelessness. In his account of the world around him, people are interested only in celebrities if they are embroiled in some scandal or suffer a tragic death, hunger pervades the Third World, and protest has lost its ability to affect change. The only options that he—or his character—sees are partying to escape reality or giving up and simply being "driven to tears." A strength of a song such as "Driven to Tears" is that it is broad enough in its social commentary that it need not be understood solely in the context of 1980. However, it is not so much the social commentary itself that draws the listener into the song; it is the musical setting. The band begins with an up-tempo groove that features virtuosic percussion playing from Stewart Copeland. Copeland, Sting, and Summers all contribute to the ostinato groove; however, Summers adds sparse added-note chords that suggest the influence of jazz. The band moves between the up-tempo feel and a half-time feel, which breaks up the potential monotony of a piece based primarily on a short ostinato.

"When the World Is Running Down" turns in the direction of disco in its tempo, Sting's bass groove, and Copeland's drum part. Over this groove—which runs throughout the entire three-and-a-half-minute song—Summers adds a strummed added-note chord on the downbeat of each measure. The accompaniment is meant to be highly repetitive and aligns with Sting's lyrics, which dwell on the boredom on daily life.

Turning from the subject of boredom, Sting next addresses an individual who lives life "like a canary in a coal mine." Specifically, Sting accuses this character of suffering from delusions and debilitating fears of danger and illness. The fast pace of the song suggests the character's frantic search for safety from the multitude of dangers that seem to be flying at the person from every direction.

The high number of groove-based songs on *Zenyatta Mondatta* might be symptomatic of the fact that the Police had a limited amount of time in which to record the album because of a previously scheduled concert tour. For the most part, however, the pieces worked very well. The album's fifth track, "Voices in My Head," might not be as much of an unquestioned success. Once again, the piece is based on a one-measure groove. This time, the vocals enter more than one minute into the four-minute piece and then consist only of a background harmonized chant; there is no lead vocal per se. The texture changes from time to time, with Copeland adding cymbal patterns and playing several brief but virtuosic drum solos, Summers adding an overdubbed rhythm guitar figure, and Sting varying his electric bass pattern and adding some shouts. Although

"SO YOU DON'T FORGET ..."

Particularly in the late 1970s and the early 1980s, American television viewers who were channel surfing could not avoid commercials for albums by artists such as Boxcar Willie, Slim Whitman, Nana Mouskouri, and Gheorge Zamfir. Some of these artists had built up strong reputations in the United Kingdom and Europe but were virtually unknown in the United States, while others were relative newcomers to the world stage. The country performer Boxcar Willie (1931–1999) had done some recording and live and television entertaining but came to nationwide attention as a result of direct-to-consumer advertising on television. Like the other entertainers who were hyped on television commercials of the time, Boxcar Willie's commercials most frequently appeared on cable television, which apparently offered a market-to-cost value that was favorable to record companies. Despite the fact that Boxcar Willie's highest charting album reached only No. 27 on the country charts, he become an oft-parodied part of American popular culture for a brief period, nearly completely on the basis of the television commercials for his recordings. The American country performer Slim Whitman (b. 1924) had a significantly stronger pedigree within the music industry than did Boxcar Willie. Whitman's chart success dated to the early 1950s; however, by the late 1950s and beyond, he was more successful as a recording artist in the United Kingdom than he was in the United States. Television commercials for Whitman, which aired in the late 1970s and early 1980s, were notable for their claims that, in England, Slim Whitman was a more successful recording artist than the Beatles. Whitman's style owed much to the 1940s' and early 1950s' focus on the "western" side of country and western and in the United States might have seemed quite dated. Nevertheless, Slim Whitman was pitched, largely on cable television, nearly endlessly. The Greek classically trained vocalist Nana Mouskouri (b. 1934) truly was an international singing star when commercials for her albums aired in the United States. Despite her amazing success in several European markets, however, Mouskouri was not widely known in the United States. The Romanian pan pipes player Gheorge Zamfir (b. 1941), who is known professionally solely by his last name, is another artist who came to the attention of U.S. audiences largely as a result of television advertising. Zamfir's recordings of popular songs helped to popularize an instrument that, at the time, was not widely known to the American public.

the piece as it stands evokes images of the persistent psychological distress that voices in one's head might cause, it also tends to sound like a backing track for which lyrics and a lead vocal melody were not written.

Copeland's song "Bombs Away," while somewhat thin in the lyrics department, presents the listener with images of military generals, attractive female guerrilla fighters, and the general uncertainty that surrounds a time of war.

Copeland name-checks Afghanistan in his lyrics, which suggests that he might have been influenced at least in part with the Soviet Union's war in Afghanistan, which had commenced just before the recording and release of *Zenyatta Mondatta*. Copeland's melody is built from short, almost childlike motives—a similar approach taken by Sting in some of his compositions. The narrow-range sing along tune that this creates combines effectively with the refrain "Bombs away; we're OK" and suggests the cavalier, couldn't-care-less attitude of citizens of a country that is carrying on a bombing campaign in a faraway land. The problem that "Bombs Away" presents is that it can be taken as making light of the gruesome horror of war. It does not seem that was the intent of the song. Rather, it seems as though it was meant to illustrate the lack of connection that the citizenry at large can have if the warfare does not directly impact them.

The next song, Sting's "De Do Do Do, De Da Da Da," is another piece that is open to misinterpretation. In fact, it is quite easy to dismiss it out of hand as an example of the kind of "Silly Love Songs" about which Paul McCartney sang back in the 1970s. In the verses of "De Do Do Do, De Da Da Da," Sting clarifies the point of his song and the point of the title line. If one listens to the totality of the lyrics (and not just the title line), then it becomes clearer that the piece is about the fact that some human emotions—romantic love, for example—sometimes cannot be communicated through verbal "eloquence." The celebration of unadorned human nonverbal communication betrays a romanticism that illustrates why the Police were not fully a part of the generally somewhat jaded British punk movement. This romanticism really is the stuff of British new wave rock. Regardless of whether listeners were drawn to Sting's point or to the catchy title-line refrain, "De Do Do Do, De Da Da Da" made it into the Top 10 of the *Billboard* Hot 100 singles charts.

The Summers instrumental composition "Behind My Camel" was one of two Grammy Award–winning pieces on *Zenyatta Mondatta*, the other being the song "Don't Stand So Close to Me." A pop musician composing and recording an abstract instrumental composition actually was nothing new in 1980; David Bowie's 1977 album *"Heroes"* and Stevie Wonder's 1979 album *Journey through the Secret Life of Plants* both contain several abstract/experimental instrumental tracks. The Summers piece features extensive electronic processing of his electric guitar lines, a heavy four-to-the-bar beat from Copeland, and a dissonant and highly disjunct minor-key melody. In fact, it comes right out of the same school of experimental instrumental rock as David Bowie's work, both on *"Heroes"* and on Bowie's other 1977 album, *Low*.

Sting returns to the upbeat reggae style for which the Police are better known in "Man in a Suitcase." This is a brief song, 2 minutes and 20 seconds long, in which Sting paints the picture of a hectic life on the road. While the upbeat tempo and the extensive use of syncopation help to complete the picture, the song is so short relative to the rest of the album that it sounds like a vignette—a brief character sketch.

"Shadows in the Rain," which is five minutes long, is a much more substantial piece. In this dark song, Sting portrays a man who suffers from paranoid delusions. Sting sings and Summers plays some atonal improvisatory lines, which are in keeping with the meaning of the lyrics but stand in sharp relief to the more pop-oriented songs on the album.

Zenyatta Mondatta concludes with Copeland's composition, "The Other Way of Stopping." This instrumental follows in the footsteps of the surf instrumental recordings of the early 1960s. However, although there are a few references to Dick Dale–style surf music in the arrangement, some of the tone colors, and some of Copeland's drum figures, it is in no way a remake of the style. Copeland's minimalistic melody consists primarily of half notes, and throughout most of the song the real interest lies in the variety of brief fills and phrase-ending flams that Copeland adds on the drums.

The Police reached the peak of their commercial success a few years after the release of *Zenyatta Mondatta*; however, this 1980 release might be the band's best, most creative, and most underappreciated album. The songs mix darkness, intrigue, political and social commentary, and romanticism. It takes careful listening to fully experience the depth of the album, because so many of the songs are so snappy that there is a tendency only to listen on the surface level. The two instrumentals, while not the most memorable tracks on the album, show that the members of the Police were solid players who thought outside the proverbial box of what a commercial pop album was supposed to be.

Note

1. Greg Prato, review of *Zenyatta Mondatta*, All Music Guide, http://allmusic.com/album/zenyatta-mondatta-r15505.

28

Laurie Anderson

Big Science (1982)

James E. Perone

While some critics have dismissed popular music of the 1980s, there were some truly innovative things going on musically in that decade, and they tended to reach wider audiences than might otherwise have been expected. For example, with the advent of music television (e.g., MTV and other related networks) beginning in the early 1980s, viewers across America could hear the experimental music of classically trained minimalists such as Philip Glass and Laurie Anderson in addition to the hits of hair bands. Albums such as Glass's *Glassworks* (1982) and Anderson's *Big Science* (1982), which might have been expected to have been purchased by fans of the classical avant-garde, made the pop charts. Videos for tracks from both albums were part of the regular rotation of music television networks of the time. One of the tracks from the Anderson album, "O Superman," had been released in 1981 as a single in the United Kingdom and became an unlikely Top 10 hit. *Big Science*, perhaps better than any other album, reflects the New York City avant-garde loft performance art scene of the day and is as challenging, eerie, and evocative in the 21st century as it was in 1982.

The 1983 independent film *Liquid Sky* parodied the postpunk New York performance art scene. Scenes in which a spike-haired young woman half sung and half spoke spacey, minimalistic, repetitive text accompanied by a rhythm machine would seem to have taken their inspiration directly from Anderson. Unlike the performance art of the character in *Liquid Sky*, however, Anderson's compositions, arrangements, and performances on *Big Science* are rich in lyrical imagery, humor, and meaning that speak well beyond the period; her music, too, exhibits a sophisticated level of detail that goes beyond the work of some of her contemporaries and especially beyond that of the apparent *Liquid Sky* parody. *Big Science* not only captures the spirit of its time and place but also speaks to the concept of American and personal identity in a way that is unlike most recorded work of the past or present. While Anderson's use of vocoder, Farfisa organ, and ambient electronics and her additive poetic style might seem quaint and maybe somewhat dated to later audiences, it is in part the home-spun, contemplative (yet never entirely serious) quality of *Big Science* (as well as its celebration of the mundane) that makes it just as fascinating in the 21st century as it was in 1982.

The album begins with "From the Air," a composition in which the music is based on a short one-measure riff in the saxophones, clarinet, and keyboards. Over the course of the piece, Anderson adds sustained synthesizer lines over the C minor riff. These added tones resolve from the second scale step back down to C. This gives the piece a feeling of recurring harmonic resolution, despite the fact that the riff itself almost entirely just makes use of the C minor triad. As is customary in Anderson's work, the additive nature of the piece also finds the riff itself expanded through the use of overdubs. Over this gradually expanding instrumental accompaniment, Anderson recites her text. She begins by identifying herself as the captain of an airplane that is going to attempt a risky crash landing. The ominous message, accompanied by the minor-key riff, takes an unexpected turn as Anderson moves from giving entirely appropriate instructions for the scenario to giving instructions such as "Put your hands on your hips" with a chuckle. Suddenly her character becomes not so much the real captain of a doomed airliner but more of a puppeteer pulling the strings of a marionette. Eventually Anderson's character tells her passengers to jump out of the plane, because no one is piloting it. Depending upon one's political beliefs, it might be tempting for some listeners to read this as a commentary on the United States early in the Reagan era. However, this would limit "From the Air" to a piece that only speaks for its time. Anderson's poetry is perhaps best read as a questioning of blind obedience to authority figures and a suggestion that situations are not necessarily what they appear to be on the surface. Taken in that light, the piece remains vital.

In the years since the release of "From the Air," the American public has wit-nessed and experienced a number of air travel–related tragedies that involved pilots becoming incapacitated. For example, in 1999 some Americans followed ongoing media coverage of the doomed small jet in which professional golfer Payne Stewart, three fellow passengers, and two pilots apparently died shortly after takeoff from lack of oxygen, only to fly hundreds of miles, from Florida to South Dakota, before the plane finally crashed when it ran out of fuel. Ander-son's composition, however, took on an especially eerie feel after the September 11, 2001, terrorist attacks. When Anderson says at the end of the piece, "This is the time, and this is the record of the time," such indelible disasters cannot help but be recalled.

Although Anderson frequently uses non sequiturs, the album's title track is perhaps as good an example as any of her use of the technique. The piece begins with a wolf howl, after which Anderson sings "Coo, coo, it's cold outside." After this suggestion of a desolate location, possibly in the American Southwest, Anderson portrays two characters, the first of whom asks for directions to an unnamed town and the second of whom provides the answer. The answer comes in the form of directions that refer to the locations where a new shopping mall, a new freeway, a new bank, and a new sports facility are planned. Of course, the joke is that none of these things yet exist—they are just in the planning stages. The meat behind these absurdist directions is not just the fact that the stranger to the area will never find her way to town (although she is unlikely to do so, given these instructions) but also that the directions speak to the unbridled expansion of some towns and cities of the time, more specifically the intrusion of suburbs into pristine areas.

The lure of such expanding cities and towns is confirmed when Anderson sings the phrase "Golden cities, golden towns." Her text also includes the phrase "Every man for himself," which suggests that the allure of these "golden cities" is not in the human connections they provide but rather in the glamour of the commercial opportunities they provide. The people in Anderson's scenario at first pay homage to their "golden cities" by singing "Hallelujah," to which Anderson tacks on "Yodellayheehoo." This at once mocks the serious "Hallelujah" that is sung to the deity of the "golden city," with its massive income-producing promise; however, it also reinforces the southwestern motif of the composition. Anderson then sings "Hallelujah" to "Big Science." Her emphasis on synthesizer and electronic sound manipulation shifts the focus from the expanding city to the allure of technology. Again, she adds the "Yodellayheehoo." As is the case with her compositions throughout *Big Science*, Anderson does not question blind adherence to technology or commercialism and consumerism in direct terms. Instead, her use of non sequiturs and (in this composition) mournful electronic music provide the questions or at the very least seem to be designed to encourage the listener to question the stereotypical American Dream.

In the brief song "Sweaters," Anderson sings in an intentionally edgy, grating voice—not unlike that used by performance artist Yoko Ono on some of her recordings from the late 1960s—that she no longer loves her former lover's mouth, eyes, or the color of his sweaters. The piece does not fit in particularly well with the album's focus on technology, adherence to authority, and the bright and dark sides of the American Dream; however, it is notable for a spirited blues/rock bagpipe solo by Rufus Harley.

The even shorter composition "Walking & Falling" (2 minutes and 10 seconds long) features Anderson's quiet, slowly evolving ambient electronic sounds supporting her slow space-filled recitation. Her text begins with a brief exploration of the idea of wanting someone, looking for that person, but not

AUDIOPHILE PRESSINGS

In the late 1970s and early 1980s—the predigital pre-CD days—listeners who wanted the absolute best in sound reproduction purchased vinyl albums produced by several companies that went back to the original master tapes, mastered them at half speed in order to preserve the highest possible audio fidelity, and pressed their albums on special ultraquality vinyl. In the United States, perhaps the most highly regarded company was Mobile Fidelity Sound Lab. Consumers of the era could purchase albums such as the Beatles' *Abbey Road*, Pink Floyd's *The Dark Side of the Moon*, Kenny Rogers' *Greatest Hits* or a wide variety of classical music that frankly sounded clearer, more intimate, and more true than the original releases. While these reissues cost more than the regular pressings, the vinyl albums were less susceptible to scratches, the frequency range was wider, and all in all the sound quality was better than anything else imaginable. Cassette tapes, too, received similar treatment at the time, with special remastering to cassette and special chromium dioxide tape and equalization that maximized the audio possibilities for that more portable medium. It seemed that serious audiophiles had everything that they needed until the dawn of the age of digital remastering and the CD. Since the start of the early 1980s' CD era, companies such as Mobile Fidelity have turned to reissuing albums on special higher-quality discs. Interestingly, the 21st century has seen a return to interest in high-quality vinyl reissues and new releases.

finding him. Because Anderson goes no further, this section of the text takes on a Zen-like state-of-being feeling; she allows the listener to try to figure out the point of her statements. In the second section, which is lengthier, she observes that the act of walking is really the act of controlled falling. It is a glorification of the mundane that connects conceptually to the pop art of the 1950s and 1960s, just as it connects to the 21st-century world of mundane observations on Twitter.

Because it begins with an unaccompanied spoken introduction, "Born, Never Asked" shares a connection with "Walking & Falling." In "Born, Never Asked," however, Anderson's text sets a scene: "a large room, full of people." She tells the listener that it is a diverse group of people and implies that they just happened to come to this place by chance at approximately the same time. Apparently the room in which they gather contains a curtain, because each person asks himself or herself, "what is behind that curtain?" On the surface, this scenario might seem to be another example of simply glorifying the mundane. In the context of the work's time, however, the strange intersection of randomness and structure becomes the more important focus. *Big Science* was issued the same year as Benoit Mandelbrot's classic book *The Fractal Geometry of Nature.*[1] The 1980s' fascination with the relationships between chance and tight structure perhaps reached a high point in 1987 with the release of James Gleick's best-selling book *Chaos: Making a New Science*,[2] but certainly the concept was in the air at the time of the major label release of *Big Science*.

The bulk of "Born, Never Asked," however, is instrumental. Harmonically, Anderson uses an oscillation between a G minor triad and an F major triad. This pairing of harmonies is inherently vague within the traditional Western tonal system. Because of the hypermetrical placement of the chords and because of the use of a repeated rhythmic pattern on the pitch G (the ostinato pattern on G is sounded beneath both chords), the piece seems to be in G minor. Anderson's use of the F major chord, though, gives the piece a modal feel. The marimba rhythmic pattern (the "and" of beat two, beat three, the "and" of four, and beat one) is reinforced by an identical pattern in hand claps. Over this ostinato, Anderson plays multitracked violins. In the spirit of the minimalistic school of composition, the violin parts (they play in harmony) are highly repetitive on the surface; however, Anderson provides slight variation with each repetition. Because Anderson's approach to minimalism is considerably sparser than that of composers such as Terry Riley, Steve Reich, and Philip Glass, a piece such as "Born, Never Asked" is striking as a Zen-like state-of-being musical expression.

Of all of Laurie Anderson's work, she is still primarily remembered for "O Superman," the lengthy composition that made the unexpected leap to the singles charts in the United Kingdom after its independent label release in 1975. The piece begins with a repeated quarter-note pulse, which consists of Anderson singing "ha" on the pitch C. On the surface, this is reminiscent of perhaps the first masterpiece of minimalism: Terry Riley's *In C*. In Riley's 1964 composition, however, the double-timed pulse is played on the highest C on the piano keyboard, and C is the opening tonal reference point of the composition. When Anderson enters on her heavily electronically processed vocal melody, she establishes the tonal center as A flat major. The melody itself is not the focal point of the piece: it consists of short narrow-range phrases but is catchy. The real meat of the music is in the ever-evolving instrumental accompaniment, with Anderson's expansion of the texture to include a super–low-range synthesized bass close to the end of the song, an especially dramatic structural point. Her text includes numerous references to American culture of the day, such as the question "Smoking, or non-smoking?" Including references to the commercial airline industry, telephone answering machines, and from-the-script utterances from flight attendants and others, the piece juxtaposes the scripted and technology-based with the human (e.g., "Hi, mom."). Anderson does not analyze this intersection of human and machine or go into the ramifications of the technology of the time. Instead, she paints impressions of an eerie world in which the listener probably feels some unexplainable unease about the inherent conflicts between the human and the electronic. This is perhaps most likely to happen when the communications between mother and daughter seem to get lost in the answering machine.

While some of Anderson's text seems to celebrate the mundane by repeating expressions commonly heard around America at the time (e.g., "Smoking, or non-smoking" and "Hi, mom"), the text "Here come the planes; they're American planes" has a wider connotation. In the last iteration of this text, Anderson's voice suggests something vaguely ominous about the arrival of the planes; this is supported by a more mysterious synthesizer accompaniment supporting her singing. In the context of the time, this could be understood as a reference to some of the early saber rattling of the Reagan administration. The lines take on an even more ominous tone in the post-9/11 world: two of the four jets that were hijacked by terrorists on September 11, 2001, were owned by American Airlines, and, of course, all four planes were "American planes," in the sense that they were owned by American companies.

In "Example #22," Anderson sings in her best Yoko Ono imitation over a German spoken text about paranormal occurrences. On one level, Anderson's sung text focuses on possessiveness in relationships and about the intersections of consumerism and human relationships. She sings in an edgy voice, "Honey, you're my one and only, so pay me what you owe me." Anderson's use of Latin, English, and German reinforces a concept that comes directly from her text: "I don't understand the languages. I hear only your sound." In other words, what is said is not as important as how it is said. Anderson's use of repetition, variation, and canon in the multitracked flute, piccolo, clarinet, and saxophone parts stands in sharp relief to the harshness of the singing style that she adopts. The dissonance that the conflicts between vocal and instrumental form, style, and timbre create can also cause the listener to question whether the most important messages are those that come from words themselves or from the way in which words are conveyed.

The background rhythm pattern in the marimba and hand claps of "Let X=X" is drawn from that of "Born, Never Asked." In "Let X=X," however, Anderson achieves a major mode feel by means of her oscillations between a C major chord and an F major chord. Ordinarily, an oscillation between these two harmonies would be quite vague—both chords are standard frequently used harmonies both in the key of F major and in the key of C major. Anderson adds to the tonal vagueness by including a rhythmic pattern in the marimba that drones the pitch G throughout the piece. Because of the metrical placement of the chords on C and F, F seems as though it should be the tonal center; however, any sense of C resolving to F is undermined at every turn by the marimba's reiterations of G. Anderson's text reinforces this feeling of lack of resolution. At the beginning of the piece, her character seemingly cannot enter a relationship with any man except for the stereotype of a loser ("a hat check clerk at an ice rink"). At the end of the piece, her character feels like she is "in a burning building" and has to leave, with the implication being that she cannot leave. She is locked into a life filled with emotional/relational unfulfillment. Also of note in the piece is the use of hocket in the multitracked trombone parts, which on a slow-paced stripped-down level is somewhat reminiscent of the rhythmic interplay between the hand clappers in Steve Reich's earlier minimalistic classic, "Clapping Music."

"Let X = X" makes a direct segue into "It Tango," a composition that retains the same background rhythmic riff. Here, the pitched instruments focus on a slow oscillation between G and F over a C bass, which offers its own feeling of incomplete resolution. Whatever feeling of unease the sense of somewhat unfulfilled harmonic progression might cause, this feeling aligns with the text, which deals with a couple's failure to communicate. In the late 1970s and early 1980s a number of lyricists were using an additive approach to constructing lines of text, such that several varying meanings might emerge as more and more words are added to the sentences. Anderson and Elvis Costello are perhaps the most notable such lyricists of the period. Anderson's use of the technique on *Big Science* largely is limited to "It Tango," but the technique is so pervasive in the composition (except for the last two lines of the piece, which sum up the couple's communications failures) that it would be impossible to fully document without printing the complete text. However, as is also the case with the similarly constructed lyrics of Costello, it is not nearly as effective to read the text as it is to hear the construction and the multiple evolving meanings that emerge. This is especially true because Anderson relies heavily on homophones and heterographs to achieve the evolving meanings.

Laurie Anderson's range of expression, which runs the gamut from taciturn to emotionally charged, as well as her sparse, eerie musical settings and her exploration of the intersections of humanity and technology both reflect the early 1980s and speak to a later time in which technology plays an even greater role in daily life. It is a challenge for listeners who are used to conventional pop music; however, it is a challenge that is worth stretching one's ears.

Notes

1. Benoit Mandelbrot, *The Fractal Geometry of Nature* (San Francisco: W. H. Freeman, 1982).
2. James Gleick, *Chaos: Making a New Science* (New York: Viking, 1987).

29

Michael Jackson

Thriller (1982)

James E. Perone

If any single performer and any single album can be said to represent 1980s'
pop, then a good argument can be made for Michael Jackson and his 1982
release *Thriller*. The album contained high-energy funk, rock, ballads, soul, and
even made–for–Top 40 middle-of-the-road pop. Seven of the tracks were hits
as singles, and the album itself sold tens of millions of copies during its initial run. Eventually *Thriller* became the biggest-selling album in history. Music
videos were produced for the most commercially successful single tracks, and
these Michael Jackson videos virtually defined the genre and were staples of
MTV in the first half of the 1980s. The lyrics are sometimes fun, sometimes
dark, and sometimes silly but always engaging, and the music and arrangements are filled with hooks that remain fresh and catchy nearly three decades
after *Thriller*'s release. To the extent that Jackson really was the King of Pop in
the 1980s, then this is the album that crowned him thusly.

Thriller begins with Jackson's high-energy composition "Wanna Be Startin'
Somethin'." The lyrics concern Jackson's "baby" and rumors that surround her,
attempts that various people make "to start [his] baby cryin'." All-in-all, however, the real theme is that of stardom and dealing with it. As Jackson sings
"You're stuck in the middle," the listener—and especially the listener who considers Jackson's post-*Thriller* life, trials, tribulations, and death—can be struck
with the fact that even coming out of success as a child star and on the edge of
superstardom and turning into a pop culture icon, Jackson saw that stardom
was not necessarily all that it was cracked up to be. Be that as it may, the real
meat of the song is not even in the lyrics: it is in the arrangement and copro-
duction by Quincy Jones and Jackson and in Jackson's performance. Jackson's

vocals are rhythmically alive with guttural explosions absolutely made for the recording studio. Using nonverbal vocalizations in recorded performances in itself was nothing new in the soul/R&B world: James Brown was doing it in the 1950s, and Stevie Wonder used the studio to emphasize nonverbal vocal interjections in the funk songs he wrote, sang, and produced in the first half of the 1970s (e.g., "Living for the City"). Jackson, however, placed even more emphasis on using his voice almost as a percussion instrument in between lines of text. This is one aspect of his performance style that shines on all of the faster tracks on *Thriller.* And on "Wanna Be Startin' Somethin'," the overall impact does not come solely from Jackson: the rhythm section and the horn section also drive the piece along so that the entire song *becomes* the frantic lifestyle of the pop star.

British songwriter Rod Temperton supplied three songs for *Thriller*, including the album's title track. The first Temperton song to appear, however, is "Baby Be Mine." The piece itself is a fairly conventional love song, with some unexpected harmonic resolutions at the conclusions of the verses that are reminiscent of the earlier work of Stevie Wonder. While Jackson shows that he was a convincing singer of this type of midtempo material, the performance tends to pale in comparison to his work on funkier songs with less conventional lyrics and on slow ballads.

Curiously, Jackson's own compositions for this album run the gamut from the syrupy to the edgy. The best-known example from the entire Jackson canon is "The Girl Is Mine," a song on which he duets with Paul McCartney. The concept—putting two of the great male song stylists of the 1960s–1980s together for a piece about competition for the attentions of a woman—might seem to be a guaranteed success. In the commercial sense, it was. "The Girl Is Mine" was an enormously popular Top 40 radio staple of the day. However, the song and the performance are somewhat mixed in artistic merits. For one thing, Jackson's text tends to reduce the woman over whom Jackson and McCartney are in competition to the level of a commodity. This singing is, as one might expect from two expert pop singers, strong throughout; however, the spoken dialogue and especially Jackson's "I'm a lover, not a fighter" are real groaners.

Rod Temperton's "Thriller" stands in sharp contrast to the preceding Jackson and McCartney ballad performance. The piece is a musical encapsulation of scenes from movie thrillers, counterpointed with the suggestion that Jackson's character can provide his movie date with more of a "thriller night" than that which they enjoy in the cinema. Actor Vincent Price, the star of many a thriller throughout his long career, appears as a guest "rapper" and delivers a text that speaks of ghouls, ghosts, hell, creatures, and doom—all the stuff of B-movies. Unfortunately, the piece has not aged particularly well. The heavy use of synthesizers practically screams "1980s," and the Price performance tends today to sound more silly than dark and sinister. Perhaps the main reason that the song itself has not aged well, however, is that the video for the song became

THE AGE OF THE MUSIC VIDEO

The beginning of the 1980s saw the advent of music television. Originally limited to cable television, such networks as MTV, VH1, and others played music videos of the latest hits. The concept of promoting singles through short films was not entirely new: even well-established artists such as the Beatles were producing promotional films in the 1960s. Some promotional films and early music videos, though, consisted of little more than the artists miming (or lip-synching) along with the recording. The concept of the music video grew to a full-fledged medium that more fully integrated the music and video imagery. In the early 1980s, however, there were relatively few music videos. Therefore, networks such as MTV worked experimental music videos from such artists as Laurie Anderson and Philip Glass into their rotation. The medium seemed to be tailor-made for some of the quirky new wave groups of the early 1980s, such as the B-52's, Talking Heads, and Devo. However, dance-oriented artists such as Michael Jackson and Madonna took the medium to new heights and popularity. In fact, it can be argued that the videos from such albums as Jackson's *Thriller* and Madonna's *Like a Virgin* and *Like a Prayer* were as well known as the songs themselves. And, in fact, the most iconic music videos of the 1980s tended to shape viewers' understandings of the meanings of the songs.

so popular and so deeply etched into the memory of fans who experienced "Thriller" when it was originally released that just listening to the song itself can give the impression that something is missing.

Although "Wanna Be Startin' Somethin'" is a potent funk track and although "The Girl Is Mine" was all over the radio airwaves in the early 1980s, the real meat of *Thriller* is found on side two of the original vinyl release. The second side begins with one of Michael Jackson's most iconic compositions and performances: "Beat It." Here, Jackson takes on the persona of a street fighter who warns another to "just beat it." It is a considerably edgier take on his earlier "I'm a lover, not a fighter" statement in "The Girl Is Mine," and the arrangement and the performance break free of traditional musical boundaries. Much like some of Prince's work from the same time period, "Beat It" is part funk, part new wave rock with a touch of pop-metal. Whereas Prince, a singer-songwriter and multi-instrumentalist, achieved his mixture of rock and funk in part with his virtuosic electric guitar playing, Jackson brought in Eddie Van Halen for the guitar solo on "Beat It." That "Beat It" quickly became an iconic piece of American popular culture is evidenced by the fact that Weird Al Yankovic's parody, "Eat It," became one of the best-remembered and most successful comedy singles ever. The video that was produced for "Beat It" was one of Jackson's best and was in heavy rotation on music television networks in the early 1980s. When Jackson died in 2009, the "Beat It" video accompanied numerous television news reports on the singer's demise.

Perhaps there is no scientific evidence to back this up, but it may be the case that many listeners think of Michael Jackson as a songwriter who achieved more in the way of overall effect than as a writer of melodies, harmonies, arrangements, and lyrics. In other words, the conventional wisdom might be that the whole is always significantly more important than the sum of its parts. To a large extent, "Beat It" is one example. The lyrical sentiments and the tune mean far less than the overall dramatic impact of the performance and the recording. With the song "Billie Jean," however, Jackson balanced overall danceable sonic impact and energetic rhythmically incisive singing with darker, deeper lyrics than those of his other *Thriller*-era compositions.

In "Billie Jean," Jackson begins by describing a girl whom he sees dancing "on the floor in the round." His description of her as a "queen from a movie scene" reflects back to the film-oriented fantasy world of the song "Thriller"; however, this girl is very real. Jackson's character dreams of being "the one" who ends up dancing with her. In the second stanza, Jackson's character becomes the envy of the other men in the club because he is the one with whom Billie Jean dances. Jackson's vocal performance and the musical setting in the bridge section take on a darker, more troubling tone. Here, he tells the listener that people, including his mother, have warned him that he should not "go around breaking young girls' hearts" and that he should be careful who he "loves" (apparently, in the physical sense). He succumbs, though, to the desirability of Billie Jean and the smell of her "sweet perfume." Eventually it is revealed that Billie Jean claims that Jackson's character has fathered a child with her, apparently after their one-night stand. Despite the fact that Jackson's character sees a photo of the baby and recognizes that the child's eyes are "just like mine," he remains in denial. Ultimately the question that remains at the end of the song is this: Is Jackson's character the father of the child, or did Billie Jean (a girl who "is in demand") simply pin paternity on him because he broke her heart? The openness of the song is part of its success. It can be understood as at once an indictment of unprotected sexual intercourse, an indictment of men who break women's hearts, and an indictment of women who use lies about sex and paternity to get even, depending on how the listener chooses to hear it.

The musical setting of "Billie Jean" is sparse, at least compared with the rest of the tracks on *Thriller*. This tends to direct the listener in the direction of Jackson's voice, which is especially important given their relative importance. Curiously, the album's liner notes credit Jackson with the vocal, rhythm, and synthesizer arrangement, as opposed to coproducer Quincy Jones. The strings, arranged by Jeremy Lubbock, generally play unison interjections. Of all of Jackson's recordings of the early 1980s, the period of his greatest success and popularity, this is perhaps the best example of his use of vocables (nontext syllables and utterances) to turn his voice into both a melodic and a sort of percussion instrument. Although the technique became a stereotypical part of the Jackson style, here it works effectively: it gives his story energy and emotion, and the interjections are timed so as to give the piece a rhythmic vitality that transcends the moderate tempo. Interestingly, "Beat It" and "Billie Jean," Jackson's *Thriller* compositions that find him portraying characters of the street, share a melodic motive in the verses, in which emphasis is placed on scale step five.

The next song, the Jeff Porcaro and John Bettis song "Human Nature," was another successful *Thriller* track when it was released as a single. Unlike its companions, though, "Human Nature" is a ballad. A somewhat unusual love song, the piece finds Jackson telling a female stranger that if her friends ask why he stares at her or why he manages to find a reason and a way to brush up against her, she should tell them "that it's human nature." The text ends with Jackson singing that he is "dreaming of the street," which connects the piece to the clearly urban landscape of "Thriller," "Beat It," and "Billie Jean."

The next track, "P.Y.T. (Pretty Young Thing)" is a fairly straightforward dance track by James Ingram and Quincy Jones. It enjoyed commercial success as a single at the time but is not nearly as distinctive as the other hits, so it has not aged as well. The upbeat tempo and synthesizer licks are somewhat reminiscent of funk stylistic Rick James, but his music, too, has not survived particularly well into the 21st century.

To conclude one of the best-selling albums of all time, Jackson turns to Rod Temperton's "The Lady in My Life." While all of the tracks on *Thriller* make at least some use of synthesizers, "The Lady in My Life" as a production sounds particularly dated because of the abundance of electronic instruments. This is highly unfortunate, because Michael Jackson provides a solid vocal performance in which he shows that although up-tempo rock/funk songs were his drawing card, he could tackle an R&B love ballad as well.

Unlike the type of movie alluded to in the title of the album, *Thriller* ends on a gentle note. It contains, however, some of the most iconic performances that Michael Jackson ever recorded, including "Billie Jean," "Beat It," "Wanna Be Startin' Somethin'," and "Human Nature." Significantly, of those four songs, Jackson wrote three. While some aspects of *Thriller* have not aged particularly well over the nearly three decades that have passed since its release (particularly the title track and the overreliance on dated-sounding synthesizers on a couple of other tracks), it remains historically significant in having propelled Michael Jackson into orbit as a superstar, and the best tracks remain vital today.

30

Bruce Springsteen

Nebraska (1982)

Rob Kirkpatrick

In 2004, author Tennessee Jones published *Deliver Me from Nowhere*, a collection of 10 short stories that together comprise a song-for-song interpretation of Bruce Springsteen's 1982 album *Nebraska*. Although the concept seems forced and smacks of fan-fiction fanaticism, Jones's stories aren't bad. (The book seems to have opened the door for a new genre of Springsteen-inspired fiction, such as *Meeting across the River: Stories Inspired by the Haunting Bruce Springsteen Song*, edited by Jessica Kaye and Richard J. Brewer.) The *Deliver Me from Nowhere* collection came four years after Sub-Pop Records, an independent label known more for alternative bands such as Soundgarden and the Shins, released *Badlands: A Tribute to Bruce Springsteen's Nebraska*, featuring such artists as Dar Williams, Ani DiFranco, Son Volt, Ben Harper, Aimee Mann, Michael Penn, and Johnny Cash.

Today, *Nebraska* is considered a classic. But back at the time of the album's release in 1982, even longtime dedicated fans had been ill-prepared for Springsteen's sidetrack from rock and roll.

After the conclusion of the *River* tour, Springsteen returned to New Jersey to plan his next record. As he describes in *Songs*, he had grown weary of spending so much time and energy in the recording studio, where he found the atmosphere "sterile and isolating" and where he "rarely got the right group of songs" he wanted "without wasting a lot of time and expense." Looking for a way to make the process less arduous and more economical, he decided that he wanted to not only write but also hear any new material before he took it into the studio again.[1]

In December 1981 he called his guitar tech, Mike Batlan, and discussed this new process. Batlan brought a four-track Tech tape machine to Springsteen's house in Colts Neck. There, Springsteen sat in a chair with an acoustic guitar and worked through Spartan versions of new songs, singing/playing into two microphones. After laying down these two tracks he then added harmony vocals, "hit a tambourine," or added a second guitar line, using the remaining two available recording tracks.[2]

Springsteen thought that he was merely recording demo tracks for a new album to be recorded with the E Street Band. But the nature of these new songs was distinct. As he describes in *Songs*, the new songs "tapped into white gospel and early Appalachian music, as well as the blues." Such artists as Robert Johnson and John Lee Hooker—artists whose records "sounded so good with the lights out"—provided guiding influences, as did the folk balladry of Woody Guthrie. As Springsteen remembers, "I wanted to let the listener hear the characters think, to get inside their heads, so you could hear and feel their thoughts, their choices."[3]

Springsteen sent a cassette tape of his 15 favorite songs from the Colts Neck sessions to Jon Landau, along with two notebook pages of handwritten commentary. The lineup of songs on the tape was as follows:

1. "Bye Bye Johnny"
2. "Starkweather (Nebraska)"
3. "Atlantic City"
4. "Mansion on the Hill"
5. "Born in the U.S.A."
6. "Johnny 99"
7. "Downbound Train"
8. "Losin' Kind"
9. "State Trooper"
10. "Used Cars"
11. "Wanda (Open All Night)"
12. "Child Bride"
13. "Pink Cadillac"
14. "Highway Patrolman"
15. "Reason to Believe"

Soon after, Springsteen gathered the E Street Band in the studio to record band versions of the songs. But something was different about these songs; they didn't seem to lend themselves to full-band electric arrangements. Although they were larger in instrumentation and volume, Springsteen judged these amped-up versions to be inferior to the original acoustic versions recorded as demos. He tried recording the songs by himself in the studio, but even these solo arrangements didn't capture the stark ambience of the Colts Neck demo tape.

At this point, he tabled these tracks and recorded some other new material with the band. These newer songs definitely *were* rock songs, and they pointed toward the possible release of a new album with the E Street Band. It was rumored that Springsteen's next album would be titled *Murder, Incorporated*, named after a hard-driving new song about a man who stands up to organized crime, only to be killed in the final verse. (More generally, "Murder, Incorporated" explored paranoia in the face of indomitable social forces, the same territory as "Roulette.")

While Springsteen kept working with the band on a growing list of new rock-and-roll songs, he remained committed to the songs that he had written alone in New Jersey, which he considered "some of my strongest songs."[4] He selected 9 songs from the demo tape that he felt held together best as a group. He also added one more, a very personal song called "My Father's House." These 10 tracks were released as the album *Nebraska* on September 20, 1982.

The publication of Jones's *Deliver Me from Nowhere* brought the album's literary influences full circle. Sitting in his rented house in Colts Neck, New Jersey, prior to recording the material that would comprise the album, Springsteen had been reading Flannery O'Connor. (Stephen Metcalf is just one writer who suggests that Jon Landau was the one feeding Springsteen an "American Studies syllabus heavy on John Ford, Steinbeck, and Flannery O'Connor.")[5] A Catholic writer in the southern Gothic vein, O'Connor had captured Springsteen's imagination after he saw John Huston's 1979 film adaptation of her novel *Wise Blood*. The influence of O'Connor on Springsteen can be seen in a number of instances. For one, he used the title of two O'Connor short stories, "The River" and "A Good Man Is Hard to Find," for songs (the latter an unreleased song that surfaced on *Tracks*). As Geoffrey Himes observes, Springsteen learned from O'Connor the "value of plainspoken language." Himes argues that "It was better to describe young men out on the weekend in language they themselves might use . . . than to describe them in kind of high-falutin' language never heard in a barroom—as he does on 'Born to Run.'"[6] O'Connor's stories also served as a model of narrative economy for Springsteen. "They were a big revelation. She got to the heart of some part of meanness that she never spelled out, because if she spelled it out you wouldn't be getting it," he told Will Percy—the nephew of Walker Percy, another Catholic author in whom Springsteen had become interested—in 1995. "In small detail—the slow twirling of a baton, the twisting of a ring on a finger—they found their character."[7]

O'Connor's Catholicism, an uncommon faith among Southerners, held additional interest for Springsteen. O'Connor's view of Catholicism was a complex one. As Himes summarizes, "She retained an unwavering faith in Christian redemption, but nearly every story she wrote tested that faith against examples of crime, cruelty, delusion and failure of every kind."[8] Springsteen stated that "Her stories reminded me of the unknowability of God and contained a dark spirituality that resonated with my own feelings at the time."[9]

This "unknowability of God" is a theme with which O'Connor dealt in a number of her stories. In "The River," the child narrator mistakes the metaphor of river baptism with literal reality and drowns while trying to find God for himself:

The river wouldn't have him. He tried again and came up, choking. This was the way it had been when the preacher held him under—he had had to fight with something that pushed him back in the face. He stopped and thought suddenly: it's another joke, it's just another joke! He thought how far he had come for nothing and he began to hit and splash and kick the filthy river. . . . He plunged under once and this time, the waiting current caught him like a long gentle hand and pulled him swiftly forward and down.[10]

Likewise, in "Good Country People" Hulga tells a con man that "We are all damned . . . but some of us have taken off our blindfolds and see that there's nothing to see. It's a kind of salvation."[11]

In "A Good Man Is Hard to Find," the family comes to a fateful end after meeting a killer known as The Misfit. After he has the rest of her family shot—a fate that she herself seals by unwisely identifying The Misfit—she tries to appeal to him in Jesus's name, but

"Jesus was the only One that ever raised the dead," The Misfit continued, "and He shouldn't have done it. He thrown everything off balance. If He did what He said, then it's nothing for you to do but throw away everything and follow Him, and if He didn't, then it's nothing for you to do but enjoy the few minutes you got left the best way you can—by killing somebody or burning down his house or doing some other meanness to him. No pleasure but meanness," he said and his voice had become almost a snarl.

Desperately grasping at straws, she denies Christ, saying that "Maybe he didn't raise the dead."[12]

"I wasn't there so I can't say He didn't," The Misfit said. "I wisht I had of been there," he said, hitting ground with his fist. "It ain't right that I wasn't there because if I had of been there I would have known. Listen lady," he said in a high voice, "if I had of been there I would of known and I wouldn't be like I am now."[13]

Himes adds that "One of the great devices employed by O'Connor and such fellow Southern writers as William Faulkner and Eudora Welty was to tell stories through the eyes of a child." As Himes points out, children serve a unique purpose within fictional worlds because, as narrators, they observe but don't always understand what happens in front of them—often leaving it up to the reader to interpret the events narrated, to "fill in the missing information."[14]

As Springsteen wrote songs in Colts Neck, he became interested in the perspective of childhood. He explains in *Songs* that the songs from this period were "connected" to his childhood more so than any other record to that point,

THE COMPACT DISC

After development in the 1970s, the audio compact disc (CD) appeared on the scene in the early 1980s. The CD promised greater audio fidelity than vinyl records, cassette tapes, and eight-track tapes. While some early conversions of analog recordings into the digital format required for reproduction on CDs sounded thin and tinny to some listeners, as the format matured so did the richness of the sound and, in particular, full bass response. The CD also offered the opportunity to make longer albums, since the maximum amount of high-quality digital audio information that could be encoded on a disc amounted to approximately an hour's worth of music. As the 1980s moved into the 1990s, consumers seemed to expect longer albums because of the format's capabilities and because gradually albums were being released less frequently on vinyl. Artists who were used to the temporal limitations of vinyl LPs dealt with the new technology in various ways. Some artists included additional songs on their albums, some expanded rhythmic groove sections in their music so that their songs were longer in duration, and some expanded their song forms. From the packaging standpoint and from the visual standpoint, the CD was a mixed blessing: the jewel boxes in which CDs were sold required a significantly greater amount of plastic, and the cover art of reissues and new recordings had considerably less impact than that of the 12-inch vinyl albums of the past. On the other hand, CD booklets made it possible to include song lyrics as well as small photographs, illustrations, and so on. Some people predicted the demise of the CD, especially at the end of the 1990s when the downloading of audio files started to become more widespread; however, even in the second decade of the 21st century—when various legitimate download and streaming audio services are patronized by millions of consumers—the CD continues to offer information, photographs, and a tangible product that the consumer can truly own that so far has not been replaced by more recent technology.

not just in narration but in the "tone of the music." The Colts Neck songs would show the influence of these childhood memories. Three songs, "Mansion on the Hill," "Used Cars," and "My Father's House," were all told from a child's perspective, all, as Springsteen assessed, "stories that came directly out of my experience with my family."[15]

"Mansion on the Hill" is another song with a title that Springsteen borrowed from Hank Williams. In *A Race of Singers*, Bryan Garman notes that Williams's song describes a "romantic relationship thwarted by class distinctions."[16] Springsteen's song is deceivingly complex, and it deals with class distinctions, though in a different context. The lyrics describe a mansion that both rises above and looms over the rest of the town. The narrator remembers parking with his father and looking up at the mansion; in summers, he and his sister hid in cornfields and listened to rich people having fun at parties inside the house.

In "Used Cars," the singer remembers the family's purchase of a used car and, more importantly, the humbling nature of the experience. The salesman stares at the father's hands, undoubtedly worn from years of manual labor that has nevertheless left him with little income. (The salesman says that he wishes he could give the family a break on the car's price.) After buying the car, the "neighbors come from near and far" to see the family drive in their "brand new used car." The paradoxical description of the car hints at the complexity of the scenario: the mix of pride felt in purchasing an automobile and shame at having the purchase of a used car be a celebratory moment. Shame triumphs over the singer, whom we can picture cringing as he walks alone and hears his little sister blowing the horn of the car, "The sounds echoin' all down Michigan Avenue." In the end, he clings to a bitter, unrealistic dream of winning the lottery, after which he vows, "I ain't ever gonna ride in no used car again."

"My Father's House" is the most poignant of the three songs. It opens with the singer recounting a dream in which he is a child, running through a dark woods of "wild . . . tall" pines amid the rustling wind, hoping to make it home before "darkness falls." There are "ghostly voices" and, in an echo of Robert Johnson's "Hellbound on My Trail," the "devil snappin' at [his] heels." At dream's end, the singer falls shaking but safe in his father's arms. But when the singer is awoken from the dream, we learn he is estranged from his father. The dream inspires him to resolve the things that had "pulled [them] apart"; he gets dressed and drives out to his father's house. When he gets there, a woman (a stranger) speaks to him through a chained door and tells him that his father doesn't live there anymore, and the sins between father and son "lie unatoned" across the dark highway between the singer's current home and that of his childhood.

The significance of homes in both "Mansion on the Hill" and "My Father's House" is inescapable. The descriptions of both are archetypal and, it can even be said, psychoanalytic in their dreamlike imagery. In the former, the mansion emerges from out of childhood memory, standing beneath a "full moon rising." In the latter, the father's former residence "shines hard and bright," standing "like a beacon." The two houses are guarded by a steel fence and a chained door, respectively; each instance establishes the house and everything that it represents—social and familiar acceptance—as unattainable.

In *Songs*, Springsteen prefaces the lyrics to *Nebraska* with memories of his grandparents' house, where his family lived until he was six. Springsteen remembers the "lack of decoration, the almost painful plainness" of the house:

Our house was heated by a single kerosene stove in the living room. One of my earliest childhood memories was the smell of kerosene and my grandfather standing there filling the spot in the rear of the stove. All of our cooking was done on a coal stove in the kitchen. As a child, I'd shoot my watergun at its hot, iron surface and watch the steam rise.[17]

It's not a stretch to find profound psychological dimensions in both songs, especially with regard to images of the home and fatherhood and how they reflect issues with which Springsteen had to deal. As Springsteen would later say of the creative space from which the song came, "that was [the] bottom. . . . I'd hope not to be in that particular place ever again."[18]

The most shocking lyrical perspective, though, is evidenced in the song "Nebraska." The song is based on the true story of Charley Starkweather, who killed 11 people between Nebraska and Wyoming during 1958–1959 while traveling with underage girlfriend Caril Ann Fugate. Springsteen was directed to the story first by the movie *Badlands*, a fictionalized account of Starkweather and Fugate that Terrence Malick directed very much in the same antihero genre as Arthur Penn's *Bonnie and Clyde* (1967). Springsteen was so fascinated by *Badlands* that he was moved to call journalist Ninette Beaver, the author of *Caril*, a nonfiction book on the Starkweather murders, to learn more about the case. From his research sprung the song "Nebraska," which he called the "record's center."[19]

The song is told from the killer's perspective, the image is straight out of Malick's *Badlands*, and the economy of language hearkens back to O'Connor: "I saw her standin' on her front lawn just a-twirlin' her baton / Me and her went for a ride sir and ten innocent people died." After they're caught and the singer is sentenced to death, he remains unrepentant. His last wish is that his girlfriend joins him in the electric chair, and he blames his inexplicable actions on the "meanness" of the world.

"Johnny 99" is a companion piece to "Nebraska." The song is another jailhouse narrative, but this time the focus is not as much on the crime—the narrator, Ralph, kills a night clerk while in a drunken rage—as it is on the factors leading up to it. Bryan Garman argues that "Johnny 99" combines the narratives of Julius Daniels's "Ninety Nine Year Blues" (1927) and the Carter Family's "John Hardy Was a Desperate Little Man" (1930)—both from the *Anthology of American Folk Music* that Springsteen had been delving into at the time—but Springsteen's song is not really like either one, especially when considering the character's motives.[20]

Johnny (his name is Ralph, but he's dubbed with his titular nickname after receiving a life sentence) gets drunk on Tanqueray and wine while attempting to drown his worries; he loses his job when the Mahwah automobile plant where he's employed is shut down. After committing the murder, he ends up in the rough side of town ("where when you hit a red light you don't stop") waving a gun. An off-duty cop sneaks up on him and cuffs him. Johnny appears with a court-appointed defender before a hanging judge, "Mean John Brown," and is sentenced to 99 years. Unlike the perpetrator in "Nebraska," Ralph/Johnny shows remorse—he doesn't claim to be innocent and says he'd be "better off dead"—and elaborates on his road to ruin: debts that "no honest man could pay" and the house he stood to lose to foreclosure. The moral climax of the song comes at the end of the penultimate verse: "I ain't sayin' that makes me an innocent man / But it was more 'n all this that put that gun in my hand."

Jim Cullen argues that "As he himself admits, Johnny is responsible for his crime. But he also implicates the CEO of the auto company, the board of the bank, and state and federal regulators, i.e., anyone who helped create a situation in which people are saddled with debts they cannot honestly repay." In addition, the "fact that Johnny's rage unfolds in a dangerous part of town calls attention to the social forces that serve as a backdrop for, and perhaps shape, his actions."[21]

While Cullen suggests that the arrest being made by an off-duty policeman implies "a sense of responsibility that is more than official or contractual,"[22] perhaps more to the point is that the incident illustrates a keen awareness of narrative detail; only a cop dressed in civilian clothes would be able to get anywhere near a gun-wielding criminal while still having the wherewithal to apprehend him. Although the off-duty policeman acts on behalf of law and order—a cause to which we are surely sympathetic—putting ourselves in Ralph/Johnny's shoes, we can imagine his sense of betrayal at getting captured by one of his blue-collar brethren. Cullen points out that Springsteen "begins the song by yodeling—an eerie, melancholy wail. This wail, an act of musical homage, conjures up the ghost of Jimmie Rodgers, the beloved 'Singing Brakeman' of Mississippi who left the railroad to become the first major country and western singer in the 1920s. Even before he's said a word, then, Springsteen connects his story to a great working-class musical tradition."[23]

It can be said that in the six years since *Born to Run*, Springsteen had moved from street-urchin opera to blue-collar soap opera. "Atlantic City" is set amid gang warfare and to a haunting folk melody with Springsteen providing an additional vocal track of wailing harmony. The death of the "Chicken Man from Philly" refers to the murder of Philip Testa in 1981. The protagonist, like Ralph/Johnny, has "debts that no honest man can pay," and recalling the singer of "Meeting across the River," he tells his girlfriend of a guy he met and how he's going to "do a little favor for him." But unlike the small-time hoods in "Meeting," the protagonist of "Atlantic City" seems to possess an awareness that they didn't. "Well now everybody dies baby that's a fact," he tells her philosophically. "But maybe everything that dies someday comes back."

Prior to *The River*, when Springsteen had written of characters committing crimes—such as Spanish Johnny on "Incident" and the small-time crooks in "Meeting"—they came across as romantic flirtations with the wrong side of the law. Now, however, we can see how the driver from "Stolen Car" is a psychological relative to characters in "State Trooper" and "Highway Patrolman" on *Nebraska*.

Like "Stolen Car," "State Trooper" is told from the point of view of a car thief. ("License, registration, I ain't got none / But I got a clear conscience 'bout the things that I done.") Unlike the driver in "Stolen Car," the driver in "State Trooper" has no secret wish to be caught. Each of the first three stanzas ends with the driver's plea to a state trooper—who is either tailing him or is imagined—not to stop him as he drives past the glow of oil refineries on the New Jersey Turnpike during a rainy night. Like Springsteen's imagined listener, the driver is alone in the dark, yet this is not a peaceful solitude. As in its unlikely inspiration "Frankie Teardrops," a 10.5-minute song from the 1977 debut album for synth-punk band Suicide, "State Trooper" has a sense of minimalist desperation. Fervently strumming a monotonous guitar line, Springsteen sings hauntingly. His narrator imagines the approaching trooper to have a nice family and says that "the only thing that I got's been both'rin' me my whole life." He can't even get music on the radio, which plays only "talk show stations." In the end, the singer casts out an empty plea for somebody to hear his "last prayer," to "deliver me from nowhere."

The song "Highway Patrolman" has obvious connections to "State Trooper"; the protagonist, Joe Roberts, is himself a trooper. But the song bears a closer resemblance to "Losin' Kind." In that song, Frank Davis picks up a prostitute outside a barroom, and after they spend time together in a Best Western motel room, Frank robs a roadside bar and beats the bartender. Frank and his date ride away, and in an ending reminiscent of the noir classic *Out of the Past*, he wraps his car around a telephone pole during a high-speed chase. Frank and the girl are able to crawl out of the wreckage, but when the patrolman tells Frank he's "lucky to be alive," Frank says, "Well, sir, I'll think that one over if you don't mind / Luck ain't much good to you when you're the losin' kind."

In "Highway Patrolman," Joe has a brother, Franky, and "Franky ain't no good." In rhyming couplets, we learn of a recurring story of Joe getting a call on the police radio reporting of trouble with Franky downtown. "Well if it was any other man," Joe muses, "I'd put him straight away / But when it's your brother sometimes you look the other way." But this time, Franky commits a serious crime: he leaves a kid lying on the floor of a roadhouse with a girl—probably someone they were fighting over—crying nearby at a table. She tells Joe it was Franky; Joe gets in his patrol car and spots Franky "out at the crossroads" driving a (probably stolen) car with Ohio plates. Joe chases him to within five miles of the Canadian border; realizing that Frankie intends to flee the country, Joe pulls to the side of the road and lets him go, watching the taillights of the Buick disappear in the night.

Beneath the plot are many layers. We learn that in 1965 Franky joined the army, while Joe got a farm deferment and married Maria, the woman with whom (as Joe recalls in a flashback chorus that paints a sentimental scene before lost innocence) they took turns dancing to the song "Night of the Johnstown Flood." Note, then, that although we are told that one man is "honest" and the other "no good," their fates are largely shaped by a social construct—the farm deferment. With it, Joe marries Maria and (when wheat prices keep falling until they were "gettin' robbed") then takes a job as a highway patrolman. On the other hand, Franky comes home from the army in 1968 without social ties; because Joe is married to Maria, Franky is left to fight for other men's women in roadhouse bars. True, Franky is no good, but Joe, the reluctant cop who claims to do his job "as honest as I could," does not do his job and does not bring in his brother. The final irony is that Joe, who claims that any man who "turns his back on his family . . . just ain't no good," must turn his back on his brother—and his own job—to let his brother go.

Joe Roberts, we're told, is a sergeant from the barracks in "Perrineville," the name of a New Jersey town, and yet the song's setting seems to have transported Perrineville to Michigan. Bob Crane suggests that "At times, Springsteen indulges in hilarious acts of geo-play," though such play usually takes the form of highway numbers mixed up or (as in the case of Route 88 in "Spirit in the Night") conflated.[24] It's an oddity, to be sure, but one that most of us will be content to let go.

Perhaps more problematic is the moral territory that Springsteen had entered as a songwriter with *Nebraska*. One may oppose censorship (as I do) and say what one wants about the moral license given to the expression of "art," but the songwriter nevertheless does not exist within a vacuum; he is a member of society, and the defining nature of any society is based on some sense of morality. What, then, of the relatives of the victims of the real-life Charley Starkweather? According to Christopher Sandford, one of the victim's relatives termed the "Nebraska" protagonist's rationale ("there's just a meanness in this world") as being "crap."[25] (Sandford neglects to provide a citation for this quote, though it's entirely believable.) This is not to say that songs about murderers will turn a listener into a murderer any more than a 50 Cent rap will turn a listener into a gangsta or a Donny Osmond record will turn a listener into a Mormon. But the murderous songs on *Nebraska* do call into question the moral responsibility of the songwriter.

One subject interviewed for Robert Coles's controversial *Bruce Springsteen's America* raises this same question. The subject, a policeman who professes admiration for Springsteen, questions the focal points of "Johnny 99," "Highway Patrolman," and "State Trooper." Of "Johnny 99," the policeman asks:

> But who's thinking of that night clerk—he's mentioned for a half a second only at the start: "got a gun, shot a night clerk." . . . Are we supposed to start sobbing, I want to know, because a guy has lost his job—and decides to go on a killing spree after he's tanked himself up with that Tanqueray stuff! . . . Maybe I've been in too many courtrooms, and seen the families of the *victims* in there, crying their bloody hearts out! Where are *they* in that song of the Boss?[26]

The policeman also terms the description of the song's presiding judge as "Mean John Brown" as a "setup": "Bruce, pal, how about mean Johnny 99?" he asks.[27]

Our man in blue also questions "Highway Patrolman" and "State Trooper" as songs that, by their titles, might imply an interest in a policeman's perspective. As he says about the latter, "There's not a single word about the state trooper, about him, his life, even though folks like me, they'll read that title on the album and go right for it!"[28] (For the former his objection is vaguely stated, but we can understand it given the song's portrayal of a reluctant patrolman who lets his brother escape the law.) Coles's policeman does not necessarily offer esoteric insight, and his perspective is undoubtedly influenced by his occupation. But his comments do highlight the complexities that would continue to develop between Springsteen and his fans.

On an album filled with songs about a murderous road trip, the damnation of used cars, and both ends of the highway chase experience, "Open All Night" emerges as the one and only fun-filled offering on *Nebraska*. Many of the lyrics date back to a song from the *River* sessions called "Living on the Edge of the World," a light, up-tempo number. "Open All Night" is stripped down instrumentally, of course, but it retains the fast tempo of its predecessor as well as the all-out fun evoked by such *River* songs as "Cadillac Ranch" and "Ramrod." "Open All Night" can be seen as a more hopeful version of "State Trooper," with which the song shares many similarities: some identical lines, a pesky state trooper, a radio jammed with talk stations (in this case gospel stations). The driver in "Open All Night" is also alone, driving through industrial north Jersey in the early morning, where the refinery towers appear surreal, "like a lunar landscape." But here, the narrative tension derives from the singer's desire to make it home in time to see Wanda, whom he'd met at her job at the Bob's Big Boy on Route 60. (His boss doesn't dig him, we're told, so the singer was put on the night shift.) The song is lightheartedly serious: the singer repeats the prayer to be delivered from nowhere, but here the prayer is offered to the local deejay, asking for rock-and-roll music to provide company on the remaining three hours of his drive. This is a more serious concern than the state trooper he passes while speeding by; even though the trooper hits his "party light," the singer simply says "Goodnight, good luck, one two power shift" and leaves him behind in the middle of the song.

Nebraska closes on a note of circumspect hope with "Reason to Believe." The four verses of the song introduce us to a cast of characters who seem to come out of O'Connor's fiction. We see a man poking a stick into a dead dog on the highway, looking like he believes that "if he stood there long enough that dog'd get up and run." We meet two jilted lovers: one waits in vain at the end of a dirt road for her lover to return, and the other is a groom left at the altar. We witness a baby being baptized in a river while mourners stand over a dead man's grave, praying that the Lord will help them make sense of the man's death. In each case, the singer offers the same conclusion: "Still at the end of every hard earned day people find some reason to believe."

Again, we come back to O'Connor and the persistence of faith amid trials. Twice the singer says that it "Struck me kinda funny" before observing how "people find some reason to believe." In each case—even the river baptism scenario, which resonates with the knowledge that a boy drowns at the end of O'Connor's "The River"—we are not given any affirmation of faith; in fact, the singer labels these illustrations of faith as being "kinda funny." Yet as Springsteen had once said, you'd better keep riding. The point in "Reason to Believe"—and, in fact, throughout the entire album—is that people endure, that they struggle against all evidence to the contrary, because it's the only thing that they can do, or else they end up dead, spiritually or literally.

After *The River*, *Nebraska* came as a shock. For fans on the periphery, those who had come to know Bruce Springsteen through "Born to Run" and "Hungry Heart," the album's acoustic-folk sound must have seemed dreary, its lyrics disarmingly depressing. Ironically, the album did spawn Springsteen's first standard-release video (not counting the 1978 "Rosalita" video, which was really just a concert clip), though even this was not a fully commercial move. The "Atlantic City" video is a starkly atmospheric black-and-white video featuring street scenes in which neither Springsteen nor any of the E Street Band members appear. Arnold Levine, who'd shot the "Rosalita" footage, had asked Landau about possibilities for shooting a video of the song. Springsteen was unavailable for the shoot—he was headed out to California to work with Chuck Plotkin in mixing some new rock-and-roll tracks—but signed off on the project with just two conditions: it should be "kind of gritty-looking" and "it should have no images that matched up to image in the song."[29]

Nebraska is by nature the least commercially successful release that Springsteen had done since his debut record, but it would not be accurate to call the album a commercial failure. Even lacking a radio-friendly single, it reached No. 4 on the album charts and attained gold-record status soon after its release—this in the midst of an early 1980s' recession. Many critics praised the album's sincerity. The *New York Times* called it Springsteen's "most personal record, and his most disturbing." *Time* described it as "an acoustic bypass through the American heartland . . . like a Library of Congress field recording made out behind some shutdown auto plant," and *Rolling Stone* said that "This is the bravest of Springsteen's six records; it's also his most startling, direct and chilling." In *Musician*, Paul Nelson said the album sounded "demoralizing" and "murderously monotonous . . . deprived of spark or hope." In the *Los Angeles Times*, Mikal Gilmore—whose older brother Gary was executed on January 17, 1977, for the murder of a Provo, Utah, hotel manager—described the album as "dark-toned, brooding and unsparing" but said that it was "also the most successful attempt at making a sizable statement about American life that popular music has yet produced." Greil Marcus said that it was "the most complete and probably the most convincing statement of resistance and refusal that Ronald Reagan's U.S.A. has yet elicited from any artist or any politician."[30]

Nebraska continued an evolution of style and substance that began with *Darkness* and continued with *The River*. But if fans worried that the album signaled Springsteen's farewell to the popular rock music genre, they would soon learn that this was anything but the truth. In fact, the album that was Springsteen's least commercial success of the 1980s shared roots with the album that proved to be the most commercially successful of his entire career.

Notes

1. Bruce Springsteen, *Songs* (New York: Avon, 1998), 135.
2. Ibid., 138–139.
3. Ibid., 138.
4. Ibid., 165.
5. Stephen Metcalf, "Faux Americana: Why I Still Love Bruce Springsteen," *Slate*, May 2, 2005, http://www.slate.com/id/2117845/.
6. Geoffrey Himes, *Born in the U.S.A.* (New York: Continuum, 2005), 62–63.
7. June Skinner Sawyers, ed., *Racing in the Street: A Bruce Springsteen Reader* (New York: Penguin, 2004), 307.
8. Himes, *Born in the U.S.A.*, 63.
9. Springsteen, *Songs*, 136.
10. Flannery O'Connor, *A Good Man Is Hard to Find, and Other Stories* (San Diego: Harvest, n.d.), 52.
11. Ibid., 191.
12. Flannery O'Connor, *A Good Man Is Hard to Find, and Other Stories* (Orlando: Harcourt, 1977), 22.
13. Ibid., 22.
14. Himes, *Born in the U.S.A.*, 61.
15. Springsteen, *Songs*, 138.
16. Bryan K. Garman, *A Race of Singers: Whitman's Working-Class Hero from Guthrie to Springsteen* (Chapel Hill: University of North Carolina Press, 2000), 209.
17. Springsteen, *Songs*, 136.
18. Christopher Sandford, *Springsteen: Point Blank* (New York: Da Capo, 1999), 198.
19. Springsteen, *Songs*, 138.
20. Garman, *A Race of Singers*, 205.
21. Jim Cullen, *Born in the U.S.A: Bruce Springsteen and the American Tradition* (Middletown, CT: Wesleyan University Press, 2005), 21.
22. Ibid.
23. Ibid., 20.
24. Bob Crane, *A Place to Stand: A Guide to Bruce Springsteen's Sense of Place* (Silver Springs, MD: Palace Books, 2002), 2.
25. Sandford, *Springsteen*, 198.
26. Robert Coles, *Bruce Springsteen's America: The People Listening, a Poet Singing* (New York: Random House, 2004), 117–118.
27. Ibid., 119.
28. Ibid., 123.
29. Dave Marsh, *Bruce Springsteen: Two Hearts: The Definitive Biography, 1972–2003* (New York: Routledge, 2004), 378.
30. Ibid., 379–380.

31

Prince and the Revolution

Purple Rain (1984)

James E. Perone

In one of the most memorable scenes from a 1980s' pop music–related film, a crowd of diverse young people in a Minneapolis nightclub slowly begins to sway and wave their hands over their heads as they become immersed in a new song, performed by "The Kid," as it debuts. This mysterious character, The Kid, had seen his family disintegrate, his standing in the musical hierarchy of local big-name bands has recently diminished, and his new girlfriend and potential bandmate breaks ranks to form another act (and become involved with The Kid's archrival). And to top it all off, The Kid was on the verge of losing his long-standing gig and seeing his band disintegrate. The song that shows the nightclub owner, his just-about-ready-to-split bandmates, and the masses that previously had begun to shift their loyalties that he was indeed *the* star of the local scene was "Purple Rain." This concert scene was the grand finale of Prince's film *Purple Rain*. Prince and the Revolution had the No. 1 album, film, and pop single in the same week. This put the group in the most exclusive of clubs: only Elvis Presley and the Beatles had previously had a simultaneous No. 1 film, album, and single. But *Purple Rain*, the album, is about much more than commercial/popular success. The songs, written by Prince alone or in collaboration with the Revolution, aim at a wider audience than any previous Prince material and succeed across the board. Two of the songs, "Purple Rain" and "When Doves Cry," have become true classics of late 20th-century popular music and as such were included in various millennial lists of the most significant music of the entire rock era. The production, apparently influenced by members of the Revolution, is punchier and more powerful than that on any of Prince's previous self-produced solo albums.

The album's opener, "Let's Go Crazy," begins with a slow synthesized organ chorale, which supports Prince's spoken introduction. Prince portrays a preacher in his monologue. He confirms the existence of the afterlife and the bliss that it will provide. He concludes, however, by observing that in this earthly life, "you're on your own." The song itself is upbeat party material, featuring a stylistic blend of new wave rock and R&B roughly in the mold of several popular early 1980s' songs by the J. Geils Band ("Freeze Frame" and "Centerfold" are the closest stylist precedents). Like the songs of the 1981 J. Geils Band album *Freeze Frame*, the melody of "Let's Go Crazy" is built in short easy-to-remember phrases. Perhaps the most notable feature of the melody is the syncopated descending figure that accompanies the words "take us down." While this represents just a touch of musical text painting, it is not the last example on the album. The song's melody is supported by a powerful instrumental accompaniment on a minimal ostinato-like chord oscillation. Prince adds strong rocking lead guitar, especially notable for a Jimi Hendrix–like cadenza at the conclusion of the song.

Since "Let's Go Crazy" is credited to Prince and the Revolution, it is difficult to ascertain exactly who came up with what. However, the lyrical style represents a shift from the bulk of Prince's earlier material. It takes on a much more impressionistic air than is customary for Prince. Purple bananas and the Grim Reaper coming "to take us down" in his "de-elevator" provide rich imagery in the verses and chorus. The chorus, with its implied message to "hang tough" against the lure of drugs but to enjoy the fun we have with our friends by punching "a higher floor" on the elevator of life, confirms the message of the preacher in the introduction: "Get through this thing called life" but keep in mind that "He's coming," indicating that the even greater glory of the afterlife will be upon us soon. It is a 1980s' blend of the Old Testament Song of Solomon with Christian imagery in which the pursuit of physical pleasure—through the enjoyment of natural highs (such as sex)—is viewed as God's gift to humankind. It is a mix of the kind of religious philosophy that Prince expressed on the album *1999* and the kind of psychedelic impressionism that he and the Revolution would explore even more thoroughly on their next album, *Around the World in a Day.*

"Take Me with U," a duet with Apollonia Kotero, serves a clear function in the film, in which it confirms the love part of what becomes a love-hate relationship between Apollonia and Prince's character: The Kid. This is certainly not among Prince's most famous songs, and it is not among the best-known songs on *Purple Rain*. This is more a result of the strength of songs such as "Purple Rain," "Let's Go Crazy," and "When Doves Cry" and not because of any weakness in "Take Me with U." The song is, in some respects, one of the most effective pure love songs that Prince has ever written and recorded. It is catchy, like the best pop music. One of the best hooks in the song comes as a result of the metrical placement of the title line. The line is presented with each word directly on the four beats of the penultimate measure of the musical phrase. Since the line ends the chorus, its seemingly early placement captures

PARENTAL WARNING LABELS

If one scrutinizes song lyrics, even of the early 20th century, one can find references to sex, drugs, and violence. It can be argued, however, that in music that was mass marketed (some of the earliest songs with these references were more obscure blues and jazz pieces), the explicitness of these references grew into the 1980s and 1990s. By the mid-1980s the National PTA requested that record companies place warning labels on record jackets so that recordings with material deemed to be inappropriate for children could easily be identified in stores. In 1985 after observing her daughter listening to Prince's "Darling Nikki," Tipper Gore, along with other wives of Washington, D.C., politicians, formed the Parents Music Resource Center and continued to push the Recording Industry Association of America (RIAA) to place warning labels on recordings. The organization lobbied against the overt sexual references in some of Prince's and Madonna's recordings and music videos as well as against the violent images in some heavy metal and rap songs. The U.S. Senate Commerce, Science and Transportation Committee held hearings on the subject in late 1985. Musicians such as John Denver, Dee Snider, and Frank Zappa testified before the committee, all taking a firm stance against censorship. Before the end of the year, the RIAA had agreed to place "Parental Advisory" stickers on recordings with explicit lyrics, a practice that continues today.

the listener's attention: the "missing" bar of singing stands out sharply. It also helps that the childlike tune to which the line is set is so simple (it moves from scale step three up to scale step five and then down to scale step seven and up a half step to the tonic, scale step one). This makes it easy to remember, easy to sing along with, and its childlike quality suggests the innocence of the love between the two characters in the film.

Purple Rain includes three songs composed, performed, and produced by Prince, without the collaboration of the Revolution. The first of these, "The Beautiful Ones," is a Quiet Storm ballad in which Prince plays the classic role of a man whose lover has to choose between him and another man. For a Prince song, the lyrics are uncompromisingly romantic—as opposed to physical—and are supported by a beautiful melody and full-sounding synthesizer arrangement and production. As Prince sings "Is it him or me?" in a vulnerable falsetto, he is entirely believable. Although it may be something of a stereotype, this kind of falsetto singing fits a song in which the hero is in danger of losing his lover better than in a song praising the purely physical side of love and sex, something that Prince had done with mixed results on his early albums.

"Computer Blue" combines elements of R&B and heavy metal rock. Prince addresses a woman, Computer Blue, whom he believes needs to "learn love and lust." One of the notable features of the song is the synthesizer figure that tops each line of the chorus. This chromatic figure bears some resemblance to a figure in Jonathan Richman's song "Pablo Picasso." Prince's synthesizer figure is otherworldly enough to suggest the unfeeling computer-like nature of the woman Prince addresses. The real highlight of the song, however, is Prince's technically brilliant and musically powerful electric guitar playing. The recording's production, by Prince and the Revolution, gives Prince's solos and the entire sonic landscape a greater feeling of depth than that found on any of Prince's earlier solo albums.

The next track on *Purple Rain*, "Darling Nikki," gained notoriety through its association with the movement to adorn recordings that included explicit references to sex, violence, or drug use with parental warning labels. It was after finding her young daughter listening to "Darling Nikki," a song in which Prince refers to Nikki's "bumping and grinding" and masturbation, that Tipper Gore, working with other members of the Washington, D.C., political elite, founded the Parents Music Resource Center to combat references to sex, violence, and drugs in popular song lyrics.

"Darling Nikki" is a powerful, rhythmically heavy, slow, bluesy rock piece. Prince's melody for the verses has a singsong quality. He presents this in a sly voice that suggests that the childlike innocence of the melody is meant to be ironic: Nikki is anything but sexually innocent. The harder-edged rock-oriented chorus, in which Prince details Nikki's highly erotic bump and grind, features more powerful vocals and distorted hard rock–style lead guitar. Nikki is a "super freak," in the sense of the Rick James song of the same title, and she can be understood this way both through the lyrics and through Prince's musical setting. Prince abruptly switches gears for the final 45 seconds of the song. Here, he turns to a combination of a gospel-esque vocal chorale and Laurie Anderson–style minimalism. This comes as a shock after the hard rock setting of Prince's tale of Nikki's sexual escapades. This music finds Prince turning from a lyrical focus on Nikki to a focus on the even greater fulfillment that will come in the "Purple Rain," a metaphor for the afterlife. From a purely musical standpoint, the minimalistic coda to "Darling Nikki" anticipates a bit of the style of the next track, "When Doves Cry."

Prince has enjoyed a number of strong commercial hits on the pop and R&B charts over the course of his career. His most successful single to date, however, is "When Doves Cry." The single was No. 1 on the *Billboard* R&B charts for eight weeks, and it held the No. 1 position on the pop charts for five weeks. "When Doves Cry" found its way into several millennial surveys of the most important songs of the rock era.[1] In some respects, the song represents Prince's coming of age as a songwriter. The music, however, is not entirely without precedent: there is a melodic resemblance in the verses to the chorus of the 1966 Supremes hit "You Keep Me Hangin' On," and Prince's use of synthesized classically inspired keyboard lines has precedence in some of Stevie Wonder's mid-1970s' work (including "Village Ghetto Land" from *Songs in the Key of Life*). The ostinato chord oscillation and Prince's incorporation of sustained synthesizer chords suggest just a touch of the hip New York loft minimalism of the early 1980s, such as the work of Laurie Anderson. The song, however, mostly achieves the status of timeless pop/R&B classic by virtue of its lyrics and the intersection of its music and lyrics.

Prince's lyrics find him addressing his lover about their passionate, albeit turbulent, relationship. The downsides of the relationship are entirely the fault of Prince's character. In the film, in fact, the lyrics about being "just like my father" take on a deeper meaning. In the story's context, the lyrics clearly refer to the scene in which, in a fit of passionate anger, The Kid strikes Apollonia. At that moment, he realizes that he in essence has become his physically abusive father. The song accompanies The Kid's lonely motorcycle ride that follows the episode of violence. Even outside the context of the film, the lyrical images of Prince's character caught in a fight between taking on the behavior of his dysfunctional parents and doing what he knows to be the right thing are poignant. And the image of the sorrow he feels about his actions and the breakup of his own turbulent relationship being just like "what it sounds like when doves cry" remains one of his strongest lyrical metaphors.

The simple nature of the musical setting allows the lyrics to stand out. While there in nothing entirely innovative about the style, the melody, or the harmony, there is one aspect of Prince's arrangement that is likely to capture the attention of the listener: not what is there but what is absent. This is one of the very few pop songs of the entire rock era that has no bass line—Prince includes no bass guitar and no bass lines in the keyboards. This suggests the influence of classical music, which tends to emphasize the midrange and higher-range instrumental sounds more than musical styles such as rock and R&B. The thinness of the sound, literally without a bass (or base), aligns with the hollow, soulless feeling of Prince's character.

Although Prince and the Revolution's "I Would Die 4 U" might not be part of the standard canon of contemporary Christian music, it is one of the purest religious songs from this part of Prince's career. In the film *Purple Rain*, the live performance of the song tends to allow it to take on a double meaning: Prince's character can be understood at once as a personification of the Messiah and as a man who tells the love of his life that he would give the ultimate sacrifice (his life) for her. In the context of the album, however, the song's religious meaning is perhaps even stronger. The combination of Christian imagery in the lyrics and rhythmic dance music supports the overarching religious philosophy that Prince espoused in the songs "1999" and "Let's Go Crazy": the Messiah will appear at the end of the world and take believers with him, but God's purpose for us on Earth is to enjoy ourselves.

The album's next track, "Baby, I'm a Star," fits well into the context of the film. To the extent that the listener considers the album *Purple Rain* as a standalone artistic statement, however, the song contributes little. That being said, it is interesting that the song makes a direct segue from "I Would Die 4 U." The combination lends some support to the understanding of "I Would Die 4 U" as a song in which Prince represents a human being who thinks of himself as his lover's messiah. The juxtaposition of the two songs at least can raise the issue.

Throughout the rock era there have been a number of especially popular mammoth slow-tempo anthem-like hits, perhaps most notably the Beatles' "Hey Jude," Foreigner's "I Want to Know What Love Is," and Prince's "Purple Rain." While not the biggest hit single on the album—"When Doves Cry" unquestionably holds that title—it is perhaps the most memorable and iconic song on the album. Certainly it plays a most prominent role in the film. It is this song—the music of which is composed by The Kid's bandmates Wendy and Lisa[2]—to which the The Kid finally acquiesces to adding lyrics and performing at what would be his band's make-or-break performance. The lyrics, which express The Kid/Prince's regrets at hurting his former friend/lover, fit easily into the context of the relationships of the film's characters. The sentiments are both an apology to Apollonia for striking her in a fit of anger and as an apology to Wendy and Lisa for ignoring their attempts to contribute songs to the band's repertoire. The image of "purple rain" was introduced earlier in the album and seems to signify the appearance of God at the end of the world. As The Kid apologizes to Apollonia and the members of his band, he gives perhaps the ultimate expression of his true but most often hidden devotion to them, that he only wanted to see them "standing in the purple rain," in other words, making it safely to heaven.

Musically, "Purple Rain" is a mixture of the familiar and the unexpected. The chord progression of the verses and the oft-repeated chorus include the most basic of harmonies, triads (three-note chords) built on the first, fourth, fifth, and sixth notes of the major scale. This collection of harmonies would fit entirely into the pop and gospel music of decades earlier. Given the style of the setting, however, the harmony seems more timeless than retro. Likewise, the melody is generally fairly stepwise and simple. The setting on the recording finds the band breaking into gospel-style harmony in the chorus, which in part lends the song its anthem feel. Adding to this is the lengthy coda section: a repeat, over and over, of the chorus's chord progression with ever-evolving instrumental lines.

Just like "Take Me with U" had featured a feeling of unusual melodic phrase structure, "Purple Rain" does the same. The end of each verse includes what sounds like an extra measure of music. Since the overall melodic shape and the harmonic material are so typical of basic pop music, this phrase extension instantly stands out. It sets up a focus on the start of the chorus that cannot help but draw even the most casual listener in.

Although it is tempting to focus on trying to find the influence of earlier guitar heroes such as Jimi Hendrix on Prince's compositions, singing, and guitar playing in his hard rock songs, I believe that "Purple Rain" is perhaps one of the best examples of the influence of Hendrix in the entire Prince repertoire. Slower-tempo Hendrix recordings such as "Little Wing" and even "Hey Joe" (the latter of which Hendrix recorded but did not write) include double-time parlando-style phrases in the verses—something that Prince adopts in "Purple Rain." The phrase "but you can't seem 2 make up your mind" has a rhythm and a pitch falloff on the word "mind" that clearly recall the work of Hendrix. Even Prince's use of the entire range of the electric guitar, including some tasty low-register lines, suggests the influence of songs such as "Little Wing." Hendrix is not, however, the only late 1960s–early 1970s guitar god whose influence can be felt in "Purple Rain." The more highly technical high-register figures suggest the influence of Carlos Santana. Prince assimilates these influences and creates a solo lead guitar style that sounds entirely personal. In "Purple Rain" his guitar work becomes an instrumental representation of the passion he expresses in the lyrics.

The album *Purple Rain* has become a pop culture classic. The fuller arrangements, the wider range of subject matter, the strong melodic pop hooks, Prince portraying a wide range of emotions, and the strong instrumental work from Prince and his band all represent a step above Prince's previous work. Add to that the impact of the film, and *Purple Rain* remains a defining work for Prince and the one that perhaps more than any other defined him as a pop culture icon.

Notes

1. See, for example, "Pop 100," *Rolling Stone*, no. 855 (December 7, 2000): 79.
2. The real names of Prince's bandmates Wendy Melvoin and Lisa Coleman. Significantly, of the characters who are members of this fictitious band, only Prince's character, The Kid, does not use his real name.

32

Madonna

Like a Virgin (1984)

James E. Perone

Madonna's album *Like a Virgin* was one of the most talked about, popular, and visible albums of the 1980s. In addition to the music itself, videos of the songs from *Like a Virgin* seemed for a period of time to be impossible to escape. Madonna's provocative songs and videos led to discussions, controversy, and the establishment of Madonna as a popular culture icon.

Like a Virgin opens with the Peter Brown and Robert Rans composition "Material Girl," one of the best known and most highly Madonna-defining songs of the album. Madonna's character acknowledges the materialism of the modern world and that she fits in because she is a "material girl." Her choice of men comes down to what they can offer her in the way of riches. Since the album is squarely aimed at dance clubs, pop radio, and a pop audience, the tune is catchy, and the beat and rhythmic groove are infectious. However, the popularity of the track caused controversy. Like the other iconic song on the album, the title track "Material Girl" is highly open to conflicting and potentially disturbing interpretations. Had the song not been as omnipresent on the radio, in dance clubs, and on MTV, it might not have caused as much discussion. Was this an endorsement of conspicuous consumption and materialism? Was the song an endorsement of women selling out to the highest bidder? Was "Material Girl" an endorsement of prostitution; was Madonna's character empowered? Was the song an example of commentary about the state of American women in the 1980s? Was the song meant to reflect materialism of Americans of the Reagan era? It could be understood in any of these ways.

One cannot overemphasize the importance of Nile Rodgers as producer on *Like a Virgin*. Rodgers, the former guitarist of the prominent 1970s' disco band

Chic, had turned increasingly to record production and work as a studio guitarist by the 1980s. The year before Rodgers produced the Madonna album, he produced and played guitar on David Bowie's *Let's Dance*. The Bowie album yielded several major hits and established the rocker, whose career extended back into the 1960s, as a dance club favorite. Rodgers brought a similar sound to *Like a Virgin*, an album that features clear synthesizer lines, background rhythm electric guitar, strong percussion parts with a distinct reverberation on the snare drum, and clear presentation of the vocal lines.

Although the best-known commercial successes of *Like a Virgin* were written by others, Madonna wrote and cowrote five of the nine songs on the album, including the second song, "Angel." Despite the fact that Madonna became most closely associated with provocative and controversial songs throughout the 1980s, a large amount of her recorded output deals with fairly standard pop song topics. Such is the case with "Angel," which is a conventional love song in which Madonna characterizes the man she loves as "an angel." The musical setting is in standard pop song structure, with a clearly defined verse and chorus. The melody is simple, and the chorus almost invites singing along.

Billy Steinberg and Tom Kelly provided the album's most iconic song, "Like a Virgin." One of the challenges of interpreting the 1980s' recordings of artists who were as important in the world of music videos as Madonna and Michael Jackson is that the videos were so widely known that for some fans they represent the only possible interpretation/meaning of the song. The video for "Like a Virgin" was particularly strong in coloring viewers' reactions to the song. Be that as it may, the focus of this essay is on the musical recording itself. Madonna sings of a new love in her character's life, a love that makes her feel "like a virgin." In other words, this new relationship has washed away all of the emotional baggage that the character carries from previous relationships and sexual encounters. Some conservatives took the song—particularly in the context of the video—as a simple endorsement of premarital sex. However, the song really is more ambiguous than that. In fact, it is possible to interpret the lyrics as a denouncement of gratuitous premarital sex: Madonna's character celebrates the "shiny and new" feeling that this relationship brings, a feeling that hearkens back to her virginity. So, Madonna's character is sexually free, but she reflects in a positive way back to her past virginity. It can be labeled contradictory, vague, or widely open to interpretation, but this is one of the things that is so compelling about this song.

The music contains several pop song hooks, not the least of which is the tune in the chorus. The music, the lyrics, the arrangement, and Madonna's somewhat coy singing style made the piece easily recognizable—iconic—and open to parody. It is interesting and might bring at least a chuckle to fans to listen to Weird Al Yankovic's parody "Like a Surgeon."

The songwriting team of Madonna and Steve Bray wrote the album cuts "Angel," "Over and Over," "Pretender," and "Stay." In "Over and Over," an uptempo dance track, Madonna describes her work ethic: she "get[s] up again, over and over," after each failure. It probably is fully safe to say that *Like a Virgin* is a collection of individual songs, as opposed to a fully conceived concept album; however, there are some lyrical connections between some of the songs. For example, Madonna's character in "Over and Over" resembles her character from "Like a Virgin." "Over and Over," though, is a much clearer song in that the lyrics do not run much below the surface meaning. While it might be unfair to characterize Madonna's songwriting contributions to this album as generic, the best-known tracks—"Like a Virgin" and "Material Girl"—were written by others. The titles of Madonna's songs, though, are fairly generic and even somewhat confusing because they duplicate, or nearly duplicate, earlier famous popular songs by other artists. Specifically, "Over and Over" is also the title of a Bobby Day song made famous by the Dave Clark Five in 1965; the song "Stay," written by Maurice Williams of the Zodiacs, is much better known than Madonna's song of the same title; and the title "Pretender" immediately calls to mind the 1976 Jackson Browne song "The Pretender."

"Over and Over" is followed by the Mike Gregory song "Love Don't Live Here Anymore." Madonna proves that she is much more than a sexy, coy singer of dance songs in this slow, emotional, soulful ballad. Producer Nile Rodgers provided a string arrangement that helps this recording connect back to the torch songs of the past.

The Peggy Stanziale and Andrea LaRusso song "Dress You Up" reflects back to "Material Girl." Here, Madonna addresses a man of wealth who enjoys wearing fine clothing and tells him that she will "dress [him] up in [her] love." Lyrical references to kissing his body all over and wrapping him up in her body were sexually explicit enough that the Parents Resource Music Center included "Dress You Up" in the organization's initial list of the so-called Filthy Fifteen. The song features a driving new wave rock-style dance beat and became a Top 10 hit single in 1985.

In her own composition "Shoo Bee-Doo," Madonna reassures a man with whom her character is in love. She tells him that her love will help him to forget his past losses and sadness and invites him to spend the night. Because the piece deals with the healing power of love, the song shares a thread with "Like a Virgin," although "Shoo Bee-Doo" is not as distinctive and hook-oriented as the album's title track. The recording includes a saxophone solo and some saxophone obbligato playing by Lenny Pickett. The saxophone work by Pickett on this song and the string ensemble on "Love Don't Live Here Anymore" provide examples of the subtle tone color changes that producer Nile Rodgers made from track to track.

In "Pretender," an attractive man whom Madonna's character sees on the dance floor mesmerizes her. She knows that he is interested only in the dancing leading to a one-night stand; however, she is "not afraid to fall a hundred times." Torn between her desire to change him and establish a longer-lasting relationship and her knowledge that he will remain "a pretender," she decides to take a chance. Like some of the other songs on *Like a Virgin*, a song such as

"Pretender" generated controversy at the time of the album's release. However, while Madonna's character acknowledges her sexual freedom and her willingness to take a chance that her encounter will lead no further than one night of passion, the song in retrospect does not seem to be so much an endorsement of sleeping around as simply an acknowledgment of one woman's passion for sexual gratification. In fact, Madonna's character acknowledges that she knows full well that she should have taken her "friend's advice" to steer clear of the "Pretender." In fact, "Pretender," "Like a Virgin," and "Dress You Up" seem somewhat mainstream, especially when compared with the more explicit dance music that came after. Although the melodic hooks of "Pretender" are not as strong as those of the hit singles that were drawn from *Like a Virgin*, the piece is noteworthy for an especially effective full-sounding synthesizer arrangement.

Like a Virgin concludes with "Stay," a collaboration of Steve Bray and Madonna. This is a more conventional love song than most of the pieces on the album, and its 12/8 meter shuffle feel suggests the touch of earlier pop styles. Madonna's character is in a relationship that appears to be somewhat shaky, and she begs her man to stay. As is the case with virtually every song on the album, Madonna's character expresses the desire to exert control over the relationship (e.g., "I can make you love me"); however, this song is more about emotion—and less about sex—than the other up-tempo songs. It, too, can be interpreted as almost a song of atonement, because Madonna's character acknowledges that her lover "saw through [her] lies" and that she was "losing [her] way" before he came into her life. In fact, it is almost like the emotional equivalent of the sexually oriented song "Like a Virgin."

Despite the controversy that *Like a Virgin* generated back in 1984, the album seems fairly tame by 21st-century standards. The synthesizer-based dance tracks sound a bit dated, but most of the songs have strong enough melodic and arrangement hooks that they still work. *Like a Virgin* was an important work not just because it was a huge commercial success or because it helped to establish Madonna as an icon of American popular culture. It also raised questions about sexuality, empowerment, materialism, and values and it expressed the healing power of love. Still, the videos from the album made such a strong and lasting impression that popular music fans who remember them might find listening to just the music less satisfying.

33

Bruce Springsteen

Born in the U.S.A. (1984)

Rob Kirkpatrick

Of the several nonmusical works that have influenced Bruce Springsteen, one rarely discussed is Robert Frank's *The Americans*, a book of photographs originally released in 1959. In 1995, Bruce Springsteen told Will Percy that "I was twenty-four when I first saw the book—I think a friend had given me a copy—and the tone of the pictures, how he gave us a look at different kinds of people, got to me in some way. I've always wished I could write songs the way he takes pictures. I think I've got half a dozen copies of that book stashed around the house, and I pull one out once in a while to get a fresh look at the photographs."[1]

Frank had traveled the country in the 1950s on a Guggenheim grant, photographing everyday people in everyday situations and, in the words of John Szarkowski, "established a new iconography for contemporary America, comprised of bits of bus depots, lunch counters, strip developments, empty spaces, cars, and unknowable faces." Elizabeth Kunreuther tells us that "Photography before Frank was pristine: carefully focused, carefully lit. Frank would intentionally lose focus, his work was shadowy and grainy, full of unconventional cropping and angles. He broke the rules in order to be true to his vision of America he saw in his travels across the country in 1955 and 1956."[2]

Peter Marshall describes the use of visual motifs in *The Americans*:

> the recurring element of the flag, the orator followed by the listeners . . . the car and the American Dream. . . . Frank concentrates on the ordinary, the things you see on the road and along its edges, but he also deals with real issues, whether of race . . . or spiritual emptiness. . . . A petrol station

forecourt, the pumps like figures in a religious procession, carrying a tall banner that says "S A V E" in heavy capitals . . . a Fourth of July celebration in New York, where the giant hanging flag is shown to be patched, torn and threadbare.[3]

In the 1980s, Springsteen found himself more and more interested with the theme of spiritual emptiness found on Main Street, U.S.A. One early demo from Colts Neck, "Vietnam," was an up-tempo tune built around a bouncing acoustic guitar line. In this song, a returning vet discovers that he's lost his factory job to a slow economy and has also lost his girlfriend (or wife), who's run away with the singer of a rock band. Like many returning veterans, he experiences a sense of isolation from the society he returns to. Walking down Main Street, U.S.A., the veteran says that "All I seen was strangers, watchin' a stranger pass by / And that stranger was me." In a line that is more affected than realistic in its blunt cynicism, a factory foreman tells him, "Now don't you understand, you died in Vietnam."

Springsteen reworked the lyrics while keeping the basic plot for a new song. The title and chorus of this new song came from the name of a film script that director Paul Schrader had sent Springsteen in 1981. The plot revolved around a blue-collar rock band in Cleveland, and Schrader had hoped that Springsteen would write music for the film. Something about the title of the script, *Born in the U.S.A.*, resonated with Springsteen. Obviously, Springsteen's breakthrough album had begun with the same word, and as Geoffrey Himes summarizes, a string of recent music and movies—from "Born on the Bayou" to "Born to Be Wild" to "Born to Lose" to "Born to Boogie" to *Born to Kill* and *Born Free*—had established artistic statements of inborn identity as an artistic subgenre of sorts.[4] And there was also "Back in the U.S.A.," a Chuck Berry song that Springsteen and the E Street Band had covered in their early days.

More relevant were the resemblances to the title of Ron Kovic's *Born on the Fourth of July*, a book much more closely related to the subject matter that Springsteen explored in "Vietnam" and to the song it evolved into, called "Born in the U.S.A." After reading Kovic's story and meeting him, Springsteen had become especially interested in the struggles of Vietnam War vets. He met Bobby Muller, a veteran who founded Vietnam Veterans of America with future Democratic presidential nominee John Kerry. In August 1981 the band had played a benefit concert at the Los Angeles's Sports Arena for the Vietnam Veterans of America. Dating back to his Steel Mill days and in early songs such as "Lost in the Flood," Springsteen had explored the topic of returning Vietnam War veterans. Meeting Kovic and participating in the 1981 benefit concert seems to have rekindled Springsteen's interest, and he worked that into songs such as "Vietnam" and "Born in the U.S.A."

Although the *Tracks* version of "Born in the U.S.A." is performed with a feverish intensity, it doesn't exactly work as an acoustic song. Jon Landau didn't think much of the song at the time. But as Team Springsteen was struggling with its attempts to record an electric *Nebraska*, Springsteen had the band take a turn at this one. And as history would prove, unlike the other Colts Neck songs that weren't conducive to full-band arrangements, "Born in the U.S.A." was destined to be a rock-and-roll song.

The studio version of "Born in the U.S.A." that millions of fans would soon know begins with a single piano-and-bass note. Then Max Weinberg kicks in, his drumbeat keeping time for a martial six-note phrase on synthesizer, which provides the melodic hook throughout the song. Then Springsteen joins in, singing of a character from a "dead man's town" who's given a choice: serve in Vietnam or (we can assume from references to his "home-town jam") serve time. He chooses the former, goes off to "kill the yellow man," returns from war, and can't get hired back. But he's the lucky one; his brother went to Vietnam and never came back.

The song's lyrical structure shows just how far Springsteen had evolved from the extensive lyricism of his first three albums. "Born in the U.S.A." tells its story in quick four-line stanzas. The couplet "Come back home to the refinery / Hiring man says 'Son if it was up to me'" is exemplary of Springsteen's economic lyrics. We learn that the protagonist worked at a refinery before the war, that he is unable to get his job back upon his return, and (most importantly) that his foreman can't hire him back due to the larger economic situation—all without the singer telling us any of this explicitly. Similarly, one line about his brother (a "buddy" in the "Vietnam" version) packs a lot of punch: "They're still there, he's all gone." In just one line, we have an implied killed-in-action and (again, more importantly) a damning assessment of the entire war's futility: his brother, and the other Vietnam fatalities, died in vain because "they" (the Viet Cong) remain. As the world would learn conclusively by the end of the decade, the domino theory rationale for the Vietnam War proved false.

The final verse and chorus reprise include unexpected references to, respectively, Martha and the Vandellas' 1965 hit "Nowhere to Run" and Hank Williams's 1948 song "I'm a Long Gone Daddy." The first is a song about the heartbreak of lost love, and the second is a leaving lover's final tell-off. The reference to "Nowhere to Run" serves as a callout to the Top 40 hits on which Springsteen grew up (the "three-minute records" he sings about in the song "No Surrender"). According to Himes in regard to the Williams reference, "Springsteen drops the leaving but retains the swagger, using 'gone' in that beat-poet sense of being 'cool' or 'far out.' 'I'm a long gone daddy in the U.S.A.,' his protagonist sings, as if confident that all the hypocritical judges, hard-assed sergeants, and head-shaking personnel officers in the world can't break his spirit."[5]

Likewise, we take the same sense of indomitable spirit from the singer's oft-repeated declaration "I was born in the U.S.A." As Himes notes, it is as if Springsteen is echoing "Woody Guthrie's assertion that 'this land is my land,' that no one can chase him off, that the nation belongs as much to him as to anyone."[6]

The album's title track records one of the classic impromptu in-studio moments in rock music. As the song was winding down, Springsteen yelled to Weinberg to keep the drums going, and Weinberg let loose with an extended roll that allowed the band to collect its energy before kicking back in for the song's conclusion. As Springsteen remembered, "We played it two times and our second take is the record. That's why the guys are really on the edge. You can hear Max—to me, he was right up there with the best of them on that song."[7]

And that song would go right up there with the likes of "Born to Run" and "Rosalita" as one of Springsteen's signature songs. It would also provide the title, the moral center, and even the packaging of Springsteen's seventh album. In *Songs*, Springsteen notes that the song "set the mark and feel" for the other songs on *Born in the U.S.A.*[8]

Tellingly, he also says that it "more or less stood by itself. The rest of the album contains a group of songs about which I've always had some ambivalence." He almost looks back on *Born in the U.S.A.* as being an artistic failure of sorts. "I wanted to take [*Nebraska*] and electrify it," he writes. "But it really didn't flesh out like I had hoped it would."[9]

With that said, it's interesting to jump ahead a year or two, by which time *Born in the U.S.A.* had become far and away Springsteen's best-selling album—indeed, one of the best-selling albums, period. It sold 20 million copies worldwide and spawned 7 Top 10 hits (this from an artist who had scored only two to date, and those seemingly in spite of himself), not to mention several heavy-rotation MTV videos, a mammoth worldwide tour, household-name status for Springsteen, a copycat Chrysler commercial, and even a presidential campaign controversy. All of this came from a collection of 12 songs, most of which Springsteen would later come to regard with ambivalence.

This might seem ironic, but it's really not. Ever since *Born to Run*, Springsteen had been struggling with competing motivations within himself: the desire to be a popular musician versus the ramifications of becoming popular. The former is self-explanatory; the latter is more complex. For Springsteen, his concern seems to have been not so much with protecting his privacy in the face of intense media glare—though that would surely become an issue in his life and career—as it was with not having his work co-opted by the popular culture and society. This concern would prove hard to manage with the release of *Born in the U.S.A.*, an album designed to reach the broadest common denominator of American popular culture.

As Marsh records, the night in May 1982 that the band recorded "Born in the U.S.A." was when "they knew they'd really begun making an album." Over the next few weeks, Springsteen and the E Street Band hit their stride, recording a number of new songs live in the studio, with minimal overdubbing.[10]

"Working on the Highway," which grew out of "Child Bride" from the Colts Neck tape, provides a nice study of how Springsteen moved toward a wider audience with *Born in the U.S.A.* The earlier "Child Bride," another sung-from-behind-bars tale, is written from the perspective of a man who falls in love with an underage girl and runs away with her (consensually) down to Florida. But the girl's brothers track them down and call the cops, and the man is sent to jail for violating the Mann Act.

"Working on the Highway" retains the story of the man in love with a girl too young, along with several lines from the original song's lyrics. But in its full-band arrangement with its rockabilly rhythm, firecracker percussion, and five-note organ phrase, the story is transformed from a brooding acoustic tale into a snappy almost happy song. Some lines providing further exposition on the young couple's love are deleted, and the tragedy of this ill-fated love is lessened. When the singer ends up on the Charlotte County road gang at song's end, the effect is less of a hurt song than that of a blue-collar ditty, with the singer merely answering a different "work bell clang" than he had when he used to wave a red flag on County Road 95.

"Child Bride" might have worked on an album such as *Nebraska*. (And as Springsteen site webmaster Flynn McLean notes, if the producers of the *Lost Masters* bootleg volume that includes "Child Bride" were ever brought up on charges of copyright infringement, "they could play Child Bride back to back with Working on the Highway and they would be acquitted.")[11] But with its appeal to both blue-collar rock and good ol' boy country fans, "Working on the Highway" works much better as a popular song, and it provides an excellent album track, maintaining a level of energy and fun on side one of *Born in the U.S.A.*, bridging from the sing-along sha-la-las of "Darlington County" to the painful dream-love of "Downbound Train."

"Darlington County" dates back to *Darkness*. I've never heard the original version of the song, but all one has to do is to hear the cowbell at the beginning of the track on *Born in the U.S.A.* to realize that it must have evolved musically quite a bit from the original version. "Darlington County" is another song steeped in countrified blue-collarism, with the singer and his friend Wayne driving down from New York City into South Carolina in search of union jobs. In a 180-degree twist on "Kitty's Back," our dual protagonists are city boys looking to score some local girls. But these two aren't pretty boys like the one who stole Kitty; they're more mischievous than anything else. They speed through 800 miles of road "without seeing a cop," and when they reach their destination, they try to work some girls by waving rolls of cash and claiming that each of their fathers owns one of the Twin Towers. (The song stands as a relic of the pre-9/11 world.) And as the singer leaves Darlington with a "little girl" at the song's conclusion, he spots Wayne "handcuffed to the bumper of a state trooper's Ford." Jimmy Guterman says that "It's unclear whether the Ford is moving," and although that suggestion feels a bit too extreme for the song, it illustrates his point that "You could dance and shout to them or you could wonder what was going on beneath all those 'Sha-la-la's.'"[12]

"Downbound Train" might be the best song on the record. (In her 1984 review, Debby Bull called it "the saddest song he's ever written," which might explain why it was never released as a single.) In its *Nebraska* incarnation (aka the "Son You May Kiss the Bride" version, named after some lyrics that were later deleted), it doesn't quite work. (The up-tempo approach of that version doesn't quite fit its bittersweet story.) Slowed down and with full instrumentation, though, the *Born in the U.S.A.* version is a standout. The opening strums of a minor-chord guitar melody lay the foundation for one of Springsteen's most bittersweet songs. Like the protagonist of "Stolen Car" or any number of songs on *Nebraska*, the teller of "Downbound Train" once had a job, had a wife—but then it all fell apart. After he gets laid off from his job at the lumberyard, his wife leaves him; he sings to us alone, working at a car wash, "Where all it ever does is rain." It's a nice metaphor for the car wash, but it's also an echo of Credence Clearwater Revival's "Who'll Stop the Rain?"—which has nothing to do with weather and everything to do with mental hardship. Bull declared that "It's a line Sam Shepard could have written: so pathetic and so funny, you don't know how to react."[13]

The whistle of the nearby Central Line reminds the singer of his ex-wife's departure as he goes to sleep at night. A mournful synthesizer introduces a dreamlike musical element to the song. The singer hears his lover crying for him. He follows her voice through the woods to a clearing, where their "wedding house" emerges, shining in the moonlight. He runs into the house and up the stairs, but when he gets to their bedroom, it's empty—then, heartbreakingly, the train whistle awakes the singer from his dream. The singer concludes grimly "don't it feel like you're a rider on a downbound train."

From the cold-sweat passion of "Downbound Train," the album moves to the heated passion of "I'm on Fire," a two-and-a-half-minute ode to adulterous lust. The song was recorded in the minimalist country-folk style of Johnny Cash and the Tennessee Three. (Cash covered the song in a stirring version that was included as a bonus on the *Badlands* compilation.) According to Himes, Springsteen came across the song in his notebook and recorded it with Roy Bittan and Max Weinberg one evening while the rest of the band was on dinner break.[14] Springsteen sings in a sonorous Cash-like voice. The music is understated—Bittan's synthesizer lines are restrained, and Weinberg's drumming is like the ticking of a clock—and the words are what give the song its heat. "Hey little girl is your daddy home?" the singer asks, and when he asks if her "daddy" can do the same thing to her that the singer can, we know that this song has nothing to do with incest. Nor is it a simple statement of who's-your-daddy-ism. When the singer confesses that he feels like someone "cut a six-inch valley / through the middle of my soul" and that he wakes up in the middle of the night soaked with sweat, it's clear which person is really in charge of the other.

On side two, the songs speak more of nostalgia than passion. "Glory Days" best exemplifies what made *Born in the U.S.A.* work as a pop record. With its descriptions of the onetime high school baseball star sitting at a bar remembering his (long-gone) glory days as well as the once-beautiful girl who is now a divorcée raising two kids, the song touches upon the "best years of our lives" cliché that, nevertheless, rang true to many of Springsteen's listeners. It's not a happy song. The singer finds himself hoping that he won't "sit around thinking" about his own lost glory days when he gets old and then concedes "But I probably will." As Marsh says, "Despite its giddiness, 'Glory Days' is as much about the fear of death as anything on *Nebraska*."[15] Yet the song is a happy song. From the let's-get-this-party-started guitar intro to the faded beauty's ability to deal with her lost direction in life—"when she feels like crying / she starts laughing"—the song emerges as a communal statement of endurance.

Between the summer of 1982 and the spring of 1983, Springsteen had recorded a number of demos (24-track mixes, more polished than the Colts Neck Teac tapes) at the garage studio in his Hollywood Hills bungalow. A number of them had a rockabilly or country feel: songs such as "Betty Jean" ("Honey you're cute, but you sure are mean / Oh, Betty Jean"), "One Love" (a simple statement of love), "Sugarland" (a despairing farmer sings "I'm sittin' down at the Sugarland bar / Might as well bury my body right here"), "The Klansman" (from the view of a child raised in a racist family), "Delivery Man" (a comic song culminating in a truck crash and the narrator chasing chickens across a parking lot), and "Don't Back Down" (a buck-up song that Springsteen ran through in at least 10 different versions). There was also "Follow That Dream," a reworking of the 1962 Elvis Presley single by the same name, and "Baby I'm So Cold (Turn the Lights Down Low)," itself a rewrite of Springsteen's "Follow That Dream" with new lyrics.

A number of the so-called Hollywood Hills tracks had a *Nebraska*-like folk tenor. Like "Losin' Kind," "Fugitive Dreams" is inspired by *Out of the Past*: a tale of a man whose "satisfied" life with his wife and children is disrupted by the appearance of a mysterious visitor who mentions something he'd "done a long time ago." And like "Losin' Kind," the narrators of "James Lincoln Deere" and "Richfield Whistle" begin by stating their name and then touch upon a similar territory as "Johnny 99."

"Richfield Whistle" tells the story of James Lucas, a parolee from an Indiana prison. Lucas marries, and he and his wife "worked as hard as two people could," but we're told that "This didn't do no good." Lucas gets a parolee job making deliveries for a rich business owner, but he starts skimming off the top of his cargo and selling it on the side. Although he admits that he "didn't like" what he was doing, he says that "I didn't lose no sleep at night." But then his boss discovers Lucas's crime. That night Lucas fights with his wife, and he goes off driving, apparently headed on a downward spiral like the driver in "Stolen Car." He pulls into a liquor store, and (in a nice touch of Flannery O'Connor–esque detail) leaves his motor running—signaling a planned getaway for an intended robbery. But when the narrator stands before the store cashier, he changes his mind, turns around, and heads out. He goes home and reconciles with his wife, and they lie in bed, listening to the prison whistle blow in the distance.

In "James Lincoln Deere," James Deere sings from within Richfield Prison, looking back on the days when he was free—"Just a kid, no better or worse than you," he tells the listener—and the crime that took away his freedom.

Unlike Lucas, Deere says that he and his wife Terry "got by all right," but Deere is tempted by his brother-in-law, who would show off rolls of money that he made by selling stolen farm equipment. (Note the proximity of the narrator's name to the name of the leading farm equipment vendor, John Deere.) Deere resists temptation until he loses his job. The two rob a Stop and Shop supermarket, and Deere shoots a store boy while getting away.

In retrospect, we can see how "Johnny 99" works better than either of the two Richfield songs. "Richfield Whistle" tells a compelling narrative, but the couple's financial woes seem glossed over in the end. Meanwhile, Deere's crime—shooting a boy in the face and doing so while clearheaded and sober—is jarringly gruesome even when compared to Ralph/Johnny's act of drunken violence. Most significantly, perhaps, is that in both songs, the protagonist's wife sighs and tells him that "We can have anything we want." Her sigh casts her statement in dubious light—not to mention the fact that in both songs the protagonist finds himself living under his in-laws' roof. Interestingly, both contain a line that touches upon while at the same time questioning the heart of the American Dream.

In "James Lincoln Deere," the narrator hears a foreman say, "These jobs are goin' boys / And they ain't comin' back." The line would resurface in another song, "My Hometown," which closes the *Born in the U.S.A.* album. It's a very personal song, inspired by Springsteen's own hometown of Freehold. The first verse, based on Springsteen's memories of driving with his father through town, is surprisingly sentimental, given the songwriter's treatment of fathers from "Adam Raised a Cain" to "Independence Day" to "My Father's House." As the father drives his eight-year-old son through town, he "tousles" his son's hair and says, "Son take a good look around / This is your hometown."

In the song's final verse, the singer (now grown) finds himself telling the same thing to his own son as they drive through town. But with the middle verses referring to an incident of racial violence in 1965 and then the "whitewashed windows and vacant stores" on Main Street and the textile mill that's closing, the singer's message to his son is no longer a simple statement of pride (as his father's had been) but instead is advice to look around and remember something even as it's fading away.

As Springsteen was working on *Born in the U.S.A.*, he may have felt the same thing about his own career. The album would be the last one for nearly two decades in which Steve Van Zandt would have any part. Van Zandt, more given to R&B than the country-twang pop toward which Springsteen was migrating, was leaving the E Street Band to pursue different musical directions. This would be no small loss for Springsteen ("Buon viaggio, mio fratello, Little Steven," say the liner notes to the album), and two songs on the album, "No Surrender" and "Bobby Jean," served as musical farewells to Van Zandt.

"No Surrender" is a statement—maybe an overstatement—of youthful defiance, with allusions to blood brotherhood and forced warlike metaphors ("Like soldiers in the winter's night with a vow to defend / No retreat no surrender") and its oft-quoted insistence that "We learned more from a three minute record than we ever learned in school." Springsteen admitted later that even he finds the song to be a bit simplistic in its anthemic affirmation: "It was a song I was uncomfortable with. You don't hold out and triumph all the time in life. You compromise, you suffer defeat; you slip into life's gray areas." But Van Zandt persuaded Springsteen that the songs' depiction of friendship and of the "inspirational power of rock music" was integral to the new album's message, and Springsteen eventually added the song to *Born in the U.S.A.* in the 11th hour.[16]

"Bobby Jean" is more overtly a statement of good luck and good-bye. The song came along late in the sessions as Springsteen, Landau, and coproducer Chuck Plotkin were struggling to agree upon a selection of songs. As Marsh records, "The song was a breakthrough for Bruce in several ways. . . . This simple, spacious music was the essence of rock and roll: effortless, joyous, deeply grieved. It was the sound they'd spent the summer searching for."[17]

Although the title character's name is vaguely feminine, her/his name could stand in for the name of any close friend the singer has known "ever since we were sixteen." (Also note that the compounded first-and-middle name adds yet another rustic, inland touch to the album.)

In *The Mansion on the Hill*, Fred Goodman suggests that Van Zandt's departure from E Street also had something to do with tensions between himself and Landau. As Columbia A&R man Pete Philbin remembers, "Steve and Jon clashed constantly." Goodman writes that Van Zandt was the person to whom the band and crew members turned as a mediator. His friendship with Springsteen predated his involvement in the band, and he had his ear. That role only served to heighten the tension between him and Landau. Having fought to carve out his own niche as a producer when Mike Appel was the manager, Landau now appeared cool to having Van Zandt as a collaborator, reportedly fighting with him over royalties and production credits.[18]

Born in the U.S.A. might have been the album on which Landau cemented his role within the Springsteen camp. Indeed, Landau would have arguably his biggest influence on Springsteen's career toward the end of the *Born in the U.S.A.* sessions. Most important was Landau's role in getting two songs onto the album that would turn into the first two singles and effectively launch the *Born in the U.S.A.* machine.

The people for disco queen Donna Summer had asked Springsteen to write a song for her, and despite the apparent mismatch in genres, Springsteen agreed. Springsteen later alluded to his distaste for what he identified as the "veiled racism" behind the antidisco movement,[19] and no doubt writing for Summer offered him the opportunity to reach an R&B audience from which he had been steadily drifting. One song that he initially offered to Summer was "Cover Me," which evolved out of an earlier song, "Drop On Down and Cover Me." With its references to the rain and driving snow and the search for a lover's cover, "Cover Me" is a revved-up sexual answer to Dylan's "Shelter from the Storm." It might have worked for Summer, but Landau liked it so much that he persuaded Springsteen to keep it for his own. Instead, Springsteen gave Summer "Protection"—the opposite of "Cover Me," with the singer confessing to the object of his obsession that he needs protection from her love. Summer ended up recording the song, with Springsteen himself providing a strong guitar track.

The version of "Protection" recorded by the E Street Band is one of many noteworthy nonalbum tracks to emerge from the *Born in the U.S.A.* sessions, for which Springsteen reportedly wrote anywhere from 50 to 70 songs. These include:

- "My Love Will Not Let You Down," a rousing pickup line of a song with some not-so-subtle coercion ("Well hold still darling, hold still for God's sake");
- "County Fair," a melodic slice of bucolic life;
- "Brothers under the Bridge," a strong-muscled anthem that combines the sentiment of "No Surrender" with echoes of "Born in the U.S.A.";
- "None but the Brave," a variation on the aphoristic sentiment "only the strong survive," with a soaring sax solo from Clarence;
- "This Hard Land," a Guthrie-esque tune with an electric *Nebraska* sound;
- "TV Movie" and "Stand on It," two fast-paced rockabilly-style songs;
- "Shut Out the Light," a wistful harmonic song about the return of a man (most likely a veteran, though the song could just as well be about a parolee) welcomed home by his lover and his family;
- "Janey Don't You Lose Heart," a slower, more subtle, and more melodic venture into the territory of "Be True" and the first song that the E Street Band recorded with new guitarist Nils Lofgren and resident violinist Soozie Tyrell;
- "Johnny Bye Bye," the "I'm on Fire" B-side that borrows its two opening lines from Chuck Berry's "Bye Bye Johnny" (Berry got cowriting credits on the song) and serves as an ode to Elvis, with the image of Hank Williams's white Cadillac death car thrown in for good measure;
- "Lion's Den," a horn-infused R&B number in which the singer announces his triumph over a recent heartbreak;
- "Pink Cadillac," a down-tempo rockabilly rewrite of the Garden of Eden myth and a sustained sexual metaphor that nearly made the cut for *Born in the U.S.A.*; and
- "Wages of Sin," the song of a man resigned to keep paying for having wronged his lover.

In the summer of 1983, Springsteen began thinking of a lineup for the album and had Chuck Plotkin do a rough mix of "Born in the U.S.A.," "Glory Days," "My Hometown," "Downbound Train," "Follow That Dream," "Shut Out the Light," "My Love Will Not Let You Down," and "Sugarland." After Springsteen and the band recorded "No Surrender" and "Brothers under the

Bridge" that autumn, he polled people on which songs to include. According to Himes's history of the album, four songs—"Born in the U.S.A.," "Glory Days," "Downbound Train," and "This Hard Land"—made everyone's ballot. Springsteen leaned toward a lineup of "Born in the U.S.A.," "Murder Incorporated," "Downbound Train," "Glory Days," "This Hard Land," "My Love Will Not Let You Down," "Johnny Bye Bye," "Frankie," "I'm Goin' Down," "Working on the Highway," and "I'm on Fire"; B-sides were to include "Don't Back Down," "Sugarland," "Little Girl Like You," and "Follow That Dream." By the following March, the team was looking at a revised list that was very close to the final lineup except for the inclusion of "Murder Incorporated," "Frankie," "This Hard Land," and "Pink Cadillac"—and with one song still missing.[20]

The sessions had been enormously prolific, and in them Springsteen had shown an increasing pop sensibility. Yet Landau felt that they still had not produced the hit single that could effectively launch the album. He told Dave Marsh:

> The type of single I was talking about was a single that would truly represent what was going on. And I was also searching for a way to express the idea that I wanted something that was more direct than any one thing that was on the record. As I said to Bruce, a song where a person who is a Bruce fan, who stayed with you on *Nebraska*, even if it was mysterious to him, a song where that guy's gonna say, "Yeah, that's Bruce; that's what he's all about, right now, today."[21]

Now, telling Springsteen at this point that he still lacked a good hit record was incendiary stuff. They argued the point, and Springsteen reportedly left the studio, telling Landau, "I've written seventy songs. You want another one, *you* write it."[22]

But Springsteen settled down and went back to his hotel suite in search of just such a song. In fact, he began to write *about* this search. The chorus, a statement of creative frustration, came to him: "You can't start a fire without a spark / This gun's for hire, even if we're just dancin' in the dark." And thus was born "Dancing in the Dark," the song that would introduce Springsteen to a whole new generation of listeners in 1984.

The song is one of the more frank examinations of the creative process. It shows the songwriter struggling not just with writer's block but also with the very nature of being a public performer. The singer is bored with himself, he can't stand the sight of himself in the mirror, and he feels confined by the walls around him. He bids a nearby love to help provide the creative "spark" he needs. "I'm sick of sitting 'round here trying to write this book," he says. He's "dying for some action . . . a love reaction."

The admission that he is a "gun for hire" no doubt carries sexual innuendo (the song is called "Dancing in the Dark," after all) but it also comments on the reason that the song was written in the first place. Some might see it as a sardonic look at the argument that he'd had that day with the manager who demanded a commercial hit. The gun-for-hire image also casts Springsteen in the tradition of the freelance troubadour, ever in search of an audience.

As Bob Clearmountain, an engineer who culled the Rolling Stones' best-selling 1981 album *Tattoo You* from unreleased outtakes, completed mixing the rest of the album, "Dancing in the Dark" was released as an advance single in May 1984, with "Pink Cadillac" as a B-side that received radio play in its own right. Soaked in synthesizer, "Dancing in the Dark" was an instant radio hit, rising to No. 2 on the *Billboard* chart and held out of the top spot by Prince's "When Doves Cry," a crossover hit that appealed to both black and white audiences.

The *Born in the U.S.A.* tour touched off on June 29 in St. Paul, Minnesota, opening with "Thunder Road" before a sold-out crowd at the Civic Centre. The night's set list included eight songs from the new album, along with five from *Nebraska* (which hadn't had a supporting tour). After the intermission, the band performed "Dancing in the Dark" with the houselights on. Then, Springsteen announced that they were making a "movie" and that they were going to perform the song again. (At least one of these performances must have been lip-synced for the benefit of the video—something he would choose not to repeat for the video to "Born in the U.S.A.") The night before, film director Brian DePalma (*Scarface, Body Double*) had shot close-ups with the band, local extras, and a young actor named Courtney Cox, who played a fan pulled onstage by Springsteen to dance with him. DePalma's video, the first true music video to feature Springsteen, introduced a suddenly buff Spring-steen to the MTV generation. For some longtime fans, synthesizer tracks and a music video smacked of a sellout, but these things were very much within the musical zeitgeist of the early to mid-1980s, and they helped Springsteen reach the audience he had sought ever since first signing his contract with Mike Appel. As Springsteen says in the liner notes of his *Greatest Hits* collection, "A bunch of autograph seeking Catholic schoolgirls came rushing up to me on the streets of N.Y.C. screaming they'd seen the video." Bobbie Ann Mason's novel *In Country*, which includes many references to *Born in the U.S.A.*–era Spring-steen, has Sam, the teen-girl narrator, dreaming that "somewhere, out there on the road, in some big city, she would find a Bruce Springsteen concert. And he would pull her out of the crowd and dance with her in the dark."[23]

Born in the U.S.A. would top even Michael Jackson's *Thriller* as a goldmine for singles, and as with the two singles released during *The River*, Springsteen established a pattern of B-sides of previously unreleased songs. A second single, "Cover Me," reached into the Top 10 at No. 7. The flip side was a live recording of Tom Waits's "Jersey Girl" from the Meadowlands in 1981, a performance so convincing that the song sounds as if it were written for, if not by, Spring-steen. These were followed by "Born in the U.S.A."/"Shut Out the Light" (No. 9), "I'm on Fire"/"Johnny Bye Bye" (No. 6), "Glory Days"/"Stand on It" (No. 5), "I'm Goin' Down"/"Janey Don't You Lose Heart" (No. 9), and "My

Hometown"/"Santa Claus Is Comin' to Town" (No. 6), a live recording from C. W. Post College way back in 1975 that has since become a holiday classic.

As the hits mounted, the tour continued to gain momentum. The band played arenas throughout the United States in 1985. At the end of January, they played their first outdoor full-stadium shows, in consecutive nights at the Carrier Dome in Syracuse. Then, they took some time off before launching a world tour at the end of March. They played eight dates in Australia and then seven dates in Japan. In June, they played Slane Castle in Ireland and toured Europe through July, ending with dates at Wembley Stadium in London and Roudhay Park in Leeds before returning home for a full-out tour of America that was tacked on to answer ticket demand. A year before, the Brendan Byrne Arena was a typical E Street Band concert venue. This time, Springsteen and the E Street Band were selling out football stadiums such as Washington's RFK Stadium, Philadelphia's Veterans Coliseum, Detroit's Silverdome, Miami's Orange Bowl, the Cotton Bowl in Dallas, and, of course, Giants Stadium. The tour came to an end on October 2, with a 33-song show at the Los Angeles Coliseum. Fittingly, the encore for that show included covers of "Travellin' Band" and "Rockin' All over the World."

Born in the U.S.A. was recognized as an instant classic. In her initial *Rolling Stone* review, Bull gave the album five stars and praised its "indomitable spirit": "He's set songs as well drawn as those on his bleak acoustic album, *Nebraska*, to music that incorporates new electronic textures while keeping as its heart all of the American rock & roll from the early Sixties."[24] At year's end, the magazine's readers voted Artist of the Year, Band of the Year, Album of the Year, Single of the Year ("Dancing in the Dark"), and Music Video of the Year (ditto) to Springsteen and the E Street Band. The cornucopia of hit singles and the mammoth world tour created a phenomenon around *Born in the U.S.A.* that endured for more than a year and a half. In 1985, *Rolling Stone* magazine's readers again named Bruce Springsteen Artist of the Year despite his not having a new album (an unprecedented feat), as well as Best Songwriter, Best Male Singer, and Best Live Performance (with the E Street Band), and ranked "Glory Days" the third-best single of the year.

The Springsteen/*Born in the U.S.A.* machine helped proliferate a pop culture emergence of American heartland rock, and artists such as John Mellencamp, Tom Petty, and Bob Seger would all reap benefits. Madison Avenue sought to exploit the trend, and Lee Iococca reportedly offered Springsteen $12 million to transform "Born in the U.S.A." into a commercial jingle for Chrysler. Springsteen turned down the offer, and Chrysler turned to Plan B with a generic "Made in the U.S.A." slogan.

While Springsteen was able to prevent Madison Avenue from co-opting his songs, he couldn't prevent politicians from doing the same. At a campaign stop in Hammonton, New Jersey, in September 1984, Ronald Reagan told a cheering crowd that "America's future rests in a thousand dreams inside your hearts; it rests in the message of hope in songs so many young Americans admire: New Jersey's own Bruce Springsteen. And helping you make those dreams come true is what this job of mine is all about." Later, when asked what his favorite Bruce Springsteen song was, the 73-year-old Reagan implausibly responded "Born to Run." Democratic nominee Walter Mondale answered that Springsteen "may have been 'born to run,' but he wasn't born yesterday."[25]

Larry David Smith argues that "Reagan—in no way—co-opted Springsteen's view or implied any type of association" but merely "did what all public speakers do when visiting a particular area: He mentioned a local hero's name as an applause line."[26] Smith's rationalization might well illustrate how Reagan earned his nickname as the "Teflon president," as Reagan's allusion is a textbook example of a candidate attempting to co-opt a celebrity's popularity for political sound bite—which is exactly what it became on the evening news that night. Surely the famously jingoistic Reagan summoned Springsteen not just because he was a "local hero" but because he was a pop culture icon who transcended localities—and voting-age demographics. The implied message was that Springsteen's songs are about hope, and Reagan would fulfill that hope. Reagan was telling the American public that he and Springsteen were working for the same thing.

Performing onstage at Pittsburgh's Civic Arena on September 22, Springsteen said that "The President mentioned my name the other day, and I kinda got to wondering what his favorite album must have been. I don't think it was the *Nebraska* album. I don't think he's been listening to this one." And then he played "Johnny 99."[27]

The mass media began to take notice of the growing phenomenon of the *Born in the U.S.A.* tour. On September 12, 1984, Bernard Goldberg had profiled Springsteen on the CBS *Evening News*, saying that "His shows are like old-time revivals with the same old-time message: If they work hard enough and long enough, like Springsteen himself, they can also make it to the promised land."[28] For anyone who had been paying attention, Springsteen's lyrics carried none of the "Be like me and you can make it, too!" message that Goldberg saw. It would be easy to write off Goldberg's analysis if not for the column that George Will published the following day titled "Yankee Doodle Springsteen." Will, a conservative syndicated columnist, took in the Springsteen concert at the Capitol Center in Landover, Maryland, and reported that Springsteen "is no whiner, and the recitation of closed factories and other problems always seems punctuated by a grand, cheerful affirmation: 'Born in the U.S.A.!'" Will then went off on a tangent, arguing that "If all Americans—in labor and management, who make steel or cars or shoes or textiles—made their products with as much energy and confidence as Springsteen and his merry band make music, there would be no need for Congress to be thinking about protectionism." Granted, Will admitted, "I have not got a clue about Springsteen's politics," and surely Will's column said more about his own politics than Springsteen's. The off-point observation that Springsteen is "no whiner" plainly bespeaks a certain conservative mind-set, one that would label any questioning of the eco-nomic status quo as unmanly. At the 2004 Republican Convention, Arnold Schwarzenegger—who followed in Reagan's footsteps as a questionable actor turned even more questionable governor of California—drew the same insult-ing comparison when he called those who would complain about a struggling economy "girly men." Back in 1984, Will had prefaced his column by saying that "There is not a smidgen of androgyny in Springsteen."[29]

Will's observation placed Springsteen firmly within the 1980s political-cultural zeitgeist. Reagan had attempted to co-opt Springsteen's popularity, just as he had similarly done in alluding to popular 1980s' movie characters such as Clint Eastwood's Dirty Harry ("make my day") and Sylvester Stallone's Rambo. Stallone's character, a muscular Vietnam War vet who spoke in the equivalent of sound bites, was especially symbolic of everything with which the jingoistic Reagan attempted to identify himself. As explained by historian Bryan Garman, media theorist Susan Jeffords argues in *Hard Bodies: Hollywood Masculinity in the Reagan Era* that "the distinction between 'soft bodies' and 'hard bodies' was an important one in Reagan's ideology."[30] Garman further explains that "Reagan's combination of masculinity and nationalism shaped and was reinforced by a popular culture that 'remasculinized' the country's image of itself."[31]

Whereas the stereotypically "soft," languid bodies of "lazy" welfare mothers, drug addicts, the unemployed, and gay men were represented and perceived as being either female or African American, the determined, individualistic, patriotic, and authoritative "hard body" was associated with white men such as Reagan and Rambo.[32] Garman further notes that "Even though Springsteen questioned the moral and political motives and ramifications of the war, his masculinity, patriotism, and identification with the working class were enough to attach him to the Reagan-Rambo bandwagon."[33]

Indeed, for those who did not look beneath the message of the chorus to "Born in the U.S.A.," Springsteen must have resembled John Rambo more than Johnny 99. The character of Rambo was an Italian American Vietnam War vet who wore a headband in battle. On the *Born in the U.S.A.* tour, Spring-steen, an Italian American, sang about Vietnam War vets, sported a muscular frame, and occasionally wore a bandana around his forehead (an apparent nod to the Vietnam War soldier). For many—especially his new fans—Springsteen was the Rambo of rock, and his "Born in the U.S.A." anthem was a "celebration of a resurgent American militarism."[34]

To be fair, Springsteen himself knew the risks he was taking in soliciting a wider audience, and (as he himself would admit in retrospect) he was not entirely innocent in how his music was perceived. As Garman points out:

> With the Summer Olympic Games being held in Los Angeles and a presi-dential election slated for November, 1984 was a year of patriotic rheto-ric and the flag, a "powerful image" that Springsteen certainly used to

242 Adding Punk Attitude to the Mix, 1974–1988

his advantage. Although he would try to clarify his cultural politics during the tour, he personally benefited from and helped create the patriotic fervor that swept the nation. The flag appeared on his album cover and hung behind his concert stage, and when he sang the chorus of "Born in the U.S.A." in his performances, he and his audience rhythmically and triumphantly pumped their fists in the air.[35]

In 1975, Springsteen had landed on the rock-and-roll map with his release of *Born to Run*. Ten years down the road, he had rewritten that map. *Born in the U.S.A.* brought Springsteen unimaginable success as a recording and performing artist. Yet Springsteen's on-the-record ambiguousness hints at the double-edged nature of the album's success. "I put a lot of pressure on myself over a long period of time to reproduce the intensity of *Nebraska* on *Born in the U.S.A.* I never got it. But 'Born in the U.S.A.' is probably one of my five or six best songs, and there was something about the grab-bag nature of the rest of the album that probably made it one of my purest pop records."[36]

Today, the album remains a litmus test among fans. Several songs, including "Dancing in the Dark," "Glory Days," and (despite its awkward transition to stadium settings) "My Hometown" draw rousing ovation from concert audiences. Still, the album is often shrugged off by hardcore fans who remember with a touch of embarrassment the muscular patriotism—real or perceived—of the title song, the fashion faux pas (bandana headbands, jean vest over leather jacket), and the 18 months of nonstop airplay on Top 40 radio that had pastel-wearing girls singing Springsteen in school hallways. In many ways, the album is very much a time capsule of the 1980s' music scene that favored jingly pop songs and in which a "grab-bag" album such as *Born in the U.S.A.* would become a blockbuster success. But regardless of one's viewpoint, the album became the proverbial lion in the road—one that Springsteen himself would have to confront as he planned the next step in his career.

Notes

1. Quoted in June Skinner Sawyers, ed., *Racing in the Street: A Bruce Springsteen Reader* (New York: Penguin, 2004), 307.
2. Elizabeth Kunreuther, Center for Documentary Studies, Duke University, www-cds.aas.duke.edu/exhibits/past/frank.html.
3. Peter Marshall, "Robert Frank—The Americans and After," About.com, archived at WayBackMachine.org, http://web.archive.org/web/20060618094840/ http://photography.about.com/library/weekly/aa071000c.htm.
4. Geoffrey Himes, *Born in the U.S.A.* (New York: Continuum, 2005), 18.
5. Ibid., 23.
6. Ibid.
7. Ibid., 31.
8. Bruce Springsteen, *Songs* (New York: Avon, 1998), 165.
9. Ibid.

10. Dave Marsh, *Bruce Springsteen: Two Hearts; The Definitive Biography, 1972–2003* (New York: Routledge, 2004), 354.
11. Flynn McLean, "The Lost Masters: Introduction," archived at WayBackMachine .org, http://web.archive.org/web/20060701195854/http://home.theboots.net/the boots/lostmasters/default.html.
12. Jimmy Guterman, *Runaway American Dream: Listening to Bruce Springsteen* (New York: Da Capo, 2005), 151–152.
13. Debby Bull, quoted in Parke Puterbaugh, ed., *Bruce Springsteen, the Rolling Stone File: The Ultimate Compendium of Interviews, Articles, Facts and Opinions from the Files of Rolling Stone* (New York: Hyperion, 1996), 144.
14. Himes, *Born in the U.S.A.*, 49.
15. Marsh, *Bruce Springsteen*, 427.
16. Springsteen, *Songs*, 166.
17. Marsh, *Bruce Springsteen*, 400.
18. Fred Goodman, *The Mansion on the Hill: Dylan, Young, Geffen, Springsteen, and the Head-On Collision of Rock and Commerce* (New York: Vintage, 1997), 335.
19. Springsteen, *Songs*, 167.
20. Himes, *Born in the U.S.A.*, 101–102.
21. Marsh, *Bruce Springsteen*, 409.
22. Ibid., 410.
23. Bobbie Ann Mason, *In Country* (New York: HarperCollins, 1985), 190.
24. Bull, quoted in Puterbaugh, *Bruce Springsteen*, 142.
25. Christopher Connell, "Springsteen's Washington Concert: Beyond Politics," Associated Press wire report, August 4, 1985, http://news.google.com/newspapers?id =g4VGAAAAIBAJ&sjid=QTMNAAAAIBAJ&pg=1329,388415&dq.
26. Larry David Smith, *Bob Dylan, Bruce Springsteen, and American Song* (Westport, CT: Praeger, 2002), 138.
27. Marsh, *Bruce Springsteen*, 486–487.
28. Ibid., 479.
29. George Will, quoted in Sawyers, *Racing in the Street*, 107–109.
30. Bryan K. Garman, *A Race of Singers: Whitman's Working-Class Hero from Guthrie to Springsteen* (Chapel Hill: University of North Carolina Press), 217.
31. Ibid., 216.
32. Ibid., 217.
33. Ibid., 219.
34. Ibid., 212.
35. Ibid., 213.
36. Springsteen, *Songs*, 167.

John Fogerty

Centerfield (1985)

James E. Perone

John Fogerty, the lead singer, lead guitarist, and principal songwriter of Creedence Clearwater Revival (CCR), has been in and out of the recording industry since the breakup of his extraordinarily popular swamp rock band back in 1972. In 1985 Fogerty wrote, recorded, and released the album *Centerfield*, a collection that reflected back on the 1950s and 1960s in general, reflected back to his work with CCR, and commented on his ongoing legal battles with Fantasy Records (to which he had signed over the royalties to all of his lucrative CCR compositions in order to be released from a contract). Therefore, throughout *Centerfield* Fogerty mixes fond memories, bittersweet reminiscences, and anger. Also, throughout the album Fogerty re-creates the swamp rock and rockabilly styles that helped to make CCR stand apart from most other rock bands a decade and a half before. Most extraordinarily, this was an album performed solely by Fogerty. True, some of the drum tracks sound as though they were sequenced on a synthesizer, but the guitar, bass, and vocal overdubs give the impression of a fully functioning rock band. Although he played all of the instruments on some of his other solo projects, Fogerty's work and production on *Centerfield* represented an unparalleled success for a popular well-loved rock musician who at times seemed lost after having at one time enjoyed three solid years at the top of the charts.

Centerfield opens with one of its three hit singles, "The Old Man down the Road." In an instant, it seems as though 15 years have disappeared and the John Fogerty who sang about mysterious characters and southern superstitions over rural blues–based electric swamp rock has taken up right where he left off. The musical setting in style, tempo, guitar figures, and some of the melodic material comes right out of the tradition of Fogerty's CCR composition "Run through the Jungle." In fact, the resemblance led to a lawsuit from Fantasy Records (which owned the rights to Fogerty's CCR-era songs). Ultimately Fogerty won the lawsuit by demonstrating in court how his compositions tend to be built around certain figures—in short, he demonstrated that the resemblance was because of his compositional style and not because he directly plagiarized his earlier work. In any case, the spirit of CCR runs throughout the song. The "old man" of whom Fogerty sings is a mysterious character who "speaks in riddles," appears to be dangerous, carries a rattlesnake-covered suitcase, and so on. The "old man down the road" is the embodiment of evil and a character who comes out of the early 20th-century rural blues tradition.

Fogerty next turns to nostalgia for the innocence of youth in "Rock and Roll Girls," another hit single from the album. Listeners may notice that most of the songs on *Centerfield* conjure up a notion of earlier blues, rock, and pop musical styles. In the case of "Rock and Roll Girls," the British Invasion–era Chad and Jeremy hit "A Summer Song" might come to mind. In particular, the chord progression that runs throughout the Fogerty song is reminiscent of the chord progression of the verses of "A Summer Song." Likewise, both songs are nostalgic. However, Fogerty does not focus on a summer romance; he creates impressions of an intertwining of love, pop music, and the beautiful young women of (presumably) the 1960s.

One of the things that has been most impressive about Fogerty—who was born and raised in Berkeley, California—throughout his career is his ability to make his audience believe that he grew up in the South, surrounded by rural blues musicians such as Robert Johnson. Fogerty adopted southern themes and thoroughly integrated blues into his electric guitar playing, his vocal inflection, and his writing and continued to do so on *Centerfield*. "Big Train (From Memphis)" is a song in which Fogerty's character recounts his youth, in which one of the highlights of summer days was seeing and hearing the "big train from Memphis." He laments the fact that the train is "gone, gone, gone." And while the piece ostensibly is about a memory of the sights and sounds of the trains of the past, it can be understood metaphorically as a lamentation about the passing of time and childhood innocence and wonder. Fogerty's musical setting is pure retro-sounding rockabilly. In fact, the opening of the melody for the verse sections bears more than a passing resemblance to the opening of the melody of the old Elvis Presley hit "I'm Left, You're Right, She's Gone."

Back when CCR was at the top of the charts, John Fogerty had already written songs in which he reminisced about the past, the best-remembered of which may be "Who'll Stop the Rain." In any case, in "I Saw It on T.V." Fogerty recounts significant events from the Eisenhower era up through the Vietnam War that he (and other Americans of his generation) saw unfold on television. The bittersweet quality of Fogerty's plaintive singing and the understated accompaniment suggest both the previously mentioned song "Who'll Stop the Rain" and the CCR song "Have You Ever Seen the Rain."

Among the images that Fogerty recalls are President Dwight Eisenhower, *Howdy Doody*, Annette Funicello as a Mouseketeer, the assassination of President John F. Kennedy, the Beatles' first appearance on *The Ed Sullivan Show*, the disproval of the domino theory, and the nightly body count updates on the evening news during the Vietnam War. At the end of the song, Fogerty identifies his character as an old man who is bitter that his only son was killed in the war. "I Saw It on T.V." contains several interesting instrumental touches. On the negative side, the drum track seems to be just a touch too perfect and consistent, suggesting a synthesizer. On the positive side, Fogerty works a clever quote of the instrumental introduction of the Beatles' "Please Please Me" into the bass line he plays at the end of the first statement of the chorus section. In addition, the instrumental fade-out consists of a near-quotation of the introduction of "Who'll Stop the Rain."

On "Mr. Greed," Fogerty steps outside of the quasi-CCR sound that he had established on the previous tracks and turns to a darker upbeat electric blues style. Fogerty's lyrical approach also contrasts with that of the earlier songs. Gone are the metaphors and the bittersweet recollections of the past. In their place are firm, unyielding accusations of "Mr. Greed." If one is aware of Fogerty's ongoing legal battles with Fantasy Records CEO Saul Zaentz regarding royalties, then this song can be understood as an indictment of Zaentz. However, the antagonist of the song's title is characterized so broadly throughout the piece that his identity would have been open to interpretation back in the 1980s, as it is today. The piece is notable for Fogerty's impassioned vocals as well as his searing electric guitar licks.

Fogerty establishes a very different mood in "Searchlight." In fact, a reading of the lyrics without having first heard the song might suggest the work of a member of the introspective, confessional 1970s' singer-songwriter genre. While Fogerty ostensibly refers to a searchlight "along the rocky shore," in the final verse it becomes clear that the "searchlight" is really a metaphor for self-realization and self-knowledge. The musical setting comes out of the 1960s' soul/R&B tradition, and Fogerty sings in the style convincingly. The track is marred, however, by the electronic percussion that, unfortunately, dates this as a clearly 1980s' recording.

"The Old Man down the Road" and "Rock and Roll Girls" were major hits and are still effective and well-remembered songs in the 21st century. However, the *Centerfield* track that perhaps is most frequently heard more than a quarter century since the release of the album is its title track. "Centerfield" has remained an important baseball anthem not just because it is about the game but more importantly because Fogerty reenacts the dream of every young boy who was never quite good enough to be in the starting lineup of a baseball team. In this story, the boy gains the skill and the self-confidence to ask his coach to put him into the game, which makes the song a suitable companion for "Searchlight." Like the best of Fogerty's work, the music is engaging and instantly recognizable, and the melody is easy enough to sing along with.

The next song, "I Can't Help Myself," is less successful. The musical style—country rock—is pleasant enough and recalls some of Fogerty's album cuts with CCR, but there are several weaknesses. For one thing, Fogerty retained the synthesized hand claps from "Centerfield," and the style begs for live human beings to provide the auxiliary percussion effect. Likewise, the synthesized tuned drums practically scream "1980s" and in retrospect make the song sound like a match of two styles (1970s' country rock and 1980s' synth pop) that really do not gel particularly well. The other thing that sets the song apart from the most successful pieces on *Centerfield* is the vagueness of the lyrics. Even the songs in which Fogerty focuses on somewhat hazy metaphors provide the listener with just enough tangible detail that they can read between the lines and fill in the gaps with their imagination. Establishing the fact that Fogerty's character sees "a whirlwind up ahead" and that he can barely contain himself just is not enough.

Unfortunately, the album's final track, "Vanz Can't Dance," is another song that sounds especially dated, mostly because of Fogerty's overreliance on synthesizers. This is especially ironic, because the piece features a reggae style, and one of the things that helped to make, say, Bob Marley–era reggae so powerful was the tightness and creativity of the ensembles. Back in the mid-1980s, however, Fogerty's arrangement sounded thoroughly contemporary, so any sense of the piece sounding dated because of the extensive use of synthesizers is more symptomatic of the time than the fault of writer/performer/producer Fogerty. Synthesizers aside, though, this is an effective, barely concealed poke at then–Fantasy Records head Saul Zaentz. Fogerty modifies the Dickens tale *Oliver Twist*, and "Vanz" becomes almost a combination of Fagin and the Artful Dodger, with Fogerty's "Little Billy" playing the role of Oliver Twist.

John Fogerty's *Centerfield* offered much that immediately connected with the audience who had enjoyed the enormously popular band CCR, particularly during the three years that brought them their greatest success, 1969–1971. CCR fans might have preferred an album that was entirely focused on rekindling the musical spirit of their old favorites. It is true that the most commercially successful tracks on *Centerfield* are those that obviously connect back to the past; however, the other songs (notably "Vanz Kant Danz") show that John Fogerty was not a musical one-trick pony and that his biting social and political commentary of the past (e.g., "Fortunate Son") might be aimed in a different direction, but it was still sharp and largely hit its mark. The legacy of *Centerfield*, though, always will be nostalgia and dealing with the past as one ages. For more than a quarter century, most of the songs of *Centerfield* continue to age gracefully.

35

Tom Waits

Rain Dogs (1985)

Corinne Kessel

The song "Time," from Tom Waits's *Rain Dogs*, portrays the undoing of a man who has found himself east of East St. Louis and is falling into disconsolateness as he begins to understand that his life has become desperate and elusive. He has a growing awareness of the fact that there is nothing left for him where he is, and he feels deserted as the moon looms overhead and even the band has gone home for the night. He then joins the army, where everyone pretends to be an orphan in order to evade the emotional strain of commitment and responsibility to family and friends, who are left behind to put candles in the windows and anxiously await the soldiers' return. The dreams, memories, and prayers of sailors, soldiers, and other wanderers can easily become confused with the forged reality of erasure and negation inherent in their lives, especially when they are forced to reevaluate the motivations for their actions. Soldiers and sailors protect themselves from their emotions by not becoming attached to the people they meet; the fewer personal feelings invested, the less it will cost to move on. There is a terrible beauty in the lines "So just close your eyes, son," for "this won't hurt a bit"; they evoke the deep isolation and the desperate heroism of being caught between nowhere and no one, trying to tackle the world alone.

In the song "Singapore" (*Rain Dogs*), the theme of the sea voyager is presented. Sailors who have been all over the world, from tawny moors to the sewers of Paris, leave home, and their loved ones must again say good-bye as the seafarers embark on another journey to Singapore. These men find escape from domesticity and are hardened by life on the ocean, where new recruits are quickly molded to be tough and mean. Home is now an iron ore vessel where the rules are different; all actions become much more relevant and efficacious, as "in the land of the blind, the one-eyed man is king." However, while these sailors may rove to countless exotic places and take on many new lovers while on shore, they are reminded that while partaking of the pleasurable distractions on land, they must not fall asleep and must always be alert to danger and prepared to leave whenever they hear "that steeple bell."

Violence and paranoia fill the powerful song "Hoist That Rag" (*Real Gone*), another example of Waits's newfound political commentary on the U.S. government and its ideology. The beginning of part of America's violent history is introduced in the song with references to Piggy Knowles and Sing Sing Tommy Shay Boys, who belonged to the infamous Hook Gang in New York City. Here, America is Waits's transient character, as the American government tries to become omnipresent and to impose its grandiose policies and righteous beliefs on other countries in order to protect U.S. interests. "Hoist that rag," "the cracked bell rings," and "the ghost bird sings" are all references to idols of American patriotism—the U.S. flag, the Liberty Bell, and the bald eagle—but the terms "rag," "cracked," and "ghost" indicate that perhaps these symbols have been damaged by their use as beacons of freedom in unwanted wars. The soldiers in this song appear to be reluctant participants who are ordered to open fire as soon as they step off the boat and onto the shore and who numb themselves to the daily horrors they encounter.

The trauma of experiencing war firsthand overwhelms the soldier in "Swordfishtrombone" (*Swordfishtrombones*), who returns home from the war mentally traumatized "with a party in his head" and "an idea for a fireworks display" and hides himself away in a room above a hardware store, unable to properly function and reorient himself to reality without a machete in one hand and a bottle of scotch in the other. In order to repulse the nightmares and trepidation of combat embedded in his thoughts and memories and to unearth new possibilities of life after war, he heads out to California in search of something to help him cope with things he cannot forget. The alluded-to substance and alcohol abuse may help the soldier escape the traumatic ravages of war and the constant memories that plague him, but combined with his psychological instability from his service, it also leads to violent crimes. The various events of his life all illuminate his patterns of escape and his pronounced mental instability. He is left degraded, ruined, and surrounded by colorful rumors; "some say he's doing the obituary mambo," "some say he's hanging on the wall," and some say they saw him "sleeping in a box car going by." It is a struggle to piece together the truth about this ambiguous character, whose existence seems based on uncertainty, rumors, and unknowing and who incarnates many aspects of the idea of the wanderer as he drifts through his realities and the imaginations of those who vie to tell the biggest tale.

In "Tom Traubert's Blues" (*Small Change*), the main character Tom wants to go "waltzing Matilda" to break the despondency of being a soldier. He is tired of being surrounded by other soldiers and of being in foreign lands where no one speaks English, and he is cold and miserable. The song refers to the Australian folk song "Waltzing Matilda" by Banjo Peterson, in which the term "waltzing Matilda" means to go wandering around looking for a job carrying only a pack with the bare necessities. The pack is called a matilda, and if you were to walk behind someone carrying such a pack on his back, the up and down movement of the pack would make it appear to waltz. To explore the countryside or outback with all of your possessions wrapped in a gray blanket on your shoulder in search of stark beauty, isolation, and escape from bustling urban centers fuels a deep yearning in many wanderers. Tom Traubert has lost his patron saint of safe travel, St. Christopher, and is not looking for sympathy. He just wants the simple diversion of going waltzing Matilda to escape the haunts and horrors that would otherwise occupy his mind. He is a wanderer who travels alone, nursing a "wound that will never heal" and searching for his personal dreams and aspirations.

A war veteran in the song "Soldier's Things" (*Swordfishtrombone*) has returned or retired from the service and is having a yard sale. He longingly reminisces about his glory days in battle. This song examines how people's personal belongings, such as swallowtail coats, tablecloths, patent leather shoes, and bathing suits, take on certain human characteristics; shoes or boots can hold the shape of the feet of the previous owner and visually relate the journeys he has been on. As this soldier's service memorabilia and medals are being sold off in a dollar bin, we see a chapter being closed in the life of a world traveler.

Soldiers and sailors are commanded to wander and travel the world. It is considered a duty, and therefore they often feel no guilt when they abandon their loved ones. The military offers security without a complicated emotional commitment and allows its recruits to gain a new identity and develop a sense of purpose or immediacy in their lives. Waits's military characters grapple with their difficult lives—one day, one situation, and one place at a time—while pursuing fulfillment, adventure, a sense of duty, or, in some cases, emotional freedom.

Train Songs

Trains are a recurring image in Tom Waits's music. Characters are seen leaving on trains or experiencing life jumping trains; sometimes the outside world is depicted as it would be seen through the observation window of a train. The actual physical image of the train can be found represented in the wheeze, groan, chug, and clank of songs such as "Gospel Train" (*The Black Rider*) and "Clang Boom" (*Real Gone*), in which Waits attempts to re-create the actual sound of a locomotive with train whistles, low wind and string instruments, and imaginative percussion (and mouth percussion). Rich sources of imagery and humanity are associated with trains, such as the scenes of slow, heavy departure; loved ones fading into the distance; picturesque scenery; dark tunnels; freight yards littered with hobos and vagabonds; thick, black billows of coal smoke and steam; the haunting sound of train whistle blasts; the immediate sense of being transported somewhere else and not being able to stop until you arrive at your destination; a feeling of escape; and the sensation of being conveyed from one place to another that is new and alive with possibilities. The trains in Waits's songs are also often accompanied by the dramatization of train hoppers and their insecurities and by the migratory nature of their lifestyle. Trains provide an escape route for transients, who can simply ride the rails to the next freight yard or town when life becomes too unbearably settled or filled with ruin.

Waits uses train imagery to evoke the contrast between a certain rural, industrial, or even antiquated scene and our rapidly advancing computerized and technological society. Trains are in sharp contrast to air travel, where the images are much stranger and evoke a very different sentiment. With airplanes, loved ones walk through a metal detector and disappear, so the same sense of departure and closure achieved by watching someone fade into the distance on a train is not possible. The presence of the image of a locomotive fading away is very effectively handled metaphorically in the song "Time" (*Rain Dogs*), in which soldiers pretend that they are orphans and that, to protect their emotional state, their memories must fade away like a train that you can see "getting smaller as it pulls away," and literally in "2:19" (*Orphans—Brawlers*), in which "[o]n the train you get smaller as you get further away." In a different way, this depiction of the association between fading memories and trains is also found in "Blind Love" (*Rain Dogs*); a character stands at the train station but cannot manage to step onto the train because he does not want to lose his treasured memories of his love, who has left him. Trains embody the notion of forward motion and of transporting characters to new places and new experiences. Each destination is merely a stopover for the vagabond stranger, who is "pushed from behind by hopes frustrated, and pulled forward by hopes untested."[1] But, as trains and locomotives always are moving forward, returning to a stagnant previously led life is not a simple accomplishment.

"Town with No Cheer" (*Swordfishtrombones*) is about a small miserable old town in Australia that was devastated when the Victoria Railway Company decided that the only bar in the town, which it operated, was no longer necessary and "the train stopped in Serviceton less and less often." This small town, whose existence depended upon the goods and services it provided and received as a train stop for the past 65 years, was now slowly being abandoned because there was no longer an "oasis for a dry local grazier." The townspeople were dependent upon the travelers who rode the rails; once they no longer stopped in Serviceton, they had no other way to support their tourism-based livelihood. The Freedom bell ringing at the beginning of the song, accompanied by lonely bagpipes, helps accent the feeling of gloom looming over the ghost "town with no cheer," now viewed only from the windows of the trains passing by. There are stark dichotomies between new and old, urban and rural, prosperity and regression, which are created as the train is used as a point of observation separating the "newfangled buffet cars and faster locomotives" from the dusty "long faces" of the 80 townspeople of Serviceton. The train, which once symbolized opportunity for this small town, has now become a source of heartache, and for Vic Rail, the whistle-stop is only a fleeting memory in a business ledger. The idea of the train as a point from which to observe the world is also present in "9th and Hennepin" (*Rain Dogs*), in which a vagabond describes his decrepit neighborhood and the derelicts who inhabit it in the image that he has "seen it all through the yellow windows / of the evening train."

Trains are important fixtures in the lifestyles of wandering hobos and vagabonds, as freight hopping is a primary means of transportation and survival. "Diamonds and Gold" (*Rain Dogs*) describes the difficulty that a hobo has in tearing himself away from life on the railroad, the mad dogs of summer, and everything that he knows. The song explores the desperation of life on the railroads, where survival instincts overshadow any issues of morality or ethics. Even if they are wounded or broken, hobos will keep on going and sleep at the side of the road. The lyrics also speak to the inherent greed and avarice of capitalist society—what people will do for diamonds, silver, gold, oil, stocks, a promotion. Brutality and violence occur frequently in the lives of vagabonds and railroad tramps, as shown in this song, in which one transient is attacked and has his knees shattered and, more figuratively, another character, rising to success, has his hopes destroyed and, like scavengers looking for something to get them ahead, his fellow drifters rifle through what is left of his belongings. For these railroad vagabonds and opportunists, "a hole in the ladder" renders escape from their personal turmoil impossible, as the "hills are agreen" only in stolen dreams; even then, their dreams are not safe from pillage.

The hobo lifestyle on the rails also emerges in the rowdy field holler "Cold Water" (*Mule Variations*), in which a train-hopping vagabond claims that "there ain't nothin' sweeter" in the world "than ridin' the rails." The lonely downtrodden anthem "Bottom of the World" (*Orphans—Brawlers*) is filled with boxcar transients who have had the brotherhood and freedom of railway life instilled into them early in life by their family and friends, who claimed that "[t]he best friend you'll have is a railroad track." The wanderers in this song are filled with stories to share and are simply looking for meaning in life, doing everything they can to sustain themselves and grasping at the memories of what were once dreams. These wayward vagabonds may be lost at the "bottom of the world," yet they are still held together by hope and beauty. One character, even though he slept in a field the previous night, still finds beauty in the situation as he recounts the wonder of a drop of dew balanced perfectly on a blade of grass. Home is never one place for very long; for the main character, who has been on the move since he was 13 years old, the "bottom of the world" may not be such a terrible place. It is all he knows, and he speaks not of regret but of the people he encounters and his dreams about a beautiful girl. In contrast, the soldier in "Ruby's Arms" (*Heartattack and Vine*) is filled with regret as he leaves his love in the middle of the night, taking with him nothing but his boots and leather jacket, and heads out to where "the hobos at the freight yards have kept their fires burning." Overwhelmed by his tumultuous emotions, he is torn between his need to get on a train and leave this place and the knowledge that if he leaves, he will never see his girl again. His need for independence and personal equanimity carry a greater weight than his need for stability. This character is taken away by the next train, hoping than all of his pain stays behind. This train hopper's sense of purpose is found in the life experiences he acquires while riding the rails. He keeps his adventures short but continuous, as "the shorter the trip, the greater the chance of completing it."[2]

Trains and train stations are places where hurt, lost, and dejected characters in Tom Waits's songs seek refuge, solace, and anonymity and where hopeful people may dream or create new identities for themselves. Trains also possess a strangely inexplicable allure of promise and adventure. For example, in the song "Gospel Train" from *The Black Rider*, Wilhelm, an innocent city clerk, is drawn down the path of diablerie and corruption by a train that has the devil as its conductor, asserting that there is room for one more passenger. Waits's characters who are seduced by life on the railroads end up being strangers wherever they go, governed by intuition, caution, risks, and chance, as "Satan will fool you" even though you "trust in the Lord." The lifestyle of an itinerant train hopper involves anticipating the movements of one's adversary and being flexible in the face of the obstacles that the world inevitably conjures. The trajectory of the wanderer is often determined simply by the destination of the next train, and thus every day has no advance itinerary and is unpredictably pieced together. In contrast, the main character in "Fannin Street" (*Orphans—Bawlers*) rues the day he ever got off the train and settled down, as it was not his vagabond lifestyle that was his ruin but the temptations and seduction of Fannin Street, as he realized too late the seductive power of drinking, gambling, and deception. The enticement and appeal of all the "glitter and the roar" of Fannin Street overtook his transient and adventurous nature. When he was young his instincts impelled him to seek out an itinerant lifestyle, and with ease he was able to say good-bye to family, home, and neighborhood. It was stepping off the train and staying put that brought him to this place "where the sidewalk ends," and he is now "lost and never found."

In "Downtown Train" (*Rain Dogs*), the train embodies both hope and disappointment as a person anxiously awaits the appearance of the object of his affection on the downtown train, even though he knows that "every night is just the same." The train becomes a place of expectation and disillusionment in love for this person, who believes that surely with all the people whose paths cross in the subways he will encounter someone who has more depth and insight than the usual Brooklyn girls, who "try so hard to break out of their little worlds" but do not have the richness of character who will capture his heart. He is left longing for his true desire. The train offers this individual a place of hope and anticipation where his loneliness may be overcome and two worlds can possibly collide.

Late in the exploits of Frank, as shown in "Train Song" (*Frank's Wild Years*), the train signifies the misery, hopelessness, and failure of Frank's situation, as he finally breaks down in East St. Louis with no dreams, no money, and no one. He laments that "[i]t was a train that took me away from here / but a train can't bring me back home." The train was supposed to carry him off to fame and fortune; all his problems would be obliterated, and his dreams would come true. However, although the train did succeed in transporting him somewhere far from where he began, it took him even further away from attaining his goals so that now he has traveled a great distance without accomplishing anything memorable or of worth. Trains embody the notion of propulsion, but when his dreams did not materialize as he had hoped, returning to the life he once had was difficult. The train has guilelessly failed Frank, as for all the promise that it delicately presented, he abandoned and destroyed everything that he had, ultimately determining his own fate and taking himself far beyond the reach of a train ride in order to return back home.

The grind and wheeze of the train engine and the blasts of the whistle fit snugly into Waits's musical sound scapes and add an appropriate smear of coal dust to his lyrics and characters. The sonic beauty of a train wreck and the piercing scream of metal against metal inspire many of Waits's songs. By stepping on (or off) a train, his characters are hoping to immerse themselves in the allure of unpredictability and in new and bizarre experiences.

The Wild Years

One particular character in Waits's music, an entertainer named Frank O'Brien, is subjected to extraordinary development. This recurrent character is worked into the fabric of numerous songs as early as "Frank's Song" (*The Early Years Volume 1*); depicted in depth in *Swordfishtrombones*, *Rain Dogs*, and *Frank's Wild Years*; and transformed into a powerful theatrical work. Elements of insanity, escapism, military trauma, and encounters with temptation, addiction, and failed love are the subjects and themes that Waits explored and eventually coalesced into the personality of Frank by the time he created *Frank's Wild Years*. Biographical information on Frank must be gleaned retrospectively from textual indications, as Waits scattered the obscure circumstances of Frank's past among the songs from these three albums.

Swordfishtrombones, *Rain Dogs*, and *Frank's Wild Years* can be considered a trilogy in terms of music, style, and production values. These three albums are a major departure from Waits's past musical styles and are a progressive exploration of new timbral and textural varieties seeped in exciting new instrumentation. These albums are linked by the character Frank, who is introduced in *Swordfishtrombones*, developed in *Rain Dogs*, and then followed on his ill-fated orphic quest for fame in the play *Frank's Wild Years*. Although all of the songs from *Swordfishtrombones* and *Rain Dogs* do not necessarily contain biographical material or direct references to the character Frank, they provide a foundation for the emotional and psychological development of his transient character and how it gets represented lyrically and musically. The saga of this battered musician, who abandons his small-town misery, begins on *Swordfishtrombones* with the song "Frank's Wild Years," which creates the atmosphere for Frank's seduction, forays with the devil, fabulous adventures, and perilous exploits. It is here that Frank torches his suburban southern California home and heads north on the Hollywood Freeway. An ambitious accordion player who has fallen on hard times, Frank finds himself freezing on a park bench in a snowstorm, with only fleeting memories of his imagined triumphs as a nightclub entertainer.

In "Frank's Wild Years," from *Swordfishtrombones*, Frank finds his beginnings in typical middle-class bondage. He is a used office furniture salesman who "assumed a $30,000 loan / at 15-1/4% and put a down payment on a little two bedroom place" and leads a dull, uneventful, and unsatisfying life. He has an insubstantial relationship with his wife, whose only redeeming quality is that she can make good Bloody Marys, and he is repulsed by the blind skin-diseased Chihuahua that is the family pet. Since he is leading a normal middle-class life with no major turmoil, Frank is forced into the illusion that "they were so happy." But for a suppressed nightclub entertainer, being settled down in the valley is not bringing him any closer to attaining his dreams of success and fame. One night on his way home from his unfulfilling job as a salesman, he decides that he can tolerate it no longer, and fueled by a bellyful of beer, he douses the family home with gasoline and watches it burn to the ground. This eventful night demonstrates Frank's psychological disturbance and reveals his urge to run away as a means of escaping the shackles of domesticity. His actions signal the beginning of the rash of irrational behavior to follow as he heads out on the highway and, with no indication of remorse, has one final thought— "[n]ever could stand that dog"—as he sets out to make his dreams come true.

While songs such as "Swordfishtrombone" and "Shore Leave," from *Swordfishtrombones*, and "Singapore" and "Time," from *Rain Dogs*, do not necessarily indicate that Frank was a seafaring man or a soldier, they do help to elucidate various motivations and causes behind the mental instability and irrational behavior that eventually consume him in *Frank's Wild Years*. Although it is debatable whether or not he actually is the character in "Swordfishtrombone" who comes home from "the war with a party in his head," it is undeniable that he too has "a mad dog that wouldn't sit still," which inspires his wandering spirit. Also from *Swordfishtrombones*, the song "In the Neighborhood" depicts the military as a means of escaping a mundane life in suburbia filled with trivial annoyances and works to support the underlying theme of Frank running away to evade his problems and unhappy situations. The thematic ideas of insanity, delusion, and mental instability are synthesized in songs such as "Rain Dogs," where wanderers have "always been out of [their] minds," and "Clap Hands" (*Rain Dogs*), with its lyric "Sane, sane, they're all insane." Both of these songs develop the idea of mental disintegration, which later crystallizes with Frank's downfall.

The early workings of the subject matter for Frank's chaotic encounters with temptation and his eventual undoing can be found in such songs on *Swordfish-trombones* as "Down, Down, Down," where the moonshine-drinking, tobacco-chewing, cheating, and lying character is easily swayed by the devil, who "called him by name"; "Trouble's Braids," in which the character gets into mischief one time too many and winds up a wanted fugitive; and "Union Square," which has the character "goin' down down down." The song "Jockey Full of Bourbon" (*Rain Dogs*) is imbued with the hallucinatory images and crazed situations encountered by an inebriated bourbon-drinking vagabond. The lyrics "Across the stripes of a full moon's head" and "A flamingo drinking from a cocktail glass" explore the language of hallucinations and wild imagination that, for Frank, distort his surroundings and limit his ability to distinguish illusions from reality. Prevarication and deception are manifest in "Tango Till They're Sore" (*Rain Dogs*), in which Frank admits that he will openly and freely expose all of his deep secrets, but in the interest of self-preservation and the attainment of his goals, he must lie about his past or at least give it an interesting spin. These actions predict Frank's suffocation in a web of lies and misguided truths. This song also gives a glimpse of the future circumstances of Frank's failed dreams, when the disillusioned character requests his theme song but then is forced to concede that daisies will have to suffice as he is brought back to the reality of his situation.

Failed love and loneliness have been an inspiration for many of Waits's moving and maudlin ballads. Frank's character is unsuccessful in his pursuit of love, and this aspect of his personality has long been in development, from the heartfelt devotion of "Johnsburg, Illinois" ("She's my only true love" and "she's all that I think of") to the sad "Hang Down Your Head," where the girl is blamed for the failed relationship in which she tore "the promise from [her lover's] heart" and caused him so much pain that he had to leave, to the deeply embittered "Gin Soaked Boy," in which the theme of betrayal is prevalent in the lyrics "you've been lying to me" and "[h]ow could you crawl so low." Throughout the course of the trilogy, the full spectrum of Frank's romantic interchanges is presented and explored. When faced with misfortune or adversity in his romantic involvements, Frank's impulse to flee from the source of discomfort or pain is often overwhelming. This issue is raised and questioned in "Frank's Wild Years" when he "got on the Hollywood Freeway" and in "Swordfishtrombone," where "he packed up all his expectations" and "he lit out for California." The albums *Swordfishtrombones* and *Rain Dogs* provide an initial insight into the character development of Frank, whose character emerges full force in *Frank's Wild Years*.

In "Shake It" (*Real Gone*), a convict who has "never been no good at staying out of jail" is holed up in the Strip Poker Motel with his "[h]ot ice, cold cash." Looking for distraction from his troubled life, the outlaw hides out with a woman for the night. In the song "Trouble's Braids" (*Swordfishtrombones*), the protagonist flees from a violent crime he committed and lies low until the

bleeding stops; he then is forced to immediately adopt the lifestyle of a vagabond. This song relates the phobic escapades of this fugitive, who pulled on
"trouble's braids." In order to avoid the repercussions of his actions, he hides
"in the briars," making sure he is "downwind from the bloodhounds." Similarly, in "Gun Street Girl" (*Rain Dogs*), a character named John is running from
his armed crimes. He is a fugitive, hiding in a sycamore tree and waiting for
his pursuers to end their chase. His troubles begin after he falls in love with
a Gun Street Girl and fuels his psychotic instability with alcohol and a "bran'
new michigan 20 gauge," a dangerous combination. After he shoots a hole in
a yellow Corvette, he has no choice but to buy a different car, dye "his hair in
the bathroom of a Texaco," and leave his hometown of Waukegan as quickly as
he could. Having lost his dreams, exiled in Indiana and unable to ever return
home, forever condemned to live his life constantly with one eye on his gun
and the other on the door, he numbs his pain with the sweet relief of bourbon
and becomes a fabled story to everyone back home. The cautionary tale "Don't
Go into That Barn" (*Real Gone*) is confrontational and filled with prophetic
prose and fiendish musings. It is filled with dark, foreboding scenery such as
old black trees, upside-down slave ships, black cellophane skies, shiny tooth
talons, and a big blue moon. The song also contains what is pretty much a
murderer's checklist—asking "Did you cover your tracks?" and "Did you hide
your gun?"—and has the outlaw on the run without even a shirt.

"Walking Spanish" (*Rain Dogs*) also concerns a criminal on death row who
is unable to evade persecution and ends up "walking Spanish down the hall."
"Walking Spanish" refers to the involuntary and humiliating stride of someone
whose neck and lower torso are being held and raised by someone to spur him
along in a controlled manner or, more loosely, to being forced to do something.
This criminal is a perpetrator of violence, armed with "a homemade special."
An unspecified malicious act has been committed with his blade camouflaged
"in his trick towel," and he is once again incarcerated and forced to walk that
painful and opprobrious gait, "walking Spanish" down the hall. This character
attempts to live his life consequence-free, like the vagabond who is not bound
by societal order or restraints; however, he is largely unsuccessful. He is indif-
ferent to redemption and does not disclose his past, reveal his motivations for
his actions, or substantiate rumors. Self-righteous and rebellious, he did not
submit to interrogation or torture when he was caught and would never suc-
cumb to the will of others, no matter how hard they tried. His resolve is infal-
lible only because it has to be. He faces his unavoidable execution, knowing
that there is nothing he can do to prevent it. Despite his brash humanity, as he
is forced to remove his watch and rings before his execution, he cannot help
submitting to some extent to his immense vulnerability, as "Even Jesus wanted
just a little more time" when he was forced to walk Spanish to his death.

Waits's unsettling catalog of fallen criminals comprises dreamers as well
as wanderers, in that they are always searching for a haven, a glorious abode
where their crimes are truly forgotten and forgiven, a place of grace where

sirens do not instill gut-wrenching fear and the criminals can begin to live life again without constantly having to look over their shoulder or sleep with one eye open.

Notes

1. Zygmunt Bauman, "From Pilgrim to Tourist—or a Short History of Identity," in *Questions of Cultural Identity*, edited by Stuart Hall and Paul du Gay (London: Sage, 1996), 24.
2. Ibid., 25.

36

Paul Simon

Graceland (1986)

James Bennighof

While the completion of *Hearts and Bones* may have been a significant achievement for Paul Simon in light of the personal and creative difficulties that he had faced early in its creation, its public reception, as reflected by sales, was disappointing. This result from an album into which he had invested so much (including unusually specific—at least for him—autobiographical elements) left Simon at a creative impasse. Where was he to go now for material that engaged him artistically and at the same time could communicate with a wide range of listeners? The answer came in the form of a cassette tape of South African township jive called *Gumboots: Accordion Jive Hits, Volume II* that was given to him by guitarist Heidi Berg.

As he had so often done in the past, Simon used this distinctive musical style as a springboard for his own personal explorations. The album that emerged (released in 1986) was to be named after Elvis Presley's famous Memphis mansion, Graceland. The album resulted in two Grammy awards, a transglobal political controversy, a significant contribution to interest in world music, and a decisive reversal of the decline in popularity that was suggested by the response to *Hearts and Bones*. *Graceland* also constitutes an uncommon aesthetic achievement that richly interweaves multiple musical styles, innovative arrangements, an intricate network of textual themes, and attractive melodies.

In order to achieve this integration of disparate elements, Simon collaborated with several different groups of musicians, as he had done in earlier albums. Most often, Simon worked with American artists with very distinctive talents, such as the Roche sisters, the Onward Brass Band, the Dixie Hummingbirds, the little-known roots guitar expert Stefan Grossman, and the uniquely mellow-voiced

Phoebe Snow. Never before, though, had Simon used the approach in such a thoroughgoing manner throughout an entire album. Eight of the 11 songs use musicians drawn from four South African bands: Tao Ea Matsekha, General M. D. Shirinda and the Gaza Sisters, the Boyoyo Boys Band, and Stimela. Two songs, including 1 of these 8, use the South African a cappella church group Ladysmith Black Mambazo, and the final 2 songs feature the Louisiana Zydeco band Good Rockin' Dopsie and the Twisters and the East Los Angeles Latino band Los Lobos, respectively. (As Simon explains in the liner notes, these bands resemble several of the South African groups by virtue of their use of saxophones and accordion.)[1] Simon characteristically used these various sounds as building blocks in constructing songs, sometimes starting with a rhythm track produced by one of the groups and developing a textual idea on top of it and sometimes cowriting with the other musicians in a more traditional way. In most cases, tracks were recorded in both Africa and the United States, and Simon added some of his customary American studio collaborators to the mix of many of the songs. Finally, the album includes two guest vocal appearances by iconic American pop artists: the Everly Brothers and Linda Ronstadt.

To the accompaniment of Tao Ea Matsekha, "The Boy in the Bubble," with music by Simon and Forere Motloheloa and text by Simon, introduces the album's textual complexity through a traditional verse-chorus division of labor: initially verses narrate, while choruses comment. Thus, after the characteristic wheeze of the accordion sets a tempo, soon ratified by explosive drum strokes and then a driving bass line, the first verse presents a stark description of an urban terrorist incident. The mood is partly established by pitch structure as the singer chants on only four relentless pitches—G, A, C, and D—that are harmonized in Dorian mode on A with a repeated four-measure pattern of A5, C, and D chords. Initially the text is marked off in short phrases as they describe "a slow day," but then the explosion brings with it a flurry of words that effectively convey not only the action itself but also the rush of comprehension that an onlooker might experience in the process of realizing that an innocent-appearing baby carriage had actually contained a bomb.

This horrifying scenario is relieved by the chorus, though, as the key drops a step into a warm major tonality (G major, using the same pitches as A Dorian); only one melody pitch is added—the B that fills the earlier gap between A and C—but it also reinforces the major quality of the scale. A very unusual feature here, perhaps based on the use of the accordion patterns, is the retention of the chord progression from the verse in the chorus with the single but totally transforming change whereby all the A5 chords are replaced with G harmonies. At this point the text retreats into a slightly more detached commentary on modern life. The melody takes on a folklike quality, emphasizing the B and adding a voice (overdubbed by Simon) that tracks above the lead vocal in sweet consonant harmonies, and high synthesized sounds suggest gentle choral sighs. But the commentary here presents the listener with a kaleidoscopic swirl of images that reflect the mixture of social commentary, intimate revelation, and exuberance that will ebb and flow throughout the remainder of the album. Here these "days of miracles and wonder" are characterized by a wide variety of phenomena, all connected to technological sharing of information and ranging from the familiar "long-distance call" all the way to a dying faraway constellation. The parental, omniscient voice acknowledges that these images can produce anxiety but concludes with comfort, urging "baby" not to cry.

Having established the roles of the verse and chorus, the song can then build on them to rhetorical advantage. The pattern is repeated for another round: the Dorian setting again conveys the tension of a stark scene, this time alluding to death at the hands of nature. And, again, this verse is chanted with accelerating syllables until the chorus settles into the comforting major key to repeat its initial text. Before the third round, though, the shriek of a synthesized horn section pushes the verse and chorus to new levels of intensity. Now instead of increasing throughout, the verse begins with a rush of syllables, and instead of presenting a third narrative, it further develops the chorus's commentary on technology and commercialism. And, conversely, the chorus that follows hard on its heels, while continuing the commentary perspective ("And I believe . . ."), is endowed with new lyrics that borrow from the verses. Not only does it contain some hints of violence, but it also extends the rush of syllables in "A loose affiliation of millionaires / And billionaires."

But this new text turns out to be an embellishment, not a total transformation, as it continues with a full presentation of the original chorus. Thus returned to this commentary, the song concludes with a search for resolution as it fades out with the repeated text "don't cry."

Three of the South African performers of this song also appear on the second song, the title track. They are joined by guitarist Chikapa "Ray" Phiri of Stimela and (overdubbed some months later) pedal steel guitarist Demola Adepoju from Nigeria. As Simon observes in the liner notes, the result "almost has the feel of American country music," and this flavor will be seen to be reinforced by several additional musical and textual elements.

Instrumental and stylistic differences notwithstanding, the song continues the search begun in "The Boy in the Bubble" but in a rather more personal way. The desire for comfort and reassurance in the face of senseless violence and the overwhelming profusion of modern technology is now turned inward into a search for personal redemption. Inspired by a trip that Simon had taken with his son Harper, the song tells the story of a pilgrimage, presumably from New York City, to Memphis. Over a constantly flowing conversational groove, the lyrics unfold the narrator's ruminations on past failures and his desire for redemption.

As in "The Boy in the Bubble," verses and choruses fundamentally take on the traditional roles of narrative and commentary, respectively. The first verse tells of the journey, and the second flashes back to the point at which a relationship—perhaps the "first marriage"—broke down. (Simon has said that "'Graceland' is the continuation of the same story" begun by "Hearts and Bones.")[2]

WORLD MUSIC

Paul Simon's 1986 album *Graceland* was famous for, among other things, his collaborations with black South African musicians. While the contributions of South African singers and instrumentalists helped to make *Graceland* stand apart from the vast majority of the American pop albums of the day, the concept of including world music influences was not new. Simon himself had enlisted the talents of Peruvian musicians on Simon and Garfunkel's 1970 recording of the song "El Condor Pasa (If I Could)." Even earlier, the 1964 Beatles single "I Call Your Name" referenced Jamaican ska style in the middle eight (or bridge) section. As time progressed, however, the references to world music styles other than the artist's own became more diverse stylistically and geographically. The interest in non-Western religions and philosophies of the mid-1960s coincided with the influence of the instruments and structure of Hindustani music becoming part of the repertoire of British and American rock bands. The success of Bob Marley as a musical and political force in Jamaica in the early 1970s led to a widening of the influence of reggae and ska into the songs of the Clash, the Police, and the Police's lead singer and bassist, Sting, in the late 1970s and early 1980s. With access to an increasingly diverse body of music from around the world, artists such as the Romanian pan pipes player Gheorghe Zamfir and the Tuvan throat singer Kongar-ol Ondar (to name just two) brought the sounds of their own national and ethnic heritages to a worldwide audience and collaborated with Western musicians to create interesting new hybrid styles.

Each chorus begins by reiterating in some way that "I'm going to Graceland" and concluding with an echo of the "belief" in "The Boy in the Bubble," in this case that Graceland will receive us all. However, through the course of the song these roles are blurred: the choruses contain a significant amount of expository information, and the third verse especially provides more commentary than one might ordinarily expect.

This evolution of rhetorical function is one of several means by which Simon uses the structure of the song to reflect the desire for transformation that is expressed in the lyrics. Others are more specifically musical. Most striking among these is Simon's treatment of the melody, which varies in some interesting ways from chorus to chorus but to a remarkable degree among the three verses. These variations tend to respond to specific ideas in the text, especially in the emotion-laden recounting of the breakup in the beginning of the second verse, and they result in a sense of freedom that underscores the narrator's pilgrimage of liberation.[3]

"Graceland" is, of course, an appropriate name for a place where redemption is sought. Simon expands his focus on this iconic southern mansion with several other references to southern culture. Some of these are found in the lyrics of the first verse: "the Mississippi Delta," the "National guitar" (a steel-bodied variety, often played with a bottleneck in a blues setting), and "the cradle of the civil war" (whose lack of capitalization in the lyrics provided in the liner notes reflects its possible application to domestic strife as well).

Others, though, are conveyed in musical ways. The bottleneck style of playing a National guitar connects with the pedal steel guitar that is actually used in the recording, and Simon remarks in the liner notes on the connection of the latter instrument to American country music. Perhaps even more specific is Simon's use of the Everly Brothers, with their rockabilly associations, as backup singers. They ease into the song by evoking the wind at the end of the second verse, and their presence alludes to personal redemption not only as southern references but also in their personal significance as crucial early influences on Simon and Garfunkel.

Having conveyed a search for deliverance from both external and internal demons, the album broadens its exploration into connections in life, fraught with absurdities, poignancies, exhilarations, and heartbreaks. In many of the remaining seven African-based songs, Simon apparently used extensive passages of music that had already been composed by the African musicians and added some elements, particularly lyrical and melodic, to them. This approach is similar to one that he had already used many times in constructing his songs, in which he started with a rhythm track that he liked and wrote a song over it; the only difference is that in most of those cases he was solely or at least largely responsible for the creation of the basic track.

Most of the songs that result from this approach on this album thus automatically contain typical elements of the South African township jive, since in many cases the foundation of a song is provided by the actual musicians playing music that they wrote. Moreover, many of them share a distinctive, significant characteristic: the harmonic structure of much or all of a particular song consists of a brief sequence of chords, repeated many times as an ostinato. "I Know What I Know" provides a clear example of both of these features.

This account of some flirtatious sparring that occasionally borders on the surreal is based on a song performed by General M. D. Shirinda and the Gaza Sisters (and while the words are simply credited to Simon, the music is attributed to Simon and General M. D. Shirinda). The harmonic structure for the entire song consists of a single two-measure series—three beats on a G chord, one on F, two on C, and two on F—that occurs 10 times in each of the three verse-refrain sequences in addition to running through the instrumental introduction and the instrumental/vocal coda. This is established by guitars playing in a distinctive style along with drums and bass throughout the song.

Over this accompaniment Simon sings the verses, in each of which a heavy dose of repeated notes accommodates a lot of syllables in two couplets. In the refrain the singer declares the title line as the Gaza Sisters sing and whoop exuberantly in the background. The singer goes on to insist that he will "sing what [he] said" about the way things work.

In the first verse, the singer tells of meeting a woman who asks if she met him "at the cinematographer's party"; he responds "who am I to blow against the wind." In the second verse he tries to figure out what she means when she says that he "reminds [her] of money," and in response she delivers the line about the wind. The third verse conveys a sense of return to the first verse, as the singer speaks positively of the woman; she repeats the line about the cinematographer's party, and again it is he who asks about the wind. (Moreover, the rhymes in the first couplet of the third verse match those in the first couplet of the first verse.) In sum, Simon uses the distinctive instrumental texture, the wordplay, and the uninhibited vocal style of the Gaza Sisters to support an overall lightheartedly satirical tone in the song. While to some degree the text suggests alienation and an inability to communicate in meaningful ways, the subject matter lacks the global or personal gravity, respectively, exhibited by the previous two songs.

A very similar mood, although perhaps slightly more serious from the singer's perspective, is conveyed by the following song, "Gumboots." Here the chord progression again spans two 4/4 measures. In the key of D, one measure of D is followed by two beats apiece of G and A, and this pattern repeats throughout the entire song.[4] The basic track is provided by the Boyoyo Boys, and two of them, Jonhjon Mkhalali and Lulu Masilda, share musical composition credit with Simon.

Simon, however, receives sole credit for the words. After an instrumental introduction, these are presented in three verse-refrain pairs. In each verse, the singer describes a situation in two lines that descend from D to D but incorporate many rapidly repeated notes along the way. He then gives his response, starting "I said 'hey'"; one line here stays between the Ds, and the second again retraces the D-to-D descent. All of this occupies 12 bars (six iterations of the D-G-A pattern), and then one or more statements of the plaintive refrain "You don't feel you could love me but I feel you could" are presented, with a summing-up flavor created by starting on the high F sharp and thus superseding the Ds that have started three of the lines in each verse.

The stories that are told are fairly accessible but are somewhat unusual, especially with regard to their juxtaposition with one another. In the first verse the singer describes a difficult discussion in a taxi with a friend "who had a little bit of a breakdown." The arrival of the refrain indicates that this friend may in fact be a potential lover, and some of the text in the verse indicates that the singer was doing some verbal maneuvering and glibly minimizing the friend's situation. In the next verse, now (and until the end of the song) supported by female backup singers, the singer describes "[falling] into a phone call." The following lines suggest that the conversation didn't go well, despite his cockiness, and he contemplates giving up on the relationship; this is followed by two statements of the refrain (each echoed by the backup singers).

At this point an instrumental interlude is inserted in which saxophones— "added . . . to the original track" by Simon, aware of their common use in "'township jive' music"[5]—respond, almost jeeringly, to what has preceded it. First a single sax lays out an eight-bar descending melody that ends on the dominant note A, and then this phrase is repeated by three saxes in harmony, now ending on a tonic harmony. The third verse then begins.

Here the singer describes a flirtatious encounter on the street with a "Señorita" that seems to show promise; this (again characterized by the singer's brashness) is concluded by two statements of the refrain, and it is unclear whether this is a new romantic prospect or the same woman whom the singer has been addressing earlier in the song. While the order of the verses seems to suggest the former interpretation, the latter is reinforced by the fact that following an eight-bar interlude in which the saxes play their harmonized melody, the first verse starts over and fades out. This may indicate that the "Señorita" verse is something of a flashback or that the new relationship is inevitably destined to follow essentially the same path that had been followed by the old one (or even that incidents like the Señorita situation lead to the kind of difficult discussions that the first verse describes with the original woman).

Romantic difficulties are also discussed in the next song, "Diamonds on the Soles of Her Shoes," but in this case much of the story is told in the third person, and it differs further from "I Know What I Know" and "Gumboots" in that it touches on class issues and is characterized by poignancy rather than self-ish superficiality. Here Simon combines an introduction set against a cappella African sounds, a rhythmic and harmonic groove similar to that of "Gumboots" for the main portion of the song, and the striking image of the title to paint a distinctive picture of a relationship. Furthermore, as is often the case with such portraits, the song includes enigmatic elements, along with its suggestive references to the couple's social situation.

In the introduction, cowritten by Simon and Joseph Shabalala, the leader of the South African a cappella group Ladysmith Black Mambazo, the group sings African words to create a syncopated shuffle-rhythm background in E major. Eventually Simon sings against them, introducing the characters of his story: a rich girl with diamonds on the soles of her shoes and a poor boy who is "empty as a pocket"—at this point the other singers join his English text. In a refrain-like passage, Simon and the other singers alternate between E and A and B chords to reiterate the title line a few times.

The music comes to a halt, and then a bright electric guitar line helps to lift the song into an F major groove, presented by guitars, drums, and a distinctively growling fretless bass. At this point the chord progression that ran through all of "Gumboots" begins to do the same thing in this song—now transposed to F, it presents one measure of F, followed by two beats apiece of B flat and C. Against this groove, Simon sings the first of two verses with a highly syncopated melodic line supported by periodic gentle background-vocal pulses. The first section of the verse says that people say that the girl is crazy, but wearing the diamonds helps her "to lose these walking blues." In the second section, the singer says that "she slipped into [his] pocket"; she feels that she's been taken for granted. The singer here adopts the first person, as if he were the poor boy, but this identification seems debatable because the singer mentions his car keys, which one might expect that the poor boy wouldn't have. The third section is a refrain, with falsetto singing and bass work, that dwells again on the image of the diamond-studded soles, "as if everybody knows what [the singer is] talking about."

Following an interlude characterized first by a brass section and then by more falsetto singing, background-vocal pulses, and nimble bass runs, the second verse follows the same three-section pattern as that of the first. In the first section the two lovers communicate cryptically with one another, and the boy compensates for his nondiamonded shoes with the application of aftershave. In the second section the girl asks to go dancing, but the couple instead falls asleep in a doorway "on Upper Broadway"; without further elaboration, they are now described as having "diamonds on the soles of their shoes." Apparently the boy has somehow gained these, because after the refrain and another brass-dominated interlude, a coda presents the opening lines of the first verse again, but now they describe the singer, who has already taken on the role of the boy earlier in the verse. The song closes with a lengthy coda in which at first all singers reiterate syllables from the refrain of the introduction. Eventually a falsetto voice enters above this ostinato; here the falsetto idea has evolved into an obbligato style typical of American doo-wop of the 1950s. Finally, though, all instruments and voices besides Ladysmith Black Mambazo and African drums drop out, and these remaining performers repeat to a fade.

"You Can Call Me Al," the most widely broadcast song on the album, thanks in part to its portrayal in a popular and strikingly low-key music video featuring Simon and Chevy Chase, also paints a portrait, but in this case its subject is an individual man who is extremely ill at ease with his place in the world. The refrain proposes that the listener be his "bodyguard," but it seems that he needs emotional protection as much as any other kind, because the listener is apparently a woman with whom he would like to be on personal terms, calling her "Betty" while she calls him "Al." The refrain is cast in the first person, and most of the first two verses also quote Al.

The form of the song as a whole consists of four verses with refrains (the third is a pennywhistle solo), along with an introduction and coda. As is seen in most of the songs on the album, the harmonic structure here consists of repeated two-bar chord patterns, although the pattern varies slightly from verse to refrain: both are a bit more complicated than some of the other songs, but the most important chords are F–G minor–C in the verse and F–B flat–C in the refrain. This regularity allows the main interest of the song to be found in the textual arena, as the man's haplessness is portrayed by a torrent of verbal devices that range from cross-references of sense or sound within the song to a scattergun array of references to phenomena outside the song, sprinkled liberally with so many clichés that they make things that are not clichés sound like clichés (e.g., "incidents and accidents").

After a brass section provides the distinctively syncopated hook of the introduction, the first verse starts, as will each of the succeeding verses, with a line that sets the humorous tone by sounding like the present-tense beginning of a joke: "A man walks down the street . . ." The man bemoans his paunch and his difficult life and wants a "photo opportunity" or "a shot at redemption" (offering a humorous perspective on the theme of "Graceland"); he doesn't want to be a cartoon, although the listener can tell that he already is one. In the second section other voices join him in a repetitive revving effect as he mentions additional threats to his well-being, and he conveys a sense of superiority by saying that he doesn't find it all amusing. In the refrain, which is set against the music first presented in the introduction, the singer is joined by an additional voice, sounding hollow at the octave below.

The second verse conveys more angst; the man's attention is short, and his nights are long. Furthermore, he feels that he has lost his "role model," who has gone into the alley "with some roly-poly little bat-faced girl." This phrase not only connects sonically with the word "role" but also relates this second section to each of the others, as each refers somehow to animals. After the instrumental third verse, which connects with the common use of the pennywhistle in some South African popular music, most of the final verse eschews quotation of Al in order to comment directly on how he might relate to larger issues. Perhaps his alienation comes from the fact that he's in the Third World or he's foreign, but finally there seems to be some awareness of transcendent elements as "he sees angels in the architecture" (the first two syllables of this word rhyming with an earlier Third World reference to the "marketplace").

The coda begins with a fifth trip through the chord changes of the verse and refrain. Simon sings "na, na, na" during the verse part, using pitches drawn from the earlier melody, and a two-bar bass lick is inserted before the refrain, which has no singing. Finally, the refrain continues to repeat to a fade as some of its phrases are reiterated.

The duet with Linda Ronstadt, "Under African Skies," resembles other songs on the album by repeating a single two-bar chord progression—E flat–A flat–E flat/B flat–B flat in the key of E flat—throughout. Furthermore, the song uses bass, drums, percussion, and guitars to provide a fairly strong shuffle beat throughout. (Simon says in the liner notes that "Hilton Rosenthal describes [this] as a Zulu walking rhythm.")[6] However, the general tone of the song, as established both by the vocals' slow pace during the verses and by the subject matter, is considerably gentler than is the case for songs such as "I Know What I Know" and "Gumboots."

The harmonic structure and formal units constructed from regular four-bar phrases create a simple setting for an attractive and elegant song. First, a 2-bar guitar riff repeats for 12 measures as other instruments accumulate in the introduction. This texture continues as Simon sings the first verse, with Ronstadt providing harmonies; its 16 bars describe Joseph, whose life reflects the night, moonlight, and stars of his African skies.

Against a more vigorous accompaniment, Simon then sings the chorus alone. In its 16 bars, he uses a more highly syncopated melody, with more leaps and skips, as the singer declares that this is about memory, indwelling love, dreams of identity, and "the roots of rhythm." After the guitar riff provides an 8-bar interlude, Simon and Ronstadt sing the second verse, which fills out these themes by introducing a second character, a woman, speaking in first person, who grew up hearing "mission music" in Tucson. Apparently referring to herself, she prays for "the wings to fly through harmony."

After this verse, the two singers repeat the phrase "Ka-oombah oombah oombah oh" through an exuberant 16-bar bridge. This leads into a recapitulation of the first verse, after which the guitar riff is absorbed into atmospheric sustained sounds to conclude the song. The song thus addresses the general themes of alienation and cultural angst that pervade the album by implying that the two characters have found each other through a deeply ingrained connection with a musical impulse that transcends cultural and geographical boundaries.

These same themes are addressed in different ways in "Homeless," whose text expresses unease but whose structure reflects a fruitful collaboration between Simon and Joseph Shabalala and Ladysmith Black Mambazo. This entire song is performed a cappella, using various textures, with some African vocal effects and antiphonal singing. English and Zulu texts alternate in the song, and this results in large measure from the compositional process, which Simon describes in the liner notes.[7] The overall form is a kind of block structure in which loosely related texts follow one another.

The entire song is based on an F sharp major scale, and lines tend to gravitate toward important notes in that scale, especially F sharp and C sharp. The introduction, written by the group, uses a harmonized traditional Zulu wedding melody with Zulu words that describe people living in deprivation in caves. This leads to the title section, originally written by Simon and modified and extended in Zulu by Shabalala, that uses descending phrases to develop Simon's textual idea, "we are homeless, homeless / moonlight sleeping on a midnight lake."

The next section is an antiphonal passage that Simon wrote to provide a transition to musical material from a preexistent Ladysmith Black Mambazo song. After that is sung, Simon's transition appears again. This time it is followed by another preexisting element, a declaration that the group is the best at singing in this style, and this concludes the song.

Simon has said that the latter part of the title of "Crazy Love, Vol. II" was intended to distinguish the song from Van Morrison's similarly titled song as well as to relate to an idea that love had started and stopped twice.[8] But it might also highlight for the listener the fact that the song develops a character similar to the one depicted in "You Can Call Me Al." In this case, the story of "Fat Charlie the Archangel" is told in three verses, each followed by a chorus in which Charlie declares repeatedly that "I don't want no part of your crazy love." As was the case for other songs on the album, simple and repetitive chord changes lend a sense of simplicity to this vignette. But it is made arresting by a profusion of captivating textual images and a continuously evolving tapestry of attractive accompanimental effects. This latter attribute, combined with the jaded subject matter, exemplifies Simon's penchant for mixing unlike features within a single song, as has been mentioned in connection with the album *Paul Simon*; in fact, as Simon noted with reference to "Peace Like a River" in his 1972 *Rolling Stone* interview with Jon Landau, "That's just a thing with me, to do something that sounds pretty or light to have a nastiness in it. That's just a style; I don't do it consciously, it just comes out naturally with me."[9]

The song resembles "Under African Skies" in that it begins with a 12-bar introduction based on a 2-bar guitar riff as other instruments join in. (This riff includes two guitars, but both songs feature the performer Chikapa "Ray" Phiri, who is credited with coarranging both songs as well as "You Can Call Me Al.") The chord progression for these two bars is G–A minor seventh–G(or G/D)–D in the key of G, again reminiscent of the tonic-predominant-dominant motion of "Under African Skies," "Gumboots," the main section of "Diamonds on the Soles of Her Shoes," and the general motion of both sections of "You Can Call Me Al." This two-bar sequence continues into the verse, which consists of four 4-bar phrases, but it is replaced at the end of the first and third of these by E minor–D–C–D sequences. The deceptively approached E minor chord in each of these accompanies the last word of a line of text and colors it with a sense of dismay (a bright splash of guitar notes each time notwithstanding); in the first verse, these include the striking images of Fat Charlie "slop[ing] into the room" and being compared to a "lonely little wrinkled balloon." Although Fat Charlie claims to have no opinions, he can perceive that he is unhappy.

The verse ends on a dominant D chord, but rather than beginning with the G that would resolve it, the chorus drops suddenly into F, and Charlie's dismissals of "this crazy love" come out in four 4-bar phrases. Each of them begins with a simple F–B flat–C–F cycle; the first three end by moving through B flat to the dominant C, but the last one resolves the C to F before the G major riff begins to set up the second verse. The chorus is propelled by heavy drums on the weak beats. At the same time, though, the texture is sweetened by some swirling guitars and a high harmony voice.

The riff before the second verse is similarly sweetened by wordless vocalizing and Synclavier piping. These sounds and sustained harmonies continue into the second verse, in which Charlie has no opinion about verbal sparring with his wife and imagines that the evening news could be reporting that his life is on fire. The second chorus follows, although its second half is now replaced by "oohs" rather than text. In the following riff, a soprano saxophone subtly joins the texture and continues along with the Synclavier to warm up the third verse. Now Charlie files for divorce and regrets the time that this will cost him and the weight that he will have to lose; he now expresses his lack of opinion in the second half of the verse rather than the first. The sax also appears in the final chorus, in which Fat Charlie's exasperation and vehemence are emphasized by Simon's melody reaching up into a falsetto range, and the sax leads the way into a brief instrumental repeat-and-fade.

The final two songs on *Graceland* are collaborations similar to those of the first nine, but each of them uses an American band. Simon says in the liner notes that he chose two bands and styles that used saxophone and accordion so as to have a "musical connection to home" from the sax-and-accordion–heavy South African music.[10] The first of these was the Cajun Zydeco band Good Rockin' Dopsie and the Twisters, with whom Simon created "That Was Your Mother."

This song is a celebration of le bon temps musically and, as it turns out, textually as well. Only two chords are used, F and C in the key of F, and the entire song is based on 8-bar units: four of F, two of C, and two of F. These provide the backdrop for the band's jamming and for the singer's syncopated tale, which employs a lot of skips among chord tones in the 16-bar narrative verses and additional rapid repeated notes in the choruses (also 16 bars) that describe the joys of partying in Cajun country.

After the song is kicked off by an eight-bar accordion solo with a four-bar extension, the singer, accompanied by the band with prominent accordion, bass, drums, and washboard, begins to tell the listener a story that took place "before you was born, dude." In the story the singer was a traveling salesman, always on the move. The chorus finds him standing on a city corner looking for a place to have a good time, and then the sax provides an interlude with three eight-bar solo passes.

In the second verse the singer tells of encountering a pretty girl, and the chorus is altered to describe him wondering how he can pick her up. The accordion provides an eight-bar interlude this time. In the third verse, the title line reveals that the singer is addressing his son, and the punch line is that although the singer loves him, he wants to make clear that the son is the "burden of [the singer's] generation," and it was before the son was born that "life was great." Following a last take on the chorus and an eight-bar drum solo, the accordion leads the instruments on a final eight-bar rideout.

Simon created the final song on *Graceland*, "All around the World or the Myth of Fingerprints," with Los Lobos, an East Los Angeles–based Latino rock band. The lyrics of this song are as elusive as those of any track on the album, as they connect rather elliptically both within the song and with the themes developed in the other songs. These lyrics are distributed among verses and choruses, all of which connect with other songs by using only three chords, in this case G, C, and D in the key of G. The verses are accompanied by an acoustic guitar–dominated texture, while the accompaniment for the choruses focuses on accordion and saxophone; as was the case in "You Can Call Me Al," this accompaniment is first heard in an instrumental introduction.

The first verse, with a syncopated folklike melody, tells of a reclusive famous "former talk-show host." He declares that "it was the myth of fingerprints" (although the identity of "it" is left unspecified) and that "they're all the same." The sense of Weltschmerz suggested here is developed a bit in the chorus, which uses a more propulsive melody to describe the routine of a weary sun setting and a "black pit town" being lit up at night and ends with the first part of the title, by way of suggesting that the mundane passage of time is universally inescapable.

In the second line two of the band members add vocal harmonies to Simon's melody. This verse talks about the Indian Ocean, thus reinforcing the idea—first conveyed by the "black pit town"—that the story is located in South Africa. The verse describes an army post that is "abandoned . . . just like the war." This, too, is somehow attributed to the myth of fingerprints, and the following chorus varies slightly from the first one by changing the weary sun to a "bloody" one. The last verse, again with three singers, recapitulates the first one, except that a small reordering in a line at the halfway point sets up the last line to rhyme by saying that "we must learn to live alone" rather than the earlier "they're all the same." This is the closing thought of the song, although it is echoed by a repeated vocal coda that is mostly textless but includes the words "live on, live on, live on" as it fades out. On this note, then, that is somewhat whimsical because of the loosely connected images but ultimately pessimistic with respect to themes of alienation in an industrial technological culture, *Graceland* ends.

On a purely artistic level, the *Graceland* project proved congenial for Simon for a number of reasons. Throughout his career as a songwriter, he had demonstrated a penchant for finding new musical materials and incorporating them into his music or, more radically, using them as basis for his music. The latter approach worked better for him than it might have for some other writers, because while many might routinely begin with text and melodic ideas, Simon often started with a swatch of musical material, as it were, and created textual and melodic ideas against it. Furthermore, not only did this inclination facilitate his appropriation of various elements of South African music as starting points for the songs on the album, but these materials themselves were very attractive. In addition to the fact that their relative simplicity probably enhanced their flexibility, their combination of familiar consonant harmonies with novel rhythms and textures was naturally appealing to listeners.

Notes

1. Paul Simon, liner notes for *Graceland*, Warner Bros. 9 25447-2 (1986), 4.
2. Paul Zollo, *Songwriters on Songwriting* (New York: Da Capo, 1997), 110.
3. An extended discussion of these ideas is found in James Bennighof, "Fluidity in Paul Simon's 'Graceland': On Text and Music in a Popular Song," *College Music Symposium* 33/34 (1993/1994): 212–236.
4. At least one sheet music source, *The Definitive Paul Simon Songbook* (New York: Amsco Publications, 2005), 182–183, places bar lines differently so that the four beats of D are split and thus one bar consists of two beats of D and two of G, and the next includes two beats of A and two of D. However, it is much easier to hear

the strongest beats of measures as falling on the initial D harmony (as the point of arrival after the dominant A harmony), rather than on the third beat of D, and on the G harmony (as the initial departure from the tonic D), rather than on the A harmony.

5. Simon, liner notes for *Graceland*, 3.
6. Ibid.
7. Ibid., 4.
8. Zollo, *Songwriters on Songwriting*, 101.
9. Stacey Luftig, *The Paul Simon Companion: Four Decades of Commentary* (New York: Schirmer Books, 1997), 92.
10. Simon, liner notes for *Graceland*, 4.

37

Prince

Sign o' the Times (1987)

James E. Perone

The 1987 album *Sign o' the Times* represented the start of a problematic period for Prince: he reached a new high level of creative output that at times put him at odds with Warner Bros. Records. *Sign o' the Times* is a two-disc set, and it was to be quickly followed by another 1987 album, the so-called *Black Album*. The amount of material that Prince was writing and recording broke every rule in the recording industry about the amount of time that needed to elapse between releases in order for albums to be commercially successful. Prince wanted his material released as it was produced, and his record company wanted to maintain the space that was the corporate paradigm of the time. It is important to note that *Sign o' the Times* and the albums that followed it in quick succession were not written, recorded, and produced by Prince so quickly because they were in any way thrown together. Some of the material, recording, and production—on *Sign o' the Times* especially—was state of the art. Prince managed to be both the most prolific artist of the era and a detail-oriented perfectionist. *Sign o' the Times* has been compared to some of the famous mammoth, eclectic multidisc packages of the late 1960s and early 1970s. In particular, critics have noted its structural resemblance to the Beatles' 1968 double album *The Beatles* (commonly know as *The White Album*) and the Rolling Stones' 1972 double album *Exile on Main Street*. Like those earlier collections by the Beatles and the Rolling Stones, *Sign o' the Times* includes songs that cross numerous stylistic boundaries and deal with a wide array of lyrical subjects. *The Beatles*, *Exile on Main Street*, and *Sign o' the Times* all present the listener with so much material and such diversity of styles that the totality is challenging to take in. However, *Sign o' the Times* is one of Prince's greatest achievements.

The album begins with the title track. Here, the musical emphasis is on a melodic descent from the flatted seventh scale step. A long stepwise melodic descent, while not common at the start of a tune, was nothing new: the famous Christmas hymn "Joy to the World," attributed to the Baroque-era composer George Frederic Handel (but perhaps just based on Handel's style by American hymn composer Lowell Mason), begins with a stepwise descent through an octave. Other composers have made noteworthy use of the flatted seventh scale step and/or the seventh of the dominant-seventh chord: Hank Williams's 1947 song "Move It On Over" features a melodic arpeggiation up to the flatted step, a melodic figure that was copied almost verbatim for the 1954 song "(We're Gonna) Rock around the Clock." Leonard Bernstein's song "Somewhere," from *West Side Story*, opens with a leap of the interval of a minor seventh. Other songs such as Chuck Berry's "Reelin' and Rockin'," Badfinger's "Day after Day," and Elvis Costello's "Green Shirt" also emphasize the flatted seventh as an upper pitch limit. The Costello song, in fact, features a dramatic leap up to the note and then a stepwise descent from it. What really marks "Sign o' the Times" is the amount of almost insistent emphasis that Prince places on the flatted seventh step. All of the other songs mentioned above eventually move off in other directions, but "Sign o' the Times" reemphasizes the note again and again. This constant fall from what would ordinarily be considered an unstable, slightly dissonant scale step gives it rare emphasis as the principal melodic tone of the piece. Prince's arrangement is not quite as minimalist as the drum and bass style that became fashionable in the 1990s, but it is quite sparse. This allows the subtle details of Prince's bluesy electric guitar solos to stand out in sharp relief to the rest of the texture. It also allows the message of the lyrics to emerge easily.

Prince addresses a number of social issues in "Sign o' the Times," some that clearly define the song as a product of the 1980s and some that are more universal. At the time of the song, the disease AIDS had been recognized for only approximately a half decade. The song begins with Prince's description of a "skinny man" who dies of a "big disease with a little name." He does not identify AIDS by name, but his description leaves little doubt as to the cause of the death of the young man and the girlfriend who shared his needle. There is even an easy-to-miss subtext in Prince's lyrics. Back in 1987, a fair number of Americans still thought of AIDS as largely, if not exclusively, a disease of homosexual men. Prince, by means of his choice of characters, tells the listener (in not so many words) that AIDS is a danger to heterosexuals (the skinny man's girlfriend dies of the disease, too).

Prince also takes on gang violence in "Sign o' the Times" as well as the proliferation of guns among youths, the *Challenger* disaster, terrorist attacks on airliners, weather disasters, inner-city poverty, crack cocaine, illegal drug usage in general, the international arms race, the human tendency to inflict and risk death, and so on. He contrasts this gloomy scenario with a reference at the end of the song to the stereotypical American Dream of getting married, having a baby, and living in a house with a white picket fence (actually, he does not mention the house with the fence, but the image fits in). Prince's singing style in the verses is deliberately offhanded—almost conversational—which gives the listener the impression that he plays the role of the dispassionate social observer. One of the structural kickers of the song, though, is that Prince uses the last line of each verse to deliver a sort of punch line. Perhaps the best example of this is in the verse about his cousin's drug abuse.

The song is powerful and considerably more effective than Prince's earlier stabs at social commentary, principally because of the musical setting and arrangement and Prince's offhanded vocal performance. The overall effect is stark, thought-provoking, and somewhat eerie, especially in light of the events of the years that have passed between the recording and today.

The next song, "Play in the Sunshine," finds Prince combining elements of J. Geils Band–style party rock and Stray Cats–style neorockabilly. The lyrics speak of having fun but without the aid of alcohol and drugs. Prince also warns against the sins of envy and the collection of wealth for wealth's sake metaphorically by stating that "the color green will make your best friends leave you." Prince's conception of partying and fun revolve around dancing, enjoying music, and love. Musically, the piece is a combination of the conventional and the experimental. The harmonic progression and melody are standard rock-and-roll fare. The arrangement and production make use of speaker-to-speaker panning. This combined with Prince's hard rock/heavy metal guitar solo, sparse sections with stop-time drumming, and the sound of the marimba all provide a sort of progressive contrast. The near sonic overload of the arrangement in the middle of the song suggests the extent to which Prince wants the listener to believe that consciousness expansion and a so-called high can be achieved strictly through nonchemical means. It is very easy, however, to miss the antidrug, antienvy, and anticonsumerism message of the song, as the lyrics tend to be overshadowed by the arrangement. Fortunately, *Sign o' the Times* includes a lengthy booklet with all the lyrics printed.

Over the years, Prince has been taken to task for his perceived inability to sound thoroughly convincing in the hip-hop genre. In particular, he has been on the receiving end of derisive comments about his attempts to incorporate rap into his music. The third track on *Sign o' the Times*, "Housequake," can be read in two ways: as a serious attempt to create a dance track in the prevailing club style of the late 1980s or as a parody of the style. To the extent that the listener reads it as the former, it can reinforce every negative stereotype about Prince's place in the dance genre. As a parody of house party music, however, it is successful. Prince includes just about every kind of stereotypical dance music phrase in the lyrics that one can imagine, from "rock this mother" to "in this funky town" to "U put your foot down on the 2" to references to rock-steady music, "let's jam, y'all," and "the baddest groove." There are enough off-the-wall references in some of the rhyming couplets, such as "green eggs and ham" (rhyming with "jam") and "the saxophone is not the fault" (rhyming with "check it out"), to let the listener know that this is not a piece to be taken particularly seriously.

One the other hand, "The Ballad of Dorothy Parker" is a song that is meant to be taken seriously. Here, Prince describes his rather fetish-like sexual encounter with a waitress named Dorothy Parker. Dorothy's character mentions that Joni Mitchell's "Help Me" is her favorite song. Prince quotes a melodic phrase from the 1974 Mitchell song, but more interestingly, he sets the entire piece to the kind of light jazz-influenced music that marked some of the work of such artists as Mitchell and Carole King in the first half of the 1970s.

Given Prince's reputation for fixating on sex in his lyrics, the listener might assume that the song "It" is about, well, "it." That assumption is absolutely correct. Prince's lyrics are not particularly substantial, consisting mostly of phrases such as "gonna do IT all night long," "I wanna do IT every day," and "feels so good, IT must be a crime." The funky music, too, establishes a heavy rhythmic groove (balanced with a lighter, higher-pitched synthesizer overlay) but avoids the subtleties of Prince's more interesting songs. Simply put, this is visceral, physical music, and as such it suggests an absolute emphasis on sexual pleasure for its own sake. Interestingly, this is at odds with the ultimate conclusion of the *Around the World in a Day* (Prince and the Revolution's 1985 neopsychedelic album) track "Temptation," in which Prince states that "love is more important than sex." This apparent conflict, however, has been at the core of Prince's treatment of love and sex throughout his career. He has explored every extreme of love and sex, including their differences and their complex interrelationships. To the extent that he is inconsistent, Prince reflects the very real human confusion about the intersections of love and sex, emotional desire and physical desire.

"Starfish and Coffee" is a very different kind of song. Here, Prince's character describes a girl he knew in school: Cynthia Rose. She has an open and active imagination (she says that she starts every day with a breakfast consisting of "starfish and coffee") and a simple innocence (she enjoys drawing smiley faces on the wall) that contrasts sharply with the attitudes of her classmates. Prince's music is simple, with few chords and a narrow-range, childlike melody. The musical simplicity complements the way in which the lyrics portray the character. While Cynthia Rose perhaps is not as vivid as some of Prince's other characters, her personality and the ways in which it makes her stand out from the other students at school are clear.

"Slow Love" is a moderately slow 12/8-meter ballad in which Prince tells his lover that tonight is a night for "making slow love." It is unabashedly romantic (in sharp contrast to the earlier song, "It") and is most notable for the jazzy saxophone and trumpet arrangement. It is not a piece without its peculiarities: in particular, the clang of the finger cymbal at one point in the song reminds the listener of Prince and the Revolution's use of that particular percussion instrument to link the first several songs of *Around the World in a Day*.

The next track, the funky "Hot Thing," calls to mind the funk style of Rick James. The lyrics are not substantial: they mostly find Prince telling the "Hot

Thing" of the song's title how much she turns him on. Musically, it breaks out of the straight 1980s' funk mold by means of some interesting vocal harmony by Prince—in open fifths and octaves—that provides another suggestion that Prince was not entirely ready to leave behind the psychedelia of *Around the World in a Day*.

Disc one of *Sign o' the Times* concludes with "Forever in My Life," a song in which Prince tells his lover that he is finally ready to settle down and make a commitment to one woman. Since the lyrics are filled with clichés, the most interesting features are in the arrangement and performance. With its steady, repeated eighth note bass part and Prince's soulful vocals, "Forever in My Life" is an amalgamation of the styles of new wave rock and R&B.

Disc two of the album begins with "U Got the Look," a rare Prince song that falls pretty much into 12-bar blues form. Actually, Prince takes a some-what minimalistic approach to the form by simplifying the conventional chord progression in the third four-measure phrase. It is not the most profound song Prince has ever written: it finds him simply telling a young woman that he finds her sexually desirable because (to paraphrase) she has the look. Sheena Easton provides backing vocals, and part of the song's appeal comes from her counter-point to Prince. Despite the apparent simplicity of a musical setting of what on the surface level is a straightforward expression of desire, deeper deconstruction of the lyrics suggests a subtle subtext. Prince describes the "pretty" qualities of Easton's character as "natural"; however, he also sings that it looks as though she "took an hour just to make up [her] face." This suggests that the beauty actu-ally is far from "natural"; it is a painted on—artificial—beauty. Therefore, on a deeper, more hidden level, Prince suggests that his character confuses "natural beauty" with fashion; he is a product of consumerism to the core.

"U Got the Look" is an appealing song with strong pop hooks. It was one of the two big hit singles on *Sign o' the Times*, the title track being the other. "U Got the Look" reached No. 2 on the *Billboard* pop charts, besting the title track by one position. Despite its pop nature, however, "U Got the Look" includes a few traces of Prince's still-present neopsychedelic inclinations, including some deliberately discordant electric guitar and synthesizer licks and some spoken material (with electronic processing) that proclaims Prince's come-on lines as yet another episode in the boy-versus-girl game. Incidentally, it should be noted that Prince had been in part responsible for guest vocalist Sheena Easton's career transformation from that of a somewhat lightweight pop diva ("Morning Train") to that of a sassy sex symbol when he wrote (under the pseudonym Alexander Nevermind) the song "Sugar Walls" for her in 1984.

The next track, "If I Was Your Girlfriend," reprises the basic theme of the early Prince song "I Wanna Be Your Lover" in that it finds Prince's character thinking across gender lines. In "I Wanna Be Your Lover," Prince's character intimated that he wanted to be everything to the woman of his desires: a lover, a mother, a sister, and so on. Here, he wishes that he could share the kinds of things with his former lover that female friends share. Interestingly, Prince leaves the references vague enough that it is never clear whether he means for the term "girlfriends" to refer to lesbian lovers or platonic girlfriends. On one hand, then, the song can be read as a desire to break down the barriers that gender and previous sexual involvement can place in a relationship. On the other hand, the song can be read as the ruminations of a man whose lover left him for another woman, although that is probably quite a bit of an interpretational stretch. After the sound of orchestral string instruments tuning up (a reminder of the opening of the Beatles' *Sgt. Pepper's Lonely Hearts Club Band*) and a snippet of Felix Mendelssohn's "Wedding March," Prince establishes a gentle R&B feel. "If I Was Your Girlfriend" is truly an intriguing song, mostly because of the ambiguity with which Prince treats the meaning of the phrase "If I was your girlfriend." It forces the listener to grapple with questions of gender roles and sexual orientation.

Prince jumps headlong into an even more controversial aspect of sexuality in "Strange Relationship." In this song Prince's character apologizes to his "lover" for using her sexually. The implication is that his continuing treatment of her revolves around sex as control, if not outright violence. Even if one gives Prince's character the greatest benefit of the doubt, this is certainly an unhealthy codependent relationship: he is a user/abuser, and she seems subconsciously to thrive on being on the receiving end of his use/abuse. The thing that really makes the song seem even more vivid and alarming is that Prince sets his tale of such a dysfunctional relationship to such catchy, vaguely Caribbean-sounding music. The more one delves into the possible implications of the lyrics, the more unsettling the song becomes. It is the kind of writing and arrangement that is easy to hear as a purely musical statement on the first listening: the musical setting is so catchy that it dominates the message at first. The song then evolves with each listening as the full implications of the lyrics gradually come into greater focus.

Prince moves firmly into the new wave pop style of the 1980s for "I Could Never Take the Place of Your Man." The happy-sounding musical setting is very similar to the Bangles' arrangement of Prince's composition "Manic Monday," a recording from the previous year. Interestingly, though, "I Could Never Take the Place of Your Man" dates from the early 1980s, with the original 1982 version evolving over the years. Despite its genesis at the height of the popularity of new wave in the early 1980s and its ties to the style of "Manic Monday," structurally "I Could Never Take the Place of Your Man" breaks out of the confines of the pop new wave mold at the 3:47 mark of the recording. At that point, Prince moves into a sparse minimalistic jam in which he suspends the song's chord progression and trades multitracked, economical, bluesy electric guitar licks with himself. Prince then counts off the lead-in into the song's brief coda section, which lasts the final 25 seconds. This coda recaps the hook-heavy instrumental introduction. In this album version of the composition, the proportion of the first section to the second section is relatively close to the classical proportions of the golden mean, a relationship in which one section of a work of art is approximately 1.618 times as large as another section. While this numerical proportion and its importance in the arts dates back to ancient Greece, it was especially important to artists in the European Renaissance and to some 20th-century composers, most notably Béla Bartók. Although the listener might not think of Prince as a structuralist, some of his compositions did from time to time exhibit close ties to the proportions of the golden mean in particular and the narrative curve in general. "I Could Never Take the Place of Your Man" and the instrumental pieces that form his 2003 album *N.E.W.S.* are perhaps the clearest examples.

The lyrics of "I Could Never Take the Place of Your Man" tell the story of a woman whose lover has left her. Prince's character meets her in a bar on a Friday night. After he asks her to dance, she intimates that she is looking for someone to take the place of the man who left her, but Prince's character knows that neither one of them ultimately will be satisfied with this and that he will never be able to replace her former lover in her heart. As is the case with many of his songs, "I Could Never Take the Place of Your Man" finds Prince's character in command of his sexual destiny; however, this is a rare example of Prince portraying a character who declines a sexual encounter. It is possible to draw connections between this story and the story of Adam and Eve's fall from grace in the Old Testament book of Genesis. Interestingly, though, while Adam yields to Eve's temptation, Prince's character in this song rejects a cheap sexual encounter because he realizes that it cannot lead to a fulfilling long-term relationship. The song reinforces the message of the *Around the World in a Day* track "Temptation" ("Love is more important than sex"). Because of the song's contrasting musical style and the way in which Prince's character differs from all the other characters on *Sign o' the Times*, "I Could Never Take the Place of Your Man" plays an important structural role on the album: it adds to the collection's rich diversity.

Overall, *Sign o' the Times* does not include a large amount of the overt spirituality of its immediate predecessors or Prince's 21st-century albums. This tends to make "The Cross" stand out. It is impossible to take it for granted since it contrasts so starkly with the material that surrounds it. The song is marked by Prince's simple sustained electric guitar melodic figure, which closely resembles one of the Hindustani ragas and the Western Mixolydian mode.[1] "The Cross" begins quietly, but just over 2 minutes and 30 seconds into the piece, Prince repeats the entire text, singing with more intensity over a hard rock feel in the drums and distorted rhythm guitar. The high level of contrast between the quiet two-beat feel of the opening and the heavy, and louder, four-beat feel of the second section resembles what alternative and grunge bands would be doing on a regular basis within a few years. Certainly the style was already somewhat in the air in the late 1980s, but this high degree of dynamic and intensity contrast would not be mainstream and commonplace until the 1990s. In the last minute of the nearly 5-minute song, Prince doubles the Hindustani-influenced/Mixolydian-mode guitar figure with what sounds like a sitar, which emphasizes the musical ties to the Indian subcontinent even more. The final

10 seconds of the song consist of a chorus singing the words "the cross" in complex barbershop-style harmony. The lyrics of the song look at the concept of "the cross" in two contrasting ways: a metaphor for the burdens that people have to bear in life and a symbol of the release that God provides from those same burdens according to the Christian tradition.

The next song, "It's Gonna Be a Beautiful Night," is a collaborative composition of Prince, keyboardist Dr. Fink, and saxophonist Eric Leeds. The recording is an eight-minute-plus live performance by Prince and the Revolution. In fact, it is the only track on the album on which all members of the Revolution appear. The song itself is a James Brown–style funk dance jam, stylistically suggesting both some of the groove-type songs of Prince's first two albums and the dance-based work he would release on *The Black Album.*

Sign o' the Times concludes with "Adore," a Quiet Storm R&B love ballad. The composition and arrangement are marked by a couple of unexpected chromatic harmonic shifts and a slightly unpredictable collection of musical instrument tone color changes. The piece meanders melodically and moves from a predictable verse structure into a more unpredictable midsong almost psychedelic section. It is a recording that would probably rarely find itself on the radio or even on the stereo as make-out music: it is just too quirky and demands the listener's attention. It is best appreciated as Prince's experimentation with a specific type of genre piece. If the song is listened to in that way, it is brilliant how Prince moves out of and back into the structural confines of the genre. His use of unusual instrumental textures and a horn section that seems to appear and disappear at unexpected times also plays around with the genre.

In two CDs' worth of music Prince explores sex as part of love, sex for purely physical pleasure, the dangers of drug abuse, various other social ills, childlike innocence, the emotional side of love, religious salvation, and the dangers of codependency. He also experiments with the Quiet Storm genre and parodies contemporary dance club music. *Sign o' the Times* is a widely eclectic mix of lyrical themes and musical styles. The material covers a fairly wide range of time: the 1982 song "I Could Never Take the Place of Your Man," new songs, and songs that were left over and reworked from the shelved triple-disc set *Crystal Ball.* Prince ties it all together, though, through the implications of the album's title. If studied and enjoyed as a wide-ranging snapshot of emotions, sexual mores, social issues, and musical styles of the 1980s, it is one of the most intriguing albums of the era. It also remains one of Prince's most essential albums.

Note

1. The Mixolydian mode (or scale) closely resembles the major scale except that the seventh note is a half step lower. For example, the C major scale consists of the notes C, D, E, F, G, A, B, C; the C Mixolydian scale consists of C, D, E, F, G, A, B flat, C.

38

Sting

. . . *Nothing Like the Sun* (1987)

Christopher Gable

Sting's second solo studio album, . . . *Nothing Like the Sun*, was released in October 1987. On the whole it feels more like a typical solo album in that the supporting musicians are for the most part different on every song, very unlike *The Dream of the Blue Turtles* on which the core band remained the same. Some key figures from the first band make a reappearance, saxophonist Branford Marsalis and keyboardist Kenny Kirkland most prominently but also vocalists Dolette McDonald and Janice Pendarvis, who were both integral parts of the band during the previous tour, film, and live album. For this album Sting switches back to bass, which gives room to highlight several guest guitarists, most notably Andy Summers. Sting remains primarily on bass for subsequent solo albums.

Generally, . . . *Nothing Like the Sun* feels a bit more coherent than the first album. This is in part due to a common theme that many of the songs share: the mother-son relationship. During the writing of these songs, Sting's mother was dying of cancer; she died while he was recording the album on Montserrat. Women feature prominently in many songs. In the periodical *Timeout*, Sting observes that "I look back on this album and I realize that the record is about my mother, although I didn't see it at the time. It's about mothers and daughters, mistresses and wives, sisters. . . . It's all about women."[1]

The album title is another Shakespeare quote, this time from the opening of sonnet 130: "My mistress's eyes are nothing like the sun." This poem is about the author's perception of his love as imperfect but ends with the couplet "And yet, by heaven, I think my love as rare / as any she belied with false compare." So in the end, it is not one of the bitter poems but rather a sweet love poem and meditation on the beauty of imperfection. Sting also isolates this line as the title of his album (even though he uses the full-line quotation in the track "Sister Moon") in order to emphasize the pun on the words "sun" and "son." Sting was very close to his mother as a boy, and they stayed in touch throughout his professional life and during his parents' divorce and remarriage.

The album sold well, despite its initial release as a two-record set in the LP version. The year 1987 was still a transitional time for the music industry, and artists were releasing albums in three formats: LP, cassette, and CD. The album . . . *Nothing Like the Sun* peaked at No. 9 on the *Billboard* chart, thanks to its only truly successful single (by Sting's standards), "We'll Be Together," which reached No. 7. Other singles did not fare as well: "Englishman in New York," "Fragile," and "They Dance Alone" did not chart. "Be Still My Beating Heart" charted at No. 15. Given the generally somber mood of the album, this is not surprising. There are wonderful songs on this album, but most would not be considered radio-friendly from a Top 40 radio format perspective. Indeed, "We'll Be Together" was retooled, rerecorded, and generally funked up after the original version was deemed not sufficient to fulfill the important slot of first single; A&M Records brought in producer Bryan Loren to help Sting rework this song. The first version of this song can be heard on the greatest-hits collection *Fields of Gold*, released in 1994.

The album . . . *Nothing Like the Sun* starts off with a fittingly exuberant elegy to Sting's mother, "The Lazarus Heart." This is one of those Sting songs that in my opinion are his best: those that have a deep and rather dark (but thematically rich) lyric but with a pop-savvy exuberance that one can dance to. The song is in C but uses the Mixolydian scale, which is a major scale with a lowered seventh. This scale is frequently used in jazz and popular and folk music, and it has a quality that may be described as happy but relaxed. The main tune of the verse sounds quite folk song–like. In "The Lazarus Heart" there are also occasional flashes of dissonance (in the synthesizer and in Andy Summers's guitar) that seem to me to be bright glints in this sonic landscape of polished bronze. The vaguely West African groove is supplied by French drummer Manu Katché, who had previously played with Peter Gabriel and has since become one of the industry's most sought-after studio drummers. The African influence is not surprising, given the year the album was recorded: a year after the phenomenal success of Paul Simon's *Graceland*.

Structurally, the song does not do much of note. After an introduction, verse and chorus alternate, with a soprano sax solo after the second chorus and more solos during the fade at the end. However, right before the third verse at the end of Marsalis's solo, the band speeds up the groove by 75 percent so that they squeeze four measures into the space of three. This kind of rhythmic play (called metric modulation) is common in postwar jazz and serves the function of momentary disorientation, purely in the spirit of fun.

Sting mentions in the liner notes to the album and in many subsequent interviews that this lyric grew out of a dream he had. Like the dream of the blue

TIME-LIFE RECORDS

Several direct marketing concerns—in other words, companies whose releases were not available in stores—have sold albums directly to consumers since the 1950s. In the 1980s, Time-Life Records was known for various series of albums that were advertised on television. Most notably, Time-Life assembled collections of hit singles based on genres and based on years. These collections were otherwise unavailable on individual albums. Admittedly, the connections between Time-Life's approach and the 21st-century playlist mentality are tenuous; however, the success of Time-Life and other companies—some of which assembled similar collections that were available in stores—illustrates that the importance that American consumers place on individual hit songs is not a new phenomenon, nor was it a phenomenon that was solely associated with the 1950s and early 1960s, the era in which the music industry viewed the 45-rpm single as the primary medium for music distribution. The Time-Life collections in particular were well researched, with liner notes and CD booklets that provided information on the artists as well as information about the songs' performance on the record charts. One of the notable features of these collections, though, was the absence of recordings by some of the major bands of the 1960s (e.g., the Beatles and the Rolling Stones), whose music was not licensed to other record companies.

turtles destroying his garden, he interpreted it as being of great importance and created a piece of music out of it. In this case, his dream involved a real person from his life: his mother. She has "cut him open," giving him a wound that gives him "courage and pain." This wound most probably represents her death, which we know affected him deeply: "It was a real nightmare about my mother's death because I was feeling totally powerless."[2] The "lovely flower" that grows from the wound is, quite possibly, the album that follows. In this light, "The Lazarus Heart" is a perfect opener for this album that explores various aspects of the mother-son relationship.

Lazarus is the man Jesus raises from the dead in the New Testament miracle story. In this song, Sting is wishing that he could be the blood of this man's heart, coursing through his resurrected body. Blood is a common image through the whole song, not just in the chorus: Sting mentions the "wound" in the first and second verses; in the third verse he mentions his mother counting her children as a shield against the pain. Indirectly, this verse refers to the blood, courage, and pain of childbirth.

Moreover, by this time Sting had four children of his own. He could now count them as a shield against his own pain. Are the birds on his mother's house in the third verse possibly symbols for children? Or are they symbols of death who will eventually visit him? It almost goes without saying that this is deep subject matter, yet each individual image in the song has its own internal logic, much like the surreal logic of a dream.

The next song shares the word "heart" in its title but could not be more different. "Be Still My Beating Heart" is about eros, or the sexual form of love. In some situations it can be called lust. The situation that Sting describes is left unclear so that he can focus on the physical and psychological effects of eros. One of the first things to go by the wayside is logic, so the speaker's search for knowledge about lust is fruitless. His "logic has drowned in a sea of emotion," like the stone that sinks in the previous line of the chorus. The use of ocean and water imagery is fitting, as in Jungian terms water represents the unconscious, irrational mind.

The music that accompanies this lyric about self-restraint and inaction has a wonderful sense of bubbling under the surface. The bass part is a crucial element in this representation of contained energy. Sting plays two basic patterns, one each for the verse and the chorus. They both seem to belong to a faster song, as though the groove established by Katché is the representation of self-restraint. During the faded-in introduction (implying a continuous state), Sting plays the chorus bass riff. The change to the new riff signals the coming of the verse.

The few times when the music seems to relax are during the chorus (when the speaker attempts to calm himself using logic and reason) and during the middle eight (where the speaker comments on the futility of perfection). In each of these spots the animated bass line is absent, which implies that the bass represents the "beating heart" of the title. Also, as we have seen in previous Sting songs, the middle eight is used as an attempted escape from the song's situation. Here, he uses the brighter relative major key, C, to illustrate the idea of futility, as mentioned above. This section slips effortlessly back into the second half of the chorus: "I sink like a stone that's been thrown in the ocean." We leave the song with a still-restrained but almost bursting coda that features Andy Summers and Kirkland soloing over a double-time beat by Katché. The fade-out implies continuation, and here the implication is that this sexual tension will ultimately boil over.

The mood is lightened considerably by the next song, "Englishman in New York." Even though it is in a minor key, Sting's buoyant melody and snappy rhythm capture the quiet and crisp elegance of the subject: Sting's fellow Englishman in New York, Quentin Crisp (1908–1999). By this time Sting had purchased an apartment in Manhattan and had written most of these songs there.[3] Crisp was an openly gay eccentric author and actor with a wicked sense of humor and fun, as can be seen in Jonathan Nossiter's documentary about Crisp's life as a homosexual British expatriate, *Resident Alien*. Sting was interviewed for the documentary and appears in a few snippets. Sting and Crisp met while working on *The Bride*, a Franc Roddam–directed adaptation of the Frankenstein story. The movie bombed and was deservedly torn apart by the critics. Crisp had just a bit part, despite his much greater acting experience than

Sting—one of Crisp's most memorable roles was as Queen Elizabeth I in Sally Potter's *Orlando* (1992). The two men hit it off and met several times while Sting was in New York.

"Englishman in New York" is a song that seems to deliberately confuse the speaker with the author. On the surface, if a listener knew nothing about the origins of the song, he or she might think that it was purely autobiographical. However, Sting's explanation that it's about Quentin Crisp seems to settle the matter. But over the course of the song, the line "Be yourself, no matter what they say" emerges as the main message. It first appears at the end of verse three, returns on the reprise of that verse (after verse four), and then is repeated underneath the coda's repetition of the chorus during the fade-out. Sting has increasingly needed to remember to be himself over the years, having endured mountains of criticism (mainly from the mainstream rock press) for changing styles upon going solo, not to mention the breakup of both the Police and his first marriage. So, the speaker of this song and its author are conflated, but in the end it is Sting's voice that comes through.

Sting takes the adage "Manners maketh man," coined by William of Wykeham (1324–1404),[4] and teases more layers out of this expression. Sting probably heard it during childhood at the dinner table and at St. Cuthbert's Grammar School, exhorting young people to use etiquette to distinguish themselves from animals. ("Don't eat like a pig" would be the American equivalent.) But in this song, Sting narrows the scope of the adage to the male sex and uses it as a springboard to explore the idea of masculinity.

But Sting refers to a kind of contemporary masculinity that is in some ways a throwback to Victorian England's values. For many, the ideal contemporary man is not necessarily marked by physical strength or many of the other traditional masculine virtues, the kind referred to in verse four as "combat gear" and "a license for a gun." Masculinity today is a complex set of qualities, many of which in other times might have been seen as feminine and also in the late 20th century became even more complex with the more public addition of homosexuality to the mix. A full exploration of this topic is beyond the scope of this essay, but this song does ultimately ask the question, "What is a man?"

Seen in this light, one can hear the song's opening groove as a wonderful combination of masculine and feminine symbols. Since this is a layered rhythm (with off-beat eighth notes in the synthesized string part, the bass on every quarter note, and the bass drum on every other quarter, that is, twice as slow), it feels like a reggae-derived rhythm. But the use of a pizzicato (plucked) string sound in Kirkland's keyboard gives it a light bounce and, in my opinion, a certain feminine quality. I think that Sting was trying to capture the essence of Quentin Crisp musically, walking down the street with a calm, slightly odd, and effeminate ease and of course a civilized walking cane.

The song's structure is fairly typical: alternating verse-chorus with a middle eight that begins in the brighter relative major key of D (the main key of the song is B minor). This middle section winds up, however, after a sequence of classically inspired chords, back at B minor. Then, there is a complete change of style and groove (although still using the same chords as the verse) into a bebop-style Marsalis solo, accompanied by the rhythm section of Sting, Kirkland, and Katché. After four times through the changes (the jazz term for chord progression), we hear yet another huge stylistic shift into that of a rap or hip-hop drum pattern. And then, just as suddenly, we enter back into the cultured world of refinement and etiquette for verse four. After the coda of the repeated chorus, simultaneous with the moral of the song (mentioned above), Marsalis's lonely sax solo fades away like a solitary musician on a balcony somewhere in Greenwich Village.

Sting has said that for the middle of this song, he wanted to create the effect of looking into doors of nightclubs as the listener is walking down the street.[5] This is quite effective in portraying Crisp (as well as the listeners) as an outsider looking in at various musical styles as well as in providing a brief snapshot of the popular music scene of New York at the time. On another level, though (and connecting to the theme of the lyrics), it can be heard as observing various expressions of masculinity: the cool bebop style first and the heavy rap beat second. Both of these styles can safely be labeled primarily masculine in nature (especially in the male-dominated world of 1987 rap). Ultimately, the moral of "be yourself" shines through musically with Marsalis's lonely solo during the fade-out. This also expresses a third traditional quality of masculinity: the occasional and necessary desire for solitude.

The next song, "History Will Teach Us Nothing," is a good example of Sting's cynical side. He mentions in the liner notes that he was disillusioned by the subject of history in school. It's easy to see how. A browse through any history book does in fact seem like a "monotonous and sordid succession of robber baron scumbags."[6] This view of history can certainly challenge any optimist.

Sting does, in fact, end the song on a note of hope, but along the way he focuses on successions of power struggles with the common features of war and fear. Each verse in turn discusses freedom, religion, power, and war. The chorus of "sooner or later" is rather opaque (except generally addressing the subject of time) until just after the fourth verse. At this point we hear the title of the song for the first time (despite the incorrect printing in the CD booklet, only partially corrected in 2007's *Lyrics by Sting*), and then a change of key from a minor to A major. With the brightening of the key, we hear the more hopeful completion of the fragment "sooner or later." There is a hint of Jamaican patois in the line "Just like the world first day," with its dropped possessive. Also, Sting channels Bob Marley on the line from verse two "Without the voice of reason." As in earlier Police songs, I believe that this is not mockery but instead is homage.

The song does not remain in the happier key of A major but keeps returning to the minor sound as if to remind us that history keeps repeating itself. Even during the coda, after an assertion of the power of human rights, the music returns to a minor, following a final "sooner or later." So, this is optimism tempered by realism.

Although not one of his strongest lyrics, the reggae groove is one of the best on the album. Katché's hits during the choruses are very effective, as everything else he plays is quite subdued. Percussionist Mino Cinelu also plays an important role in this track. Sting plays electric guitar in addition to bass on this song, and he obviously had fun with the wah-wah pedal (a foot-controlled device that squelches or opens up the overtones of the sound, depending on how far back or forward one's heel is). Marsalis contributes a mournful soprano sax refrain, first heard in the introduction and later combined with the title words.

"History Will Teach Us Nothing" is one of a handful of songs in Sting's catalog that seems to have been changed in the latter stages of recording and production. The printed lyrics in both the CD and LP versions do not exactly match what is sung on the recording.[7] In this case the difference is slight but significant. The first chorus is sung as "sooner or later," still in the minor key that we started with. In the CD booklet, the longer later version of the chorus (in the major mode) is printed at this point in the song. It is my belief that Sting changed his mind about the placement of the chorus, and thus also the change of key, after the lyric sheet was laid out and sent to the printer. Either that or it was simply an oversight. The final version makes for a much more effective structure, saving the major key for later on in the song and also reducing the overall number of key changes.

Changing gears somewhat, the next track, "They Dance Alone," seems to be a response to the question posed by the previous song: Are we doomed to repeat history? In the case of South America, the unfortunate answer seems to be yes. The continent struggled throughout the 20th century to break the cycle of corruption, chaos, and dictatorship, with a few success stories and signs of hope. Yet it still seems that these countries have one foot planted in the Third World.

One country that is far better off now than in 1987 is Chile. Augusto Pinochet's CIA-backed military junta wrested power from the legitimately elected Allende government in 1973. Their practice of disappearing people (arresting, imprisoning, torturing, and executing political opponents and innocent people without trial) was still being used as late as 1986, when Sting toured the world and visited Chile as part of Amnesty International's Conspiracy of Hope tour. Pinochet's regime was finally toppled in 1990, and he died peacefully in exile in 2006, despite several attempts to convict him of crimes against humanity.

This regime suppressed not only any and all political opposition but also every art form and artist deemed dangerous or offensive in any way. This included the playing of traditional Chilean and Andean folk music.[8] The *cueca*[9] is one of the most popular folk-dance songs in the country and was outlawed in 1973. However, Sting learned firsthand during his 1986 tour that mothers, wives, and daughters of these disappeared men would dance this dance, silently, with giant photographs of their loved ones hanging from their necks. This brave act was simultaneously protest, mourning, and an expression of love.[10]

The faded-in introduction sets the stage. The ominous military-style snare drum flourishes, countered by the synthesized pan flute (a traditional Andean instrument), which represents the grieving women, some of whom were indigenous Chileans.[11] The choice of this synthesizer patch is apt, if a bit of a cliché, since all of the traditional Andean music and, by extension, instruments were banned by the regime. Thus, the instrument itself becomes part of the protest.

Sting uses each verse to address an aspect of the scene. In the first, he wonders why these women are dancing alone a dance normally done with a partner. In the second, the focus is on their enforced silence: If they speak out they could be arrested. The third verse is directed at the man responsible for this situation, Pinochet himself. It speaks of this man's tenuous hold on power, based as it is on foreign investment from like-minded regimes. This verse also brings the song full circle thematically, asking Pinochet directly to imagine his own mother performing the *cueca* solo.[12] Once again, Sting is infusing a bleak situation with hope.

The middle section, beginning with "One day we'll dance on their graves," becomes more important after the last chorus. Here, in a moment of exhilarating musical transformation, the same chord progression is used to create a samba, another South American dance but one of pure joy. The beat gets doubled exactly, but the chord changes do not speed up, and so the transition is smooth and magical. The band lets the groove build, with repeated vocal parts of "And we'll dance," until Marsalis enters with a buoyant soprano saxophone. It is hard to find a better representation of hope for the future in a popular song.

One frustrating element of this track is the mix. Sting has several guests in the studio with him, most audibly actor and musician Ruben Blades, who speaks the words of the chorus in Spanish (over music from the introduction).[13] The other three guests are notable guitarists Fareed Haque, Mark Knopfler, and Eric Clapton (all playing acoustic guitar), who unfortunately are so low in the final mix that they are practically inaudible. They play most audibly during the spoken section, under Blades, but in general don't ultimately contribute much to the sound.

"They Dance Alone" and the following song, "Fragile," are both significant in Sting's output for being some of the first to address human rights and their abuses. The Conspiracy of Hope tour, including meeting with victims of torture and the Mothers of the Disappeared, had a profound impact on his output and his career. These two songs are also the most Latin-influenced songs on the album, which led some early reviews to dub . . . *Nothing Like the Sun* his "South American" album. In truth, it is only these two songs, plus possibly "Straight to My Heart," that explicitly use this style.

In any case, "Fragile" is a straightforward minor-key *balada*-style track, featuring Sting on acoustic guitar. The song is framed by an introductory section, which becomes the coda at the end. This introduction alternates two synth chords while Sting plays fragments of the vocal melody on guitar. The main guitar melody, once the rhythm section starts, is a lovely, haunting series of parallel sixths. This interval is typical of Spanish classical guitar music; it is relatively easy to play and yet has melodic and harmonic interest.

This guitar pattern becomes a countermelody to the vocal line, which is deliberately soft and understated. "Too many cooks can spoil the pot," as the saying goes, and so it is true in songwriting also. If you have too many melodies and musical ideas in one song, it can become confusing for the listener. Here Sting wisely opts for simplicity, both in musical material and in the song's structure. Aside from the introduction, there really are only two musical sections: the verse and the chorus. The impressive guitar solo uses the same chordal pattern as the verse. The chorus is very similar to the second half of the verse, using the same last three chords of A Minor, B, and E minor. Also, the harmonization of the melody in parallel sixths continues. The only difference happens during the last two repetitions of the line "how fragile we are," when Sting descends from E minor down to C and back up. This is a typical move in this style, and he saves it for the end to provide contrast to the following coda.

The framing coda is almost exactly like the introduction except for the addition of some guitar arpeggios (rapid broken cords) and, at the very end, a final cadence on the home chord of E minor. The very last gesture is a quick ascending harp-like arpeggio that ends with a musical question: The passage ends on the F sharp, or a dissonant scale degree two in this key of E minor. The energy and direction of this gesture really point toward another note in the pattern, a G, but it is left unfulfilled. This has the psychoacoustic effect of being unfinished, despite the final low E bass note, and thus ends the song with a question mark.

The question seems to be the eternal "why?": Why do people still resort to violence to attempt to solve their problems? Will violence ever stop? Why do people kill? Sting keeps the point of view of the song very general, which is perhaps why it has been taken up by the environmental movement[14] and by people grieving after the 9/11 terrorist attacks. In 2001 during the rehearsals and recording of the live album . . . *All This Time*, Sting fashioned a new version of "Fragile" with expanded instrumentation and harmonies.

As general as the lyrics seem, there may be a touch of Sting's voice here. The ultimate message is that violence begets violence and that people "born beneath an angry star" need to exercise restraint in the face of that animalistic fighting instinct. Sting has described himself as full of rage as a young man: "One of the biggest influences the Sex Pistols had on me was that they were destroying something which had held me back. . . . I could relate to that anti-establishment feeling. The energy and aggression—hatred!"[15] A revealing scene in Stewart Copeland's 2006 documentary *Everyone Stares: The Police Inside and Out* shows a bit of that rage. In a partially staged sequence, Copeland films Summers "nonchalantly" exploring the train compartment that Sting is sitting in, listening to music through headphones. As Summers gets closer and increasingly annoying, Sting explodes in profanity-laced fury at Summers and tackles him to the floor. The episode soon dissolves into adolescent laughter, but Sting's anger is visceral and almost palpable.

A complete contrast, "We'll Be Together," began the original side two of the cassette version of the album and disc two (or side three) of the original LP pressing. In the LP era, the first song on the second side was crucial: It was a new beginning in the middle of a record, but of course people had the choice of just listening to side one. The song in that spot had to keep people listening and was often therefore an up-tempo annunciatory type of song.[16]

"We'll Be Together" is very blatantly a dance track, with a heavy funk-derived beat that was typical for mid-1980s' pop. Also from funk, it borrows a bass effect that simultaneously duplicates the note an octave up (the octave duplicator). This gives the bass note a more biting presence in the mix. Musically, the most notable thing is Sting's voice. Compared to many of his earlier solo tracks, his vocal style seems much looser and more playful on this song. The backing vocalists during the chorus focus on a high D,[17] and Sting in the coda actually surpasses that note to sing an F above it. This is the highest note he has sung on record.

The song's structure is nothing special: a verse-chorus alternation with a middle eight using some contrasting chords. The most interesting thing that happens harmonically is the coda. After a final break chorus (with no musical accompaniment, just drums), the chord pattern changes to B flat, G minor–D minor, and continues under the backing vocalists' repetition of the song title. In between these repetitions, Sting does another of his self-quotations, this time from the previous album's first single, "If You Love Somebody Set Them Free." In fact, up to now his pattern was to quote the previous album's hit single in the coda of a song on the new album, a pattern that will be broken on the following album, *The Soul Cages*.

It is quite revealing to compare the single version of "We'll Be Together" with the original version included on the greatest-hits compilation *Fields of Gold*. This version is sparer, a tick slower, and includes a prominent electric guitar (played by Eric Clapton). The bass and drums are not as present, there is no coda with the self-quotation, and in general the song sounds rather anemic. Like the rest of the album, this track was produced by Neil Dorfsman. Bryan Loren was brought in to create a more marketable radio-friendly version.

Although no one would consider "We'll Be Together" subversive, it does bend the rules a bit. Dance music is naturally associated with the body and thus carries connotations and both implicit and explicit sexual messages in the lyrics and overall style. Most dance tracks could generally be classified as love songs although of the lusty libidinous kind. This song, while using the musical style associated with sexual love and lust, has lyrics that are purely about romantic love. It is about staying together, not philandering, flirting, or physical intimacy. This is why the quote from "If You Love Somebody Set Them Free" is apt. This is a love song for an established couple, celebrating their love on the dance floor.

"Straight to My Heart" is another song that has a vaguely South American flavor, mainly due to Mino Cinelu's percussion. This song is one of the first Sting songs to use an unusual time signature: 7/8.[18] On later albums he will show a predilection for asymmetrical meters (the number of beats in a measure, which is a basic unit of musical time). The use of these time signatures probably comes from his jazz rock roots and playing with Last Exit. It actually has very little to do with Latin American music.

But this hybrid creates a great song. The percussion-only introduction deliberately obscures the beat and really only functions to establish the 16th note constant. Soon the keyboards and bass introduce the musical germ of the song: an elaboration of a B minor chord harmonized with a descending chromatic internal line. The two phrases played twice through make up one verse. After another verse we get a verse/refrain, which begins on a chord a step below and descends to an F sharp before bouncing back up to the tonic of B and the statement of the title words (the refrain).

This pattern of verse and verse/refrain (so-named because of the title words appearing at the end of the stanza) repeats and leads to the joyous midsection in the relative major key of D. This section almost functions as a chorus, since the words are identical each time it appears: "Come in to my door / Be the light of my life." The addition of clapping and a flute sound serve to further lighten the mood. At the end of this middle section the texture thins, and on the words "I'll be true" Sting sings an ascending stepwise melody that is mirrored in the bass (i.e., stepwise down).

Then, at this halfway point in the song, we go back to the beginning, and the whole structure repeats (with new words and with the exception of one verse at the beginning of the structure instead of two). This type of musical structure is called binary, meaning "two parts." The song can be divided roughly in half, with the same musical events happening in sequence in each half. After the final "I'll be true," the cycle begins again. This time, however, the opening music becomes the coda of the song, and we fade out in essentially the same way we began, except that here the verse and the refrain are overlaid and repeated. A large part of what makes this song so fun to listen to is the rhythmic interplay between the consistent bass/keyboard pattern and Cinelu's and Katché's percussive additions to the mix.

This is a song where the music outweighs the lyrics in terms of quality. In a songwriter's craft there are generally three methods of working: Write the music first and put some words onto the melody, write the music and words simultaneously, or write the words first (or have someone else write them) and then set them to music. Any of these approaches can be appropriate for any given song. "Straight to My Heart" feels like the first type, where the music came first. The lyrics seem to be about biotechnology creating love in some future time. The speaker is telling his lover that even though "they" may someday invent this technology, his love is true. Although there are several forced rhymes along the way, it is essentially a courting song, with the clearest section being the joyful middle: "Come into my door . . . come and be my wife."

"Rock Steady" is another one of the weaker songs on the album. The title puns on the intermediate style of Jamaican popular music, between ska and reggae. This style had its heyday in the mid-1960s, before the full flowering of reggae in 1969.[19] The title more strongly refers to several elements of the song, as rather than having a rock steady rhythm, this song is in a 12/8 shuffle, propelled constantly by Sting's upright bass and Katché's playing. It is also a story song with no variation in the verse-chorus alternating structure. The end of each verse has a descending chromatic bass line that ends up on the dominant before returning to the tonic for the chorus.

Sting's version of the Noah and the flood story seems to be updated to the present day, or else Sting is using contemporary language—such as "newspaper" and "radio"—to tell his version of this ancient story. Either way, Sting compresses the main elements into three verses, which leaves little room for development or detail. The speaker is an additional character who, accompanied by his girlfriend, signs up to help the Noah figure. They help and do get saved from the flood, but they feel trapped and enslaved, so they send a bird to find land (in the original, it is Noah who sends the dove).

The chorus, which happens after every verse, alternately refers to "Noah's" confidence in the ark, the speaker's confidence in "Noah," and the rock that the dove finds at the end of the song. But the musical setting of the words "rock steady" deliberately go against the apparent solidity of the rock. This musical text painting of an unspoken unease with the Noah figure (at least at the beginning) is clever, but the use of the same unstable music for the final chorus does not offer any comfort. So, it seems that the speakers are in the same place that they began, despite being saved from the flood.

What does make "Rock Steady" fun to listen to is the sonic variety of the track: the interplay between Marsalis and Kirkland, animal sounds, storm sounds, and vocalizations of the backing vocalists. For me, these details save the song from dullness. In the hands of a lesser songwriter and producer, a song like this would not make the final cut.

"Sister Moon" was originally the first track on the last side of the two-LP version of . . . Nothing Like the Sun and has a sort of homestretch feel to it. The nocturnal setting seems to fit at this point in the album: a night song after the "rebirth" of the "Lazarus Heart" and daytime songs such as "Englishman in New York" and "Fragile." This view of the order of songs following the arc of the day is perhaps tenuous, but track order is in many cases an agonizing decision process, and this may have served as a loose template on which to place the songs. Moreover, song order can greatly affect how listeners perceive and remember an album.[20]

Sting says in the liner notes that "Sister Moon" is "a song for lunatics everywhere," and he is possibly including himself in that category.[21] The song contains the kernel of this album: his love for his recently deceased mother and his explanation of why he has chosen the path that he has. In relation to the album as a whole it points to a strong thematic connection to the mother figure. Despite the title's reference to the moon as a sister, the women in this song are also mother (verse two) and mistress (verse three). This implies that Sting is singing about the eternal feminine, a Jungian concept with which he is undoubtedly familiar; an individual woman, after all, can be all three at once (mother of children, sister, and lover).

In verse three, Sting's choice of album title becomes clear. "My mistress's eyes are nothing like the sun" is the first line of Shakespeare's sonnet 130, which lists how the lover's qualities do not measure up to this or that, but ends with the couplet "And yet I think my love as rare / As any she belied with false compare." In other words, the poet's love is unique, special, and cannot be described through conventional comparisons.

Sting's use of this line is telling, because it speaks to the idea of false compare—comparison of people to some idea of perfection (also referred to in "Consider Me Gone"). Sting's comparison here, on the surface, is of the moon and the sun, but it works on a deeper level of comparing the mother with the son (along with the pun on "sun"). Typically, in many mythologies the sun is seen as masculine and the moon as feminine. Sting's next line, forming a couplet with the Shakespeare line, relates his career as a musician, songwriter, and performer to his "hunger" for the feminine. The "howling" of the next line could be a reference to his singing career as well as an image of a lunatic, and the last statement of the refrain ("I'd go out of my mind but for you") makes more sense in relation to a female figure serving as an anchor for his life and emotional state.

The music of "Sister Moon" heightens the connections among the many levels of the song. The nocturnal mood is ushered in by the solo soprano saxophone in one of Marsalis's best contributions to the album. Kirkland's synthesized strings are full of lush Gershwin-esque harmonies that swell and fade over Sting's upright bass. The atmosphere is masterfully created before the first note is sung. The two opening chords (F sharp minor^{79} and B^{79}) serve as an anchor for the whole song in that they underscore the first part of the verse and return on the refrain.

The most interesting section of the song happens at the beginning of verse three (which initially feels like the middle eight, but in retrospect we realize that it is an altered verse) on the crucial line from Shakespeare. The key changes up a third, and Sting's vocal line is therefore higher than the rest of the song. The third line of this verse effects the change back into the original key (of F sharp minor), and it is done so smoothly that we don't even realize that it is happening. During the last refrain, Sting sings the line "And they really don't care if I do" instead of the established refrain. On the word "do" there is what is called a deceptive cadence (from classical terminology): the chord pattern, instead of moving V-I like a typical cadence, does V-VI, thus deceiving the listener into expecting the phrase to end on the home chord of I (but it doesn't). Here, the final cadence does not happen until the last note of the refrain, thus reestablishing the home key and returning to the F sharp–B anchor of the opening. Thus, the metaphoric connection between the home key, the moon, the eternal feminine, and Sting's career and emotional life are crystallized in this one moment. Heard this way, it is hard to imagine a more personal and emotionally powerful song in his catalog.

Another personal song, even though it is not an original, is the next track, Jimi Hendrix's "Little Wing." Since this essay focuses on Sting as a songwriter, I will not discuss the music of this song per se but will instead talk about the reasons for its inclusion on the album. Among Sting's solo albums it is the only cover that he has done, and therefore it must be regarded as an important song to him.

The path that this song took to make it onto . . . *Nothing Like the Sun* is a circuitous one. Sting heard the Jimi Hendrix Experience live as a 16-year-old in 1967 in Newcastle. It was a transformative experience for him:

> The Jimi Hendrix Experience was an overwhelming, deafening wave of sound that simply obliterated analysis. I think I remember snatches of "Hey Joe" and "Foxy Lady," but that event remains a blur of noise and breathtaking virtuosity, of Afro'd hair, wild clothes, and towers of Marshall amplifiers. It was also the first time I'd ever seen a black man. . . . I lay in my bed that night with my ears ringing and my worldview significantly altered.[22]

Almost 20 years later, Sting introduced himself to Gil Evans (1912–1988), one of the 20th century's greatest big band leaders and arrangers. Evans had previously done an entire album of Jimi Hendrix arrangements (1974's *The Gil Evans Orchestra Plays the Music of Jimi Hendrix*).[23] Evans invited Sting to sing with his band, which eventually led to an evening-length concert at the 1987 Umbria Jazz Festival in Perugia, Italy. This concert recording is only available as a bootleg; the track listing tells us that in addition to Hendrix covers and standards, they did a few Police and Sting songs as well, arranged for big band by Evans and his assistant, Maria Schneider.[24]

One of the songs they did together was "Little Wing." The original studio version appears on Hendrix's 1967 album *Axis: Bold as Love*. Evans had arranged it for his 1974 album and again for his 1985 *Farewell* album,[25] and he expanded the original song's structure to include space for soloists. Indeed, the original Hendrix studio version is only two and a half minutes long. Evans (and Sting) gives the song more shape by essentially playing the song twice, with a guitar solo in the middle. The guitar player on the . . . *Nothing Like the Sun* version was Hiram Bullock, at that time a young rising star of the jazz-funk scene. Bullock certainly delivers a fiery performance, with a conscious homage to Hendrix's original solo during the final fade-out.

A confusing credit in the booklet of this album states that "Gil Evans and his orchestra play on this track."[26] But if one listens closely, one is hard-pressed to hear any big band at all. The music seems to be all created by Kirkland's synthesizers. Since this album was exclusively recorded at Air Studios in Montserrat (no other recording locations are mentioned), it would have been too expensive to hire and transport an entire big band to record just one song. My contention is that Sting used Evans's arrangement of the song (the 1985 version, which Bullock and Egan had recorded with Evans), and Kirkland emulated the sound of a big band with his keyboards. The "orchestra" credited is really just Hiram Bullock, Mark Egan on bass, and Kenwood Dennard on drums. Bullock and Egan had played with Evans's band for a few years and had performed this song several times, and Dennard is a much sought-after studio drummer.

What is most important for our purposes is the meaning of the song. The fantastic and psychedelic-influenced lyrics could either suggest a drug-induced seduction or a supernatural communication. The most significant lines for the latter interpretation is "When I'm sad she comes to me / with a thousand smiles she gives to me free." In this way, "Little Wing" has a similar sentiment as "Sister Moon." Connection or communication with a female muse will help him get through this time of sorrow and depression, and he will channel that grief into music making.

As "Little Wing" fits nicely into . . . *Nothing Like the Sun*'s theme of the spectrum of female figures, so does the final song, "The Secret Marriage." As Sting states in the liner notes, the melody was adapted from a song by German expatriate composer Hanns Eisler (1898–1962). "An dem kleinem Radio-apparat" ("To the Little Radio") was one of the collaborations between Eisler and Bertolt Brecht, who together created several communist musical-theater pieces in the 1930s.[27] This particular song is from the collection titled *Die Hollywood-Elegien* (*Hollywood Elegies*), published in 1942 while Eisler and Brecht were both living in Hollywood. The subject of the original poem is living in exile, and it is a bittersweet ode to a radio brought from the old country. The sentiment is "please don't fall silent, little radio, even if I have to still hear from my enemies and about everything I've lost."

Sting chose to expand this short song, similarly to "Little Wing." Instead of the one and a half verses of the original, Sting creates three verses plus a chorus by repeating and expanding the music.

Although Sting's words have nothing to do with living in exile, they do retain the longing beauty of the original mood and suit his purposes well.

Sting says that this song is for Trudie Styler, who at the time was still unmarried (they married in 1992). "We expressed our vows to each other every day, but not in a big public ceremony."[28] This album progresses from the opening song about a mother (the first woman a child knows) to a song about marriage (the embodiment of the Jungian concept of anima). It is a wonderful ending to one of the strongest albums in Sting's catalog.

Eisler	Sting
A	A (verse 1)
A'	A (verse 2)
B	B (chorus)
	A' (verse 3)
	B (chorus)

Notes

1. *Timeout*, October 1987, quoted on Sting.com, Discography, "Sting: . . . Nothing Like the Sun," http://sting.com/discography/index/ablum/albumId/18/tagName/Albums.
2. Vic Garbarini, "Invisible Son," *Spin*, November–December 1987, 51.
3. Sting, *Lyrics by Sting* (New York: Dial, 2007), 122.
4. *Oxford Dictionary of Quotations*, 5th ed. (London: Oxford University Press, 1999), 606.
5. Peter Watrous, "How Can You Not Dump on a Guy Like Sting?," *Musician* 110 (December 1987): 64.
6. Sting, liner notes to . . . *Nothing Like the Sun*, CD, A&M 75021-6402-2, 1987.
7. "We Work the Black Seam" also includes a verse in the booklet that was cut from the final version.
8. Peter Manuel, *Popular Musics of the Non-Western World* (New York: Oxford University Press, 1988), 70.
9. Misspelled in the CD booklet as "Gueca."
10. U2, in the song "Mothers of the Disappeared," addressed this same topic on *The Joshua Tree* album a few months before Sting's album was released.
11. The political opposition, being a Marxist-Socialist group, identified strongly with the indigenous people, even if most of the politically active Chileans at this time were not Indians themselves.
12. This point is also made by Christian Jahl, *Sting: die Musik eines Rockstars* (Stuttgart: Ibidem Verlag, 2003), 86.
13. Blades is one of the preeminent band leaders, composers, and voices in salsa. He has also infused salsa with a unique social and political consciousness; previously it was simply thought of as "party music" (Manuel, *Popular Musics of the Non-Western World*, 48–49).
14. "Fragile" was included on the soundtrack to the IMAX documentary film *The Living Sea* (1995).
15. Phil Sutcliffe and Hugh Fiedler, *The Police: L'historia Bandido* (London and New York: Proteus Books, 1981), 36.
16. "Here Comes the Sun," the song that begins side two of the Beatles' *Abbey Road*, is a great example.
17. This is the highest harmony note in the second half of "So Lonely."
18. "Synchronicity I" is in six, and Andy Summers's "Mother" from the same album is in a loping seven.
19. Manuel, *Popular Musics of the Non-Western World*, 75.
20. The original order of side one of *Sgt. Pepper's Lonely Hearts Club Band*, for example, has a much different effect than the published order: "Sgt. Pepper," "With a Little Help," "A Benefit for Mr. Kite," "Fixing a Hole," "Lucy in the Sky with Diamonds," "Getting Better," and "She's Leaving Home" (CD liner notes by Peter Blake). This is a huge topic in and of itself and is beyond the scope of this entry. Suffice it to say that many factors go into choosing the best song sequence, including tempo, mood, key, texture, stylistic genre, song topic, emotional content, and sound quality.
21. Sting, liner notes to . . . *Nothing Like the Sun*, CD, A&M 75021-6402-2, 1987.
22. Sting, *Broken Music: A Memoir* (New York: Dial, 2003), 85.

23. "Little Wing" was originally released on the Evans LP *There Comes a Time* (1976). It has since been included on the CD reissues of the Hendrix sessions.

24. The track listing for the Gil Evans Orchestra Featuring Sting in Perugia (one of several bootlegs of this concert) is given on Amazon.com as "Up from the Skies," "Strange Fruit," "Shadows in the Rain," "Little Wing," "There Comes a Time," "Consider Me Gone," "Synchronicity I," "Roxanne," "Tea in the Sahara/Walking on the Moon," "Instrumental," and "Message in a Bottle." http://www.amazon.com/In-Perugia-Sting/dp/B000I5YUX0.

25. Richard Cook and Brian Morton, *The Penguin Guide to Jazz on CD, LP and Cassette* (London: Penguin, 1992), 356.

26. Sting, liner notes to . . . *Nothing Like the Sun*, CD, A&M 75021-6402-2, 1987.

27. David Blake, "Hanns Eisler," Grove Music Online, edited by Laura Macy, http://www.oxfordmusiconline.com.

28. *All This Time CD-ROM*, Starwave, A&M Records and Philips Media 70904 25, 1995.

39

U2

The Joshua Tree (1987)

James E. Perone

The Irish rock band U2 has roots that go back before the British punk era; however, it took some time for U2 to become stars in the United Kingdom and the United States. The band's first couple of albums generated considerable critical and commercial interest, but the 1987 album *The Joshua Tree* established U2 as superstars. The album included a mix of Christian imagery, secular imagery that can be interpreted as philosophical or religious statements, social commentary, and explorations of self-identity as well as the heavily processed electric guitar of the Edge, Bono's passionate vocals, a broad stylistic range, and an accessibility that not only contributed to the commercial impact of the album but also generated significant sales of singles and a level of radio airplay not previously enjoyed by U2. Perhaps more than any other U2 album, *The Joshua Tree* exhibits a tempo, dynamic, and thematic progression that, with its buildups and releases of tension, keep the listener thoroughly engaged throughout. Not only was *The Joshua Tree* crucial in establishing U2 as perhaps the premiere band of the era, but the aural sound scape that permeates most of the songs also influenced later artists and the production, and guitar effects style of *The Joshua Tree* especially can still be heard in Christian rock music into the second decade of the 21st century. The production by Daniel Lanois and Brian Eno combines the sound of rock with experimental textures that reflect back to Eno's work with David Bowie (e.g., *"Heroes"*) in the 1970s.

The Joshua Tree begins with "Where the Streets Have No Name." The song emerges from silence via a slow crescendo. This establishes a pattern to which U2, Lanois, and Eno return throughout the album. In fact, the band and the producers use the contrast between this sort of slow fade and more abrupt cuts into songs to enhance the moods—and the transitions between the moods—of the songs. Like most of Bono's texts for this album, "Where the Streets Have No Name" is open to interpretation. He sings of wanting to escape from the feeling that life might be meaningless by using metaphors of walls and nameless, apparently random, streets. The image of the nameless streets in particular is interesting. For example, one listener might hear this to mean that this place is nameless and impersonal; however, another listener might hear this to mean that the borders between streets (whether actual or metaphorical) have broken down to the point at which all are part of the same larger universe. The lyrics also highlight the dualism that runs through the album. Bono sings of "building then burning down love." We want to do the right thing, but as humans we make mistakes. The one constant is that "when I go there, I go there with you." In this song, then, there is at least a partial resolution to the conflict that comes from existing in the middle of a dualistic situation. The Edge's electric guitar parts are heavily overdubbed and electronically processed so as to produce a whirlwind of activity, as if musically portraying the dizzy, confusing world of Bono's lyrics and the confusion of the real world of the time. Like the constancy of the "you" with whom Bono's character ventures into the maelstrom, the melody of "Where the Streets Have No Name" is built largely around repetition, expansion, and variation of one primary motive, thus giving the piece a structural coherence that seems to hold forth in the face of the processed guitars.

"I Still Haven't Found What I'm Looking For" also finds U2 exploring the challenges of life. Since Bono sings in the final verse of believing in "Kingdom Come" and of "you" breaking "the bonds" and carrying "the cross," the song's lyrics suggest the quest for the meaning of life through Christianity. Experiencing the good and the evil of the world, experiencing success in love and loss in love, still leaves the singer searching for meaning. It is as if he believes but finds his faith tested and, like Jesus of Nazareth's apostle Thomas, longs for proof. This grappling with faith and the internal conflict between good and evil reemerges in more oblique ways in later songs.

The album's third track, "With or Without You," finds U2 creating a similar type of musical texture as that of "Where the Streets Have No Name" and "I Still Haven't Found What I'm Looking For," even though the pieces feature contrasting tempi and rhythmic feels. What binds them is the contrast between the rather lyrical nature of the vocal melodies and the agitated and much more rhythmically active instrumental accompaniments. The lyrics, which speak of not being able to live "with or without you," suggest the strange irony of having to decide whether to continue in a relationship that will never be completely healthy or to break up the relationship and have to live with the lingering pain of the breakup. It is an exploration of the complexity of being in the middle of a dualistic situation. The situation that Bono and his bandmates lay out is more hopeless than that of "Where the Streets Have No Name." The musical writing and performing style support the complex and competing emotions:

the melodic material for the verses is resigned-sounding, in a narrow range and low tessitura. However, Bono cries out in a higher range at the end of an instrumental and vocal crescendo in the chorus. The fade-out at the end suggests the ongoing resignation and indecision: this painful state of limbo continues on with no resolution.

In "Bullet the Blue Sky," U2 creates the image of a dangerous, apocalyptic world that, in the last lines of the song, is revealed to the "America." Once again, the images incorporate the concept of dualism. The listener hears about a character, identified as "suit and tie," who counts out dollars in increments of 100, juxtaposed with images of starving children in "mud huts." Likewise, the sound of a man playing the saxophone is juxtaposed against the sound of the "groan" of a city. The imagery runs the gamut from the highly impressionistic and abstract to the immediate and obvious and is not entirely successful. For example, All Music Guide critic Stephen Thomas Erlewine writes that generally *The Joshua Tree* is a classic album and that "only the clumsy, heavy rock and portentous lyrics of 'Bullet the Blue Sky' fall flat."[1] While some listeners might not find the track quite as objectionable as Erlewine, it is disturbing. The images, unlike those of many of the songs on *The Joshua Tree*, suggest utter hopelessness and a place absent beauty of any kind. The instrumental texture is thick and lacks the subtlety of the album's other songs; however, it is befitting the in-your-face dramatic impact of the lyrics.

"Running to Stand Still" begins with a sparse slide guitar solo that suggests a rural American scene; however, the lyrics and the rest of the musical setting are essentially placeless. The principal character is a woman who realizes that all is not right with her life. The nonsense syllable part of the refrain suggests a childlike innocence; however, the woman seems not to be able to fully express herself, and there are hints that she takes refuge through the use of drugs (the "poison" that causes her to "float out of here"). The song features a dramatic crescendo, and then just as dramatic, a diminuendo as the final two lines, in which Bono confirms the pointlessness of the woman's addiction, are heard. There is a sense of resignation about her plight. Despite this, the simplicity of the melody line and the childlike refrain suggest that there may still be at least a glimmer of hope for her. The lyrics also revisit the dualism that is present in earlier songs. Here, Bono sings "sweet the sin, but bitter the taste." The implication is that yielding to temptation carries with it satisfaction on some level; however, it also carries the bitterness of guilt or (depending on the extent to which the listener hears this as a song about drug abuse) the long-term pain of addiction. Because the lyrics of "Running to Stand Still" include a mixture of short lines and some that are more extended thoughts, it is perhaps one of the best examples on *The Joshua Tree* of the skill with which the members of U2 set texts to melodies with natural speech-like rhythms.

Although the lyrics are a touch oblique, "Red Hill Mining Town" deals with life in a formerly vibrant mining town. It seems as though all Bono's character has "to hold on to" is a mysterious "you," who is never fully identified. In other

RHINO ENTERTAINMENT COMPANY

Over the course of the digital music age of the past 30 years, record companies had serious issues with which to contend. One of the issues was how to deal with past catalogs of recordings that had been issued on vinyl LPs, cassettes, and eight-track tapes. Some of the major record labels made the transition to CD smoothly and by the late 1980s had reissued some of the most significant and most popular albums of the 1960s and 1970s on CD. For one reason or another, however, some of the more popular albums of the past were not issued on CD. Rhino Records was one company that aggressively took to the new medium and obtained the rights to reissue albums and compilations of singles that the original companies had not reissued. Many of the Rhino albums included digitally remastered recordings that, in some cases, offered superior audio fidelity compared to the reissues that major labels rereleased on CD. In the 1980s and 1990s, Rhino reissued everything from 1950s' R&B to 1960s' pop (e.g., the Monkees' catalog) and also reissued pop music films and pop culture cult classic films on DVD.

words, it could be the love of a person or the love for the town itself that is all that is left to make life livable. Once again, dualism is heard in several stanzas but perhaps most clearly in the statement "we . . . stoop so low to reach so high." There is also an implication that environmental degradation, perhaps in emptying the mine of all saleable material, is responsible for the current state of the town. One of the more notable phrases that Bono sings in the chorus, "I'm still waiting," is not included in the CD booklet. Bono sings this in the high register with intensity, suggesting that his character still holds hope for the reemergence of his town. The line also connects the song with the earlier "I Still Haven't Found What I'm Looking For." Whereas in the earlier song there was hope for finding the answer to life's questions (although perhaps only in the "Kingdom Come" afterlife), there is little hope that Bono's character will have much more than the mysterious "you" to save him in "Red Hill Mining Town."

A mixture of oblique and rather more concrete imagery makes "In God's Country" a particularly rich song. The lyrics begin by painting a desert scene with a mixture of desolation and beneath-the-surface beauty. Even this beauty, however, is not all that it seems to be: the desert rose calls "like a siren," the mythological woman who called sailors to death on rocky shorelines. Part of the scenery of "God's Country" includes "sad eyes" and "crooked crosses." Perhaps these crosses are swastikas; the phrase "crooked cross" is sometimes applied to the symbol that in the 20th century came to be associated with the racism of Nazi Germany. There is some support for this image in the earlier song "Bullet the Blue Sky," in which the similarly racist image of the burning cross (of the Ku Klux Klan) is described. The conflicts and contradictory images are heightened by juxtaposition of the pop-like mostly lyrical melody and the driving instrumental background.

"Trip through Your Wires" features a quicker harmonic rhythm than the other songs on *The Joshua Tree*, which is especially notable because of the fact that the song is built around an oft-repeated short harmonic pattern. The metrical feel of the song, in which U2 explores a triple subdivision of the larger beats, also stands in contrast to the rest of the album. In the lyrics, however, dualism once again can be found. In "Trip through Your Wires," salvation comes to the lonely, naked, and thirsty. Interestingly, though, the one who comes to the aid of the person in need might be either "angel or devil."

U2 dedicated *The Joshua Tree* to their friend and roadie Greg Carroll (1960–1986) and specifically link the song "One Tree Hill" to Carroll's funeral in the CD booklet.[2] The band also honors the memory of slain Chilean political activist and singer-songwriter Victor Jara (1932–1973) in the song. Most of the songs on *The Joshua Tree* feature memorable melodic hooks that provide a relief from some of the darkness of the lyrics. "One Tree Hill" is no exception and in fact is one of the catchiest tunes. Part of the appeal and part of what makes this song stand out is the heavy use of Mixolydian mode in the vocal melody and guitar accompaniment. The lowered seventh scale step that distinguishes Mixolydian from the conventional major scale is featured prominently. Other songs make use of the lowered seventh (or subtonic) scale step (such as "Trip through Your Wires"), but here its use is more noticeable. In the context of the lyrics this mode functions particularly well, suggesting the bittersweet quality of remembering those who died young.

Although it did not enjoy its highest degree of commercial success until the early 1990s, American grunge music had at least emerged by the time of U2's *The Joshua Tree*. The song "Exit," with its high degree of stylistic and dynamic contrast and its lyrics that imply depression and violence in the wake of loss of hope, is at least in the same stylistic ballpark as the rock music that members of Generation X were popularizing at the time. It is a haunting track although not as musically accessible as the bulk of the album.

Throughout *The Joshua Tree*, Bono's lyrics explore the grappling within dualistic systems of behavior, feelings, and beliefs that make up the reality of life and mixes a gradually increasing dose of references to the plight of political activists and prisoners. By the time of "Mothers of the Disappeared," the focus is on politics and the suffering of the mothers of political prisoners. That the album concludes with this focus cannot be missed by someone who owns the original CD release of *The Joshua Tree*: an invitation to join Amnesty International—as well as contact information for the organization—immediately follows the lyrics of "Mothers of the Disappeared" in the CD booklet. The music of this song is relatively slow, understated, and reverent. The simplicity of the melody gives the piece a folk/protest song–like feel. The wash of sound in the guitars and synthesizers draws no attention to itself, providing an almost ambient music–style backdrop to the listener's imagined mental images of heartbroken mothers mourning the loss of their politically active sons and daughters.

The invitation to join Amnesty International that appears in the CD booklet of *The Joshua Tree* was not a one-off for U2: the band—and especially lyricist and lead singer Bono—has continued to support Amnesty International as well as various international relief efforts to battle hunger and homelessness up to the present. *The Joshua Tree* can be a challenging listening experience; however, this is because it deals in song after song with the very real grappling with faith and hope that people go through. Although Bono as a lyricist does not say so in so many words, these are songs about the confusing shades of gray between polar extremes. Although the musical settings of lyrical melodies set off against agitated, electronically processed instrumental writing and playing was distinctive at the time, these settings somehow refuse to sound overly dated even a quarter century after the album's release. In part this may be because of the impact that U2's style has had on later musicians: musicians of the second decade of the 21st century are still using the same juxtapositions and the same kinds of instrumental effects.

Notes

1. Stephen Thomas Erlewine, review of *The Joshua Tree*, All Music Guide, http://allmusic.com/cg/amg.dll?p = amg&sql = 10:0pfyxq95ldde.
2. U2, liner notes for *The Joshua Tree*, CD, Island Records A2-90581, 1987.

40

Suzanne Vega

Solitude Standing (1987)

James E. Perone

In retrospect, it seems as though the 1980s are remembered for flashy dance music and videos. Throughout the decade, however, a new introspective singer-songwriter movement developed. Joni Mitchell, James Taylor, Carole King, Jackson Browne, Carly Simon, Cat Stevens, and others dominated the singer-songwriter movement of the 1970s. The singer-songwriter movement of the 1980s developed more slowly and eventually came to be dominated by Suzanne Vega, Tracy Chapman, and other female artists. That the undercurrent of activity took several years to reach its fruition in the late 1980s can be seen in the fact that Vega's 1987 *Solitude Standing* contains songs written over a 10-year period, and Chapman's self-titled 1988 debut album contains material written over a 7-year period. *Solitude Standing* contains haunting songs in which Vega explores everything from the mundane activities of daily life to domestic violence, love, the nature of solitude, childhood memories and intergenerational connections, and so on. Vega, and producers Steve Addabbo and Lenny Kaye, organized the album in such a way as to suggest that the entire range of subjects reflects the reality of daily life. Throughout *Solitude Standing*, Vega spins out lyrics filled with imagery, sometimes immediate and vivid and sometimes hazy and impressionistic, and her music is engaging and at times haunting.

The album opens with "Tom's Diner," a minor-key strophic-form a cappella song built principally on a simple four-note motive. The simplicity of the music—almost like Laurie Anderson–style minimalism without the electronic effects—matches the lyrics perfectly. Vega describes her observations while "sitting . . . at the diner on the corner." She witnesses a fleeting romantic encounter between the "man behind the counter" and a customer, reads an article in the newspaper about the death of an actor, reads her horoscope and the comics, sees a woman adjusting her hair and stockings while using the reflection of the diner's window as a makeshift mirror, and so on. The mundane activities of this rainy day, however, are interrupted by thoughts of (presumably) a former lover now gone from Vega's life. This type of song, which on the surface seems simply to be a quirky celebration of the mundane, and the entire female-dominated coffeehouse singer-songwriter movement would come to be parodied over the course of a decade (1994–2004) in the form of the character Phoebe Buffay on the television situation comedy *Friends*. However, there is more to this song than what appears on the surface. The album concludes with an instrumental reprise of "Tom's Diner," which is dominated by the tone color of synthesizers. In tone color, in the first additive and then subtractive way in which the piece is shaped, and in its repetitiveness the reprise hints at the Laurie Anderson New York loft scene of the 1980s. This reprise can give the listener the impression that everything that Vega explores between the "Tom's Diner" bookends reflects other deeper and sometimes hidden and darker aspects of the real daily life, just as the album's first track reflects the surface realities of life.

Surprisingly, it was the second track on *Solitude Standing*, "Luka," that became the album's hit single. In this song, Vega deals with the topic of domestic violence from the viewpoint of the victim. She portrays the title character, and the lyrics of the verses sound like Luka's rehearsal of what she will tell her downstairs neighbors if they hear arguments, fights, and possible violence from overhead or if they see that she appears to have sustained an injury. In the chorus Luka thinks to herself about her predicament, with perhaps the most haunting line being "They only hit until you cry." Vega's character does not ask for or want help and in her chorus ruminations leans in the direction of believing that the abuse is her own fault. In fact, Luka seems to exhibit the classic wide range of feelings of abuse victims: denial, shame, low self-esteem, and so on. Vega sings her pop-like melody in a low-key style, with little change of inflection or intensity. Some listeners might hear it as emotionless, while others might hear it as resigned. The musical arrangement moves beyond the confines of that of a solo acoustic singer-songwriter; however, the texture of keyboards, acoustic and electric guitars, bass, and drums is sparse enough to help lend the song a personal-feeling touch.

For the song "Ironbound/Fancy Poultry," Vega shares songwriting credits with her synthesizer player Anton Sanko. It should be noted that several of the songs on *Solitude Standing* are collaborations, with various members of the band sharing credit with Vega for the music. Despite this, there is a stylistic consistency of pop-oriented gently rising and falling melodies and subtle harmony and arrangements that runs throughout the album. In addition, the spirit of a gently hypnotic minimalism ties the songs together. This particular song paints a picture of the Ironbound section of Newark, New Jersey, an area with a large Portuguese population. In fact, in the second section of the piece, which begins approximately 3 minutes and 36 seconds into the song, Vega portrays a Portuguese poultry seller. Vega's portrayals of the common scenes of daily life on the album generally contain at least one quirky lyrical touch. On this song, this feature occurs at the end of the song. Here, the character of the vendor tells the passersby that the chicken "wings are nearly free." Then, outside of the quotation marks that delineate the vendor's words in the liner notes, Vega repeats the words "nearly free," which some listeners might hear as a highlight of the irony of the word "free"—while the wings might be "nearly free" in the sense of inexpensive, the irony is that wings, which can symbolize freedom, have been turned into a cheap commodity.

Marc Shulman, who played the electric guitar parts on *Solitude Standing*, cowrote the music of "In the Eye" with Vega. In perhaps the ultimate expression of empowerment in the face of danger, Vega warns the person to whom she sings that were the person to kill her, she would "look you in the eye" and indelibly burn her image "into your memory." Considering the potential circumstance in which Vega's character finds herself and the inferred tension of the relationship between the two characters, her understated delivery truly is eerie. The arrangement makes the song sound even more detached through heavy use of synthesizers. Some 1980s' synthesizer-based popular music has not aged particularly well because of the fact that the synthesizers too narrowly define the music by its decade. "In the Eye" actually seems to benefit because of the slightly nonhuman, artificial sound of the instruments.

The Anton Sanko/Suzanne Vega collaboration "Night Vision" is one of the shorter tracks on *Solitude Standing*. Vega's text was inspired by the poem "Juan Gris" by Paul Eluard.[1] The lyrics reflect on the contrast between the "sweetness" of the day and the "fear" of the night as Vega's character watches her lover fall asleep. More than the earlier songs on the album, "Night Vision" moves into the world of acoustic ambient music. The setting reflects a state of being and is evocative of the twilight feeling as one is just on the verge of sleep.

The music of the album's title track is credited to Vega and the members of her backing band. Based on the ever-changing, ever-evolving instrumental arrangement of the piece, it sounds as though the attribution might have been meant to acknowledge the band's role in creating the arrangement. Interestingly, this is another song in which Vega features a deliberate disconnection between the lyrics and the music. In this case, however, the disconnection occurs because although her lyrics reflect on meeting solitude in the form of a visible spirit-being, the music is fast-paced and, although gentle in rhythm, does not stereotypically reflect solitude.

In the next song Vega portrays "Calypso," a character who seems to be particularly open to interpretation. Vega's character in this 1978 song seems, though, possibly to be a sort of siren in reverse. In other words, instead of luring a sailor to his death, she rescues him from his "struggle with the sea." Eventually, though, she lets him "sail away" with a new knowledge of the sea and the waves. The character of Calypso, however, could be a metaphor for any woman who takes in a man as lover or friend, helps him better himself, and then willingly lets him go. Aside from the a cappella opening track, "Calypso" is one of the sparsest arrangements on *Solitude Standing* and is another of Vega's trademark haunting combinations of words and lyrics.

As one listens through *Solitude Standing* track by track, it becomes increasingly clear that a significant part of the album's appeal comes from Vega and her band's creation of various atmospheres. The totality of music, words, and arrangement is more important than the component parts. The song "Language" is a particularly strong example. Vega deals with the necessity for silence—wordless communication—and concludes that this silence can be "more eloquent than any word could ever be." The minimalistic, repetitive arrangement adds significantly to the atmosphere, to the feeling of a suspension of time.

According to Vega, the 1978 song "Gypsy" was inspired by a fellow camp counselor from Liverpool, England, she met and with whom she became friends.[2] Be that as it may, "Gypsy" resonates with anyone who has had a lover who leaves for a far-off land and both people know that they will never see each other again. It is also the most lyrically and musically conventional song on the album. It is a simple, sparse composition and arrangement, which adds to the personal, autobiographical-sounding feel of the song.

Vega turns from personal experience to a fantastic but true story from the 19th century for "Wooden Horse (Caspar Hauser's Song)." As a teenager, Kaspar Hauser mysteriously appeared in Nuremberg, Germany, and claimed that he had lived his entire life up to just shortly before that time locked in a dark cell. His story and mysterious death at the age of 21 have inspired books, films, and music in the more than 150 years that passed between his death and Vega's song. As Vega recounts Hauser's saga, the small wooden horse that the boy had as his only toy becomes the metaphor for Hauser's freedom and his connections to the father he claimed never to have known.

The musical arrangement of "Wooden Horse" might take some listeners time to get used to, primarily because the bass and drum-heavy arrangement in no way connects directly to a story from the first third of the 19th century. However, that very well may have been the point of Vega and her band, for the connection of Hauser to the toy can be projected into a late 20th-century setting, particularly in light of the album's earlier track, "Luka." It is possible to hear "Wooden Horse (Caspar Hauser's Song)" as the story of a modern tale of child abuse and the psychological damage that it does—the only thing with which Hauser (or the present-day abuse victim) can connect is an inanimate object, something that can do him no harm, and is in fact the only friend he has.

The final track on *Solitude Standing* is the instrumental version of "Tom's Diner," which effectively ties all of the other songs together. This is an album with pain, hopelessness, nostalgia, love that continues after a relationship ends, self-doubt, and empowerment. While some of the synthesizer tone colors have not aged well, Vega's somewhat detached vocal delivery and the atmospheric nature of the songs make *Solitude Standing* not just perhaps the first major hit album of the late 1980s–1990s female singer-songwriter genre but also an album that remains vital and haunting today.

Notes

1. Liner notes for *Solitude Standing*, CD, A&M Records CD 5136, 1987.
2. Interview with Suzanne Vega, "'Gypsy': The Story behind the Song," http://www .youtube.com/watch?v=ZlS6cvkM4Mw.

41

Enya

Watermark (1988)

James E. Perone

From the work of minimalist composers such as Terry Riley, LaMonte Young, and Steve Reich to the work of the group Tangerine Dream, Mike Oldfield's *Tubular Bells* album, various acoustic jazz artists on the Windham Hill label, Yanni, and various artists who have come to embrace the label "New Age," repetitive trance-like music has enjoyed popularity since the early 1960s. At the same time, some artists have increasingly sought to explore both world music and their own ethnic roots more fully than in the popular music of the past. This has sometimes created interesting but unlikely hybrids, such as R. Carlos Nakai's work in merging the sound of the traditional Native American flute with jazz rock fusion. After she left the Irish band Clannad, Enya emerged as a star of a brand of trance–New Age music that combines the more standard sounds of New Age—acoustic piano and synthesizer—with a melodic and vocal style that sometimes owes a debt to Celtic folk music, a natural synergism that has allowed her to become a popular recording artist.

Although subsequently she has enjoyed greater sales success, the recording that really pushed Enya into stardom was her 1988 album *Watermark*. The album begins with its title track, an instrumental piece that weighs in at a bit less than two and a half minutes. "Watermark" features a simple melody of a fairly narrow range in the right hand of the piano. Enya supports this melody with slow arpeggiated figures in the left hand and ethereal sustained chords in the synthesizer. The piece does not stray far from its opening tonality of F major. In fact, the piece is so focused on largely diatonic harmony that Enya's use of the bVII chord (an E flat major chord in the key of F major) at the final cadences of the verses (although "Watermark" is an instrumental composition, its AABAA structure is closely related to song form) tends to stand out. The modal flavor that the bVII lends and Enya's use of diatonic minor chords call to mind the piano compositions of Erik Satie (1866–1925), who, with his so-called furniture music, was the antecedent for later trance music.

The simplicity of the piece is also enhanced by Enya's approach to form. Each of the sections (A and B) consists of a parallel period, meaning that each section consists of two equal-length phrases that begin with the same melodic material. While the use entirely of parallel periods certainly is not exclusive to this piece—some late 19th-century waltzes and rags, for example, share this trait—it tends to lend "Watermark" a feeling of simple, organic wholeness, particularly because the B section in this AABAA-form piece shares motivic connections with the A section.

The next piece, "Cursum Perficio," was, according to Enya, "inspired by the inscription on the portico of Marilyn Monroe's last home—my journey ends here."[1] Roma Ryan wrote the Latin lyrics as well as the rest of the lyrics on *Watermark*.[2] The gist of the lyrics translate into English roughly as "I finish my course; the more one has, the more one wants; after the rain, Phoebus." It should be noted that Phoebus is often used as the Latin equivalent of either Apollo or Helios and thereby is the god perhaps most closely associated with the sun. In light of the tragedy of Marilyn Monroe's life (once one gets behind the glitter of the public image), the text suggests the rebirth out of darkness that could only come through the actress's death. Enya's setting, complete with the mysterious incantations that mark many of her compositions, is centered around dark tone colors in the synthesizers and the tonality of C minor. Because Enya sings the lyrics in Latin, provides no translation in the liner notes, includes incantations that fall outside the Latin text, and uses extensive repetition and extensive overdubbing of vocal lines, the listener cannot follow the meaning of lyrics like in a traditional pop song. Instead, one gets the meaning of the piece from the overall gestalt, effect, or feel. It is an example of what Frank Zappa said in relationship to what he believe represented the real content and meaning of recorded pieces:

> On a record, the overall timbre of the piece (determined by equalization of individual parts and their proportions in the mix) tells you, in a subtle way, *WHAT* the song is about. The orchestration provides *important information* about what the composition *IS* and, in some instances, assumes a greater importance than *the composition itself*.[3]

In other words, the piece is about texture and timbre (tone color) as much as, if not more than, it is about the text, the harmony, and the melody. While "Cursum Perficio" is an example of this, especially as the text is in what is today an obscure language with no printed translation, it is not the only piece on *Watermark* on which the overall feel comes more from the arrangement and manner of performance than from the text. Especially for the listener who does not understand Gaelic, "Storms in Africa," for example, is similar. One can understand the meaning of the piece just from the arrangement, texture, and style of playing and singing. One thing to keep in mind about Enya's work throughout the album, however, is that even in the pieces on which the listener can understand the lyrics—from the printed CD booklet and/or from listening—coproducers Nicky Ryan, Ross Cullum, and Enya bathe Enya's voice in significant studio reverberation, and some of the pieces include several multi-tracked contrapuntal vocal lines, both of which tend to make the text deliberately hazy and impressionistic.

It should be noted that the moderate-tempo rhythmic drive of the cello-like synthesizer bass line, the emphasis on modality, and Enya's clipped chanting of the narrow-range melodic figures in "Cursum Perficio" are both reminiscent of several movements of Carl Orff's famous *Carmina Burana*; however, because Enya avoids using synthesized percussion sounds, the drive is always more reserved.

The next track, "On Your Shore," finds Enya turning more in the direction of folk song. The strophic-form song may have an original melody, but the simple melodic setting, accompanied by minimal harmonic change, suggests the influence of folk music. "On Your Shore" is perhaps the most understated song on *Watermark*, so it can be overlooked; however, the song exhibits an elegant simplicity. The retrospective nature of the tune and the simplicity of the accompaniment fit Roma Ryan's lyrics in which the singer longs for the days of childhood. "On Your Shore" is the first song on *Watermark* to include Ryan's references to water, in this case waves washing over the shore and waves that "drift away with dreams of youth." Considering the twin major influences in Enya's work—synthesizer-based New Age music and Gaelic folk music—it is curious that "On Your Shore" contains a brief clarinet solo from Neil Buckley. Interestingly (and perhaps meant as an inside joke), Buckley's open tone suggests the playing of British clarinetist Mr. Acker Bilk on his 1961–1962 instrumental megahit "Stranger on the Shore."

In "Storms in Africa," one of the album's Gaelic pieces, Enya focuses on building several layers of material above a repeated harmonic in E flat major: IV-V-I, although occasionally the V chord resolves deceptively to the vi chord. She includes dramatic imitations of thunder in the synthesized cello and bass parts. The piece, with its minimalistic text about walking through a storm and its static harmonic pattern, creates the feeling of a long journey. Enya reprises the piece for *Watermark*'s final track. If anything, however, "Storms in Africa II" is more dramatic, with its loud crack of thunder near the start of the piece, more intense percussion parts, the overdubbed lead vocal line in octaves, and changes of texture in which the instruments abruptly drop out.

In "Exile," Enya evokes ancient folk music, particularly through a feel of modality as well as through melodic rhythms that emphasize gentle short-long patterns. The folk nature of the piece is also confirmed by Davy Spillane's low-pitched whistle solo. The piece moves beyond traditional strophic folk song, however, because of the high degree of tonal contrast in the chorus. The minor modal verses contain impressionistic text that deals with the coldness (physically and emotionally) of winter and being away from presumably one's lover. The chorus, however, concerns the hope that the singer feels for the prospect of sailing home. Here, Enya turns to major-inflected tonality and makes heavy use of the major third scale step. As such, the piece presents almost a bipolar mood: the melancholy of the present, with its distance and physical coldness, contrasted with the hope for reunion.

At just one tick under two minutes in length, "Miss Clare Remembers" is the shortest track on *Watermark*. Enya returns to the focus on a simple melody-plus-accompaniment texture in the piano that was heard on the album's title track. In "Miss Clare Remembers," however, she makes noticeable use of major sevenths in the chords as well as unexpected harmonic shifts. The piece is also melodically less predictable—almost improvisatory—compared with most of the compositions on *Watermark*. Still, the melodic motion to high-range chord roots in the tune reflects a melodic characteristic of the title track and suggests that perhaps conceptually the two works are related.

The next track, "Orinoco Flow," is the best-known piece on *Watermark*. While the title refers to a Venezuelan river, the text also mentions sailing away to "the shores of Tripoli," Bali, the Coral Sea, Babylon, and other locations from around the world, including "lands I've never seen." This suggests that the Orinoco plays the role of a mythological river that can take one to exotic locations—a sort of dream-world Orinoco. Roma Ryan's text also contains such inside-joke touches as references to *Watermark*'s coproducer Ross Cullum and executive producer Rob Dickins. However, nearly all of the text of the verses is obscured by Enya's delivery, the jumpy melody, and studio reverberation. The clearest text is the phrase "sail away, sail away, sail away," which basically is part of the backing vocal texture in what amounts to the chorus section. But then, this is in keeping with most of the pieces on the album: the "sail away" text, as general as it might be, captures the overall mood of the piece to the extent that all the other details of the lyrics come close to becoming a succession of tone colors whose primary purpose is to give Enya vowel, diphthong, and consonant sounds to adorn the vocal melody line.

It should be noted that the basic backing figure throughout most of the piece features the melodic descent b7–6–5. In large part because of its emphasis on the lowered seventh scale step, this figure links "Orinoco Flow" with "The Longships," a track that contains brief motion to the minor seventh scale step as well as to "Na Laetha Geal M'óige," a song that includes upward leaps to the minor seventh scale step. "Orinoco Flow" was released as a single and played an important role in bringing Enya to a wider audience. Curiously, although the song is catchy, it is not as interesting for in-depth listening as most of the other vocal pieces on *Watermark*, in part because it is perhaps the most mainstream song on the album and in part because one can too easily zone out with the "sail away" chorus and tonality shifts that come right out of the technique of Philip Glass.

In the next piece, "Evening Falls," Enya uses conventional AABA song structure. Unlike AABA pop songs that come out of the Tin Pan Alley and jazz traditions, however, the modal harmonies and the heavy use of parallel phrase construction reflect the influence of folk song. Significantly, "Evening Falls" perhaps is the clearest setting of lyrics on the album, with Enya's solo vocal supported by block synthesizer chords. The effect is very similar to the simple settings of traditional folk material that some of the folk-revival singers of the 1960s—Enya's vocal quality and singing style vaguely call to mind Judy Collins—used in order to place the emphasis on the text.

Watermark is an album that tends to invite the listener to experience the whole as one interrelated composition rather than as a series of shorter pieces. In part this is because of the simple technique of reprise ("Storms in Africa" is the 4th piece, and "Storms in Africa II" is the 12th and final piece), but it is also because of Enya's inclusion of closely related compositions. Specifically, the album's 9th track, "River," is an instrumental piece that shares some rhythmic motives with "Orinoco Flow." Although "River" might remind the listener of the earlier song, it adds little else to the album. One of the ironies of some relatively static New Age/minimalist music is that lengthier pieces can sometimes work more effectively than relatively short ones. At 3 minutes and 10 seconds in length, "River" seems short: there is very little development through the piece, but it also is not quite long enough to create a lasting mood. By contrast, "The Longships," with Enya's haunting singing, mysterious background chanting, unexpected chromatic harmonic shifts, and subtly evolving synthesizer textures, effectively evokes the ghost of Viking longships and their passengers.

In the Gaelic-language song "Na Laetha Geal M'óige," Enya longs for the innocent days of youth, when the reality of death and true sorrow were unknown. Although the song is not the last track on *Watermark*—it is followed by the dramatic reprise and elaboration on "Storms in Africa"—"Na Laetha Geal M'óige" sums up the general sense of melancholy and longing for the innocence of a former time that can be felt in several of Roma Ryan's poems throughout the album. And as mentioned earlier, the upward leap of a minor seventh that is part of Enya's melody connects the musical materials of this piece to several of the other songs on *Watermark*. Because of their placement within the phrases, some listeners might hear these upward leaps as reminiscent of those in Harry Chapin's song "Taxi," in which Chapin sings "I needed one more fare to make my night." While the melodic parallels probably are purely accidental, it is interesting to note that in a sense, the 1972 Chapin song also concerns nostalgic remembrances of better times.

For listeners who enjoy atmospheric New Age–style mood pieces in small packages, Enya's *Watermark* fits the bill in that the individual tracks are fairly short. However, the album is much more than a collection of a dozen individual pieces. Enya's musical connections and Roma Ryan's lyrical connections tie the pieces together so as to make a unified and touching statement about dealing with the present by means of remembering the past.

Notes

1. Enya, liner notes to *Watermark*, CD, Reprise 9 26774-2, 1988.
2. Enya provided Irish Gaelic translations for some of the texts.
3. Frank Zappa, with Peter Occhiogrosso, *The Real Frank Zappa Book* (New York: Poseidon, 1989), 188 (capitalization and italics in the original).

42

Melissa Etheridge

Melissa Etheridge (1988)

James E. Perone

Over the years, Melissa Etheridge has been known as a frequent Grammy nominee, for her decision to candidly discuss her private life, as a gay rights activist, as an environmental activist, and as a cancer survivor. Her 1988 self-titled debut album presented a collection of 10 self-penned strong rock songs of loss, alienation, and identity in the face of betrayal. As noted by critics at the time, *Melissa Etheridge* reflected some of the same aesthetics as found in the contemporary work of already established rock singer-songwriters such as John Mellencamp and Bruce Springsteen. Like these musicians, Etheridge championed independence, sang with powerful emotional expression, and presented a welcome alternative to the synthesizer-laden dance music of the time. In the words of All Music Guide critic Vik Iyengar, these attributes helped to make Etheridge "a role model for a generation of young women who found her to be an uncompromising artist unafraid to expose (and celebrate) her strengths and weaknesses."[1]

The album opens with "Similar Features." Etheridge's character sings to a former lover, who is now with another woman who has "similar features with longer hair." Like the other songs about loss in love on the album, "Similar Features" finds Etheridge at once defiant, jealous, hurt, sarcastic, and angry. In short, the failure of her character's relationship elicits the range of human emotions that might reflect the complexity of real life. Part of the challenge of listening to the entire album in sequence, though, is that Etheridge so unrelentingly works her way through a similar range of emotions in song after song. This might tend to force some listeners away from the lyrics somewhat and experience the songs as musical pieces outside of their lyrical contexts. If the emotional jockeying becomes too much, it perhaps is best to experience the album as a collection of individual songs.

The second song on the album, "Chrome Plated Heart," finds Etheridge dealing with loss and desire more impressionistically and metaphorically. Here, she uses the image of "scratches and stains on [her] chrome-plated heart" to symbolize her past losses. Perhaps even more interesting is the somewhat fatalistic image she creates when she sings, "The only way I know where the train will go is when I'm sleeping on the tracks." The musical setting is stripped-down acoustic guitar and rhythm section–based blues, albeit in a modified blues form. It is this kind of texture—as well as her blues-inflected vocals—that made Etheridge's sound stand out from the more obviously commercially motivated artists of the late 1980s.

The rhythm section arrangement on "Chrome Plated Heart" hinted at funk, particularly with the syncopations at the 16th-note level. The next song, "Like the Way I Do," also includes a mixture of rock and funk rhythmic styles. In the lyrics, Etheridge addresses a lover who is now with another woman. She puts her own prowess as a passionate lover and as a seducer up against that of her rival. Etheridge captures the bravado of the lyrics in her edgy, pointed singing. One of four songs on the album to make the record charts as singles, "Like the Way I Do" is a standout. It is not the most commercially successful of the lot at the time ("Chrome Plated Heart" and "Bring Me Some Water" rose higher in the charts), but the emotion and the engaging and memorable tune wear very well more than 20 years later.

Curiously, the next piece, "Precious Pain," bears a motivic resemblance to the Kansas hit "Dust in the Wind," a song written by Kerry Livgren. Like the well-known Livgren piece, "Precious Pain" is what can only be described as a "downer." While Livgren writes that "all we are is dust in the wind," Etheridge basically equates feeling pain in life with knowing that one is alive. The slow, largely acoustic setting and the dark lyrics of hopelessness suggest the 1970s' singer-songwriter movement stretched to an extreme. What really makes the piece work is Etheridge's understated singing style; she is entirely believable as the woman whose life has been filled with, and only with, such intense personal pain that were the pain to be absent, she might not be sure that she is still alive.

"Don't You Need" is one of the more interesting songs on the album from a structural standpoint. Etheridge includes tempo and texture changes as she contrasts her needs and desires with what would seem to be the lack of the same in an estranged lover. While the clearest connection between the songs on Etheridge's debut album is the emphasis on deeply seated emotions revolving around broken and dysfunctional relationships, some of the songs share specific imagery. For example, in "Don't You Need," Etheridge frames her explorations around a dream in which "the water was running low," thus allowing the heat of the desires of her heart to "abduct" her mind. In "The Late September Dogs," which is six and a half minutes long, Etheridge portrays a character who must now, after her loss, only dream that "the hand that touches you is mine, and mine alone." In the chorus, she pleads with the rain to "fall down on [her]" and thus to "set [her] free." In fact, despite its slow tempo, "The Late September Dogs" is one of the most potent songs on Etheridge's debut album, particularly because of the contrast between the quiet sparseness of the verses and the sharp edginess of Etheridge's plea to the rain in the chorus sections. Etheridge returns to the metaphor of water on the album's penultimate track, "Bring Me Some Water," probably the best-known song in this collection.

"The Late September Dogs" is followed by "Occasionally," the shortest track on the album. Here, accompanied solely by her own percussion work on the back of her guitar, Etheridge sings to a former lover (who she happens to see with the person's "new friends" and "new envoy") that she "only feel[s] lonely occasionally." She provides a short litany of these "occasional" times, such as driving her car, watching television, and "after dark." As she does in earlier songs, Etheridge conveys a feeling of sarcasm, hurt, anger, contempt, and so on. Her character seems to realize that she "is addicted" to being drawn into new relationships in which she ultimately will be hurt. The stark a cappella setting is haunting. Etheridge sings the verses in the key of F major and the chorus in B flat major. The modulation to the key of the subdominant (F to B flat) is not in and of itself unusual in pop or rock music; however, the fact that the song ends with the chorus and that Etheridge establishes the F major tonality of the verses more strongly than the B flat major tonality of the chorus (which is somewhat vague until the final cadence of the chorus sections) tends to give the piece a somewhat unresolved sound. To the extent that the listener perceives it, the unresolved feeling of tonality supports the unresolved nature of the pain of which Etheridge sings in her lyrics.

"Watching You," a slow ballad, is one of the richest pieces lyrically on the album. Etheridge's character can be read several ways. She braves even the harshest weather to watch someone else through their window. She sings that "if I can't love you, I don't want to love you," which suggests that she may be stalking a former lover. However, Etheridge includes several hints that her character lives in poverty and is homeless. In this scenario, the person she watches may be someone with whom she is fixated, even if they have never met. The sparse musical arrangement supports the image of the loneliness of Etheridge's character. The setting is also made more effective by Etheridge's performance of the opening few words of each verse as spoken text—this helps to give the piece a greater feeling of authenticity. The melody of the verses, too, with their short rise and fall, supports the text, in this case by suggesting the passing of time as Etheridge's character gives the object of her desire her secret scrutiny.

In part because of the timbre of her singing voice and in part because she specializes in songs about brokenness, Melissa Etheridge sometimes has been compared with the late 1960s' icon Janis Joplin. Because the song more closely resembles the hard rock style associated with Joplin when she was a member of Big Brother and the Holding Company than any other on this album, the Etheridge song "Bring Me Some Water" is perhaps the most Joplin-like piece here. In her lyrics, Etheridge expresses how "weak" she feels because her former lover is now in the arms of another woman. However, the chorus plea "somebody bring me some water" is so powerfully sung and performed with so much instrumental drive that the listener might feel that Etheridge is not just weakened by the breakup; she is also angry.

Etheridge's debut album concludes with "I Want You," a funky musical setting for the singer-songwriter's raw expression of desire. Despite an initial night of passion, Etheridge sings that now "satisfaction never comes," suggesting that her partner treated the event as a one-night stand. Interestingly, in this song—the most obvious statement of sexual desire—as well as in every other song on the album, Etheridge never defines the gender of the object of her desire. Even if Etheridge had never openly discussed her sexuality as she did in the early 1990s, the gender-neutral nature of the relationships makes for interesting listening. This aspect of the songs allows the listener to imagine the characters whom Etheridge sets up in her songs in a wider variety of ways than would be possible if she explicitly told the listener that the character opposite her own was male or female.

Melissa Etheridge is a strong debut album with nothing that can be labeled as filler. Etheridge was unrelenting in her exploration of a wide range of emotions, all of which are caused by broken relationships; however, this is perhaps one of the most emotionally cathartic albums of the era and one that rocks throughout.

Note

1. Vik Iyengar, review of *Melissa Etheridge*, All Music Guide, http://allmusic.com/album/melissa-etheridge-r6881/review.

43

Tracy Chapman

Tracy Chapman (1988)

James E. Perone

Tracy Chapman's self-titled 1988 debut album immediately established the singer-songwriter-guitarist as a star. Chapman was one of several female singer-songwriters whose careers developed throughout the 1980s, only to reach fruition late in the decade. Chapman's work on this album, because the recording focused on her voice and rhythm guitar and was relatively free of dated-sounding 1980s' synthesizers, has an immediacy and an intimacy that were rare in that decade. However, it is that intimacy, the relative lack of electronic gimmickry, and Chapman's lyrics about still-persisting personal and social issues that continue to persist that help to make *Tracy Chapman* an album that sounds fresh and relevant more than 20 years after its release.

Part of the continuing success of *Tracy Chapman* comes from the fact that although Chapman focused her attention more fully on specific social issues than did other singer-songwriters who emerged in the second half of the 1980s (e.g., Suzanne Vega), they are social issues that remain in public consciousness and headlines in the second decade of the 21st century. Such is the case with the album's opening track, "Talkin' bout a Revolution." At the beginning of the song, Chapman describes the undercurrents of a revolution as "a whisper." As the song progresses, Chapman details the reasons for this revolution—poverty, unemployment, underemployment, lack of social services—and by the end of the piece she tells the listener that the revolution now is imminent. On this track, Chapman (who sings and plays acoustic guitar, electric rhythm guitar, and percussion) is backed by drums, electric guitar, Hammond organ, and bass. The texture, however, is clear and closer to the feel that one might expect from a deeply personal coffeehouse singer-songwriter than what the personnel list might imply. To put it another way, the guitars, organ, bass, drums, and auxiliary percussion parts are well balanced and understated.

Interestingly, the copyright dates given in the liner notes show that "Talkin' bout a Revolution" was the product of 1982, early in the Reagan era and just after the United States had experienced high inflation and high unemployment. In fact, 1981–1982 was the time of a prolonged economic recession in the country. At the time of the album's release, the United States was in the middle of the savings and loan crisis and the attendant downturn in people's ability to secure mortgages, which made Chapman's lyrics once again seem relevant. More recently, Chapman's words reflect the reality of the high unemployment, homelessness, and increasingly dissonant political discourse associated with 2008–2009.

That Tracy Chapman's 1987 song "Fast Car" became a bona fide hit seems unlikely in the world of 1980s' pop music, which for some people meant dance music dominated by the likes of Michael Jackson and Madonna. In verses of the song, Chapman's voice is accompanied by little more than her guitar. While the other guitar parts, bass, and drums enter for the chorus, the overall texture is sparse, far more sparse than what one might stereotypically expect from a 1980s' Top 10 single. As she did in the album's opening track, Chapman deals with poverty; however, in this song she portrays a victim of poverty. Her character works as a checkout clerk in a store, her "old man" is unemployed and "live[s] with the bottle," and the only escape from her feelings of disappointment and even desperation is driving in "a fast car." Ultimately she sees the escapism as a dead end and at the end of the song concludes that with or without her "old man" her life is going to change. Chapman embeds poverty, codependency issues, escapism, desperation, depression, and other issues and emotions in her text. Her music, too, supports the various unreconcilable states, with its alternation of introspective fully acoustic singer-songwriter style and full rock band sound. It is a thoughtful, highly emotionally charged song.

In "Across the Lines," Chapman focuses her attention on racism and more specifically on the divisions between blacks and whites. As Chapman sees the situation, riots that ensue after a young black girl is assaulted work to undermine the American Dream. There is much more beneath the surface of the text, however, and the key is the phrase "gets assaulted." As the song concludes, Chapman focuses her attention more fully on the girl and takes the phrase "gets assaulted" to its illogical conclusion by singing that the girl herself is the one to blame for the situation. In context of singer, situation, and song, obviously the song's concluding line reflects the social blame game. And as has happened on more than one occasion, the victim of a racially motivated crime becomes in the eyes of some observers the cause of the incident (e.g., "She must have been asking for it"). Tracy Chapman's musical style adds a special touch to the song. As a black woman singing in what was commonly—and stereotypically—considered a white style (the acoustic singer-songwriter style), Chapman clearly cut across the proverbial race lines as a writer and performer.

None of the arrangements on *Tracy Chapman* are particularly flashy or lush; however, the a cappella setting of "Behind the Wall" is so stark that it stands in sharp relief to the other tracks. This is a brief song in which Chapman deals with domestic violence. Unlike Suzanne Vega's 1987 recording "Luka," which was written from the perspective of the victim, Chapman sings from the perspective of the one who hears "the screaming" night after night. As Chapman's character sees the situation, it is pointless to call the police because either they will not respond, they will respond after the situation cools, or they will say that they cannot "interfere with domestic affairs" between husband and wife. In the final stanza that is printed in the album's liner notes (the recording ends with a repeat of the first stanza), Chapman's character once again hears the screaming, but this time it is followed by an eerie silence and then the sound of an approaching ambulance. In a twist of irony, this time the police do respond; however, they do so only to disperse the crowd in order to "keep the peace." Ultimately, then, Chapman deals with domestic violence, the feeling of powerlessness of her third-party character, and society's lack of resolve to solve the root problem. Since Chapman performs "Behind the Wall" a cappella, it is a particularly good track with which to focus on her melodic style. Like most of the other songs on the album, "Behind the Wall" has a memorable melody; however, like the others, it does not move in the direction of pop-oriented tunes that invite singing along. Chapman's melodies throughout the album tend to feel thoroughly original and lacking in easy clichés, and in many cases they contain unexpected rhythmic turns. Likewise, Chapman's lyrics and music work together in several songs to create unexpected extensions and elisions of phrases.

The album's first two tracks were its most commercially successful singles; however, "Baby Can I Hold You" also enjoyed some success, particularly on the adult contemporary charts. Chapman deals with her lover's inability to say "I'm sorry" and "I love you." These deeply emotional expressions are replaced by the song's title line, and her partner's communication challenges stand in the way of the relationship moving forward.

In "Mountains o' Things," Chapman's character dreams of a life of material wealth, a life that she never will be able to achieve. The title line refers to the "mountains of things" about which she dreams. Throughout the song, Chapman's character grows less and less lovable on the surface as she enumerates her materialistic desires and admits that in her dreams "good people are only my stepping stones." However, this is a life about which the character only dreams. It is easy to imagine the character's dreams as simply a turnaround of the situation in which she actually finds herself: she is the good person others have used on their ascent of the social and economic ladder. This is the most synthesizer-driven song on the album; however, like some of the dance music of the 1980s, the synthesizer arrangement does not sound particularly dated today. This is because most of the synthesized sounds are low strings and percussion—tone colors that are not among the most artificial sounding on the equipment of the late 1980s. The percussion parts lend the piece an African/world music feel.

Throughout the album, Chapman returns to the familiar theme of escape from desperation. In "She's Got Her Ticket," Chapman observes a young runaway who is about to board an airplane to escape to "her place in the sun." The girl looks to escape greed, hatred, and a belief that she does not belong. For this story, Chapman and her band turn to reggae style. One of the most notable strengths of the recording is Jack Holder's work on electric guitar.

In "Why?" Chapman asks why there are such things as poverty, missiles that are called "Peacekeepers," starvation among babies, and the continuing danger of violence against women, particularly in domestic situations. She predicts that victims, the poor, and the disenfranchised will rise up if their (and her) questions are not answered. As such, the song recalls "Talkin' bout a Revolution." Chapman breaks free of conventional pop song rhyme schemes in her lyrics, which tends to focus the listener's attention on her words. The musical setting leans in the direction of soul, although the texture remains consistent with the Tracy Chapman singer-songwriter style, that is to say, sparser than conventional soul music.

Over the decades, countless singers have performed songs in which they portray a character who is in love with someone whom all of their friends and family tell them is bound to be bad for the character—the inexplicable love. "For My Lover" represents Tracy Chapman's take on the theme. She uses syncopated, bluesy minor key music for this song. Another feature that sets "For My Lover" apart from the previous songs is the fact that the melody of the verses is based on ABAB phrase structure, in which the B parts serve as a brief refrain of the song's title line. That the piece comes closer to the American roots music tradition than any other earlier tracks is confirmed by the presence of steel guitar and Dobro. However, the steel guitar, quite unlike the role that it usually plays in electric blues or in country, here provides a wash of harmony. Likewise, the Dobro playing is understated, thus providing just a roots-music touch.

Technically, *Tracy Chapman* cannot be labeled a concept album; it really is a collection of individual songs. However, there are several thematic connections that run throughout (e.g., the theme of rebellion against poverty). "If Not Now . . ." connects to the earlier "Baby Can I Hold You" in that "If Not Now . . ." concerns the inability to express feelings of love. In this case, Chapman ponders when to make a declaration of love. She concludes that while she can "wait and lose this heart," "the moment has arrived." Chapman leaves the exact nature of her declaration of love vague. In fact, she seems to imply that a verbal declaration is not enough, which might suggest that her declaration represents a commitment. Part of the beauty of the lyrics is that they invite multiple readings and understandings. "If Not Now . . ." is another song in which Chapman defies conventions of pop song structure. The song contains two distinct musical sections in ABABA (coda) form. The A sections are mellow and relatively quiet, much like what one ordinarily would expect from a verse section, and conversely the B sections are more intense and sound like the chorus. However, the lyrics for each of the A sections are the same, and those of each of the two B sections are different. Lyrically, then, the A sections play the role of chorus, and the B sections play the role of verse. For some listeners, the easygoing jazz-oriented style and unconventional formal arrangement of lyrics and music might bring to mind some of the jazz-influenced songs of Joni Mitchell and Carole King in the early 1970s.

Chapman continues her focus on love in the album's final song, "For You." In this song, Chapman's acoustic guitar provides the sole accompaniment for her voice. As she does on other songs—but perhaps most effectively here—Chapman breaks free of conventional pop song rhyme schemes. Similarly, the ABAB structure of the lyrics (both "verses" are exactly the same, and both chorus statements are exactly the same) breaks free of the conventions of late 20th-century verse-chorus-break structure. This gives the song the feeling of a through-composed piece that is based on pure emotional expression.

Tracy Chapman may have written the songs that graced her self-titled debut album over the course of approximately seven years, but *Tracy Chapman* made her an instant star. The album earned three Grammy Awards, was a huge commercial success, and spawned the somewhat unlikely Top 10 hit single "Fast Car." More than that, however, the album—although a collection of individual songs—has an overarching shape that emphasizes the deeply felt personal nature of the material. It is an album that speaks to the personal and social issues not only of its time but also of today.

Index